The Confederates of
Chappell Hill, Texas

The Confederates of Chappell Hill, Texas

Prosperity, Civil War and Decline

STEPHEN CHICOINE

McFarland & Company, Inc., Publishers
Jefferson, North Carolina, and London

The present work is a reprint of the illustrated case bound edition of The Confederates of Chappell Hill, Texas: Prosperity, Civil War and Decline, *first published in 2005 by McFarland.*

LIBRARY OF CONGRESS CATALOGUING-IN-PUBLICATION DATA

Chicoine, Stephen.
The Confederates of Chappell Hill, Texas :
prosperity, Civil War and decline / Stephen Chicoine.
p. cm.
Includes bibliographical references and index.

ISBN 978-0-7864-6418-0
softcover : acid free paper ∞

1. Chappell Hill (Tex.) — History — 19th century.
2. Texas — History — Civil War, 1861–1865. I. Title.

F394.C46 C48 2012   976.4'245 — dc22   2004018785

BRITISH LIBRARY CATALOGUING DATA ARE AVAILABLE

© 2005 Stephen Chicoine. All rights reserved

No part of this book may be reproduced or transmitted in any form or by any means, electronic or mechanical, including photocopying or recording, or by any information storage and retrieval system, without permission in writing from the publisher.

Cover photograph: 1913 Reunion of Terry's Texas Rangers (courtesy of Ruth and Rice Buchanan of Navasota, Texas); inset Terry's Texas Rangers flag (www.galleryoftherepublic.com)

Manufactured in the United States of America

*McFarland & Company, Inc., Publishers
Box 611, Jefferson, North Carolina 28640
www.mcfarlandpub.com*

To Judy and the late Nath Winfield
of Chappell Hill, Texas.

Their tireless accumulation of historical details
through the course of their lives helped to preserve
the true story of Chappell Hill for posterity.
The real history of our great nation lies in the personal
details of the lives and struggles of forgotten individuals,
rather than in gross characterizations.

Contents

Preface 1
Introduction 5

1. Texas Secedes 13
2. Terry's Texas Rangers' First Blood 28
3. Sibley's Brigade and Waller's Regiment 37
4. Hood's Texas Brigade Moves into Action 45
5. Capture at Arkansas Post 58
6. Glory at Galveston 66
7. Marauding Cavalry 75
8. Vicksburg and Gettysburg — The Turning Points 87
9. The Home Front 1863–1864 95
10. Eastern Tennessee Campaign 106
11. The Defense of Atlanta 118
12. The Wilderness and Petersburg 129
13. The End of the War 136
14. Texas at the Close of the War 144
15. Texas Homecomings 155

16. Occupation and Reconstruction 166
17. Yellow Fever 181
18. National Reconciliation 187

Epilogue 219
Notes 227
Bibliography 243
Index 253

Preface

I first came to the realization that there was a story worth telling in Chappell Hill on a warm October day. I drove with my family from Houston to Chappell Hill for the annual Scarecrow Festival. Several thousand attend the Chappell Hill event each year. My wife and daughter were making their way through the crowd on Main Street to view as many of the arts and crafts booths as possible. I chose to go for a stroll away from the bustling crowd and ended up at the Masonic Cemetery, where I meandered among the old headstones. As an historian, I tried, while reading the names and paying my respects, to imagine from the dates what the life of each of the deceased might have been. Most striking in the cemetery are the white marble headstones scattered throughout. Each prominently marks the grave of a Confederate veteran. Nath and Judy Winfield, Chappell Hill's well-regarded historians, arranged for the stones to be properly inscribed and placed in their appropriate locations in the cemetery next to the small, faded markers from many years past.

I realized rather quickly that the men of Chappell Hill served in many distinguished Confederate units during the War Between the States. The men of Chappell Hill, unlike those of so many other Southern towns, did not march off in one company of a particular regiment. The diversity of the experiences of these men from a single town struck me as unique and was what initially attracted me to concept of a book on Chappell Hill. Appealing as it seemed, however, I knew this concept would never become a good book project unless I was able to locate considerable biographical information on a number of these Confederates. It was even more critical to locate personal papers, such as letters, journals and memoirs. I wanted to convey the human experience, the personal side of history. I hoped in an extremely optimistic way that I might be fortunate enough to find photographic images of some of the Confederates of Chappell Hill. Look in a man's eyes, and read his letters, and he comes to life.

I wandered back through the bustling crowd on Chappell Hill's Main Street and headed toward the old elementary school, which had been converted into an historical museum. I found exactly what I was looking for in one of the small exhibition rooms. There were photos of young men in Confederate uniforms, a few weapons, and a few pieces of correspondence from these men, which had been enlarged and mounted in the display cases. I was overjoyed.

My preliminary research upon returning to Houston took place at Rice University's Fondren Library. I found references to a few of the men in some old, musty Texas biographical volumes from the late 1800s and early 1900s. I became familiar with the regimental histories of the various units represented in the Masonic Cemetery. Internet research yielded information on a few more men and their units. I accumulated enough notes within a month's time to fill a box with file folders.

It was at this point that I felt prepared to return to Chappell Hill and introduce myself to Nath Winfield. I was prepared for the possibility that he might not want an outsider writing about the town. Chappell Hill, after all, was this man's birthplace and lifelong home, as it had been for his daddy and his granddaddy, Joseph Eugene Routt. The Routts raised Nath and instilled in him his passion for the history of the local families and the town of Chappell Hill.

Nath Winfield greeted me warmly upon my arrival at the Chappell Hill Historical Society Museum. An intelligent man with a dry sense of humor, he spoke carefully and with confidence. I understood, as I came to know Nath, that he was a gentleman, steeped in the honor and tradition of the past. Nath told me that long ago he envisioned writing a book on the Confederates of Chappell Hill. He assured me that that time was past for him and that he would embrace and support my efforts to bring such a project to fruition. The material Nath shared with me that day made clear that there was sufficient information to seriously imagine a book.

My research took me far beyond the archives of the Chappell Hill Historical Society. As always, the Center for American History at the University of Texas, Austin, provided important material. The Harold B. Simpson History Complex at Hill College in Hillsboro, Texas, was the source of two very significant collections, as well as of some important photos. The Texas State Archives and Library were important on several accounts. I pursued leads from notes and references through myriad phone calls in the hopes of securing one more letter or one more photograph. Judy Winfield tirelessly came up with additional papers from the archives, or the name and phone number of some folks in the next county or across the country who were related to one Confederate or another.

One of the great joys of writing a book is the sudden discovery of the concept. Another is seeing the depth and breadth of the story reveal itself over time. I can never be certain that I will find enough quality material, but good book projects just come together. Equally exciting are the people I come across and come to know while compiling history. I was privileged to see a painted bunting in Fred and Mary Brandt's backyard in the Texas countryside. I had the pleasure of visiting with Rice and Ruth Buchanan at their home. I will never forget listening to Rice recall his granddaddy, a trooper in Terry's Texas Rangers, telling his grandchildren tales from the war with the Yankees. Rice would laugh and laugh, thinking about the tall tales he heard, and tell me with a gleam in his eyes that he sure enjoyed his granddaddy. I came to know Nath and Judy Winfield and recognize them for the Texas treasures they will always be. I was also fortunate to be able to share unabashedly my passion for history with Ladonna Vest at the Museum and Archives and with Tom Stevens, former president of the Chappell Hill Historical Society.

I thank my loving wife, Mary Ann, and my daughter, Maddie, for their wonderful patience and understanding through the long course of this work. I also must thank Dr. Joe Chance for his encouragement and his insistence that this book was an important work and needed to be published.

This book is not all-inclusive. It only just touches on the African American perspective of this period. Slavery was an important institution in Washington County before the war. There were many freedmen and freedwomen in and around Chappell Hill in the aftermath of the Federal government's defeat of the Southern Confederacy. The important periods of Federal occupation and Reconstruction deserve far more space than given in this book. All of this will have to wait for another book.

The vast majority of the archival material available pertains to the Confederates of Chappell Hill, proud Texans, Southerners and Americans, who made their stand against all odds and suffered either death or the humiliation of defeat. I have made every effort to bring to life for the reader the people of Chappell Hill from over 100 years ago: their hopes and dreams for the future, their painful suffering, the character they showed, the tragic losses they endured. Their story has never been told. The human experiences during this most important of times are what make up the real history of our great nation.

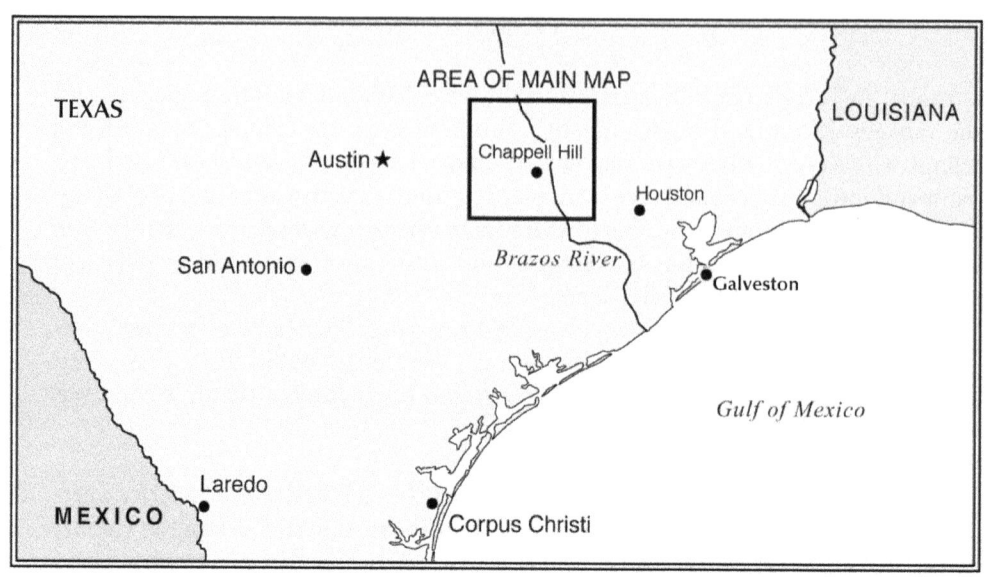

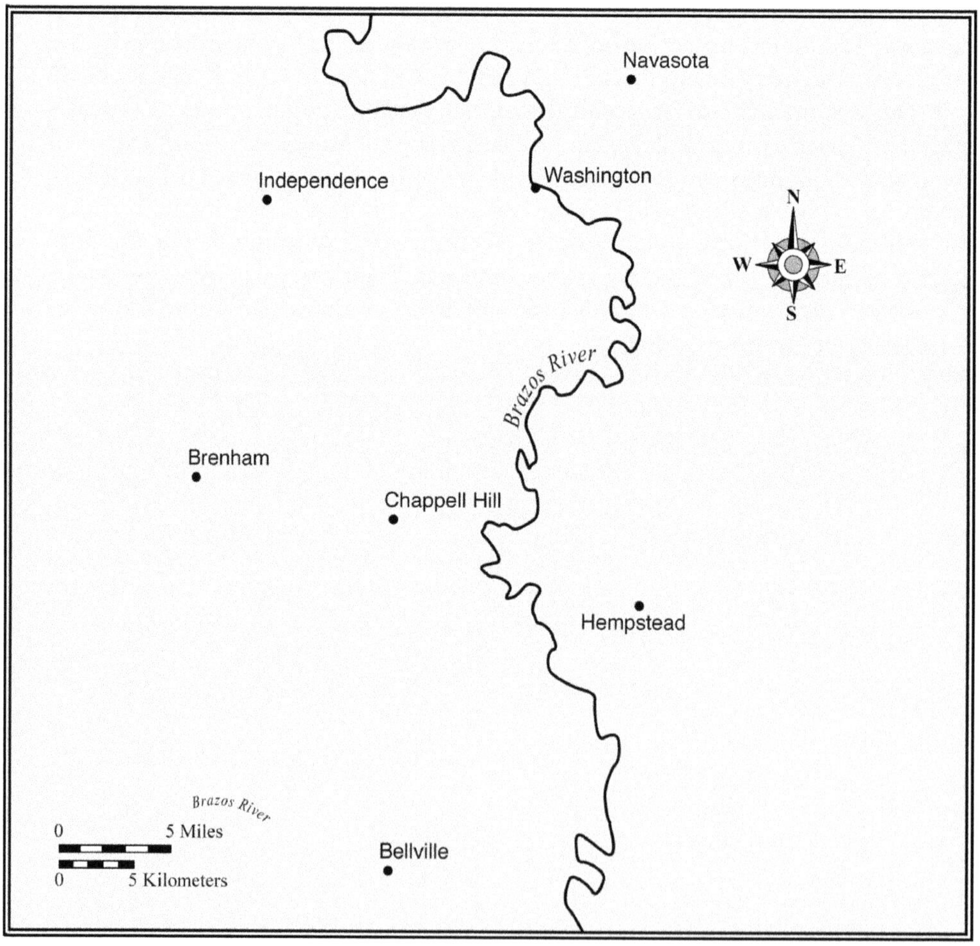

Maps by Patti Isaacs

Introduction

In the first half of the nineteenth century, cotton was king in the American South. Eighty percent of the world's cotton came from this region. By the mid-nineteenth century, the soil in the cotton fields of the Deep South was depleted and the yield was in serious decline. This problem was compounded by the boll weevil infestation. Foresighted planters began to move westward to the rich, virgin soils of Texas, where they could expect higher yields and perhaps escape the boll weevil for a time.

Texas was the South's frontier in the antebellum period. The vast new state represented the hope and future of many Southern planters. As a result, Texas changed greatly during the 1850s as increasing numbers of Southern planters moved westward and settled there. Planters brought with them large numbers of slaves to plant, cultivate and pick this cotton. No state in the South grew nearly as fast as Texas from 1850 to 1860, and the booming economy for this valuable cash crop led the economic development. By 1860, slaves made up 30 percent of the total population of Texas, rising from 58,000 in 1850 to well over 180,000. As cotton became more and more an important part of its economy, Texas became increasingly embroiled in the national debate as to whether slavery should exist within a democratic republic dedicated to the freedom and independence of man.

The fertile soil of the central Texas coast was ideal for growing cotton. Prime acreage lay within "the bottoms," the broad floodplains of the mighty Brazos and Colorado rivers. Washington County encompassed some of the most prolific cotton-producing soil in Texas by virtue of the Brazos River bottoms. In a relatively short period of time, ambitious men added considerable wealth to their estates, as evidenced by the magnificent Southern-style mansions they built along the Brazos Valley. Each plantation owner had his own mule-powered cotton gin in those days. The

THE STAGECOACH INN. The Stagecoach Inn was built in 1850 by Jacob and Mary Haller. Mary's mother operated the inn until 1859. The inn was a favorite stopping place for stagecoach travelers between Houston and Austin from 1851 to 1871. The stone and cedar building has 14 rooms, including six bedrooms upstairs. The entire framework is pegged — nails were used only for finish work. The downspout heads around the house bear the Lone Star of Texas. (Photograph by Thomas G. Stevens of Chappell Hill.)

Brazos River not only provided rich river-bottom soil for cotton, but also allowed transportation of cotton via steamboats to the port of Galveston. The planters helped build two steam-powered sternwheelers, the *Washington* and the *Brazos*, which made regular runs down to Galveston. Warren Town, founded by Jesse Bartlett on the west bank of the Brazos River (near where today's Highway 290 crosses the Brazos), became the chief river port for the cotton plantations of surrounding Washington County until the railroad came into the area in the late 1850s.[1] Major James H. Cocke[2] was president of the Warren Town (Development) Co. in 1850, his partners including Richard J. Swearingen, William Keesee and William Hargrove of Chappell Hill, among others. Cotton shipped down river to Galveston made its way into the markets of New England and across the ocean to Great Britain. Houston and Galveston existed to house brokerage merchants and to ship the cotton of the central Texas coast to the world market.

Introduction

The town of Chappell Hill grew up amid this period of booming prosperity in the middle Brazos Valley. In the early 1840s, William Hargrove and his son-in-law Jacob Haller built an inn at a stagecoach stop halfway between Houston and Austin. The Jackson Brothers' sawmill on nearby New Year's Creek provided lumber for the inn and later for the town that grew up around the inn. In 1847, Haller's wife, Mary, purchased 100 acres and established a settlement, naming it for her grandfather, Robert Wooding Chappell. A post office was opened there in that same year.

Several heroes of the Texas Revolution made Chappell Hill their home. Among these was John Cloud, who fought at Velasco in 1832,[3] Major William Edward Howth,[4] who took part in the capture of San Antonio in 1835, and Captain William Jones Heard,[5] who led Company F of the First Regiment, Texas Volunteers, into battle at San Jacinto in 1836. Other veterans of San Jacinto included Francis Jarvis Cooke, a charter member of Chappell Hill's Masonic Lodge in 1850 and a town alderman in 1856,[6] and Judge Benjamin Thomas,[7] who bought the old Hargrove House hotel in 1859 and operated the inn until 1870. Thomas also served Chappell Hill as an alderman through the Civil War.[8] All of these men were buried in Chappell Hill's historic Masonic Cemetery.[9] Chappell Hill's Texan character was further accentuated by Sam Houston's home just up the road in Independence.[10] The General often visited friends in Chappell Hill; John Washington Lockhart and Major James H. Cocke were among his closest friends.[11] The Lockhart House, which Houston frequented, still stands in Chappell Hill.

Chappell Hill developed a decidedly Southern character. The town grew dramatically, becoming a center of wealth and privilege during the 1850s as a result of the flourishing cotton economy. The majority of Texans during this period were not plantation owners (generally defined as owning 20 or more slaves) or even slaveholders. The federal census indicated there were just over 2,000 plantation owners in Texas in 1860, representing three percent of all Texas families. Those families owning slaves were only 27 percent of Texas families.[12] Texas planters, although a small part of the total population in the state, dominated the economy and state politics. The more prominent men of Chappell Hill were among those who wielded considerable influence in antebellum Texas.

Cotton production centered in Texas' Washington County rivaled that of anywhere in the South with in excess of 45 bales per square mile in 1860. T. H. Justice wrote his brother, John Justice, "the health of the country is very good ... crops as good as you ever saw and rain aplenty, girls fat and saucy."[13] Chappell Hill planter Thomas Banks reported making 12 bales of cotton "to the hand" during his first season after moving to Texas from Alabama.[14] The average for the Texas counties along the Brazos River was seven bales "to the hand," while the states of the Deep South averaged three bales "to the hand."[15] This rich yield enticed a number of prominent Southern planters to relocate to the Brazos River Valley. The 1860 federal census indicates that Banks owned 99 slaves and had a net worth of $278,000. Joseph Toland, formerly of South Carolina, had a net worth of only slightly less and owned 68 slaves. It was Toland who brought the fragrant huisache tree to the locale of Chappell Hill after a trip to Mexico.[16] William Westcot Browning, who moved from Mississippi,

The grave marker of Major Howth (Texas Revolution), an early Texan hero, who resided in Chappell Hill.

was worth well over $200,000 and owned 62 slaves. Other prominent planters included Gabriel Felder from South Carolina with 130 slaves, R. J. Swearingen, also of South Carolina, with 65 slaves, T. J. Jackson of Georgia with 47 slaves and Dr. John Lockhart of Alabama with 51 slaves.[17] There was one Yankee among the most prominent planters of Chappell Hill. Dr. Bartley Stanchfield, a Mainer, owned 27 slaves and listed a net worth over $200,000.[18] Much of the net worth of these planters was in human property, what people of the era referred to as "that peculiar institution." A male slave was worth $1,300 to $1,500,[19] while Chappell Hill acreage was readily available for the reasonable price of $25 to $35 an acre.[20]

Planters from the Deep South brought more than slaves with them when they moved to Texas and into the Brazos Valley. They brought the Southern way of life. Prosperity from cotton led to Chappell Hill becoming not only a center of wealth and aristocracy, but also one of scholarship and culture. Southerners assigned great importance to the refinement of an individual through classical education and they carried this with them to Texas. Chappell Hill Male and Female Institute opened in 1850, becoming Chappell Hill Male and Female College in 1852.[21] The Methodist Texas Conference acquired the college in 1854. They formed Soule University from the college's male faculty and students and Chappell Hill Female College from the female faculty and students.[22] Soule University opened its doors in Chappell Hill in 1856 with the intention of becoming *the* Methodist university for all of Texas. The wealthy planters of Chappell Hill and vicinity saw to it that these schools were well endowed. The cornerstone was laid in 1858 for the main building. Soule University student William Colbert wrote his sister on June 11, 1859, "A great many people were expected to move to Chappell Hill because of the three-story building to be completed within twelve months."[23] In fact, the imposing building was described as "spacious and perhaps the largest in the South."[24] The school had a faculty of six professors. Gabriel Felder, the largest slave owner in the county,[25] endowed a chair for Ancient and Modern Languages and Colonel Jared Kirby of nearby Alta Vista endowed a chair in Mathematics. The *Bellville Countryman*, published in adjacent Austin County, reported, "Washington County is one of the wealthiest and most intelligent counties in the State."[26]

Southerners also brought to Texas their code of honor. A man held to his word and expected others to do the same. People, as a matter of course, left their homes unlocked. Hospitality was offered to strangers, no matter how poor the host might be, and "to offer to pay for such hospitality was the quickest way to provoke a fight."[27] Strangers rarely took anything. At the same time, thieves were not tolerated and justice was dispensed quickly. Dr. John Washington Lockhart recalled two men in Chappell Hill being taken across the Brazos, where they were tied to large cottonwood trees and whipped in punishment for theft before being sent away.[28] A Southerner felt bound to challenge to a duel any man whom he felt had in any way impugned his honor. One might argue that the intense temperament and the tendency towards physical response to perceived harm done led Texans to enter into a fight that more reasonable men, like Sam Houston, knew they could not win.

The writings of Sir Walter Scott greatly influenced the Southern ethos. The repeated theme of Scott's historical novels was one of individual heroic action in

The grave marker of William Jones Heard (Texas Revolution), an early Texan hero, who resided in Chappell Hill.

the face of overbearing power threatening one's independence, home and family. Southerners easily translated this theme to their impassioned stand on states' rights. The aristocrats of Chappell Hill annually held a colorful costumed pageant, the highlight of which was a tournament in which young men performed feats of skill on horseback. One event involved riders attempting to collect small steel rings with a seven-foot lance as they raced by at full speed on their horse.[29] When the war began, Southerners carried over the romantic image of Scott's chivalrous knight to that of the gallant Confederate cavalryman.

The planters of Chappell Hill followed closely the fiery arguments in the United States Congress and Senate that threatened their privileged way of life. There was more involved than just slavery. Yankee manufacturers used their considerable influence in the federal government to obtain tariffs to protect their finished goods from foreign competition. Southern planters, including Texans, exported agricultural products to Europe and, in turn, imported manufactured goods from that continent. They favored free trade, as tariffs cost them dearly. The tariffs imposed by the federal government on European goods enabled Yankees to offer their goods at inflated prices that otherwise were unrealistic. Southerners argued with some justification that much of the money generated by the tariff was spent on federal projects in the North.

Planters throughout the South, including Texas, prepared to fight to defend their life of privilege built on the backs of slaves when Abraham Lincoln and the antislavery Republican Party gained power in 1860. They influenced the proud men of the South, whether or not planters or even slaveholders, to serve the newly formed Confederacy when the War Between the States began in the spring of 1861. Texans did so with enthusiasm. The proud men of Chappell Hill were determined to prove worthy of the reputation of Texans as fighting men, whether to defend their privileged way of life, their home state, their families or simply their own manly honor.

Numerous men from Chappell Hill served in Hood's Texas Brigade and Terry's Texas Rangers, two of the most renowned Texas units in the Confederate Army during the War Between the States. Several men from Chappell Hill served the entire course of the war with Hood's Texas Brigade and were paroled at Appomattox. A man from Chappell Hill led the Rangers in the last great cavalry charge of the war at Bentonville in North Carolina in March 1865. The Twenty-First, Twenty-Fourth and Twenty-Fifth Texas Cavalry Regiments were formed at Chappell Hill and led by men from Chappell Hill. Men from Chappell Hill were involved in Sibley's ill-fated expedition to win New Mexico for the Confederacy. They defended Vicksburg through Grant's long siege. An aging veteran of the Mexican border wars organized a company of middle-aged men and barely of-age boys from Chappell Hill that took part in the Battle of Galveston and restored that important port to the Confederacy. Men from Chappell Hill gave their lives at Murfreesboro, Gettysburg, Chickamauga and Knoxville. They were wounded at Second Manassas and the Wilderness and taken prisoner at Arkansas Post and Vicksburg. They served in Walker's Greyhounds in Louisiana and Granbury's Brigade in Cleburne's Fighting Division in Tennessee and Georgia. One man from Chappell Hill was the regimental flag bearer for the veteran Tenth Texas Infantry regiment that fought Sherman every step of the way in his drive to Atlanta.

Well over 100 men of Chappell Hill fought for the Confederacy in the war that reshaped our nation. That so many men from one small town fought in so many different regiments in so many important battles and campaigns may be unique. That so much of their experience was preserved in words and photos surely must be. This is their story and the story of their families. It is not a local history. It is a collective personal account of the Texan experience in the War Between the States.

1

Texas Secedes

The right to own slaves was one of the issues that drove Texans to fight for independence from Mexico. This same issue prevented for a time the admission of Texas into the Union. While Texans voted overwhelmingly in favor of annexation just months after winning independence, the administration of Martin Van Buren, a New Yorker and the first ever non-slaveholding president, refused Texas admission. It was not until 1845, when the United States became alarmed about British involvement in Texas, that the Northern bloc finally relented. Texas, upon admission, aligned itself with the other Southern slaveholding states. This relationship deepened as cotton and slaves became increasingly important to Texas.

The addition of Texas buoyed Southern control of the U.S. Senate at a time when rapid population increase in the North from immigration had cost the South control of the U.S. House of Representatives. Men like John C. Calhoun of South Carolina fought desperately to hammer out the Missouri Compromise, the Kansas-Nebraska Act and numerous other bills intended to protect the South's institution of slavery. The Southern bloc recognized that their power in the Senate would diminish over time if they did not continue to add to the number of Southern states in the Union. They looked to Texas, the frontier of the South, as their vehicle to this end. When serious expansion westward beyond Texas was cut off, prominent Southerners determined that expansion to the south into Mexico and across the Caribbean and the Gulf of Mexico was their only hope to maintain political control.

Texans needed little encouragement from neighboring Southern states to consider seizing control of Mexico. Slaveowners were infuriated by the protection that the Mexican border offered runaway slaves from Texas. Newspaper publisher Rip Ford estimated that as many as 4,000 fugitives lived just south of the Rio Grande[1]

BROWNING PLANTATION MANOR HOUSE. Colonel William Westcot Browning built his manor house of native-cut cedar in 1857. The house is held together with pegs, notched joints and square nails. The two-story house has eight large rooms, four up and four down, with a fireplace in each and a wide hall down the center of each floor. The Browning home, one of the finest residences in Chappell Hill, was the center of the antebellum town's social life. (Photograph by Thomas G. Stevens of Chappell Hill.)

and referred to the subjugation of Mexico as a "political necessity" for Texas.[2] There was some encouragement in this regard in 1855 upon the overthrow of dictator Santa Anna. Later that fall, there was strong public sentiment to cross the Rio Grande after a major fight along the border between Texas Rangers and Mexicans. Ford advised Ed Burleson, the leader of the Texas Rangers, "If you or McCulloch or Callahan would go up on the Brazos you could get money" for an invasion of Mexico.[3] The powerful cotton planters of the Brazos River Valley, men in Chappell Hill and the surrounding settlements, had both the money and the inclination to support such a move. However, by this time Texas, as part of the United States, no longer had the ability to declare war.

In the period between independence and statehood, Texans had attempted invasions of Mexico on several occasions. Claudius Buster arrived in Texas with his father in 1836 just after the hostilities with Mexico had ended. He settled in Washington

County, near what later would become the town site for Chappell Hill. Buster, the great-grandson of one of George Washington's Continental soldiers, was perhaps more inclined to fighting than farming. He eagerly volunteered to become a part of Somervell's 1842 expedition into Mexico. President Sam Houston ordered this punitive expedition after the Mexican Army made significant advances into Texas in three separate incidents. Somervell, after taking Guerrero, fell back across the border into Texas and disbanded. Claudius Buster was among those Texans who insisted on continuing the fight. Buster and four other elected captains led three hundred Texans back across the Mexican border into the town of Mier, where they engaged units of the Mexican Army. A Texan diarist wrote that Claudius Buster's Washington County company was most exposed in the fighting and that Mexican bullets "fell like hail against a wall immediately in the rear of Buster's Company, which was not over five feet high."[4] In the end, the greatly outnumbered Texans, exhausted and low on powder, food and water, surrendered. Buster wrote: "Although we lost the battle after fighting 18 hours, no one who participated in it is ashamed of it...." Many of the Texans in chains died in imprisonment. The last of the prisoners, including Claudius Buster, were not released until September 1844.

When Mexico severed relations with the United States in March 1845 after the U.S. annexation of Texas, Texans rushed to join the resulting war between the two nations that lasted from April 1846 until February 1848. Among those was James Nicholson, who lived at Chappell Hill until his death in 1903.[5] Terrell A. Jackson was another. In 1841, his father and uncles built a sawmill on New Year's Creek, just north of what would become the Chappell Hill town site. Terrell Jackson was 23 years old in May 1846 when he enlisted in the Washington County Rangers organizing at nearby Brenham.[6] The Rangers became Early's Company of the First Texas Cavalry.[7] Sergeant Jackson and his comrades saw considerable action in September 1846 at Monterrey, which the American Army captured after three days of fierce fighting in the streets.

In the aftermath of the war, the victorious United States forced Mexico to concede the Rio Grande River as the Texas-Mexico border and added vast amounts of land to the United States across the southwest. There was considerable debate after the Mexican War as to whether the United States should continue the occupation of Mexico and incorporate that country into the United States. But Northern statesmen would not consider annexing Mexico after the Democratic Party refused to agree that slavery would not be established within the new territory.[8]

While the politicians battled in Washington, Terrell A. Jackson and many other Mexican War veterans headed to California in 1849 and 1850 to seek their fortune in gold. Jackson, like most "49ers," found little gold. His wife died giving birth to their daughter while he was gone and he returned to Chappell Hill to become a prominent member of the community.[9] John A. Hargrove and a number of other Chappell Hill men, including John D. Rogers, left for California in February 1850. They took a steamboat from Warren down the Brazos and around to Galveston, where they fell in with Frank Terry and Tom Lubbock (who later would form Terry's Texas Rangers for the Confederacy). Hargrove was wintering in California in anticipation of the following season when a letter from Chappell Hill arrived, advising him of the death of his father. He honored his father's dying request that he return home to take care of the family business. The decision would bring him back to Texas in time to become embroiled in the fight.

While some young men dreamed of gold, men of power continued to direct their attention to adding new slave states to the Union. Filibustering, expeditions of private armies, became a popular vehicle. A force of 300 men departed from New Orleans in 1851 to "liberate" Cuba from Spain. Americans rioted and destroyed the Spanish consulate office in New Orleans upon learning that Cuban authorities had executed all those involved.[10] Nicaragua became a new focus for filibustering in the mid–1850s. Corpus Christi real estate entrepreneur Henry Kinney confided to a friend: "It requires but a few hundred Americans and particularly Texans to take control of all that country [Nicaragua]. I have grants of land and enough to make a start upon safely and legally. I intend to make a suitable government and the rest will follow."[11] The pro-slavery administration of President Franklin Pierce at first was supportive of Kinney's intentions, stating: "It would be difficult to suggest a single object of interest, external or internal, more important to the United States."[12] But Kinney lost political support and his followers deserted him to join another American.

William Walker, a former newspaper editor from Tennessee, took advantage of civil war in Nicaragua and seized control of that Central American country by the end of 1855. Yankee tycoon Cornelius Vanderbilt provided the initial backing for the adventurer in the hopes of securing a transportation route from the Atlantic to the Pacific Ocean. But when Vanderbilt pulled back, Walker was able to obtain support from Southerners. The *Galveston Daily News* editorialized:

> We believe the great question of slavery must be seriously affected, if not, controlled by the changes that are now going on and must, sooner or later, be consummated, in the territory of Central America and Mexico.... The present ... occupants ... [of the] unproductive wilderness, must sooner or later, give way to a more enlightened race.[13]

Many other Texas papers agreed. President Franklin Pierce's formal recognition of Walker's regime in May 1856 legitimized the adventurer's filibustering success.

Prominent Chappell Hill planter R. J. Swearingen, a former Texas state representative, traveled to Nicaragua after Walker had taken control to evaluate the potential of the soil and the land. Upon his return, Swearingen addressed a gathering in Galveston on April 9 concerning "the prospects in this land of promise." The Houston *Telegraph* editor noted that "Dr. Swearingen is well known here and his statements will command confidence."[14]

The Austin *State Gazette* published Swearingen's account of his trip in its May 17, 1856, issue. Swearingen began his front page with the comment that "Since my return from Central America, I have been frequently interrogated, both orally and by letter." Swearingen referred to "the chivalric Walker" with direct reference to Walker's efforts "to Americanize this country." The article offered detailed observations, including Swearingen's belief that "its fertility is superior to that of the Nile Delta." In closing, Swearingen delivered a powerful vision: "'Tis here where young America shall have the prerogative ... leaving in its tracks the foot-prints of

Americans, large plantations, State-houses and Colleges, with domes pointing toward the skies, together with all the concomitants of American greatness."[15]

Other supporters of Walker held public meetings in Galveston on May 24 and 26. Prominent Texans, including General Sidney Sherman and Judge David Burnet, former president of the Texas republic, pledged support and discussed sending emigrants to Nicaragua.[16] Such meetings continued on a regular weekly basis in Galveston and Houston throughout the summer. Walker realized that he was striking a chord with powerful Southerners and officially re-established slavery in Nicaragua in late 1856. He sent an official commissioner to the State of Texas in January 1857 to solicit funds and enlist soldiers. The U.S. government nervously assessed the volatile situation as expeditions of armed Texans began leaving Galveston for Nicaragua.

The grand scheme suffered a setback in May 1857 when Nicaraguans drove Walker out of their country. He returned to America a hero and began a speaking tour intended to gather renewed support. Walker used his slavery decree more than ever to establish himself as the champion of the South. In a speech in Mobile he told a crowd he was seeking to "extend your institution."[17] His subsequent expedition in December 1858 was a dismal failure. Although he was arrested and delivered to U.S. authorities as a prisoner, Walker was soon free and reorganizing. He led an invasion of Honduras in the spring of 1860, but his luck ran out. The Royal British Navy captured Walker and handed him over to the Honduran government, who promptly executed the filibuster.

Texans did not give up on Nicaragua after Walker's demise. Mirabeau Lamar, who had succeeded Sam Houston as president of the Texas republic, applied to President James Buchanan for a diplomatic posting to Nicaragua. Upon obtaining the posting, Lamar spoke openly and vehemently about the need for an American protectorate in Nicaragua.[18] Even Sam Houston, Lamar's old enemy, publicly supported Lamar's position. Houston went so far as to offer that he might even lead the filibuster himself if he was not so old.[19]

While Texans entertained filibustering schemes, there was yet little talk of secession. Washington County's own Sam Houston was the man most responsible for Texans remaining calm. Texas' greatest hero made his home in Independence, just north of Chappell Hill, and counted numerous Chappell Hill men among his closest friends and strongest supporters. When Houston lost his bid for re-election to represent Texas in the U.S. Senate, he ran for governor in 1859 as an independent candidate. Houston won "with little effort on his part"[20] on a platform of "The Constitution and the Union." But events were moving too quickly for even a man like Sam Houston to maintain control in Texas.

The abolitionist John Brown's raid on the U.S. Army arsenal at Harper's Ferry in October 1859 sent a shock wave across the South. The realization that prominent New Englanders financed John Brown and that many other Northerners justified his actions heightened fears of slave uprisings.[21] Many became convinced that the hope of settling differences through the democratic process was disappearing. Paramilitary groups began drilling in both North and South in anticipation of war. Rural townspeople throughout the South became increasingly suspicious of and hostile toward outsiders. Transplanted Yankees were threatened and some were run off. Travelers were turned away or carefully searched.

The Texas Senate responded by amending the criminal code on February 11, 1860. Anyone found distributing abolitionist literature could expect two to five years imprisonment. Anyone subscribing to such literature could be jailed for up to six months.[22] A man faced jail time up to three months for playing a game of chance with a slave or a free person of color and imprisonment of two to five years for discussing a slave's situation "to endeavor to render such slave discontented with his state of slavery."[23] In July 1860, authorities in Chappell Hill arrested three men who "were convicted of having confessed to be Abolitionists ... and had been seen to take negroes privately into their rooms."[24] Local authorities ordered them to leave the state and showed them the way out of town.

The summer of 1860 has been compared to the Nat Turner insurrection.[25] The Texas Troubles, as the events became known, began when a series of urban fires were attributed to abolitionists.[26] The most significant fire destroyed downtown Dallas, a city that had been the scene of the whipping of two abolitionist Methodist ministers the previous year. The Austin *State Gazette* and the Houston *Telegraph* published an inflammatory letter from the editor of the Dallas *Herald* that claimed the interrogation of "certain negroes" had revealed a statewide plot to kill whites and destroy their homes.[27] Slaveowners across the state responded with violence and force at the slightest indication of a potential problem in "one of the greatest witch hunts in American history."[28] In all, vigilante groups comprised of leading citizens[29] killed at least 30, and perhaps as many as 100, blacks and whites in Texas that summer.[30] The extent of the hangings and whippings led one New York paper to warn, "Texas is no place for Northern people just now."[31]

Many travelers passed through Chappell Hill, a thriving commercial center on the main route between Austin and Houston. A letter from Chappell Hill, dated August 20, 1860, and published in the Goliad *Messenger*, related one of many incidents that summer:

> A man from New York, who was employed in making engagements for maps through the country last winter, while delivering them during the summer, was suspected of having something more dangerous than the maps he was vending; his trunk was examined and found to contain a large number of revolvers, which he acknowledged had been brought to supply negroes with fighting implements. He was summarily disposed of by the use of a "two bit" rope. His wife in a short time after came on laden with "more of the same sort" and she is now in prison.[32]

Chappell Hill, as the Methodist center of Texas, was a standard stopping point for traveling Methodist circuit riders. These itinerant preachers on horseback carried the Word of God to rural communities. Any man able to preach effectively and ride a horse could become a circuit rider.[33] The Methodist Church had split over the issue of slavery and it is likely that at least some of these circuit riders passing through Chappell Hill were abolitionists. U.S. congressman John H. Reagan of Texas laid the blame clearly on the Methodists when he spoke before his colleagues in Congress on January 15, 1861:

1. Texas Secedes

> We found, for the last two or three years, that the members of the Methodist Church North and others, living in Texas, were propagating abolition doctrines there. We warned them not to carry on their schemes of producing disaffection among our Negroes; but they persisted, and did not cease until they had organized a society called the "Mystic Red." Under its auspices, the night before the last of August election the towns were to be burned and the people murdered. There now lie in ashes near a dozen towns and villages in my district…. The poisonings were only arrested by information which came to light before the plan could be carried into execution. The citizens were forced to stand guard for months, so that no man could have passed through the towns between dark and daylight without making himself known. A portion of them paid the penalty of their crimes. Others were driven out of the country … the results of abolition teaching; a part of the irrepressible conflict; a part of the legitimate fruits of Republicanism.[34]

The events of the summer of 1860 led even moderate Texans to consider secession. The unrest in Texas created opportunity for George Bickley, a Cincinnati physician. Bickley founded a secret society, the Knights of the Golden Circle, in 1854 to appeal to Southern dreams of expansion. His grand objective was to establish a slave empire extending from the southern United States across Mexico and Central America and including Cuba and the West Indies—"Golden Circle" deriving from this broad circular area, some 2,400 miles in diameter. Bickley foresaw the possibility of an empire that would become a key player in the world's supply of a number of commodities, including cotton, but also tobacco, sugar, rice and coffee. He left Cincinnati in 1859 to escape creditors and headed into the South.

There was considerable interest in Texas in Bickley's movement. The Knights in Texas felt sufficiently strong in the spring of 1860 to make plans to invade Mexico. Albert and Pryor Lea of Goliad approached Governor Sam Houston to win favor for their bold move.[35] Houston, instead, requested U.S. Army assistance to block the illegal venture. Colonel Robert E. Lee, the commanding military officer in Texas, insisted that Houston was exaggerating the threat and refused any help.[36] Houston then resorted to a public proclamation on March 21, 1860, against the Knights and their activities in Texas. The move worked and the Knights failed to gather sufficient support. Bickley, who had promised to arrive at the head of a large force, failed to show. Houston sent out the Texas Rangers, who dispersed those few Knights assembled, and the crisis evaporated for the moment. The events of the summer of 1860 offered Bickley a second chance in Texas.

George Bickley finally made his appearance in Texas on October 10, 1860, arriving at the port of Galveston. He spent the remainder of the year organizing in Texas, where powerful planter interests warmly received him. Bickley spoke in Houston on October 30 and the meeting was reported in most positive terms in that town's *Telegraph* on the following day. The paper reported that 40 men joined Bickley's ranks following his address. The *Telegraph* served as a means of communication for Bickley for the next two months, allowing him free advertisement, providing regular information on his activities to its readers and even publishing Bickley's letters.[37]

One such letter Bickley sent to the editor of the *Telegraph*, dated November 3, 1860, "to keep the Texas Division fully advised of the movements …"[38] noted that he had visited and established castles (local chapters) in Houston, Austin, Brenham, LaGrange, Navasota, Huntsville and Chappell Hill. Bickley identified George W. Chappell as the leader of the Knights in Chappell Hill with 17 members.[39] Bickley reported establishing 32 castles in Texas. He left his nephew, Charles, and a Dr. George Cupples to continue his work from the Knights' state headquarters in San Antonio.[40]

While the Knights of the Golden Circle were planning a second attempt at an invasion of Mexico, events on the national level were overtaking their movement. The Republican Party nominated Illinois lawyer Abraham Lincoln, an avowed opponent of slavery, in May 1860 as its candidate for president. Influential men across the South roused crowds to prepare for war. Texas Attorney General George Flournoy told a large crowd gathered in Austin on September 22:

> What will you do if Lincoln is elected? That, I know, is what you want to hear about. I say, secede from the Union![41]

The Southern states refused even to put Lincoln's name on the ballot. Abraham Lincoln swept the Northern states in the election held on November 6, 1860, and in so doing secured enough electoral votes to win the presidency. Word of the results reached Galveston two days after the election. Galveston authorities sent word to Houston via a telegraph line that had been completed just two months earlier. E. E. Cushing published an extra edition of his *Telegraph* and sent his paper out to Brenham, Chappell Hill, Navasota, Washington, Independence and all the surrounding towns.

Governor Sam Houston tried to calm the situation, telling a crowd at Huntsville on November 14, 1860, "So long as the Constitution is maintained by Federal authority and Texas is not made the victim of 'Federal wrong,' I am for the Union as it is."[42] Not all Texans were so calm. Planter Burrel B. Hutchinson of Chappell Hill chaired a convention in nearby Washington that declared its intention to "withdraw all our relations from non-slaveholding states."[43] Conventions across the South passed similar resolutions in favor of seceding from the Union.

The impact of Lincoln's election was immediate in other ways. Al Baines, a mechanic in Chappell Hill, received a letter from his brother in December 1860:

> [I]f not for the Money Crisis which has been brought about by the Elections of Lincoln. In Houston & Galveston the Merchants have all closed down and will not sell for anything but money. Cotton has always been just as good as money until now.... The Banks in New Orleans have almost entirely suspended business and we depend on them for what paper money we use. So we are cut off of the use of much money until we see how Old Abe's Election will go with the People. The excitement is very high here in favor of Secession ... I am not. I am in favor of Taxing Every kind and all goods of all kinds that come from any of the Northern cities that have passed Laws in opposition to the fugitive Slave Law and by retaliating in that way I think that they can be made to observe the rights of our Property.[44]

Secessionists in Texas demanded that Governor Houston order a state convention to allow debate as to the formal secession of Texas from the Union, but Houston refused. The December 17, 1860, Brenham *The Texas Ranger* asked, "Have We a Dictator?" and charged, "The treatment of Governor Houston, towards the Houston Committee ... calling for a session of the Legislature, was characterized by his usual contemptuous manner." The article added fuel to the fire of secession, opining: "Our sister Southern States, who are more fortunate than we, in having men at their head who reflect their will, and lead them in the remedial course they are adopting, have left us far behind in the general movement of resistance to Republican rule."[45] A letter to the editor printed directly under the anti–Houston editorial in *The Texas Ranger* reported that a committee of citizens had "passed a resolution requesting the Governor to resign and permit some other person to fill the Executive chair who would comply with the manifest wishes of the people of the State ... without a dissenting voice."[46] Another small piece noted, "[A] military company has been organized in Washington County, composed of sixty men." The state legislators ultimately endorsed a convention without the governor's consent. The convention convened in Austin on January 28, 1861.

Reverend George Washington Carter, president of Chappell Hill's Soule University, was among those who went to Austin for the secession convention. The native Virginian had been at Chappell Hill only since May 1860.[47] Carter was a gifted orator who had been preaching since the age of 17.[48] He was a presiding elder while still a boy when Bishop Paine took him on a series of engagements across the South "to exhibit his rare gifts."[49] Carter became a professor of ethics at the University of Mississippi with a well-established reputation as one of the most prominent intellectual minds in the country. Comparisons were even drawn between Carter and Alexander Hamilton and Yale Divinity School's renowned Jonathan Edwards.[50] George Washington Carter was 32 years old when the Texas Conference and the board of Soule University approached him to become the new president of Soule University.[51]

George Washington Carter, although not a Chappell Hill slaveowner, was a fiery advocate of secession. While not an elected delegate to the secession convention, he managed to gain an opportunity to speak during the recess on the opening day. His style was quiet, not loud, but those who knew Reverend Carter remarked that he "had phenomenal endowments ... no match in the forum of logic."[52] His remarks to the convention were recorded as "an address which for closeness of logic, beauty of diction, anecdote and pathos, all present coincided in the opinion was rarely equaled, never excelled."[53] That Chappell Hill could send such a prominent orator to the secession convention further enhanced the town's reputation as a sophisticated center of education and culture.

The Austin convention passed an ordinance of secession on February 1 by a vote of 166 to 8, resolving:

> [T]his abolition organization has been actively sowing the seeds of discord....
> By consolidating their strength, they have placed the slave-holding states in a hopeless minority in the federal congress and rendered representation to no avail in protecting Southern rights.... They have proclaimed, and at the ballot box sustained, the revolutionary doctrine that there is a "higher law" than the constitution and laws of our Federal Union, and virtually that they will disregard their oaths and trample upon our rights.... We the delegates of the people of Texas, in

> Convention assembled, have passed an ordinance dissolving all political connection with the government of the United States of America and ... appeal to the intelligence and patriotism of the freemen of Texas to ratify the same at the ballot.[54]

The convention set February 23, 1861, as the date for a statewide referendum to ratify the ordinance by popular vote. Men across Texas debated the merits of the ordinance. Governor Houston's unwavering loyalty to the United States was well known and he was met with anger and sometimes threats wherever he spoke. Planter Burrel B. Hutchinson debated Houston on the steps of his plantation home outside Chappell Hill.[55] By February 1861, the general sentiment in the Brazos River Valley was overwhelmingly for secession and few men in Chappell Hill or anywhere else shared sentiments with their old friend and governor. Over 62 percent of the Texan electorate cast their vote on February 23, 1861. The final tally was 46,129 to secede from the Union and 14,697 to remain.[56] Ninety-six percent of the voters in Washington County voted for secession. The men of Chappell Hill voted 175 in favor of and 2 against. Voting in those days was not by secret ballot. The names of those against secession have been lost to history. They left town and never returned.

Upon the results of the referendum, the convention declared Texas independent on March 5, 1861. The official response to the Federal authorities in Washington, D.C. was:

> Texas is therefore a separate sovereign State ... and ... her citizens and people are absolved from all allegiance to the government known as the United States of America.[57]

By the time of the ratification of Texan secession, six states of the Deep South already had withdrawn from the Union and formed the Confederate States of America. Representatives of South Carolina, Georgia, Alabama, Florida, Mississippi and Louisiana met in Montgomery, Alabama, at the beginning of February 1861 to set up a new provisional government. Representatives from Texas joined them soon afterwards. The secret society of the Knights of the Golden Circle seem to have played an important role in the secessionist movement in Texas by providing a rallying point and an organization in place when the time came for action. They likely were a factor not only at the polls, but also afterwards. The Knights merged into the military organizations, which formed as the war began.[58] Southerners took up arms throughout January and February, seizing U.S. Army installations and munitions. On the night of February 15, 1861, two weeks before the inauguration of Lincoln as president and two months before the firing upon Fort Sumter, 1,000 Texan volunteers under Ben McCulloch seized the U.S. Army military supplies at the Alamo in San Antonio without a shot being fired.[59] They lowered the U.S. flag and replaced it with the Lone Star flag. Many of McCulloch's volunteers were from the various Knight castles that had been organized in towns across Texas.

Dick Swearingen, the son of prominent Chappell Hill planter R. J. Swearingen, was a law student when the troubles began. After Ben McCulloch's crowd seized the Alamo, the Texas Committee on Public Safety authorized the forming of regiments of volunteer cavalry. Swearingen was among 500 men who enlisted in Houston to serve under the command of Rip Ford. He was assigned to Captain Ed Waller's company.

Ford's objective was the U.S. Army base at Brazos Santiago, a fortified position not far from Brownsville at the mouth of the Rio Grande River. The small army of Texan volunteers boarded two ships at Galveston on February 28, 1861, just two weeks after McCulloch's seizure of the Alamo. They sailed south along the coast, landed on the beach and stormed Brazos Santiago. The 12 men within the walls surrendered without a shot. The Texans gathered in the parade ground to watch the lowering of the Stars and Stripes and cheer the raising of the Lone Star flag. Swearingen referred to Brazos Santiago in his journal as "that miserable little island"[60] and was delighted ten days later when Ford gave the order to march to Brownsville. Ford negotiated an agreement with the outnumbered Federal troops at Brownsville on March 15 and for the second time relieved Federal troops of their weapons without firing a shot. It was still a month before the shelling of Fort Sumter that would propel the nation into war.

At first, the prospects at Brownsville were encouraging for Swearingen.

> I was never more charmed with a camp and pictured for myself a wild but joyous future with dark eyed senoritas wandering by moonlight along the grassy banks of our lovely lake while soft notes from sweet guitars would wake the infant stars.... But alas for human expectations so gaudy and glorious soon melted into nothingness— disease fastened its loving arms around me Oh! and embraced with more zeal and devotion was ever given a Mexican beauty to a Texas soldier. For two long months I lay upon a bed of straw, friendless and penniless racked by a thousand pains, and almost consumed by burning fevers. Verily I thought the dark angel would close my career — but He who does all things well — had his duties for me to perform and restored my health and hopes.[61]

Ford's soldiers were put to work improving the earthen embankments. Swearingen wrote:

> Remained in Brownsville six months, most of the time employed in erecting ... a picturesque mud-daubers nest.... We soon became worn out with the humdrum life and having completed our mud monument of folly, were discharged on 15 Sept. (1861).[62]

He returned home to Chappell Hill, as he described his return, "telling of bloodless victories and valueless trophies." The preliminary contests fought by Texan volunteer soldiers to seize Federal arsenals and drive Federal troops from Texas soil were but the beginning of a long contest.

Governor Sam Houston remained a symbol of Texan resistance to secession. In late March 1861, Texans deposed Governor Sam Houston from office for refusing to take the oath of allegiance to the Confederate States. Houston was en route by stage from Austin to his home near the San Jacinto battlefield when his friends and former comrades in Washington County asked him to stop and speak in Brenham, near Chappell Hill. Houston did not want to speak, but agreed to do so when he heard angry secessionists yelling that they would not let him. News spread throughout the county that Houston would speak on the next day, Easter Sunday.[63] People flowed into Brenham from Chappell Hill and the other neighboring towns. A huge crowd of excited men pressed into the Washington County courthouse to hear Houston.

Dr. John Washington Lockhart of Chappell Hill grew up knowing General Sam, a close friend of his father's.[64] He remembered Houston as:

> the finest looking man that I ever saw. After serving in the civil war and seeing many of the leading military men on both sides, he was, in my judgment, vastly the superior of them all. General R. E. Lee came nearer him in soldierly bearing and commanding appearance than any man I ever saw. He was a natural born ruler, both in the field and forum.[65]

But Sam Houston in 1861 was past his prime and a tired man. When Houston entered the courthouse to address the crowd on the following day, some men in the crowd cried out, "Don't let him speak." Others yelled, "Kill him." Hugh McIntyre, a wealthy Brenham planter and an ardent secessionist, leaped onto a table and drew his Colt revolver. He answered the crowd,

> I and 100 other friends of Governor Houston have invited him to address us, and we will kill the first man who insults, or who may, in any way attempt to injure him.... There is no other man alive who has more right to be heard by the people of Texas. Now, fellow-citizens, give him your close attention; and you ruffians, keep quiet, or I will kill you.[66]

The crowd settled down and Houston spoke. The old Texan defiantly told the crowd, "The hiss of the mob and the howls of their jackal leaders cannot deter me nor compel me to take the oath of allegiance to a so-called Confederate Government."[67] He protested "surrendering the Federal Constitution, its Government and its glorious flag,"[68] to which he referred as "glorious heritages bequeathed to the South,"[69] and reminded the crowd "Washington declared for an indivisible union."[70] Houston urged those listening to understand that no government could survive if its Constitution permitted a state to secede at any time that it chose. Houston stressed his belief that the majority of the South opposed secession. In closing, the former president and governor of Texas told his audience that, as a result of secession, war was inevitable and foretold:

> [T]he civil war which is now near at hand will be stubborn and of long duration ... the fearful conflict will fill our fair land with untold suffering, misfortune and disaster. The soil of our beloved South will drink deep the precious blood of our sons and brethren.... The die has been cast by your secession leaders.[71]

Houston rode off into retirement with Texas in the hands of secessionists presenting a solid front.

Abraham Lincoln was inaugurated president of the United States on March 4, 1861. On April 12, 1861, as Federal supply ships approached, Confederate artillery opened fire upon Fort Sumter, marking the commencement of hostilities. When

Lincoln called for volunteers to defend the Union, the four states of the Upper South, Arkansas, North Carolina, Tennessee, and Virginia, seceded and joined the Confederacy. The *Brenham Enquirer* of April 18, 1861, reported to the citizens of Washington County "The War Begun!" and "The Ball in Motion":

> A large number of our citizens gathered around the stopping point of the [rail] cars on Monday evening last, evincing an unusual eagerness to hear from Charleston through the extras of the *Telegraph* feeling that some decisive action had certainly taken place. In this they were not doomed to disappointment. The gratifying news of an attack upon Fort Sumpter [sic] and the almost certain victory that awaited the forces of the Southern Confederacy was most enthusiastically received. At night several rounds were fired, when Judge Oldham being waited upon appeared in the court house and delivered an appropriate address amid the cheers of a most enthusiastic auditory....[72]

A cannon salute was fired in Houston's courthouse square, "rejoicing at the fall of Fort Sumpter [sic]." Reference was made that "The citizens of Galveston are inaugurating measures for the defence of that city." The paper reported, "The State Convention of the supporters of the Southern Confederate States in opposition to Black Republicans alias, unionists, will be held at Dallas on the 27th May next," and that a convention would be held in Brenham on May 4 to appoint delegates.[73] The Confederacy's secretary of war was quoted as saying, "In less than three months the Confederate forces would be in possession of the City of Washington."

On April 17, just five days after Confederate forces fired on Fort Sumter in Charleston harbor, George Washington Carter's native state of Virginia seceded from the Union. Carter had not yet been president of Soule University for a year. On June 24, 1861, Carter delivered a "plan" to the board of trustees "for the future management of the university."[74] In the plan, Carter suggested that the university could expect half of the enrollment in the coming school year "for reasons affecting the students," i.e., the war. He suggested that the reduced student body he expected could be managed with only three professors. Carter told the board, "I may find it necessary for religious, political, patriotic and necessary reasons to take part in the war," but made clear that he wanted to retain his position. He proposed that he and two other professors retain their positions with the university but draw no salary until their return at the end of the war. Carter told the board that he and the two others "are not only fully in heart, and actually identified with Texas, but with the University and with Methodists in Texas—we never more fully felt all this than now."[75]

George Washington Carter's ninth and final point of his lengthy, well-laid plan was to advise the board to "get my wife to read this memorandum as I fear you will not be able to decipher my scribbling." The board approved the plan and further agreed that it be published in the *Texas Christian Advocate*.[76] George Washington Carter resigned his position as president of Soule University and headed home to serve Virginia. Carter, much to the regret of the board of trustees, spoke in Chappell Hill before departing. He delivered an impassioned appeal to the students to join him in enlisting to serve in the Confederate Army. Edmund Duggan, who later became a captain in the Fourth Infantry of Hood's Brigade,[77] was among the many students who did go off to war. It was the beginning of the end for Soule University. There had been 166 students enrolled at Soule University when the school year began in the fall of 1860, and the school had plans to add departments of law, medicine and theology, and even offer post-graduate study. The academic institution was a centerpiece of Chappell Hill's prestige in Texas. Its demise would foreshadow that of Chappell Hill itself.

As Texas prepared for war, Sam Houston warned friends at Independence on May 10, 1861:

> [T]here must be discipline and subordination to law and order. Without this, armies will be raised in vain.... The Northern people by their nature and occupation are subordinate to law and order. They are capable of great endurance and a high state of discipline ... Never underrate the strength of your enemy. The South claims superiority over them in point of fearless courage. Equal them in discipline ... I give this advice as an old soldier. I know the value of subordination and discipline.[78]

Few Americans at the outset of the conflict understood the grim realities of war as well as old General Sam. His foresight would prove to be only too correct. Yet, in the spring of 1861, men on both sides rushed to enlist and achieve glory in battle before the war ended. The men of Chappell Hill were no exception.

Some men of Chappell Hill enlisted to fight in defense of their way of life. The slave-based cotton economy allowed the planters a life of wealth and privilege. But there were also other reasons for these men to enlist. Not all of the Chappell Hill men who served in the Confederate Army owned slaves. For some, the war simply offered an opportunity for adventure, a chance to escape the daily routine of life on the farm or in the shop. Volunteering was often motivated by personal honor. Those who chose not to enlist found their manhood questioned. A young man from a small town such as Chappell Hill would have found it difficult to charm the ladies had he hesitated to fight for his homeland. Lieutenant J. B. Wheeler wrote to Miss Nannie back in Chappell Hill from his posting in Louisiana:

> It is with feelings, commingled with fear and pleasure, that I attempt to address you for the first time.... It is one of my greatest pleasures to have the honor of corresponding with you. I arrived in this land of frogs, mosquitoes, alligators, cajins [Cajuns] and Jayhawkers on yesterday morning ... we are confident of success, our cause is just and feeling that God always assists those that are in the right.... It is her bright smile that animates me to do my whole duty without complaining. It is the hope of gaining her favor that makes me lively in performing the laborious duties of the soldier....[79]

Many men from Chappell Hill volunteered simply to fight for Texas. This may or may not have been related to the concept of states' rights. But there certainly was more loyalty to Texas than to the Federal government based in far-off Washington. The defense of Texas and of their homes and their families was one motive the men of Chappell Hill had in common.

These men, flawed mortals that they were, gave up all that they valued in life to serve. They left behind their families, their homes, and whether or not they realized it, some gave up their futures. They enlisted with their friends to risk their lives together with honor. They were gallant, courageous men ... all of them.

2

Terry's Texas Rangers' First Blood

They were hellions on horseback. A high-ranking Confederate officer referred to them as "a damned armed mob."[1] They shunned the traditional saber of the cavalryman and armed themselves instead with double-barreled shotguns, pistols and bowie knives. They earned a reputation for courage and recklessness, charging boldly at the enemy and opening fire with their shotguns at point-blank range. They were the troopers of the Eighth Texas Cavalry Regiment, better known as Terry's Texas Rangers.

The Eighth Texas Cavalry, C. S. A., was conceived in April 1861 on a stage between Austin and Brenham. Benjamin Franklin "Frank" Terry, a wealthy Fort Bend County planter, John Wharton, a Brazoria County attorney, and Thomas Lubbock, a Houston cotton broker, were returning home from the state secession convention when they resolved to organize a cavalry regiment for the Confederacy.[2] The three went to Montgomery, Alabama, to petition Jefferson Davis for commissions. They were initially unsuccessful. The determined men followed the Confederate government when it moved to Richmond, Virginia, in June. All three ended up serving on the staff of General James Longstreet at First Manassas, the first big battle of the war. In the aftermath, Davis gave them a commission to raise a regiment.

The call for volunteers that Terry posted in the Houston newspaper in August 1861 was for "mounted rangers ... for service in Virginia." The opportunity to serve as cavalry and to take part in what was expected to be the big fight attracted a great deal of interest. Nearly 1,200 men responded.

Twenty-year-old Daniel Harvie Browning of Chappell Hill was among those who volunteered to fight with Frank Terry. Some critics referred to the Confederacy's effort as "a rich man's war and a poor man's fight." Daniel Harvie Browning's family was among the wealthiest in Washington County. Numerous others from Chappell Hill, who fought alongside Browning in Company K, Terry's Eighth Texas Cavalry, were also well-to-do and cultured men. Daniel's father, William Westcot Browning, was a wealthy planter from Mississippi who moved to Texas in 1856. He was of an aristocratic line, his mother's family, the Westcots, having founded Providence, Rhode Island, in pre-colonial times. The Brownings' 6,000 square foot Greek Revival manor house was one of the finest homes in Chappell Hill. William Browning was known around the state as Colonel Browning. The origin of his title, which may have come from the Mississippi militia or perhaps the Mexican War, is not clear. He was "a great lover of horse flesh,"[3] which he raised himself on his 2,000 acre plantation just south of the town center. His son, Daniel, shared his love of horses and was anxious to join the Confederate cavalry.

The Brownings were deeply religious. Colonel Browning read a chapter of the Bible in the morning and at night and led his family in daily prayer. He was a man who had promised his mother as a young boy to never take a drink of alcohol and held to his word throughout his life.[4] His wife shared his strong beliefs. She was close to Daniel, her only son. She gave him a small copy of the New Testament to take with him to war and inscribed it "My Dear Son, Read this Book carefully every day and remember your Mother."[5] Daniel Harvie Browning carried the book on campaign in his breast pocket.

Perhaps the best known of the Chappell Hill boys that served in Terry's Eighth Texas Cavalry was James Fiske "Doc" Matthews, who late in the war rose to the rank of captain. The Brownings and Matthews had lived near each other in Sharon, Mississippi. James's father, the Reverend Jacob Matthews, was a close friend of Colonel Browning. The Brownings moved to Texas in 1856. Reverend Matthews followed in 1859 after the death of his wife.[6] Three men of Chappell Hill's Routt family enlisted in Terry's Texas Rangers and served in Company K with Daniel Browning, while a fourth fought in Company A. Company K also included Hammond and Green Bouldin from Chappell Hill. The Routts and Bouldins migrated together from Alabama to Chappell Hill.

Hammond Bouldin was among the first of the family to arrive in the Chappell Hill area, traveling with James Wilburn and Edmund Bouldin. Hammond married his cousin, Martha, and their only child was born in Washington County in 1847. Martha died in February 1851 of childbirth complications. Hammond, a practicing physician, professed his love to Mary Chappell, founder of Chappell Hill, in a poem in September 1851.[7] When nothing developed, Bouldin set his sight on Colonel Browning's daughter, Eliza. Family tradition relates that Colonel Browning wanted better for his daughter than a poor country doctor such as Hammond. The determined young man rode up to Browning mansion on his horse, Eliza climbed on back and the couple eloped.[8]

The Iankes brothers, Albert and Charles, natives of Sweden and sons of Chappell Hill's silversmith, were non-slaveholders who served in Company K. A. L. Baines became a sergeant in Company K. There was John Grissett, who married Susan Travis,

HAMMOND BOULDIN. Dr. Hammond Bouldin enlisted with his brother, Green, in Terry's Texas Rangers. The two served in Company K alongside many other men of Chappell Hill. Hammond was promoted to lieutenant in 1862. He died in 1905. (From *Confederate Veteran*, 1905.)

daughter of the famous Alamo hero, and Robert Elgin, Hiram Rice, Theodore Coffield and R. N. Condren. Brothers Austin and Presley Baker enlisted in Company A. Austin was the town treasurer for Chappell Hill and owned a paint shop on Main Street with his brother Milton,[9] and Presley was an attorney. In February 1861, Presley had just joined Chappell Hill's Masonic Lodge to which his older brothers belonged.[10] John Justice served in Company F. These were a few, though not all, of the men of Chappell Hill who served in Terry's Texas Rangers.

One thousand men were sworn into service as the Eighth Texas Cavalry Regiment in downtown Houston on September 7, 1861. All had signed up "for the duration of the war" and were proud to note that fact. They were horsemen born to the saddle, Texans by every measure. The Rangers wore distinctive jackets trimmed in red and proudly displayed the insignia of the Lone Star on their broad-rimmed hats. The regimental battle flag was dark blue with a white circle in the center. In the circle were a red cross with eleven gold stars and the words "God defend the right."[11] The entertainer Harry McCarthy wrote the song "The Bonnie Blue Flag" in the spring of 1861. The song became extremely popular in the South, rivaling even "Dixie." Terry's Texas Rangers adopted the song.

> We are a band of brothers,
> Native to the soil
> Fighting for the property
> We gained by honest toil.
> And when our rights were threatened,
> The cry rose near and far;
> Hurrah for the Bonnie Blue Flag
> That bears a single star!

2. Terry's Texas Rangers' First Blood

Chorus:
Hurrah! Hurrah!
For Southern rights, Hurrah!
Hurrah for the Bonnie Blue Flag
That bears a single star!

Terry's Rangers advanced to New Orleans after being sworn into the service of the Confederacy. Private Daniel Harvie Browning wrote his father from New Orleans on September 29, 1861:

> Dear Pa, As I have not written home since I left, and it has been nearly two weeks since, I have taken this opportunity of letting you know that we are all well but do not know where we shall be sent. We received orders this morning to be ready to start tomorrow morning for Grand Junction at six o'clock and from thence it was uncertain whether we would go to Virginia, Kentucky or Kansas. Col. Terry is in favor of going to Kentucky. There is some talk of an attempt being made to turn

JOHN C. JUSTICE · AUSTIN CLAY BAKER

John Justice enlisted in Terry's Texas Rangers with many other men of Chappell Hill on September 7, 1861. He was a long-time merchant in Chappell Hill and served as alderman on at least two separate occasions before his death in 1885. Austin Baker with his brother Milton ran a paint shop in Chappell Hill before the war. Austin, town treasurer before the war, enlisted in Terry's Texas Rangers and served in Company A. He and his wife Susan lost two infants before the war and one during the war. Austin and Milton were quite successful in the cotton business in Galveston after the war. (From the Archives of the Chappell Hill Historical Society.)

us into infantry but our officers say that the regiment shall be disbanded first, if it is I reckon that I will come back to Texas very soon. It is all doubt and uncertainty before us. Although I am discouraged still I think there is something wrong about, or our officers would know what is going to be done. There is now 4 companies of the regiment in the City and we start tomorrow for we don't know where. I have to go. My love to all. I will write soon. Your son, Dan.[12]

There was some disappointment among the Rangers when they learned that they were not going to Virginia, as there was a general sense that the major fighting would be in the east. The Texas Brigade, composed of three regiments of Texas infantry, had only just preceded the Rangers by a few days and was on its way to Virginia. But General Albert Sidney Johnston was gathering an army for the Confederacy near Bowling Green, Kentucky, and specifically had requested the Rangers.

The Rangers camped for a week at the fair grounds just outside Nashville. The people of Nashville would head out to watch the Rangers perform feats of horsemanship. One of the favorite tricks was for a man riding his horse at full tilt across a field to reach down and pick up a lady's handkerchief from the ground. Pvt. John A. Jackson of Chappell Hill wrote home from near Bowling Green on November 11, 1861:

JOHN JACKSON. John Jackson, son of prominent Chappell Hill planter Terrell J. Jackson, enlisted in Terry's Texas Rangers in September 1861 at the age of 18. He was wounded in action at Woodsonville, Kentucky, but later returned to serve out the war. He took charge of his father's ruined estate after the war and restored the family fortune. John Jackson moved to Sealy, Texas, in 1899 and died there in 1927. (From *A History of Texas and Texans*, 1916, vol. IV, courtesy of the Texas State Library.)

Ther is three hundred sick with the measles. A. M. Thaxton will die we all suppose with them [Ed. note: Thaxton did not]. Spell Routt & John Routt & Bill Morse, Phil Milton are all gone to the Hospital but not daingerous [*sic*], all doing well. W. Billingsley is sick with them but doing well ... all the rest of the C. Hill boys are ingayin [enjoying] fine health....[13]

2. Terry's Texas Rangers' First Blood

Jackson added at the end of his letter, "I begin to feel myself a man."[14] John was the cousin of Terrell A. Jackson. His father, Terrell J. Jackson, was one of Washington County's wealthiest and most influential businessmen. The Jackson brothers had all come to Texas in 1840 from Pickens County, Alabama. Terrell was one of the officers of the Washington County Railroad Company. John was 20 years old in 1861 and had led a carefree life. His love of fast horses led to his enlisting in Terry's Rangers.

The Rangers were assigned to General Thomas Hindman's infantry brigade for whom they marched in the vanguard. On December 9, 1861, the Confederates moved towards the Federal Army in the vicinity of Woodsonville, Kentucky. Several companies of the Thirty-Second Indiana Infantry were constructing a pontoon bridge across the Green River to replace the Louisville & Nashville Railroad bridge, which previously had been damaged by Confederate forces. The Indiana infantry moved toward the Confederates upon spotting them, not realizing that they were facing a much larger force. Hindman set up his infantry and artillery and ordered the Rangers to fall back and decoy the Federal infantry into a trap. But the Rangers were spoiling for their first fight. Colonel Terry advised Brigadier General Hindman, "This is no place for you; go back to your infantry." As one Ranger later recalled, "... (we) thought we would devil them some before we left them."[15] Terry formed his Rangers into ranks and led a charge into the Federal line. Colonel August von Willich, commanding the Thirty-Second Indiana, later recalled, "With lightning speed, under infernal yelling, great numbers of Texas Rangers rushed upon our whole force. They advanced to fifteen

John Jackson of Terry's Texas Rangers. (Courtesy of Rice and Ruth Buchanan of Navasota, Texas.)

or twenty yards of our lines, some of them even between them, and opened fire with rifles and revolvers." The charging mustangs and point-blank shotgun blasts shocked the Federal line and threw it back. The Indiana men, although reeling from the Texans' wild cavalry charge, maintained some semblance of order. Many were recent German immigrants and more than a few had some military experience. They formed into hollow infantry squares with bayonets at the "kneel-and-parry" position upon being given the order "guard against cavalry."[16] The maneuver repulsed the Rangers' wild charge and Von Willich managed to remove his men in an orderly fashion to a stronger position under cover of his artillery and move up additional infantry to support their position at the bridge.

While this first engagement by Terry's Texas Rangers was relatively insignificant in the overall perspective of the war, there was a price paid. The Thirty-Second Indiana lost 10 dead and another 22 wounded. The Confederates lost 33 killed in the action and 50 others were wounded. Colonel Terry was among the Confederate dead.[17] The Rangers learned the high cost of the glorious charge in their first action. Yet they would continue to charge infantry throughout the war. Private John A. Jackson was wounded in the action at Woodsonville when a musket ball hit him in the left arm, passed through both lungs and lodged in his ribs.[18] He would not be back in action with his comrades until 1863.

Disease was often as dangerous as a wound in the Civil War. Daniel Harvie Browning became ill on December 17. He spent the remainder of the year and most of January recuperating. Browning, while homesick, was in good spirits when he wrote his sister Fannie back in Chappell Hill on January 10, 1862: "I was very glad to receive a letter from you ... I should have liked very much to have been at your concert on New Year's night and I hope it will not be long before I can come home and see you all ... Give my love to all of my old sweethearts ... I have been with some very nice ladies and the Dr. thinks that I am in love with Miss Ermine Ford."[19] The "Dr." was Daniel's good friend from Chappell Hill, Lt. Hammond Bouldin. However unrealistic his plans, Private Browning told his sister, "I will try to come home for your examination and then I can see all the young ladies. I shall try very hard to come home then if not before."[20] The best he could realistically offer was a proxy, his comrade: "Mr. Stokes will be home in a few days and tell Ma the first time he comes to our house to set out some Mustang wine for him and then he can tell her all the news. ... I am very anxious to hear from you all. Dr. joins me in love to you all. Write soon. Your brother, Dan"[21]

Daniel was much better nearly two weeks later, when he wrote family friend Dr. John Lockhart: "I am again able to eat my full rations (that is when I can get them). ... I was with Miss Ellen and Ermine Ford for two or three weeks and the balance of the time with Miss Lizzie Blewett and I am not very anxious to get to camp. Our boys are back again on Issen river and probably they will have some fighting before very long."[22] He noted that he had seen Terrell Jackson in camp to accompany his wounded son, John, home to Chappell Hill. That caused Daniel to reflect, "I don't see much prospect of getting home shortly and no more prospect of a fight at B-G [Bowling Green] now than when we first came here.... Sometimes I think the summer campaign will certainly end the war and then again I think it doubtful about its ending for three or four years.... It is true I would like very much to see the young ladies about C.H. [Chappell Hill].[23]

When General Ulysses S. Grant took the Mississippi River strongholds of Fort Henry and Fort Donelson in February 1862, Confederate General Albert Sidney Johnston withdrew his Confederate forces to the south. Terry's Texas Rangers covered Johnston's army as it withdrew. Private Daniel Browning returned to his unit as the withdrawal commenced. He related the regiment's retreat in a letter he wrote to Dr. John Lockhart in Chappell Hill: "After evacuating Bowling Green (double quick) we retreated to Nashville travelling until three o'clock at night in a gallop to cross the cumberland river before the Yankeys should reach Nashville and thus cut us off from Dixie. This being accomplished we stayed at Nashville the next day and then started on a scout toward fort Donelson (which had fallen) to protect the soldiers who had escaped from the cavalry of the enemy which were supposed to be pursuing them ... then to this place and we leave here next Tuesday for some point farther south I suppose." The young trooper added, "I never saw men more willing in any life to fight than our army is at the present and both officers and men are looking for a big fight before very long."[24]

The Rangers were already under their third commander. Thomas Lubbock, who took command after Terry's death at Woodsonville, died in January 1862[25] and was replaced by John Wharton. Wharton lived for a time in his youth at Hempstead with his Uncle Leonard Groce and practiced law at Brazoria with Clinton Terry, brother of Frank.[26] Thomas Harrison of Waco moved up under Wharton as the Rangers' second-in-command. Harrison was a disciplinarian and became most unpopular with many of the unruly Rangers.[27] Daniel Browning, raised a gentleman of one of Chappell Hill's aristocratic families, seemed not to have a problem with Harrison's discipline, in contrast to the opinion of his comrades. He wrote: "Colonel Wharton is sick and not with the regiment and the command falls upon Major Harrison who is the best officer we have. Some of our men have been acting very badly and have caused the name of Texas Rangers to be dreaded by both friend and foe and Maj. Harrison has been trying to correct these men and part of the regiment has turned against him."[28]

Albert Sidney Johnston, having lulled the Federals into a sense of confidence by the beginning of April, ceased his withdrawal. He moved his army to the west and caught Grant by surprise, attacking the Federal forces at Shiloh on April 6. The Confederates routed the Federals in fierce fighting on the first day. Word of the bloody battle spread across the nation. Daniel Browning reported home: "As I have just returned from the battlefield I concluded to write you a few lines to let you know I am well. For two days I was exposed to the fire of the enemy but escaped without being hurt ... None of the CH boys hurt." But there were considerable Confederate lives lost. Browning wrote of the death of General Albert Sidney Johnston, which all knew to be a serious blow. He also related his experience on the bloody first day at Shiloh:

> On last Sunday we charged the enemy and I was within fifty yards of the Yankees. We lost 6 or 7 killed and 10 or 12 wounded in the charge on that same evening. We were drawn up to charge a battery when Genl. Hardee ordered us to fall back

under the hill and while we were falling back I was riding by the side of Capt. Christian when a bombshell from the enemy's gunboat shot my horse's legs off and left me dismounted on the field. I got a man to take my saddle and I footed it for a while but I came across a yankee mule I mounted.[29]

Major General Don Carlos Buell's Army of the Ohio arrived during the night and the strengthened Federal forces severely punished the Confederates on the second day of the battle. Private Browning wrote: "On Monday I had to make a charge at the enemy on my mule but I got along finely and we had to dismount and go into the woods to skirmish and I got behind a tree that was hardly large enough to cover and it seemed to me that about forty balls hit the tree that I was behind."[30] Daniel Browning managed to survive the battle and took part in the final action.

The Confederates withdrew from the battlefield of Shiloh on the morning of Tuesday, April 8. Terry's Texas Rangers with several other companies of cavalry were ordered to cover the Confederate withdrawal. General Nathan Bedford Forrest was in command. He was just beginning to develop his reputation in the field. He deployed the small force for an ambush of the advance units of the pursuing Federal Army. The Federals, intent on pressuring the Confederates, fell right into General Forrest's trap. The Confederate cavalry gave a fierce yell and charged into the Seventy-Seventh Ohio Infantry. The surprised infantrymen in the front of the advancing column fired their muskets too soon at the onrushing cavalry, who then rode down on them and shot-gunned them at close range. Panic set in and the entire regiment broke and ran, as did a cavalry battalion supporting the Seventy-Seventh Ohio. Muddy conditions hampered the Federal flight. General William Tecumseh Sherman and his staff barely escaped capture and lost a bit of pride in the process. That action ended the Federal pursuit and allowed the Confederate Army to withdraw without further engagement.

Pvt. Daniel Browning wrote his mother back in Chappell Hill on April 10, 1862, from Corinth, Mississippi: "This is yankee paper and I am writing with yankee pen and ink. I would be very happy to see you all but suppose that it will be next winter before I shall be able unless I am wounded. Give my love to all. Your son, Daniel."[31]

The reality of a long war was just beginning to set in for the brave men of Chappell Hill and the many other Texans fighting for the Confederacy.

3

Sibley's Brigade and Waller's Regiment

In the early days of the war, Brigadier General Henry Hopkins Sibley convinced the Confederate command in Richmond of the merits of a Confederate invasion of New Mexico. The ultimate objectives were the conquest of Colorado and California, whose vast gold reserves would stabilize the Confederate government's treasury. Access to California's ports on the Pacific Ocean also would make it much more difficult for the Federal Navy to successfully continue its naval blockade of the Confederacy. The Confederacy hoped for considerable support among the populace once a Confederate Army presented itself in these states.

Sibley established recruiting headquarters just outside San Antonio on August 12, 1861, and sent captains into the surrounding counties. The primary challenge was that many Texans preferred to fight in the east, where everyone recognized the major fighting was taking place. Many saw Sibley's expedition as a march off into obscurity in the west, despite the fact that the west was vulnerable and critical to whichever side held it.

Colonel Tom Green raised what would become the Fifth Texas Mounted Volunteers to become a part of Sibley's Brigade. "Daddy" Green was a near-legendary Texan. As a 21-year-old private in the Texian Army, he helped man the famous "Twin Sisters" battery at the decisive Battle of San Jacinto in 1836. In 1842, Green led Claudius Buster and other men from Chappell Hill and vicinity in the Somervell Expedition into Mexico. Men from Washington County enlisted in Companies E and F of the Fifth Texas Mounted Volunteers. At least three men from Chappell Hill signed up with Green. William C. Chappell and A. J. Robinson enrolled as privates in Captain Hugh McPhail's Company E at Brenham.[1] William was a son of Robert Wooding Chappell, for whom Chappell Hill was named. Gideon Keesee enrolled on August 27, 1861, in Captain George Campbell's Company F formed in Washington County. The Keesees were a prominent Methodist family in Washington County. Gideon's father, William, was a trustee of the Chappell Hill Male and Female Institute as early as 1850.

The Fifth Texas Mounted Volunteers had its share of color. Samuel "Nicaragua" Lockridge joined the regiment with the rank of major. His abilities as a military man were perhaps questionable, but he was a noted filibuster and soldier of fortune, having fought with William Walker in Nicaragua. Lockridge was active in Texas with the Knights of the Golden Circle in the years leading up to the Civil War.

Green's cavalry regiment joined three other regiments at San Antonio, including Lt. Colonel William Scurry's Fourth Texas Mounted Volunteers. Sibley's brigade was 3,700 strong. Gideon Keesee, William Chappell, A. J. Robinson and their comrades-in-arms were mustered into service there on October 5, 1861.[2] Weapons were in short supply. State officials either already had dispersed the weapons seized from Federal bases upon secession or were reluctant to allocate such precious supplies for a foray westward into the forsaken desert. Volunteer soldiers were ordered to supply their own arms. The result was a wide collection of arms requiring varying caliber of ammunition. Two companies, including Company G raised by Captain Jerome McCown on Clear Creek in the Hempstead-Bellville area,[3] were outfitted with nine-foot lances adorned with red pennants. All recruits furnished their own horses.

Sibley reviewed his small army in San Antonio on October 21 and final preparations were made. On November 7, 1861, the vanguard of Sibley's expedition marched off into the west. Their objective was 700 miles away across the vast desert expanses of West Texas. Lieutenant Benton Seat told Gideon Keesee and the men of Company F: "You'll soon be way up yonder where the wolves howl and the chickens never crow, and ye won't have mammy's apron strings to tie to."[4]

Sibley had missed the moderate days of September and October and was embarking on a winter campaign for which his men were ill-equipped. They had only the single uniform they wore and their saddle blankets. There were no tents. As for food, there was no major settlement between San Antonio and El Paso that could provide supplies. The arid land was essentially devoid of crops and forage for horses. Meanwhile, the Federal forces in New Mexico were comfortable and well-supplied. The journey westward was much slower and more difficult than Sibley's enthusiastic volunteers had imagined. Morale among the troops suffered from lack of good rations. The plundering of small settlements along the way served to antagonize the locals. Horses and mules wore down from lack of good forage. Native Apache raided and stole what horses they could, harassing stragglers and outposts. It was not until January that the Confederates reassembled in New Mexico.

Sibley's first major objective was Fort Craig, 100 miles south of Albuquerque. His strategic plan to forage off the land for supplies failed to take into consideration the arid nature and general poverty of the region. As a result, his expedition desperately needed to capture Federal supplies. However badly he needed the supplies within the walls of Fort Craig, Sibley recognized the futility of an assault on the formidable fortifications. The Confederate numbers were too small for such tactics. Some would later argue that the expedition was doomed from the beginning by poor planning.

On February 16, Green's Fifth Cavalry drew up in line before Fort Craig and attempted to draw out the Federal commander, Colonel Edward Canby. But Gideon Keesee, William Chappell and A. J. Robinson did not get their first taste of combat as the Federals refused to leave their walls to engage the invaders. Canby recognized that he needed do little more than wait out the Confederates. Sibley was forced to bypass Fort Craig and proceed north, cutting off the Federal garrison from the main force at Santa Fe. He left Green's Fifth Texas in front of Fort Craig as a diversion.

When Canby realized what was happening, he dispatched a column to Val Verde Ford, six miles north of Fort Craig, to prevent the Confederates from crossing the Rio Grande River. The first major clash in the West was fought there on February 21, 1862. Both sides charged the other across the river with little success. The Confederates found themselves at a distinct disadvantage, as the Federals' heavier artillery and rifled muskets had greater range than the light howitzers, shotguns and carbines used by the Confederates. The Confederates were forced to take the offensive in an attempt to dislodge the Federals, who were well positioned behind the embankment at the river's edge. At noon, Sibley ordered Green's regiment to withdraw from the fort to reinforce Colonel William Scurry at the ford. Canby left a small garrison at the fort and moved the rest of his troops to join the fight for the ford.

Sibley passed command to Colonel Green upon his arrival at the battlefield in early afternoon. Captain Willis Lang insisted on leading his lancers in a charge. The Federal officer shouted to his men, "Those are Texans! Give them hell!"[5] and a withering volley of musketry unleashed at close range devastated the lancers. Meanwhile, Federal artillery continued to rake through the Confederate line. Green recognized that he needed to do something quickly. He ordered an all-out assault on the artillery batteries on either flank of the Federal line that were so severely punishing his men. The attack against the Federal right was driven back with serious losses. Major Samuel Lockridge led the dismounted Fifth Texas Cavalry through a hailstorm of grapeshot and canister against the Federal left. A thousand yelling Texans refused to quit and surged into the Federal line. The regimental color bearer waved the Fifth's Stars and Bars emblazoned with the motto "Victory Awaits You."[6] The men of Chappell Hill "saw the elephant" that afternoon, their first experience of real combat. In fierce hand-to-hand fighting, the Texans broke the Federal left and carried the day. Canby ordered a retreat back to Fort Craig. The Fifth were proud victors with the six heavy guns of the Federal battery as their prizes of war.

Although the Confederates held the field of battle at its conclusion, their victory was not decisive. The men were exhausted and even more than before in need of supplies. Both sides suffered casualties of the same magnitude, but the Confederate losses could not be replaced. Major Samuel Lockridge lost his life in the glorious charge and Lt. Benton Seat, Gideon Keesee's officer in Company F,[7] was among those wounded. With the Federals again within the safety of Fort Craig's formidable walls, Sibley felt he had little choice but to proceed northward towards Santa Fe.

The Battle of Val Verde opened up New Mexico Territory to the invasion force.

The Confederates captured Socorro on February 27, Albuquerque on March 2 and Santa Fe, the territorial capital, on March 10, 1862. Fort Union, east of Santa Fe, was the last remaining Federal post in New Mexico. Its capture would complete the Confederate conquest of New Mexico. More important, Fort Union was a substantial supply depot in the Southwest. With each passing day, Sibley's need for supplies increased. The most serious problem was the lack of forage for the horses. By the time Sibley's Brigade moved out from Santa Fe, two-thirds of the horses had been lost. Many of those who managed to keep their mounts alive were forced to give them up for use hauling wagons and artillery pieces.

Sibley and several companies of Green's regiment remained in Albuquerque. The remaining companies of Green's regiment were at Santa Fe, while a force led by Colonel William Scurry advanced towards Fort Union. Sibley was unaware that 1,300 Colorado volunteers had marched south to support the beleaguered defenders of New Mexico. These troops force-marched through snow-covered mountain passes to reach Fort Union before the Confederates. By March 22, the reinforced Federal force had left Fort Union and was marching to meet the oncoming Confederate force.

The opposing sides clashed in Glorieta Pass, southeast of Santa Fe in the Sangre de Cristo Mountains, on March 26, 1862. The battle lasted six hours and involved fierce bayonet charges and brutal hand-to-hand combat. The Confederates under Scurry held their ground and drove back the Federals. Although they won the battlefield, the Confederates discovered afterwards that Federal units had slipped behind them across a mountain pass and destroyed all of their supplies and pack animals. Supplies had been the key to the entire campaign and this move became the turning point. The Confederates' victory at Glorieta Pass was meaningless. They were deep in enemy territory and had again suffered serious losses of men. The much-needed supplies at Fort Union were out of reach. Sibley learned that Canby, whom he had allowed to remain in his rear, was heading north towards Albuquerque. The Confederate leader ordered Scurry to fall back to Santa Fe. The *Texas Republican* of May 17 announced to its readers: "The Battle of Glorietta. Our gallant Scurry with his 'ragged Texians' has gained another victory over the Federals in New Mexico."[8]

On April 8, the Confederates withdrew from Santa Fe and headed south. As the Federals closed in on Sibley at Albuquerque, he gave the order to begin the long trek back to San Antonio. Sickness had plagued the Confederate force and there were many sick in the Confederate hospital at Albuquerque. Among these was William Chappell. When Sibley withdrew from Albuquerque, many of the sick and wounded chose to make the trip back, rather than be left behind and taken prisoner. William Chappell chose to stay behind and face the consequences. He probably made the right decision. The 700 mile trek back to San Antonio tested even those soldiers who were healthy and many died along the way.

A front-page article in the June 2, 1862, Houston *Tri-Weekly Telegraph* carried a letter describing the Battle of Glorieta and listing the dead and wounded. The article noted: "Col. W. R. Scurry, the hero of Glorietta, and in fact one of the bravest and most popular Texian officers in the service ... brings gratifying news that Gen. Sibley's command is safe in Arizona," and added, "He fell back, not from fear of the enemy, but for lack of provisions."[9] The article conveyed little of the agony of retreat by men desperate for food, in need of shoes and clothing and harassed by Apache.

The expedition had been poorly equipped. The ambitious strategy by necessity required more men. No one anticipated the consequences of retreating 700 miles across the West Texas desert in the blistering summer heat without adequate supplies. The survivors of Sibley's ill-fated expedition straggled into San Antonio in small groups nearly all summer. Most were on foot, their horses having succumbed to the rigors of the trail.[10] The heat claimed its share of victims. People from San Antonio rushed out to meet them with food and transportation each time word reached town of another group sighted. More than 500 of the original 3,500 had died in battle or from wounds or disease. Another 500 were missing and taken prisoner.

Sibley had ordered his small artillery pieces buried at Santa Fe and Albuquerque to prevent their capture by Federal forces. But the six artillery pieces captured in the bloody charge at Val Verde Ford were too important to be left behind. These were trophies of war, proof of their courage on the field of combat. An artillery unit was formed from men of the Fifth Regiment. Among these men transferred was A. J. Robinson of Chappell Hill, who was promoted to sergeant. Joseph Sayers, the commanding officer of the unit, later would become governor of Texas. When the mules died, these men dragged and pushed the pieces all the way across West Texas. They became known as the Val Verde Battery and would distinguish themselves in numerous battles and engagements in Louisiana in the coming years of war.

The Texans who survived Sibley's expedition re-grouped and fought for the Confederacy until the end of the war. They would have their day of glory yet. William Chappell was paroled by the Federals on August 19, 1862, and made his way home on his own. The men of Chappell Hill would head to Louisiana soon enough to defend their homeland from invasion.

While Sibley's expedition failed in the West, other men prepared to fight closer to home. Federal forces were threatening Louisiana. If they were to gain a foothold, they could use that position as a springboard to invade Texas. Edwin Waller had helped his father run the family mercantile business in Austin County before the War Between the States. He served in 1861 with Rip Ford's Texas Cavalry. At the beginning of 1862, Waller obtained permission from General Thomas Hindman, commanding the Trans-Mississippi Department, to form a cavalry unit. Waller ran an ad in the Houston *Tri-Weekly Telegraph* on March 26, 1862. It read in part:

> Texians your homes and hearthstones are now threatened from the North. You are called to the rescue ... to beat back the invader. Come now, come at once, come to the rescue.... This Regiment like the brave Rangers of Terry's will be assigned duty in the teeth of danger. Come with me, and I will lead you right.[11]

Waller wanted men who "were at home on horseback, who ride like cowboys, who shot the bull's eye with a rifle or pistol and go anywhere and stand anything like a regular Ranger."[12]

Company C was raised from Washington and Austin Counties. John R. McDade of Chappell Hill enlisted at Camp Waller near Hempstead on May 3, 1862. Lt. Colonel Edwin Waller, Jr., signed up the 20 year old. The McDades had been settled in Washington County for more than a decade and Company C became a family affair. Two first cousins of John McDade's father also enlisted in Company D, as did their nephew. The nephew, 20-year-old William A. McDade, was elected captain of the company. William represented the most prominent branch of the McDades. His father, James W. McDade, had been the first sheriff of Washington County in 1846 and later a state representative and senator in the early to mid 1850s. William McDade's two uncles served under him as officers. Thomas S. McDade, 33 years old, was elected first lieutenant and 30-year-old Jacob Cobb McDade became first sergeant.

Other Chappell Hill men joined the McDades in Company C. Madison Wear, a 37-year-old grocer and owner of the livery stable in Chappell Hill, was elected second lieutenant. Thirty-year-old Amos Allen, who had been Chappell Hill's carriage maker, became the bugler. Charles Dickens had made reference to Amos Allen and his brother in an article he wrote for *All the Year Round*, a weekly London publication. "Two Friends from Texas" told of Dickens meeting the "two brothers from Chapel-hill, Washington County, Texas" on a ship from New York bound for Liverpool.[13] The writer referred to the Texans as "perfect specimens of the American frontier settler" and described Amos as having "a bad tobacco-chewing complexion and that peculiar sort of cut beard which is all but national."[14]

Edwin Waller raised only five companies, which became Waller's Thirteenth Cavalry Battalion. Waller's Battalion left Hempstead on July 1, 1862, and moved eastward, crossing the Sabine River into Louisiana on July 20. Federal forces captured New Orleans in April 1862 and were making forays into western Louisiana towards Texas. In their first engagement, Waller's cavalry caught some Federal infantry in an ambush and soundly defeated them. That action prompted Major-General Benjamin Butler, Federal commander of the Department of the Gulf, to dispatch a sizeable force to retaliate against Waller.

On September 8, 1862, Federal troops, moving quickly by riverboat, surrounded Waller's Battalion at Bonne Carre. Waller's several hundred men were greatly outnumbered, facing a force of several thousand. The ensuing action was little more than a rout. The only escape for the Confederates was into and through the Louisiana swamp. A soldier in Waller's Battalion recounted the action in a journal:

> could not find ground sufficient to form in line of battle. Mounted so all were dismounted and then every fourth man had to hold horses. We then marched about one hundred yards and all were stationed along side of the road awaiting attack ... they opened on us with their Battery and Minnies and Waller gave the order to fall back to our horses amid Shells & balls! Some horses had got frightened and run off and some men took most any horse they first met with.... We retreated down the canal and here we come to the Swamp and Col. Waller finding it impossible to take our horses into the swamp, commanded all to leave their horses and take it a foot.... By this time the command was very much scattered and in all directions.... We come through a swamp that never was trod before by man. In some places water and mud was waist deep and some come very nigh giving up. We passed through what is called the impenetrable swamps of Louisiana."[15]

Regimental rolls indicated that Private James R. McDade, First Lt. Thomas McDade and Captain W. A. McDade all lost their horses at Bonne Carre.[16] Sergeant J. C. McDade somehow managed to save his horse. Some men were more fortunate than others. Most of Waller's men, despite the humiliation of having lost their mounts, escaped capture. Five men from McDade's company were captured at Bonne Carre, including bugler Amos Allen. Ten others of Waller's Regiment, including Captain James January of Victoria, commanding Company A, were also captured. Cox reported that January "stood his ground with sword drawn — swearing that he would not join in such an ignominious flight."[17] January, a man of 51 years and a veteran of the War for Texas Independence, returned home after being released and did not return to the conflict.[18]

Waller's men re-grouped at Camp Gillis. On September 24, Private William Craig wrote in his journal: "The Command have petitioned for 90 days furlough so they can go home & try and get an outfit." General Taylor eventually allowed one officer from each company to go back to Texas for new mounts. He was determined to keep the bulk of the men in the field. When the battalion moved out of Camp Gillis on October 4, Private Craig wrote: "We succeeded in getting carts to ride in from Mr. Gillis. The Cavalry went up on the right hand side of the Bayou (Lafourche) and the Cane Cart Cavalry on the left," referring to the men without mounts riding in the cane carts.

It was a humiliating experience for the Texas cavalrymen. For most of the remainder of the year, McDade and his comrades had to sit out the fighting and wait to be outfitted with new horses. C. C. Cox reminisced:

> [O]ur humiliation and discomforture in the presence of the Victorious Kageans [Cajuns] was very mortifying — and now we are on foot — dismounted and degraded to the infantry service — and for awhile were hauled about in La cane carts or marched on foot from place to place as the necessities of the service required — Col. Waller was very sore about the condition of his command.[19]

The Houston *Tri-Weekly Telegraph* carried an account of the "Narrow Escape of Waller's Command" in its September 22, 1862, edition that likely added to the agony of Waller and his men.

Waller's Battalion merged into Sibley's Brigade in early 1863. The men of both units had something to prove to themselves and to the Confederate command. That opportunity presented itself in 1863 when Federal forces began moving northward into the interior of Louisiana. Federal control of Louisiana would leave Texas vulnerable to invasion from the east across the Sabine River. Confederate authorities moved what regiments they could spare to Louisiana to face the threat. Sibley's Brigade, by this time commanded by Tom Green, and the Val Verde Battery were among these.

Federal General Nathaniel Banks began his advance into Louisiana in the spring of 1863. He sent the gunboat *Diana* ahead on a reconnaissance mission up the Atchafalaya River. Confederate forces engaged the *Diana* on March 28, 1863. A. J. Robinson and the Val Verde Battery played a key role in the ensuing fight. They killed, wounded or captured 150 Federal soldiers and took the *Diana* with five heavy guns intact. Banks pushed onward and Green's cavalry fought one delaying action after another to protect the smaller Confederate force as it withdrew slowly northward. When Banks finally turned eastward to help Grant at Port Hudson and Vicksburg, the threat to western Louisiana ended for the moment.

In June, Tom Green moved his force southward to attack the Federal garrison in Fort Buchanan at Brashear City (known today as Morgan City), which served as an important jumping-off point for Federal advances into the interior of Louisiana. A bold plan was put forth. The men of Waller's Battalion, still smarting from the Bonne Carre fiasco of the previous year, jumped at the opportunity. The McDades and the others crossed Grand Lake at night in small boats and waded through a swamp in waist-deep water to move behind the Federal forces. This time, the press would praise the exploits of Waller's Battalion. The Houston *Tri-Weekly Telegraph* reported:

> Theirs was the proud privilege of storming the almost impregnable fort on the opposite side of the bay.... It was a hazardous mission to cross the Lake, 12 miles, in these frail barks, to land at midnight on the enemy's side, in an almost impenetrable swamp and await the dawn of day which would insure them victory or a soldier's death.... With a real Texas yell they at once dashed with bayonets fixed and pistols drawn, full at the threatening walls of the proud Fort.... In twenty minutes they climbed the walls, dispersed the garrison. Tore down the stars and stripes and hoisted the bonnie flag on its ramparts."[20]

The surprise attack resulted in the capture of 1,300 Federal soldiers, 2,000 horses and mules, 11 siege guns and 7,000 arms.[21] Waller's Battalion established a reputation as fighting men that would stay with them for the remainder of the war.

4

Hood's Texas Brigade Moves into Action

General Robert E. Lee said of Hood's Texas Brigade, "I need them very much, rely upon them in all our tight places and fear I have to call upon them too often. They have fought grandly and nobly and we must have more of them."[1] Hood's Texas Brigade, including three regiments of Texas volunteer infantry, served with Lee in his Army of Northern Virginia. They became Lee's shock troops, one of the most distinguished units in the Confederate Army. But in the beginning, no one foresaw the glory with which these Texan men would cover themselves.

John Marshall, editor of the *Texas State Gazette* in Austin and a strong advocate of secession, convinced his old friend Jefferson Davis to levy Texas in June 1861 for 2,000 infantrymen to serve in Virginia.[2] Three regiments were formed, two of them, the Fourth and Fifth Texas Infantry, in Central Texas.[3] Davis rewarded Marshall by giving him a commission as lieutenant colonel in the Fourth Texas Infantry under John Bell Hood. Edmund Duggan, a student at Soule University in Chappell Hill, was among those who enlisted in Marshall's Fourth Infantry. By the end of the war, Duggan attained the rank of captain.[4]

Washington County men made up the majority of two companies of the Fifth Texas Infantry. Captain Jerome Bonaparte Robertson formed Company I, the Texas Aids. Robertson had been in Texas since arriving in September 1836 at the head of a company of Kentucky volunteers. He was mayor of Washington-on-the-Brazos in the early days and a state legislator. He also served in several campaigns against hostile natives and as a soldier in the Somervell expedition. Robertson was also a member of the state secession convention in Austin.[5] Robertson's first lieutenant in

Company I was his good friend Tacitus Clay, mayor of Independence, Texas. Clay was well known to his neighbors in Chappell Hill, having lived in the area since the 1830s. His home, known as Clay Castle, was a magnificent four-story structure of stone and cedar, which featured a glassed-in ballroom on the third floor.[6] A number of Chappell Hill men served in Robertson's Company I, including Del Perkins, Abraham Lee, Thomas Bates, James Deggs and Robert McRee. Captain John D. Rogers, a graduate of Tulane University, was practicing medicine at nearby Washington when the war began. He obtained a captain's commission and raised Company E, the Dixie Blues, of the Fifth Texas Infantry. Chappell Hill men in Rogers' Company E included Robert Hargrove, John Francis Williamson Toland, F. M. Williamson, Miers Felder and Rufus King Felder.

The Felder cousins belonged to a prominent South Carolina family, descended from Captain Hans Felder of the Continental Army. Judge Gabriel Felder, a wealthy South Carolina planter, relocated to the Chappell Hill area in the spring of 1851 with his wife and two sons. He accumulated holdings of nearly 2,500 acres along New Year's Creek, which he began clearing to grow cotton. In 1854, Judge Felder hired a relation, Jesse Felder to bring his large number of remaining slaves from South Carolina to Texas. Jesse Felder was a Yale graduate and a former state legislator in South Carolina. He brought along his younger brother, Miers, on the journey and Miers settled in Chappell Hill.[7] When the Methodists established Soule University in Chappell Hill, Judge Gabriel Felder was a member of the first board of trustees. He endowed the Felder Professorship, a Chair of Ancient and Modern Languages, and served as president of that board from 1858 until his death in 1868.

Rufus King Felder was the oldest son of Frank J. Felder, a wealthy South Carolina planter, and Catherine Barrilon, the daughter of a wealthy French diplomat. Frank's untimely death in 1847 left Catherine to care for five children. In 1854, when Jesse Felder was moving Judge Felder's slaves, Catherine sent her family's slaves along to begin clearing land for a cotton plantation outside Chappell Hill. Catherine and her children moved to Texas in the following year.[8] Rufus King was fifteen years old when he arrived in Texas in 1855. He grew up into manhood with his older cousin, Miers. Rufus King was a student at Chappell Hill's Soule University in 1861. He and Miers enlisted together in the Fifth Texas Infantry on July 11, 1861.

The First, Fourth and Fifth Texas Infantry Regiments formed on Buffalo Bayou near Houston in the summer of 1861. The song "The Yellow Rose of Texas," which had originated less than 10 years earlier, became popular with these men.

> There's a yellow rose of Texas
> That I am going to see
> No other fellow knows her
> No other, only me
> She cried so when I left her
> It like to broke my heart
> And if I ever find her
> We never more will part

Rufus King Felder wrote his mother in Chappell Hill from camp:

4. Hood's Texas Brigade Moves into Action

> The camp is all in a stir. No one knows what we will do. We have not been mustered into the service yet.... If you have a chance I wish you would send me my oil cloth & tell I. to send my pistol & all the buckshot that wil fit in it & also my flask.[9]

The Texas regiments moved east to Virginia in mid August. They took the train to Beaumont, but then marched across South Louisiana to New Iberia, where they boarded steamboats for New Orleans. Rufus wrote of that march as "that long & to be remembered march ... from knee to waist deep in mud & water." The Texas regiments made the rest of the long journey to Richmond, Virginia, by train.

Rufus King Felder wrote from his regiment's camp outside of Richmond:

> Sept. 12, 1861, Richmond, VA. ... We are growing quite tired of our inactivity. We are encamped three miles from the city without guns or marching orders.... It is rumored that Galveston is about to be attacked & it created in me deep feelings of regret & self condemnation that I left & will not be there to defend the state of my adoption & the home of all those on earth who are so dear to me, though my humble mite [might] would be small, yet it would be given with a prior determined will & a truer sense of an outraged people. If it is true that our state has been invaded there is not a man or boy in the lone star state, but would rise up in anger & swear to drive from our soil the last man that dare oppose us.[10]

Rufus King Felder's first encounter with Federal soldiers occurred while on furlough in Richmond. He reported home, "I also had the pleasure of seeing the yankee prisoners.... They sometimes got very insulting. Several of them had to be shot by the guards."[11] Rufus King closed with: "Tell all the Negroes howdy for me & tell them I am growing fast and harty [hearty]. Give my love to all & tell the girls I will expect letters from all of them...."[12]

On October 21, 1861, three Texas regiments were combined with the Eighteenth Georgia Infantry to become the Texas Brigade. Brigadier General Lewis Wigfall assumed command on the following day. The Confederate Army issued Enfield rifles, fitted with sword bayonets, to the men of the Texas Brigade. The arms had recently arrived on a blockade runner. The new soldiers settled into camp for the winter and suffered terribly from disease. At one point, only 25 of 800 men in the Fifth Texas Infantry were fit for duty. Thirty men in the Fifth's Company K alone died of yellow fever in the first six months of service.[13] One Washington County man, Tom Muse, was among those who died.[14]

Those of the Texas Brigade who were well were suddenly ordered to prepare to move out to the front lines on the night of November 7. Rufus King wrote that his company was the healthiest in the regiment with only 18 sick.[15] Orders stipulated that knapsacks be packed with three days' rations for a forced march, causing Felder to write that the load was "enough for a pack mule."[16] The brigade marched all night for a distance of nearly 20 miles to Dumfries, where Quantico Creek empties into the Potomac. Rufus King wrote, "We had a dreadful march of it over the worst road I ever saw."[17] The men found some relief watching each other slide and fall in the mud, but the pace was grueling and many fell out of the ranks from exhaustion.[18]

RUFUS KING FELDER and MIERS M. FELDER in uniform, shortly after enlisting in the Fifth Texas Infantry. The two cousins enlisted together in the Fifth Texas Infantry on July 11, 1861. Rufus King, at his mother's request, had this photograph taken before the regiment left Kentucky, as they moved eastward to Virginia. (From the Harold B. Simpson Research Center, Hill College, Hillsboro, Texas.)

4. Hood's Texas Brigade Moves into Action

Rufus King Felder and his comrades-in-arms "were greatly disappointed on our arrival to find that the enemy had not crossed [the Potomac River] & there was no chance for a fight. The useless order was from Gen. Wigfall & has I think the fancy of an intoxicated brain."[19] The young man wrote, "No telling what moment the long roll will be sounded to lead us forth to battle. Come when it may they will find brave hearts to meet them & men who not only feel the power of their arm, but know that the God of battles are with us & will sustain the cause of right & justice."[20]

The Texas Brigade took their place in the line along the Potomac River near Dumfries, Virginia. A week later, Felder wrote home that, per his mother's request, he had his photograph taken. "Miers and myself had ours taken together the day before we left K [Kentucky]. We will keep it & send it back by who ever brings our clothing." The photo of the two cousins made its way back to Texas and survived the passage of time as part of the Chappell Hill Historical Society collection of Nath and Judy Winfield.[21]

The brigade continued to await its chance to fight, as reflected in a December 6 letter from Tom Bates of Robertson's Company I to his grandmother, Elizabeth Cocke McRee in Chappell Hill. Bates wrote from his entrenchment overlooking the Potomac River "in this far off land of Virginia"[22]:

> I have been pretty sick ... I do not think I will leave this world very soon unless I get a ball through me from the Yankees, which I think is very probable, as we are looking for a fight any minute.... I have just got through cleaning my rifle in expectation of tomorrow's battle for we will have a battle without a doubt. And I hope to send one yankee to his long account. Every time I think of home I wish I was there but some of us are obliged to come, and I was one of them, to defend our country from the Yankees ... if we whip the Yankees this time we will be sure to take Washington ... if I am not killed I will write to you immediately afterwards to let you know that I am still in the land of the living. I do not write this way because I think I am going to get killed or anything that way, but to let you know that I am not afraid to die as I have made up my mind to that a long time ago."[23]

There again was no action that following day and the Texas Brigade continued to wait out the winter, each man trying to survive the real threat of disease so as to be fit for combat in the spring. Tom Bates wrote his grandmother that Del Perkins, his friend from home, was in good health and sent his respects.[24] But Del was discharged later that same month with a surgeon's certificate of disability after it was discovered that he was epileptic.[25] Tom also wrote, "Bob McRee is pretty nearly sick all the time when there is anything to be done and a bigger fool than ever."[26] McRee would prove to be a courageous man, suffering wounds at Freeman's Ford, Second Manassas and Cold Harbor and remaining with his regiment through the duration of the entire war.[27]

Rufus King Felder wrote his sister on February 20, 1862, that they had lost two more to disease since he had last written and optimistically added, "I hope they will be the last we shall loose [lose] until we return to the bosoms of our familys."[28] The

Texas Brigade had yet to see combat and young Felder had no idea of the loss of life he would witness in the three years ahead. The birth of a son to his sister caused him to reflect with homesickness:

> Give sister E. my congratulations & tell her to find him well that he may soon grow up & make a stout healthy soldier & make himself useful a Boregard [General P. G. T. Beauregard] for the rising generations. The farmers, I suppose, are by this time planting a new crop. It seems strange that it should be planting time in Texas. Here the ground is covered with snow.[29]

On March 12, 1862, General Robert E. Lee promoted John Bell Hood to Brigadier General and gave him command of the Texas Brigade. The brigade would be known thereafter as Hood's Texas Brigade. Hood himself, though not a native Texan, was stationed in the state as a lieutenant with the Second U.S. Cavalry before the war broke out, serving under Lieutenant Colonel Robert E. Lee.[30] The promotion of Hood allowed John Marshall to assume command for the Fourth Texas Infantry.[31] Colonel Jerome Bonaparte Robertson became commanding officer of the Fifth Texas Infantry.

Rufus King Felder's Company D of the Fifth Texas Infantry found itself with a new company commander and Rufus King was little disturbed by the loss of Captain John D. Rogers, writing:

> The Capt. has received a commission or rather an order to raise a reg. ... Some of the boys condemn Capt. R. for leaving the company, but most of them are very willing to get rid of him as he thought more of enjoyment and promotion than he did of his company. Our government certainly must be scarce of military men to appoint him Col. when he cannot drill a Company much less take care of it. We were very much disappointed in him, but I did not complain as I knew it would create uneasiness at home.[32]

Rufus became ill and was sent to Richmond's Chimborazo Hospital at the end of March. He did not return to active duty until nearly the end of April. The Texas Brigade marched without Felder to Yorktown in response to the landing on the peninsula of General George McClellan's Union Army. Felder was witness to the ensuing panic in Richmond, as the fighting was just 60 miles from the Confederate capital. Enthusiastic cheering overcame fear as Confederate troops in large numbers began to pass through Richmond on April 6 to engage McClellan's army. Rufus King Felder was just returning to his regiment when the siege of Yorktown ended at the beginning of May and the Confederate forces fell back toward Richmond to regroup. He saw action when Hood's Texas Brigade fought a delaying action at Eltham's Landing on May 7. Historian Stephen Sears noted the skirmish "was marked by the same aggressive Southern tactics that characterized Williamsburg."[33] The Fifth Texas Infantry was not engaged in the Battle of Seven Pines, which took place on May 31–June 1, 1862.

Private Felder traveled by train with the Texas Brigade to Staunton, Virginia, on June 12, 1862, to join Stonewall Jackson's army in a series of rapid movements. Felder wrote his sister Kate:

4. Hood's Texas Brigade Moves into Action

When I wrote last to mother, we were on our way to reinforce Jackson. Well we have reached him & have taken with him some of his famous forced marches.... The boys were continually breaking down & worn out with fatigue.... Among those that broke down on the march was your weakly brother.... It was about a week before I had good use of my legs.

Rufus King Felder was admitted to an army hospital in Charlottesville, Virginia, on June 20. His letter continued:

[T]he consequence was I was cut out of the fight.... It may have been best that I was not in it, as our company suffered a great deal. Out of the 42 that were in the fight, 19 were killed & wounded ... [Cousin] Miers passed through unhurt. Our brigade did damn good service & though it fought as becomes Texians the loss was very heavy.... Our brigade charged & drove the enemy from one of their strongest positions, which one or two others had failed to accomplish having been driven back by the deadly fire of the large batteries of the enemy planted on the surrounding hills & which continued to throw a shower of shot and shell into our lines.[34]

Rufus King missed the brigade's first major battle, Gaines' Mill on June 27, 1862. Hood's Texas Brigade distinguished itself by breaking a deadlocked battle with a dramatic frontal assault in which they overran two lines of entrenchments and captured an

JOHN D. ROGERS. John Rogers, a graduate of Tulane University, was practicing medicine at nearby Washington when the war began. He obtained a captain's commission and raised Company E, the Dixie Blues, of the Fifth Texas Infantry in Washington County. Chappell Hill men in Rogers' Company E included Miers Felder and Rufus King Felder, John Toland, F. M. Williamson and Robert Hargrove. Rogers rose to the rank of lieutenant colonel in Hood's Texas Brigade during the course of the war. He was a successful Galveston businessman in the post-war period. (From *A History of Texas and Texans*, 1916, vol. IV, courtesy of the Texas State Library.)

entire regiment and fourteen artillery pieces.[35] Only sunset saved the Federal Army from disaster. Other attacks that day had failed and there was little reason to expect Hood's Texans to do any better. The Confederate victory at Gaines' Mill saved Richmond and delivered victory to Robert E. Lee, who had just assumed command of the Army of Northern Virginia. Lee would never forget. He turned to Hood's Texas Brigade time and time again to serve as his shock troops.[36] The Confederates proceeded to pursue the Federals out of Virginia in what became known as the Seven Days' Battle, of which Rufus King Felder's existing correspondence makes no note. Colonel John Marshall died that day while leading the Fourth Texas Infantry in the attack.

In the aftermath of his success in the Seven Days' Battle, General Robert E. Lee marched his Army of Northern Virginia towards Washington, D.C. Pope replaced McClellan and prepared to meet Lee. North and South clashed again at Manassas Junction on August 28–30, 1862. The Battle of Second Manassas was a bloody affair. Longstreet's corps counterattacked the Federal left on the 30th with a massive assault involving nearly 25,000 men.[37] Hood's Texas Brigade led the attack, its front extending 700 yards as it marched across an open plain into the Federal line.[38] The Texans essentially destroyed two Federal brigades and successfully turned the flank of the Federal line in the process.[39]

The Fifth Texas Infantry advanced to within close range of the Fifth New York Zouaves, who were behind a creek and on higher ground. The New Yorkers fired early and high. The Fifth Texas unleashed a devastating volley that ripped through the Union line and charged with bayonet before the Federals could reload.[40] The Texans routed the Zouaves and pursued them for some distance. The Fifth New York lost nearly 300 men in 10 minutes in what was the greatest loss of life of an infantry regiment in any single battle in the entire war.[41] One veteran of the fight wrote in his memoirs that the regiment became known as "The Bloody Fifth" ever after.[42]

Rufus King Felder described the battle two weeks later in a letter to his family back in Chappell Hill:

> Our brigade was ordered in about three. We double-quickened it about a mile before we met the enemy. We first met two reg. of Zouaves. We kept advancing & shooting until we got within thirty yards of them. They then broke and fled, but few of their number were left to tell the tale. The ground was perfectly strewn with the bodies of the red breeched fellows. This was but the commencement of the carnage. We then had three successive lines of battle to charge over. This was done & when night came & put an end to the dreadful carnage it found the enemy in full retreat. Had there been a Joshua to save the setting sun, we might have made captives of almost the entire army, but when dawn came they were too far off to be followed by our worn out and exhausted troops.

Rufus shared the reality of the glorious victory, sparing little in the details:

> I walked over the battlefield this morning. The sight was indeed horrifying in the extreme, you could see corps mangled in every conceivable way & hear the moans of the wounded in every direction. The only consolation was that you could see five times as many Yanks as Rebels. Our brigade suffered dreadfully.

Our reg. lost 280 killed & wounded out of five hundred. Our company lost 25 out of about 40.⁴³

One of Felder's comrades offered a different perspective, writing of the scattered dead of the New York Zouaves: "the variegated colors of whose peculiar uniform gave the scene the appearance of a Texas hillside in spring, painted with wildflowers."⁴⁴

The Houston *Tri-Weekly Telegraph* of September 29, 1862, heralded this latest frontal assault by the Texas Brigade, stating: "The glorious Texan soldiers have again won undying fame on the battle field.... That deadly volley in the face of the Fifth would have turned any other troops that ever charged with bayonets."⁴⁵ In fact, the Fifth Texas Infantry suffered higher losses than any other Confederate regiment at Second Manassas. The regiment's 261 casualties exceeded those of any other battle in which the unit fought in the entire course

MR. AND MRS. MIERS FELDER AND CHILDREN. Miers and Catherine Felder with son Rufus and daughter (baby only partly visible) Catherine. Miers, following his serious wounds sustained at Second Manassas, was discharged from the service at Columbia, South Carolina, on February 14, 1863. He returned home and married Catherine Felder in Chappell Hill on December 31, 1863. Catherine died and Miers remarried in 1872, only to lose his second wife just a few years later. (From the Archives of the Chappell Hill Historical Society.)

of the war. Seven different flag bearers lost their lives and the regimental flag had 28 holes.⁴⁶ Yet Rufus could write that he "went through the fight of M. [Manassas] ... without a scratch." He added in his next letter home, "Miers, I suppose you have heard, was wounded at M. in the arm & foot."⁴⁷

Rufus King Felder's cousin, Miers, was first wounded in his foot. He was a big man, well over six feet tall and weighing over 200 pounds, and fell to the ground while attempting to hobble back to safety. While Miers was lying there, a musket ball struck him in the arm. He lay on the battlefield amid the wounded and dying through the night and into the next day. A detail finally came across Miers and loaded him onto an ambulance wagon, full of screaming and moaning men, which took him on a jolting, painful ride to a field hospital.[48] He lay there without care for some time, the doctors occupied with more seriously wounded men. Miers knew that he needed to remove the minie ball lodged in his arm and convinced a young man passing by to perform the extraction with an old pocketknife. Infection set in and a brother-in-law came up from South Carolina and took Miers home to recuperate. Months in recovery, he was finally discharged from the army with a disabled arm and foot and sent home to Texas.

Other men from Chappell Hill were also wounded. Among these was Sgt. F. M. Williamson of the Fifth Texas Infantry. George Kerby was in Richmond as word filtered into the Confederacy's capital in the aftermath of the Battle of Second Manassas. He wrote his Aunt Elizabeth (Cocke) McRee in Chappell Hill to report another casualty, that of her grandson:

> I received a letter from Tom Bates last night. He was wounded slightly in the leg and arm at the battle of [Second] Manassas on 30th Augst. And carried to Warrenton, Va. with the other wounded. The Yankees made a dash at the place a few days ago and took them all prisoners, but had not time to carry them away, so they paroled them and left them. Tom is still there.... He is well cared for by the ladies of the neighborhood & is doing well ... I will render Tom all the assistance I can ... I am glad that he is showing himself to be a true man.

Kerby closed by adding, "My health unfits me for the Service or I would be by his Side."[49]

Abraham Lee served in Company I with Tom Bates. He was 40 years old and had been a dentist in Chappell Hill before the war. He was detailed as a nurse at the hospital set up at Warrenton, Virginia, after Second Manassas. Like Bates, Lee was captured by Federal troops and paroled. He obtained furlough to Texas in October and never returned.

John F. W. Toland of the Fifth Texas Infantry's Company E, who called Chappell Hill home, was another casualty of Second Manassas. He was the son of Joseph Toland, a prosperous South Carolina planter who had relocated to Chappell Hill before the war. The Tolands were the second wealthiest family in Chappell Hill per the federal census of 1860 with 68 slaves and over 4,200 acres of prime Brazos River bottomland. Private Toland returned to duty for the rest of 1862. He seemed to suffer from poor health, having been in the hospital twice in the spring and summer of 1862 before Second Manassas. He again was sick several times during 1863 for extended periods. John's father passed away at Chappell Hill on July 16, 1863, at the age of 59 years. The Confederate draft allowed for a man to be excused from call-up for service if he owned more than 20 slaves and was needed to oversee the plantation, a stipulation which clearly applied to John Toland. He obtained furlough in early 1864 to go home to Texas. He never returned. It seems likely that James was needed to manage the vast family plantation, but he apparently never obtained a formal release from his regiment. The Confederate muster records of May–June 1864 officially listed him as "absent without leave since March 10, 1864." By July–August, the official listing was "deserted March 10, 1864." Private John F. W. Toland saw a great deal of action in the period that included the Seven Days Battle, Second

Manassas and Antietam. In fact, his combat experience far exceeded that of many who forever after proudly called themselves Confederate veterans of the war — men who served in the Home Guard or perhaps fought in one small engagement. Toland moved to Lampassas County, Texas, after the war and later McLennan County, where he settled down and raised a family. He did not again reside in Washington County until his later years. He died in Brenham in 1909.

Such cases were not uncommon, as men weighed their continuing responsibilities to their comrades and country relative to the needs of their family back home. In some cases, the absurdity of war with the terrible bloodletting was enough to convince a man to head home. As the war dragged on and the Confederacy found itself more and more desperate for manpower, authorities did all in their power to return such men to the ranks. A notice posted in the *Galveston Tri-Weekly News* in late 1864 was directed specifically toward the men of Hood's Brigade, stating: "The War Department is determined to arrest and bring to justice the officers and men belonging to commands East of the Mississippi River, who continue to absent themselves without a regular discharge or transfer ... it is enough to remind you that your services are needed by the side of your comrades in Virginia. It is known that many of you are anxious to return and to those of the Old Brigade ... who will report forthwith to the undersigned, at Houston, to be returned to their commands, full pardon will be extended for past offences."[50] Confederate authorities never caught up with either Abraham Lee or James Toland. The young men, by virtue of not returning to their regiments, appear to have felt it necessary to give up Chappell Hill. They were, in their own way, also casualties of war.

General Robert E. Lee followed up his success at Second Manassas with his first invasion of the north. It was, as Rufus King Felder wrote his mother, "a campaign unequalled by any thing of this war."[51] Some historians later would argue that the outlook for the Confederacy never looked brighter. But Rufus King shared an interesting observation with the home front: "I have heard a great deal of southern feeling in Ma [Maryland], but I found it a mistake. There are some trusted men there, but the majority are Union."[52] Indeed, the men of border state Maryland did not flock to the Confederate standard, as Lee hoped. Robert E. Lee's Army of Northern Virginia was exhausted and ill prepared for an invasion into the North. Colonel Jerome Robertson, suffering from a shoulder wound from Gaines' Mill and a groin wound from Second Manassas, collapsed along the way while leading his Fifth Texas Infantry.[53] Many others fell out.

Robert E. Lee pressed northward and engaged a much larger Federal army on the morning of September 17, 1862, near the town of Sharpsburg on Antietam Creek. Lee had hoped to have the advantage of surprise, but the reality was that McClellan had come into possession of Lee's plans by a stroke of luck. The serious fighting commenced at first light on the morning of September 17, 1862. John Bell Hood led the advance of his division, which included his old Texas Brigade, at 7 A.M. The Confederates rushed out of the woods, crossed Hagerstown Turnpike and poured into the Cornfield, routing the Federal troops in position there. The Fifth Texas was among several regiments which turned and advanced into the East Woods in pursuit of retreating units. The Texas Brigade fought, lost and re-took the same ground several times in the course of the bloodiest single day of the war.[54] The Army of Northern Virginia suffered 40 percent casualties.[55] Hood's division suffered 60 percent casualties. Hood, upon being asked after the fighting where his division was, was said to have replied, "Dead on the field."[56]

Rufus King Felder wrote of the fight:

> We had a very hard fought battle at Sharpsburg before we left M. [Maryland]. The enemy greatly outnumbered us. The battle raged furiously the whole day commencing early in the morning & ceasing only at night. The slaughter on both sides was terrible; there was very little ground gained on either side. Both sides were too exhausted to renew the fight next day & a flag of truce was agreed to bury the dead. This occupied all day & that night our forces fell back across the river. Next morning the Yankees thinking we were retreating crossed over a bridge which was immediately attacked & the whole except about a hundred was killed & taken.[57]

The letters of Rufus King Felder, by the time of this letter of October 1, were becoming a long litany of neighbors and friends killed or wounded. He reported the deaths of brothers Jim and Julian Hutchinson at Antietam and wrote, "What a shock it will be to the family, two sons in one fight." The wear of the war on Felder's heart and soul was further emphasized by the following comment:

> You said in your last letter that you hoped the Texians thirst for Yankee blood had been partly quenched. I can speak for the three reg. in Va. [Virginia]. Their thirst has not only been partially quenched, they have been in so many fights and have suffered so much they would be willing never to go in another fight.[58]

But the war had only just gotten underway. The years 1863 and 1864 would be marked by a number of colossal battles and terrible loss of life. America was caught in the vortex of war and there was no way out for hundreds of thousands of volunteers, including the men of Chappell Hill, Texas.

General Robert E. Lee withdrew his battered army southward after Antietam. The army crossed the Potomac River on September 18 and went into camp in Virginia. Many of the men of the Fifth Texas Infantry, as with most other regiments, were in need of warm clothing and boots for the coming winter. Lee promoted Jerome Robertson of Independence to brigadier general in November and gave him command of the Texas Brigade, succeeding John Bell Hood.

Winter camp for 1862–1863 was a welcome relief for the men from the bloody fighting. Rufus King asked his sister to "Give Miss Bell my compliments and thank her in the most affectionate manner of the gloves & tell her when I am doing my accustomed round of guard duty, the gift will add greatly to my comfort & the memory of the kind donor and cheer my heart with the hope of once more returning & enjoying the pleasant smiles of our beautiful girls."[59]

A heavy snow covered northern Virginia with a foot of snow in late January 1863, offering a break in the tedium of camp life. Rufus King Felder wrote, "The boys had a fine time yesterday, fighting battles with snowballs."[60] The First and Fourth Texas regiments started the fray by attacking Rufus King and his comrades in the Fifth Texas. "[T]he storm of battle raged with the utmost fury for two hours ... both parties having become perfectly exhausted."[61] The three regiments then joined together and swept over the Third Arkansas, which replaced the Eighteenth Georgia in the brigade in November 1862. The process continued until half of their division had joined together to march against the next division camped two miles away. Just as war had changed these boys and men into battle-hardened veterans, the experience changed how they played. The mock combat was rough with bruised and even broken limbs, not to mention varying degrees of personal insult. "Captured" officers were roughly handled. Rufus King Felder, having undergone his share of bloody combat, shared his perspective with family back home.

> When we got in sight they had the long roll sounded and their officers leading them out in force. We did not succeed in effectually subduing them but held our ground. It is indeed a grand sight to see several thousand men drawn up in line of battle fighting with snow & with as much earnestness as if the fate of our country depended on the contest.... It is more interesting to look at these battles than a real one as there are no live lost & but little blood shed.[62]

5

Capture at Arkansas Post

George Washington Carter returned to Chappell Hill from Virginia in November 1861 with a colonel's commission. He posted notice announcing his intentions to raise a regiment of lancers. Carter, no doubt, knew the skills of the men of Chappell Hill, having witnessed their skill with lances at the annual tournament. That, coupled with the South's immediate shortage of weapons, may have convinced Colonel Carter to form a regiment of Texas lancers. The recruiting poster appealed in bold letters "To the Chivalry of Texas." The finer print read: "Brave sons of Texas, the South is invaded by more than half a million fanatical mercenaries. All that is dear to us is at stake. There will be nothing to live for if we are conquered. There is no help for us but in hard fighting. Who will refuse to take part in the glorious strife?"[1] Carter's name with his rank was included on the poster. Appropriately enough, as Chappell Hill was a Methodist center, Carter's fellow officers included two other Methodist ministers, Franklin Wilkes and Clayton C. Gillespie, as lieutenant colonel and major, respectively.

The former president of Chappell Hill's prestigious Soule University could not have imagined the success that he met. The options available to soldiers may gave helped the lancers. William Zuber wrote: "I preferred cavalry service, but determined to join Carter's Lancers rather than go into the infantry." Zuber as a boy of 16 had cried when left behind prior to the Battle of San Jacinto. When the War Between the States first broke out, he could not afford to leave his family, burdened as he was with debt. He worked hard and by 1862 had settled his personal finances and was ready to fight for Texas.[2] So many men volunteered that the original plan to form one regiment was changed to include three regiments. Carter took the First Texas Lancers, which became the Twenty-First Texas Cavalry Regiment. He gave the

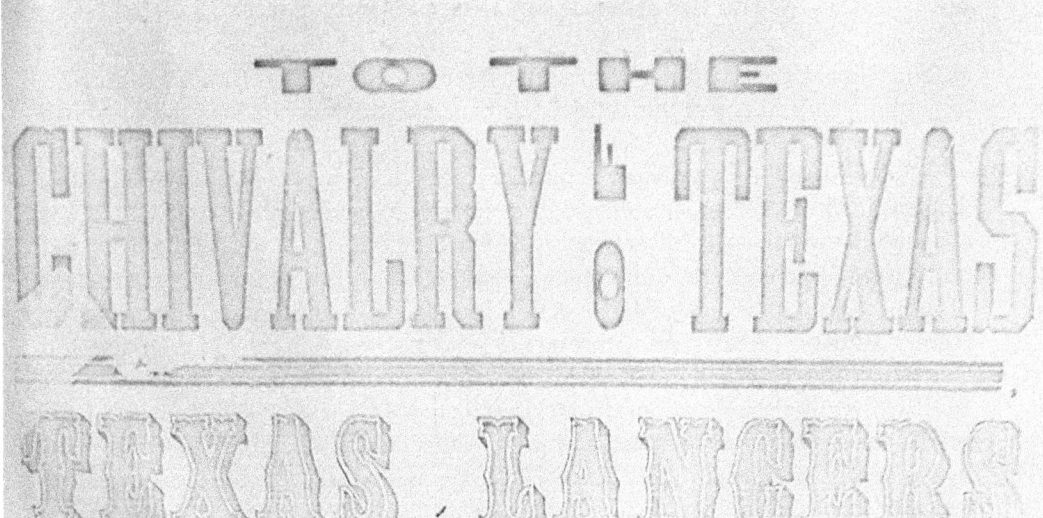

RECRUITING POSTER FOR FIRST TEXAS LANCERS. George Washington Carter, president of Soule University, returned to his native Virginia after secession. He returned to Chappell Hill, Texas, with authorization to raise a cavalry regiment. The response from Chappell Hill and the surrounding region was so strong that Carter raised three regiments. These became the Twenty-First, Twenty-Fourth and Twenty-Fifth Texas Cavalry Regiments. (Courtesy of the Chappell Hill Historical Society from their museum exhibit on the Civil War.)

Second Texas Lancers, which became the Twenty-Fourth Texas Cavalry Regiment, to Franklin C. Wilkes and the Third Texas Lancers, which became the Twenty-Fifth Texas Cavalry Regiment, to Clayton C. Gillespie.

Franklin Wilkes, a native of Tennessee, came to Texas as a Methodist minister, first assigned in 1857 as an agent for the church's Waco Female Institute.[3] He was assigned to the Chappell Hill station in 1858, riding circuit out of that town. An old catalog for Soule University announced, "Rev. F. C. Wilkes, M.D., will fill the chair of Biblical Literature and give instruction in that Department and in Elocution by regular lectures."[4] After serving through 1859 as the presiding elder in the Galveston district, Wilkes returned to Chappell Hill at the end of the year to be an agent for Soule University.[5] The board of trustees that included Gabriel Felder, William Chappell, James Presler, Joseph Routt and John Wallis concurred with the appointment by the Texas Conference of Rev. Dr. F. C. Wilkes as general agent for the university.[6] It was in that capacity that he came to know well George Washington Carter, Soule's president. Wilkes was one of Chappell Hill's numerous doctors in residence before the war. He also owned and operated the drugstore in Chappell Hill.[7]

Clayton C. Gillespie was a veteran of the Battle of San Jacinto in 1836. He was a brickmason by trade and in that capacity oversaw the construction of the Texas state penitentiary at Huntsville in 1848 and 1849. Upon its completion, Gillespie became the prison's first superintendent.[8] Gillespie became a Methodist minister sometime during this period. In 1854, Gillespie became editor of the *Texas Christian Advocate*, a Methodist paper published in Galveston.[9] He gained widespread popularity for his championing both Texas and slavery within the Christian context. Gillespie chaired a Methodist Texas Conference committee that proposed that the General Conference delete John Wesley's General Rule on slavery[10]—the rule specifically stated that Methodists would not be involved in buying or selling human beings. Gillespie was so successful as editor of the *Texas Christian Advocate* that the Methodist General Conference promoted him in 1858 to edit the *New Orleans Advocate*.[11] When the war began and Gillespie learned that Methodist minister George Washington Carter was forming a regiment, he rushed to Chappell Hill.

Company D of the Twenty-Fourth Texas Cavalry included a number of men from Chappell Hill. Thomas A. Elliott, brother-in-law of Rufus King Felder, and John F. Matthews, the brother of James Fiske Matthews of Terry's Texas Rangers, were in the Twenty-Fourth. The Keesee brothers, William Jr. and Walstein, were in the Twenty-Fourth. The Keesee family was one of the earliest to settle Chappell Hill and is mentioned in early accounts of Methodist gatherings in the area.

The Swearingens were among the most prominent families in Chappell Hill to be represented in Carter's Texas Lancers. R. J. Swearingen was one of Chappell Hill's most prominent citizens and a man respected throughout Texas. He passed away a few months before the war broke out, suffering a stroke and collapsing on the floor as he was getting up from breakfast. His family gathered around him on his deathbed but he seemed to not notice. A neighbor wrote that they all took his death very hard.[12] His son Patrick Henry Swearingen was educated at Centenary College in Louisiana. Brenham newspapers from the period carried ads for P. H. Swearingen, Attorney and Counselor at Law, Chappell Hill, Texas. He was 27 years old when he enlisted, less

5. Capture at Arkansas Post

than a year after marrying M. E. Toland, daughter of planter Joseph Toland. The men of his company elected Patrick Swearingen to be their lieutenant. Soon afterwards, Colonel Wilkes promoted young Swearingen to serve under him as lieutenant colonel of the Twenty-Fourth Texas Cavalry Regiment.

Since Carter had his authorization from Richmond, he took orders from the authorities in the Confederate capital. That caused problems from the beginning with Texas state officials. The three regiments that Carter formed organized in two camps near Hempstead. They remained separate from the infantry regiments organizing in Camp Groce and the ample provisions in the cavalry camp reflected this situation. Colonel George Flournoy of the Sixteenth Texas Infantry filed complaints with the state assistant adjutant general, but to no avail.[13] The men of Carter's brigade found themselves at a disadvantage in one respect. As Carter's authorization came from Richmond, the bounty payment for enlisting and pay had to come from Richmond. Carter's problems only multiplied when he sent Wilkes to Richmond to draw the bounties and back pay for the men of all three regiments. William Zuber, one of Carter's troopers, later wrote:

> After he had drawn the money, Wilkes told the authorities at Richmond that there was no such body as Carter's Brigade. Then he returned, bearing instructions to himself and Colonel Gillaspie which showed that they commanded unattached regiments. Colonel Wilkes then appropriated the brigade's money for the use of his own regiment.[14]

The Twenty-Fourth and Twenty-Fifth Regiments under Wilkes and Gillespie subsequently were assigned to Colonel James Deshler's brigade and relocated to Shreveport, Louisiana.

On July 3, 1862, while camped at Shreveport, Thomas Elliott wrote Emma (Felder), his pregnant wife:

> My Dearest Wife ... I am glad to see that your friends visit you so often. It is a pleasure to me to know.... I am sorry to hear that Kittie [oldest child] is so thin. Do watch her close and don't let her get sick. Don't let them spoil our little boy [six-month-old Thomas A. Elliott III] by petting him too much. Oh how I should like to see him.... Pat Swearingen went to Little Rock to try and secure arms and uniforms and get the bounty for the men. He has not returned as yet and I am afraid he is sick on the road as Capt. Fly has returned and said Pat was to meet him on the road. Capt. Fly says they told him they had no use for us up there. If we came we would be put on half rations for horse and men. He also states there is no arms or money in the place, so we will get no bounty or pay and Wilks [Colonel] & Carter [Colonel] have lied so to the men that they have lost all confidence in them and it would not surprise me to hear that some one had shot them. Some of the western boys would just as soon do it. And now dear wife I must close. Keep up your spirits and trust in God. If he wills we will soon meet once more. There is news here of an armistice of 60 days but I don't place much confidence in the report.... Kiss the little ones for me. God bless you all. Your affectionate Husband, T. A. Elliott.[15]

Later that same month, Deshler's brigade was ordered north into Arkansas. It was there that the Twenty-Fourth and Twenty-Fifth Texas Cavalry regiments learned that they were to be dismounted. Zuber insisted in his memoirs that, " He [Wilkes] and Gillaspie [sic], who preferred infantry service to that of cavalry, arranged for the dismounting of their regiments."[16] In fact, the official records of the war suggest otherwise. A Federal colonel reported, "so scarce is subsistence for horses that they have dismounted a large part of their cavalry force, including the Twenty-fourth Texas, Colonel Wilkes, and the Twenty-fifth Texas, Colonel Gillespie."[17] Further, in each instance in which Confederate authorities dismounted a unit, there was much discussion, "some large swearing and small swearing and any other kind you can think of."[18] Twenty members of the Alabama-Coushatta Nation had enlisted in Carter's Lancers. They complained so bitterly about having been misled into being in a mounted unit that they were sent back to Texas to await further orders.[19] They were the fortunate ones.

In late November 1862, the men of Chappell Hill in the Carter's Twenty-First, Wilkes's Twenty-Fourth and Gillespie's Twenty-Fifth Texas Cavalry were ordered north to Arkansas Post. While the men of the Twenty-Fourth were armed with model 1841 Mississippi rifles, the men of the Twenty-Fifth carried obsolete flintlock muskets converted to percussion ignition.[20] The Confederate force at Arkansas Post was composed of three brigades, totaling some 4,000 to 5,000 men, most of them Texan. Among the other regiments was the Tenth Texas Infantry, which included Sergeant Hosea Garrett and Lt. John V. Buster, both of Chappell Hill.

Fort Hindman, which the Confederates built on the site in late September, could fire upon Federal gunboats attempting to move up the Arkansas River to Little Rock, 100 miles to the northwest. This position was only 40 miles above the confluence with the Mississippi River and thus posed a threat to Federal forces downriver that were attempting to take the strategic river city of Vicksburg. On January 9, Confederate scouts brought reports of the approach of a vast flotilla under the command of General John McClernand. The force, in addition to transport vessels conveying 30,000 men, included six gunboats and three ironclad vessels.

The Confederates spent the night of January 9 in the earthen trenches of Fort Hindman. Lieutenant Colonel Swearingen and five companies were deployed in a skirmish line several hundred yards beyond the entrenchments.[21] It rained hard throughout the night, leaving the soldiers shivering in the morning cold. Federal gunboats and a battery on the opposite bank of the river began bombarding the Confederates early on the morning of January 10. Swearingen and his men pulled back towards the fort that afternoon, withdrawing under fire. The gunboats shelled the fort for three hours after dusk, while the Confederates frantically worked to prepare the defenses for the attack anticipated in the morning.

At sunrise on the morning of the 11th, the Federals commenced a combined attack with gunboats, artillery fire from a battery across the river and an all-out infantry assault. Colonel Deshler wrote in his report of "such an unremitting and intensely hot skirmishing fire that it was almost impossible for a man to show himself without being struck."[22] The Confederates held their ground and returned deadly fire that ripped through advancing Federal infantry and broke each attack. The Federal artillery had its range set by this time. C. H. Smith, Chief Surgeon for Brigadier General Churchill, wrote: "they kept up a terrible cross fire that swept the whole area of ground occupied by us."[23] Colonel Garland wrote: "the enemy's batteries and gunboats had complete command of the position, taking it in front, flank, and rear at the same time, literally raking our entire position."[24] Garland wrote in his report:

> [T]here was heavy and rapid firing on the left, which induced me to believe that the enemy was attempting to turn our left flank.... I ordered the alternate companies of the Twenty-Fourth and Twenty-Fifth Cavalry (dismounted) ... under ... Swearingen ... to repair to the left and report to Colonel Deshler.... Much credit is due to [Swearingen and other officers] for the prompt and gallant manner in which they led the re-enforcements [sic] from their respective regiments, ordered from left to right to re-enforce [sic] the extreme left of the line, under a most galling fire.[25]

Colonel Deshler added in his report of the action:

> under command of ... P. H. Swearingen [the men] ... had to pass through a very galling fire almost the entire length of the line, as it was on my extreme left that I wanted them, and it was necessary to crawl on all fours in our shallow trench the entire distance.[26]

The Confederates faced a withering fire from infantry and field artillery from the front, and field artillery and naval guns from the right rear. At around 4:30 P.M., white flags of surrender began to appear among Colonel Wilkes's Twenty-Fourth Texas Cavalry. No order was given to surrender. Federal infantry penetrated the Confederate lines at a number of points amid the confusion and the battle was over. Federal losses had far exceeded those of the Confederates with 1,100 dead and 800 wounded, versus 60 dead and 80 wounded. But in the end, victory belonged to the Federals, who held Fort Hindman and several thousand Confederates as prisoners. Garland and Wilkes received blame for the surrender. Garland's career never did recover, although he attempted to place full responsibility on Wilkes.

The captured Confederates expected to be exchanged. The logical place of transfer was Vicksburg. Instead, the prisoners found themselves loaded onto transport vessels and shipped up the Mississippi River to the north. Major General John McClernand, commanding the Federal force at Arkansas Post, advised General Grant: "[I]t would seem to me criminal to send the prisoners to Vicksburg ... to re-enforce [sic] a place with several thousand prisoners at the moment we are trying to reduce it."[27] The plan became to move the prisoners north and then east to eventually be exchanged in Virginia.[28]

The Confederates had spent three days exposed to the rain and freezing temperatures on the battlefield. They suffered exposure to the weather, still in their damp uniforms, in unprotected barges as they were transported upriver. When the transports reached St. Louis, the prisoners were for a time interred on Arsenal Island in the Mississippi River. Samuel Curtis, the commanding officer, was concerned, as there was no shelter on the barren island. He sent a dispatch to Grant, advising him that, as he had sent most of the men under his command southward to help at Vicksburg, Arsenal Island was the only place he could put so many prisoners with so few guards.²⁹ Sickness and death continued to take its toll on the Confederates of Arkansas Post.

The Federals transported the Confederate officers captured at Arkansas Post, among them Patrick Swearingen and Franklin Wilkes, upriver to St. Louis, where they were placed on a train for Camp Chase, a prison in Columbus, Ohio. The long train ride in the dead of winter was miserable and one officer froze to death en route. The men arrived at Columbus at midnight on January 30, 1863, and were forced to make a four-mile march in a heavy snowstorm to the prison.³⁰ During their stay, David Todd, the governor of Ohio, and Andrew Johnson, the military governor of Federal-occupied Tennessee, came to see the Confederate officers captured at Arkansas Post.³¹ General Churchill, the senior officer among the prisoners, refused an interview with the governors, which caused enthusiastic cheering among the otherwise downcast Confederates.³² The Federals transported the enlisted men captured at Arkansas Post to Camp Douglas in Chicago and Camp Morton at Indianapolis. Word had begun to filter northward about the treatment of captured soldiers in the South and Federal prison authorities had begun to develop a new, tougher attitude towards Confederate prisoners.³³ The men taken at Arkansas Post were the first affected by this change in Northern attitude.

Chicago, the site of Camp Douglas, was rife with Southern sympathizers. When the train carrying the Arkansas Post prisoners rolled into Chicago, about 200 men tried to free the prisoners.³⁴ But a band of rowdies was no match for well-armed, disciplined soldiers. The attempt ended after some minor bloodshed and several arrests and the soldiers escorted the prisoners to Camp Douglas. Many men were quite ill by the time they finally arrived at the camps. Observers in Chicago described the prisoners as "poor white trash in the main, poorly clothed and overjoyed at the sight of a fire."³⁵ There was no sense of who the men actually were or what they had just undergone.

Confinement in a prisoner-of-war camp exposed a soldier to a wide range of physical experiences and emotions. At its best, the experience was boring and monotonous with day after day of nothing but waiting for a release that never seemed to come. There was an element of guilt on the part of men who surrendered rather than having fought to the death. Imprisonment gave a man long periods to reflect on this, whether real or imagined. Prison camps in the North exposed Confederate prisoners to harsh winters with inadequate clothes, blankets or shelter. Extreme discomfort was inevitable and many became sick and died.

In April, the Federals shipped the Arkansas Post officers by train to Fort Delaware on the Delaware River, 30 miles below Philadelphia. While their slow-moving train made its way through Philadelphia, it was attacked by a mob of angry citizens.³⁶ Conditions at Fort Delaware were even worse than they had been at Camp Chase, but fortunately, the stay there was short. On April 29, the officers boarded a ship and sailed to Fortress Monroe on the coast of Virginia and from there to the Federal Army base at City Point on the James River. The officers were released at City Point, the result of a prisoner exchange. The enlisted men were likewise exchanged at about the same time.

An order issued June 5, 1863, by Lt. Gen. Edmund Kirby-Smith, commanding the Trans-Mississippi Department for the Confederacy, instructed Lt. Colonel Patrick Henry Swearingen to "proceed to Texas for the purpose of collecting the men of his regiment who may be in that district."[37] Swearingen established himself at Hempstead for that purpose.[38] Confederate Military Headquarters reassigned the Arkansas Post prisoners to Major General Patrick Cleburne's division. Word of the surrender at Arkansas Post had spread. The men faced criticism from other units and a rumor circulated that only Cleburne would accept them into his command. Colonel Francis Wilkes was given command of the Seventeenth, Eighteenth, Twenty-Fourth and Twenty-Fifth Texas regiments. The time would come soon enough for them to restore their honor.

6

Glory at Galveston

It became apparent to Confederate authorities as early as 1862 that Union forces were planning to invade Texas. Many New England mills were shut down by 1862 for lack of raw cotton. Certain influential Yankees argued that the Federal government only needed to seize Galveston and then advance inland. The Brazos River offered a route not only for an invasion force, but also to move Texas cotton to New England mills. The Confederacy accordingly authorized the formation of new regiments. As many men of fighting age had already enlisted and marched off, the men mustered in at this point were often older or even slightly underage. The Twentieth Texas Infantry Regiment was among the new units raised. Colonel Henry Elmore organized the regiment at Galveston in the summer of 1862. Claudius Buster of Chappell Hill, survivor of the ill-fated Mier Expedition, decided he had one last fight in him and led a contingent of men from Chappell Hill to Galveston to enlist.[1] Buster became the captain of Company C in Elmore's Regiment. Most of the Chappell Hill men ended up in Company B under the command of Captain John Wallis, also of Chappell Hill.

John C. Wallis was the son of Major Joseph Wallis, a prominent Chappell Hill planter, who moved his family to Texas from Mississippi in 1848. John, as the eldest son, brought the slaves overland while the rest of the family came by boat. John opened the second store in Chappell Hill in partnership with Terrell Jackson in that same year. Emily, the eldest Wallis daughter, married Joseph Toland when the family was living in Mississippi. Toland, originally from South Carolina, was a man of considerable wealth. He and his wife moved soon thereafter to Chappell Hill to join Emily's family. Elmina, the second oldest Wallis daughter, married not long after the family's arrival in Chappell Hill. Her husband, Dr. John Washington Lockhart, would serve as a lieutenant in Company B under Captain John Wallis.

6. Glory at Galveston

LOCKHART PLANTATION MANOR HOUSE. Dr. John Washington Lockhart built the manor house in 1850 on his 1,000-acre plantation. The house was built of cedar, pine, ash and black walnut cut on the plantation. This was one of the first plastered houses in rural Texas. The house features four fireplaces with slate hearths and the original hand-cut mantels. The black walnut stairway balustrade was hard-carved by plantation slaves. (Photograph by Thomas G. Stevens of Chappell Hill.)

Lockhart set up a practice in Chappell Hill in 1847 upon his graduation from Louisville Medical College. A practicing doctor spent long hours in the saddle and sometimes provided service to people who were unable to pay. Lockhart became intrigued by the substantial profits to be made in cotton. He gave up the medical profession as a livelihood and acquired 1,000 acres of land near Chappell Hill for planting cotton.[2] Fifty slaves under Lockhart's direction constructed a Greek Revival mansion from the cedar and black walnut trees growing on his property.[3]

Major Wallis helped finance the Houston & Texas Central Railroad. Among his partners was Colonel Landes, patriarch of another long-time Chappell Hill family. Major Wallis' second oldest son, Joseph, married Colonel Landes' daughter Kate in 1860. When the war began, Colonel Landes' oldest son James went to Virginia with the Texas Brigade. The Colonel's younger son, Henry Landes, not quite 18 years of age in the spring of 1862, enlisted in Elmore's Regiment to serve with his brothers-in-law. Joseph Wallis and Henry Landes served as privates under Captain John Wallis.

THOMAS CHAPPELL. Kentucky-born Sergeant Thomas Chappell was among the Chappell Hill men who served in John Wallis' Company B in the Twentieth Texas Infantry. He survived yellow fever and was deputy sheriff in Brenham for a number of years. (From the Archives of the Chappell Hill Historical Society.)

J. W. "Bill Dick" Thompson was another Chappell Hill man who enlisted in Company B of Elmore's Regiment. Bill Dick had originally been a member of Terry's Texas Rangers, but had been discharged for medical reasons. He re-enlisted when Colonel Elmore formed the Twentieth Texas Infantry. Thompson, who listed his occupation as "gentleman," had been educated at Emory and Henry College in Virginia. His education earned him a position as quartermaster's clerk.

Nineteen-year-old Del Perkins of Chappell Hill originally enlisted in the Fifth Texas Infantry on August 3, 1861, and was mustered into the company of Captain Tacitus Clay of nearby Independence. By the end of December, Del Perkins was sent home on medical disability, having been diagnosed with epilepsy. The doctor's scrawl at the bottom of the Certificate of Disability for Discharge reads "Mr. Perkins is not now, never was and never will be fit for service."[4] The Fifth Texas was in winter quarters along the Potomac River in Virginia at the time. Perkins was given a voucher from the Quartermaster's Department in Richmond, Virginia, asking the superintendent of the Danville Railroad to furnish Perkins transportation to New Orleans.[5] Del Perkins' medical condition should not have been a surprise. His father was a graduate of the medical college at Memphis, Tennessee, and a physician in Chappell Hill.[6] It is not absolutely certain that Del Perkins had been aware of being epileptic before signing up with the Fifth Infantry. But he certainly knew when he re-enlisted with the Twentieth Infantry on March 26, 1862, only three months after his discharge from Hood's Texas Brigade. Del's father was a staunch supporter of the Confederacy[7] and, no doubt, instilled the same in his young son. Del was determined to fight and was assigned to Company B with many others from Chappell Hill.

Jacob Umland, also of Chappell Hill, enlisted in Elmore's Regiment. He was, like Del Perkins, 19 years old. Jacob was the eldest son of 54-year-old Johann Umland, a cabinetmaker who had brought his wife and large family to Chappell Hill from Hanover, Germany. Chappell Hill's wealth created a demand for quality handmade furniture and there was an abundance of good hardwood for raw material. Johann Umland was one of three renowned cabinetmakers in Chappell Hill, all of whom were German. The Umlands owned no slaves and the federal census of 1860 shows they had a net worth of only $600. Their work is recognized to this day by antique collectors.[8]

There were numerous other Chappell Hill men in Elmore's Regiment, most of them in Captain John Wallis' Company B. These included Sergeant Thomas Chappell and W. C. Chappell, J. R. Crockett and Second Lieutenant John E. Crockett, George P. and J. W. Crump, James and John Walker. W. C. Chappell had survived the disastrous Sibley's expedition to New Mexico. There were H. J. Phalen, David Sallis, E. M. Smith, R. C. Tapscott and J. H. Traynham. A. W. Guyton served in Company C. Milton Baker, whose two younger brothers were gathering glory as part of Terry's Texas Rangers, enlisted with Wallis. However, the long-time alderman of Chappell Hill

JOHN E. CROCKETT. John Elijah Crockett moved from his native Alabama in the 1850s and settled in the Chappell Hill region where New Year's Creek runs into the Brazos River. His grandfather was a soldier in the Continental Army and later became governor of Virginia. John Crockett enlisted in the Twentieth Texas Infantry after the Battle of Galveston. He became a second lieutenant six months later and served in various assignments along the Texas coast for over two years without a leave of absence. He was paroled at Columbus, Texas, in late July 1865. John and his wife Sallie died of yellow fever at Chappell Hill in 1867. They left two small sons, whom John's sister Mary Davie Crockett raised.

soon found a substitute in John Martin and went to Austin to serve in the Texas legislature.[9]

When a combined Federal army and navy expedition took Galveston without a fight from the Confederates in October 1862, the reality of war struck home to many Texans. People in settlements such as Chappell Hill recognized that an invasion inland from the coast was a very real possibility. From that moment on, there was a sense that Galveston had to be recovered and Texans prepared to meet the challenge. Galveston, only slightly smaller than San Antonio in population, was the most important city in Texas by virtue of being its major port.

General John Magruder arrived in Texas to take command on November 29, 1862. He would attack and re-take Galveston in only a month's time. Magruder was known as "Prince John" for his demeanor, as well as his elaborate uniforms. He also had a deserved reputation for results. It was Magruder who had used his theatrical background at Yorktown during the Peninsula Campaign to bluff General George McClellan by constructing a large number of fake cannon from logs. Magruder began directing a major effort to organize forces and accumulate men and supplies for an attack on Galveston. The men of Chappell Hill in Elmore's Regiment soon found themselves marching into their first battle.

Magruder ordered the Twentieth and Twenty-First Texas Infantry to Virginia Point, on the mainland just across the water from Galveston Island. The Twenty-First had little more experience in combat than the untested Twentieth Regiment. On December 31, the day before Magruder's attack on Galveston, Lt. John Lockhart wrote: "Our company drew new Enfield rifles."[10] Major General Magruder met the assault force at Virginia Point at dusk on December 31, 1862. The men moved as quietly as possible across the two-mile long wooden plank bridge that crossed over from the mainland to Galveston Island. Lockhart wrote to his wife that on the eve of the battle, "My heart melted and I wept. It was not for fear, but the necessity of spilling others' blood."[11] Lockhart saw war as unnecessary and believed fervently that the gradual abolition of slavery could have been accomplished peacefully. He received a letter from his wife and read it by moonlight. "I thought it might be the last I ever should receive from you, though I did not believe that the Yankees would kill me. I had a strong presentment that I would not be hurt."[12]

Galveston was held by only 242 men of the Massachusetts Forty-Second Infantry Regiment. They withdrew into a well-barricaded position on Kuhn's Wharf when their pickets were driven back by Confederate units moving into place. Companies A and B of Elmore's Regiment with Pyron's Regiment and Griffin's were to take part in the assault on Kuhn's Wharf.[13] The opportunity for glory and death belonged to Company B with its large contingent of Chappell Hill men. Claudius Buster's Company C and the other companies of Elmore's Regiment were relegated to physically dragging artillery across Galveston Island into place for the attack. The Confederate artillery was to be positioned along Galveston's waterfront for a distance of over two miles, targeting both the Federal gunboats anchored in the water and also the Federal infantry barricaded on Kuhn's Wharf.

Magruder had decided that a frontal assault down the wharf at the Union

6. Glory at Galveston

position would be futile. Instead, the plan was for 500 men to wade into the water along the wharf, covered by rifle fire from sharpshooters on shore. The objective was to wade beyond the barricade on the wharf, then climb onto the wharf and take the Union position from behind. Lockhart recalled that when Company B was issued three ladders and for the first time came to learn the battle plan,

> [T]hings looked gloomy. We knew we had terrible work before us, a desperate and hazardous undertaking. But Texans never flinch from any duty. So we set out again for the city, as we thought, every nerve stretched and every heart resolved to conquer or die.[14]

Pyron's men were deployed as sharpshooters, leaving two companies from Elmore's Regiment and two companies from Griffin's to make the assault, a total of only 150 men.[15] Lockhart wrote:

> We marched in silence, not a whisper was heard; everyone seemed wrapped in his own meditation. The sand in the hour-glass was well-nigh run out, each tick of the clock brought us nearer the scene of blood.[16]

At 4:00 A.M., Magruder himself fired the first gun, signaling the attack, and the entire Confederate line opened fire.[17]

It is not clear from John Lockhart's summary, written six days later, exactly what happened. But one can get some sense that the attack never really got off the ground. Lockhart, to his credit, appears to have related the incident without embellishing his own role or that of his unit:

> [L]oud boomed a cannon near us. It startled us. This was our maiden fight; it shocked us; our breathing became louder, our hearts palpitated. Our commander, Captain John Wallis' voice, was heard to cheer the men. In an instant another gun was fired from the enemy. This made the confusion greater; our lines were broken. It now required the assistance of other officers to keep the men in ranks; they were disposed to scatter; some fell to the ground, others dogged, but after a time we managed to gain the advantage of an old plank fence. By this time the battle had opened in earnest; the grape and canister came so fast and thick that Colonel Cook ordered us to lie down. About this time the Yankees commenced pouring a shower of balls upon us from the wharf, which we had been detailed to storm. A few shot from our battery planted near the wharf drove them back, which enabled us to gain our feet and repair to an old building, from which we commenced pouring into them a murderous volley.... We soon attracted by our fire the peculiar notice of three vessels, which played on us for one or two hours ... so constant was their firing and so thick their grape that we were unable to form and carry out our first purpose.[18]

Colonel Joseph Cook, commanding the Confederate attack force, wrote later that the men under him "all acted well, and braver men I never desire to behold, wading into the water up to their hips under a galling fire of grape and canister and musketry, they found no chance to get at the enemy, the ladders being too short for the high barricade. It was indeed a desperate affair."[19] The attack was a dismal failure and a disaster. Magruder acknowledged: "The water was deep, the wharf proving higher than anticipated, and the scaling ladders ... were found to be too short to enable the men to accomplish their object." Little did the men of the Twentieth Texas Infantry know at the time, back on shore and pinned down by gunboat fire, that it would be the only action they would see in the entire war.

While withering fire from the Union gunboats devastated the ground troops, a makeshift flotilla of Confederate "cottonclads" made their way toward the Union fleet. The small boats were named such by virtue of the bales of cotton set on the deck for protection from enemy fire. One cottonclad was sunk, but the remaining Confederate vessel managed to ram the U.S.S. *Harriet Lane*. Tom Green's riflemen jumped onto the deck of the *Lane* and captured the Union gunboat with considerable loss of life. Joseph Wallis heard one of Green's men comment: "all of them that want to fight gunboats can do it, but he will be d____d if he will do it again."[20]

John Lockhart and his fellow Confederate infantrymen on shore witnessed the naval action and upon the capture of the U.S.S. *Harriet Lane* "a loud huzza went from every throat."[21] When the Federal flagship, the U.S.S. *Westfield*, ran aground on a sandbar, the crew scuttled her with a gunpowder blast that killed the crew and rocked the harbor. The tide of battle turned and the remaining Federal vessels left for the open sea, leaving the small garrison on Kuhn's Wharf to fend for itself. These men soon surrendered, though having suffered negligible loss in the infantry attack on their position. In fact, not a single Federal soldier had been killed. Two hundred and forty men of the Forty-Second Massachusetts Infantry marched in a column of fours before the men of the Twentieth Texas Infantry. It was the Twentieth Regiment's brief moment of glory, regardless of what had transpired on the field of battle.

Galveston was again in the hands of the Confederacy and would remain so for the duration of the war. The Chappell Hill men of the Twentieth Texas Infantry would not see any further action for the remainder of the war. They would be relegated to guard duty and defense along the Texas coast for an invasion that never came, not until after the surrender and the end of the war. The recapture of Galveston was not only strategically important, but also a significant emotional boost for Texan spirits. The victory led to great rejoicing and the men of Chappell Hill rightfully could claim credit for participating. After the war, they could refer to themselves as Confederate veterans, a point of honor in post-war Texas. Henry Landes, recalling the action years later as an aging Confederate veteran, wrote of his only experience:

> I participated in only one battle, that being the battle of Galveston ... [which] was planned and fought under great disadvantages and was won only by strategy and bulldog bravery of the Southern soldiery, and Texans especially. And its result was far reaching because it kept the Federal troops out of Texas."[22]

While the Battle of Galveston was a glorious moment for Texans, the outcome meant prisoner of war camp for the Federal soldiers captured. Confederate authorities in Texas sent the Federals taken prisoner inland. Camp Groce near Hempstead, just east of Chappell Hill, had been a recruiting camp in 1862. The authorities converted Camp Groce to a prison camp in June 1863. The initial contingent of prisoners numbered 132, that being 29 officers, 17 soldiers and 86 sailors taken prisoner at

Galveston.²³ One man, who survived, testified that the largest number of prisoners in the camp during his tenure was about 700. An estimated 1,100 men were confined within the walls during the course of the war.²⁴

Colonel Clayton Gillespie was newly returned from being paroled after his capture at Arkansas Post. He was given command of the new Confederate prison at Camp Groce on the basis of his experience as superintendent at Huntsville before the war. Gillespie's experience as a Union prisoner of war was fresh in his mind. Camp Groce was open ground surrounded by a 15-foot-high wooden stockade with sentry boxes set on top about every 50 feet. A survivor later testified:

> [There were] guards, who were instructed to shoot any coming within an imaginary distance of ten feet of the fence. Inside the pen were old barracks, not sufficient, however, for the accommodation of all the prisoners, and, but very little protection from the weather ... the high stockade preventing any air from entering, while the only well in the grounds having caved in before our arrival, our only source of water was from a muddy creek outside the camp; and since being provided with but few buckets, and but a few allowed to go to the creek, under guard, at a time, the demand being constant, this privilege was often denied to many, the officers saying that it occasioned the guards who accompanied "too much work."²⁵

The camp was garrisoned by, as one prisoner later wrote, "a company of 60 to 80 militiamen under the command of a fat officer known as Captain Buster."²⁶ Claudius Buster of Chappell Hill had been assigned to Camp Groce in the aftermath of the victory at Galveston. Later, when conscripts escorted additional prisoners to the camp, Buster and his men were reassigned to Camp Lubbock near Houston.²⁷ The first fatality occurred on July 8.²⁸ Dysentery claimed a number of lives that summer. Typhus flux, a contagious disease transmitted by body lice, was also common. There were also snakes to be dealt with, as rattlesnakes and copperheads were prevalent in the area. More prisoners arrived in September after the second Battle of Sabine Pass.

In late September 1864, as yellow fever was spreading across Central Texas, Colonel Gillespie determined it best to move the Yankee prisoners of war from Camp Groce. Accordingly, on September 20 he ordered the prisoners moved to a location west of the Brazos River near Bellville. A number of deaths at this location convinced Gillespie to again move his charges, this time to land just east of Chappell Hill on Gabriel Felder's plantation. A survivor later recalled:

> In October we were crowded into mule carts, for few could walk, and moved to Camp Felder, near Chapel Hill, several dying on the way. At this camp there was the greatest amount of sickness, and largest number of deaths. It was located on low, swampy ground, at the foot of a hill, the top of which had formerly been used for camp-meetings, and on which were many large sheds, ample for all; but no, their horses enjoyed the shelter, while dying prisoners even were not given this little protection from the winter storms. All were herded on the muddy ground, in so small a compass that it was almost impossible to walk through the camp, so near together were the sick and well lying. The suffering and mortality at

this place surpassed the others; it may be said that the ground was covered with sick and dying, and these, too, with no shelter, lying on the wet ground with chills, and diseases of every description, exposed to the winter heavy rains and chilling 'northers' .... With not clothing enough to cover them, several being chilled to death.[29]

7

Marauding Cavalry

When Don Carlos Buell's Federal Army of the Ohio threatened Chattanooga in mid 1862, Nathan Bedford Forrest led a large force of Confederate cavalry into middle Tennessee behind Buell's advancing army. Terry's Texas Rangers were among Forrest's troopers and generally regarded to be among the best fighting men in the command.[1] On July 13, 1862, Forrest captured the important Federal supply center of Murfreesboro and its 1,400-man garrison.

By the fall of 1862, Terry's Texas Rangers had been in the field for nearly a year. The hard riding and reckless frontal charges of the cavalrymen had taken its toll of men and horses. An article in the Sept. 24, 1862, issue of the Houston *Tri-Weekly Telegraph* read:

> Clothing and Horses for the Rangers. Mr. G. L. Neville of LaGrange will leave that place on the 1st of October, stopping at Mr. Affleck's in Washington County and at Navasota and will take to the Terry & Lubbock Rangers all horses and packages that may be left at these places for them.[2]

The article reported that Neville already had a large number of horses and that he was definitely making the trip. Those willing to contribute horses were asked to include sufficient money to cover expenses for the 30-day journey to Tennessee. The article also requested that clothing be packed in 30-pound boxes and that a pack saddle be included for every two pounds of clothes.[3] Two days later, the *Tri-Weekly Telegraph* received a letter from Thomas Affleck at his plantation between Chappell Hill and Brenham:

> Mr. G. L. Nevill writes me that he will start for the head-quarters of Terry's Rangers on the 17th of October, with a lot of horses, sent on by friends to those

who are badly mounted, or not mounted at all. I presume he is prepared to take any number of horses that may offer.[4]

Federal forces, after repulsing Price at Iuka, defeated Bragg's Confederates at Perryville, Kentucky, in October 1862. Bragg fell back into Tennessee and established winter quarters for his army at Murfreesboro. Some of Terry's Texas Rangers had little interest in remaining in Tennessee. Word of the Federal capture of Galveston in 1862 caused one of the Rangers to write home:

> We hear that the Yanks are comming to Texas in large forces.... We here it reported in the regiment that Col. Wharton is going to do his best to get this Regiment sent back to Texas because the Yanks have come there.[5]

The fighting in Tennessee was not over. Major General William Rosecrans moved his Federal Army of the Cumberland out of Nashville on December 26, intent on engaging the Confederates.

Bragg gave Brigadier General Joseph Wheeler, commanding the Confederate cavalry, responsibility for slowing the Federal advance. The men of Terry's Texas Rangers, commanded by Colonel Thomas Harrison, were among the 4,000 cavalrymen under Wheeler's command. It was 4,000 men against 40,000 but Wheeler took advantage of the rugged country to unleash sudden attacks on the advancing columns. The daring cavalrymen would attack, forcing the infantry to form into line for battle, then strike the flank and disappear as additional strength moved up. This was repeated over and over. There were numerous actions, many of which involved desperate fighting, in the vicinity of LaVergne, Tennessee. Wheeler delayed the Federal Army until the night of December 29, at which time the Federal Army moved into position before Bragg's army. Wheeler and his exhausted Confederate cavalry had gained Bragg four days of preparation. Bragg sent a note to Wheeler: "Your command has already done more than their duty most nobly."[6]

Both sides spent December 30 maneuvering in preparation for battle. Hardee led the Confederate left against the Federal right flank at dawn of December 31 and the Battle of Stone's River near Murfreesboro began. The fierce Confederate attack caused the Federal line to collapse. Bragg sent Wheeler on yet another mission, a midnight raid around the Federal Army to attack and destroy their supply trains. The Rangers rode down an artillery battery in a reckless charge that resulted in the capture of 1,500 men.[7] The Confederate cavalry came upon a wagon train, only to find themselves confronted by a Federal cavalry regiment. The two sides slammed into one other at full gallop.[8] The desperate melee lasted for a few minutes before the Federal troopers withdrew with the Confederates in hot pursuit. The Confederate cavalry, initially successful in capturing a supply train, were escorting the supply train to Murfreesboro when the regrouped Federal cavalry countercharged and retook the train.[9] Sgt. Alfred L. Bains of Chappell Hill was killed during one of these violent clashes. He had been a mechanic, a part-time deputy sheriff and a member of Chappell Hill's Masonic Lodge. Word traveled home slowly. Chappell Hill's Masonic Lodge officially recognized the loss of Brother Bains on March 14, 1863, bowing their heads in a moment of silence. Private James Fiske "Doc" Matthews of Chappell Hill was among those Rangers taken prisoner at Murfreesboro. He managed to escape en route to prison and return to his unit.

The Federal Army managed to re-establish their line and hold. There was a respite from the fighting on New Years Day. On the following day, both remained in position. There was more fighting on January 2 with no clear-cut result. On January 4, the Confederate Army withdrew. The North rejoiced, proclaiming victory, but an exhausted Rosecrans did not pursue. The army that held the field of battle had responsibility of the dead and wounded left on the ground. The reality was that the army that remained, whether Confederate or Federal, generally took better care in tending to their own dead and wounded than those of the enemy that had hours earlier sought to kill them. Al Bains of Chappell Hill was likely laid to rest in a mass grave, his body thrown into a trench with other butternut-uniformed corpses and quickly covered with dirt, the grave unmarked.

In late January, General Wheeler was ordered to take a position on the Cumberland River at Palmyra from which he could attack Federal vessels and disrupt shipping. However, the Federal authorities became aware of the plan and simply suspended traffic on the river. Wheeler recognized that he could not remain in the area indefinitely. He chose to attack the Federal garrison at Dover, Tennessee, which his intelligence had advised him was small. Daniel Harvie Browning of Terry's Texas Rangers wrote Dr. John W. Lockhart, his sister's husband, in Chappell Hill in February 1863:

> We have just returned from the hardest scout our regiment has ever been on. We have been on an expedition down the Cumberland River under General Wheeler. We started from Shelbyville on the twenty ninth of January and that night camped at Eagleville the next night we got to Franklin where we rested until 12 o'clock next day and then proceeded and that night camped at Smith Springs and so on to Fort Donelson where we arrived on the evening of the third of February....[10]

Wheeler's cavalry attacked the small Federal force at Dover, Tennessee, on February 3. Eight hundred Federal soldiers faced nearly 3,000 Confederate cavalrymen. The Federal men were well entrenched and supported by artillery, as well as by gunboats in the river. A deep snow had fallen the night before under a full moon.[11] Private Browning served during the action on the staff of Colonel Harrison. He wrote:

> Wharton's brigade under Wheeler and Wharton attacked the center while Forrest charged the right. I could see it all and hear plenty of bullets.... After two or three hours hard fighting we were compelled to withdraw as our ammunition was about out. Gen. Wheeler and Forrest told Wharton to bring up the Rangers to lead the charge and the balance would follow but Wharton would not do it. Wharton was slightly wounded, Forrest had two horses shot under him, Harrison had one shot. While I was riding from one part of the field to the other and the balls were flying like hail I heard one strike very near me and my horse wheeled around. I thought he was shot but I was mistaken.[12]

Many commanders recognized that the primary use of cavalry was to screen an army's movements and to scout the enemy's position. Rifled muskets allowed for an expanded killing zone and a volley from an infantry line could be devastating on an attacking line of cavalry. However, Confederate élan was based upon the bravado of defying logic and making bold attacks. The consequences to the attackers, even in victory, were severe. Terry's Texas Rangers, for their part, persisted in brave, reckless charges to the bitter end of the war. General Wheeler concluded that the enemy was too well entrenched at Dover and withdrew his Confederate force. While his decision many have been appropriate, Wheeler's failure to take Dover left the Cumberland River open to Federal traffic. Federal forces, as a result, retained control of their strategic position in middle Tennessee.

There was considerable dissension among the Confederate leaders in the aftermath of the setbacks in Tennessee. Daniel Harvie Browning wrote: "Old Harrison during the fight cursed Smith's Tennessee regiment and told them that he could take twenty Yankees and whip them and a thousand other things too numerous to write." Gen. Nathan Bedford Forrest, for his part, denounced Wheeler, saying he would not serve under him again. Despite the defeat, Daniel Browning maintained an upbeat tone. He wrote: "General Wharton says that we will all be home by September. My love to all the family. Yours fraternally, Dan Browning. In my next letter I will tell you about my stealing some bee gums, I have taken up smoking."[13] By September, the two armies would be clashing in the thick underbrush along Chickamauga Creek in Georgia. The war was far from over.

A "Letter from the Rangers" was published in the June 15, 1863, issue of the Houston *Tri-Weekly Telegraph*. The letter was dated May 16 from Sparta, Tennessee.

> One half the Rangers are with Colonel Harrison, now acting brigadier at Liberty. The other half are near Gen. Wharton's quarters.... The Rangers are in better health than usual, are well-clothed and certainly are at the head of all in cavalry service. They are a noble band of soldiers and well may any one be proud to command.[14]

The Confederate defeat in Tennessee left the strategic Mississippi River exposed. In April 1863, Brigadier General John S. Marmaduke led a combined force of 2,000 troopers into Missouri. His objective was to create sufficient havoc to somehow disrupt Federal operations down the Mississippi River threatening Vicksburg. Marmaduke was a Southern aristocrat who attended Yale and Harvard before graduating from the U.S. Military Academy. He previously had attempted to drive Federals from his home state of Missouri in November 1862 and failed.

George Washington Carter's Twenty-First Texas Cavalry, as part of Parson's Cavalry Brigade, became a part of Marmaduke's raid. One gets a sense of the former president of Soule University from a description published in the *Bellville Countryman*: " ... with his coonskin cap, his tiger blanket and top boots ... one would hardly recognize the gifted and eloquent preacher of the Gospel in Texas."[15] J. Norfolk Cocke of Chappell Hill was among those riding on Marmaduke's raid with Carter. His father, Major James H. Cocke, had been a prominent man about Chappell Hall, a friend of Sam Houston and customs collector for the District of Galveston, Republic of Texas.

7. Marauding Cavalry

Major Cocke's wife, Elizabeth Cocke, remained in Chappell Hill after his death in 1853. In the summer of 1861, her grandson Tom Bates enlisted in nearby Independence with Captain Jerome Robertson's Company I of the Fifth Texas Infantry. Bates wrote from Virginia to his grandmother in Chappell Hill on February 21, 1862, asking:

> Everybody I see here who knows Norfolk asks me what he is doing, why does he not enlist in the army and that is what I say too. He ought not to have any tobacco to chaw if he would go and fight for his country—come here to Virginia or Kentucky and he would get plenty to chew....[16]

J. Norfolk Cocke had not rushed off in the early days to enlist with Terry's Texas Rangers, Sibley's Brigade or Hood's Texas Brigade. But the situation for young men in the Confederacy changed dramatically in early 1862 when the Confederate congress began discussing conscription of white males between the ages of 18 and 35 years. The *Bellville Countryman* of March 1, 1862, urged Texans to be "honorable volunteers" before they were drafted. Volunteers were paid a bonus and also allowed to choose their regiments and their officers. The conscription act of April 1862 drew the line. Texans who wanted to get into the cavalry had to move quickly before they were drafted into the infantry. For Colonel George W. Carter, who was having some difficulty raising his regiment of lancers, the conscription act was the incentive he needed. Recruits began reporting to his camp near Hempstead to enlist. Among these was Tom Bates' cousin, 22-year-old James Norfolk Cocke of Chappell Hill. Cocke enlisted as a private at Hempstead on March 13, 1862 and assigned to Captain W. Hess Jones's Company E. Norfolk was promoted to fourth corporal later that year.

Word spread through the family of Norfolk's move. His cousin George Kerby, who attended college at Georgetown and Princeton,[17] was in the East when the war began. Federal authorities in Maryland arrested Kerby as a spy and there was no word of his situation for some time. Kerby wrote Elizabeth Cocke from Richmond in October 1862: "Norfolk I am informed is with Rev. Col. Carter's Regmt. in Arkansas."[18] Marmaduke was raiding into Missouri by April 1863.

Carter's Twenty-First Texas Cavalry rode as the advance guard as Marmaduke approached Federal forces under the command of Brig. Gen. John McNeil near Bloomfield, Missouri. Confederates knew McNeil as "the butcherer."[19] Although Marmaduke ordered Carter to avoid serious contact that might cause the Federal troops to flee, the anxious Texans were apparently looking for a fight. They attacked and McNeil withdrew into fortifications at Cape Girardeau. Colonel Carter was ordered to not follow McNeil to Cape Girardeau, which he did anyway. Marmaduke recognized at this point that any attempt to withdraw would encourage pursuit by the reinforced Federal troops. He ordered Col. John S. Shelby's brigade to demonstrate against the fortifications in an attempt to extricate Carter. The demonstration escalated into an attack and the Confederates were repulsed with losses. As Marmaduke withdrew his forces southward, the raid turned into a retreat with Federal troops in close pursuit. The only thing that saved the Confederates was a shaky bridge across the flooded St. Francis River. Carter was among the last to cross. The cables on the south side of the bridge were cut just as Federal troopers approached the opposite bank. The expedition was a complete failure and a clear illustration of the absurdity of sending cavalry against a fortified town. The Houston *Tri-Weekly Telegraph* in June published a report from Sgt. Norris of Carter's Twenty-First Cavalry in St. Francis County, Arkansas, with a list of the killed, wounded and missing in action.[20]

William Zuber, a trooper with Carter's regiment, wrote of the Battle of Taylor's Creek (Arkansas) that occurred after the crossing of the St. Francis River.

> Colonel Carter sent Burford's regiment and Morgan's squadron to attack them, ordering our men to retreat as soon as the fighting should become hot. But he held his own regiment in reserve and ordered us to be ready to charge when our comrades should emerge from the bottom. These orders were strictly obeyed, but the enemy dismounted. They hid behind trees and lay down behind logs, and sent a hailstorm of bullets among us. And so we retreated.[21]

Although the Federal casualties were slight, they withdrew. Zuber was among those who accompanied Carter across the battlefield to take care of the wounded and bury the dead. Zuber recalled that during this search, Carter confided in him:

> I know that I erred in giving the orders. If I had conducted the whole brigade together in a general charge and had pursued the enemy, we would have captured them. But through my error, we have let them escape.[22]

That Sunday, Carter preached in church not far from the brigade's encampment. William Zuber thought it a pretty good sermon and recalled Carter telling his listeners, "I was a much better preacher then than I am now, because I was a much better man." George Washington Carter, despite his ego, seemed to recognize his weaknesses.[23] "Buck" Walton, who served under Carter, wrote of him:

> Col. Carter was as simple hearted and credulous as a child—yet brave and fearless as a lion. He was a college professor and a Methodist preacher—sincere and honest, but with little aptitude for the practical affairs of a rough and tumble life.[24]

The exhausted troopers reached the safety of Arkansas and halted for several weeks to rest. "Buck" Walton wrote:

> The men being rested got mischievious, and a great many complaints were brought in of hogs disappearing. Chickens & turkeys came up missing—wagons robbed—potatoe fields invaded—& other depredations.[25]

Carter's solution was to issue an announcement that any man found guilty of plundering would receive 39 lashes on the bare back to be inflicted publicly. The result was near revolt. Walton recalled Carter's response.

> I was at headquarters with Carter. Without saying a word to me or to anyone, he issued another order for the men all to assemble in the evening to hear what he had to say.... It was under an old arbor ... Col. Carter stepped in the rude pulpit, holding me by the arm. He made a speech, such as one he alone could make—in which he scolded, shamed, arraigned & held up men, who pretended to be

7. Marauding Cavalry

soldiers — who would be guilty of the acts that were charged against them — then asked any man present to answer what he had said. No man came forward: after a pause of five or ten minutes he continued, and said — that he had been abused and animadverted on for issuing the order, complained of — his courage had been doubted, his manhood distrusted — and his honor impugned — but he said: "I will waive my rank altogether, and any man, officer or private, may have a fair fight, and we will step out, and settle the matter right now." He then went down from the pulpit, pistol in hand, and went out on the plateau, and took his stand — but no man offered to take up the challenge — not because they were afraid — not because they were not mad enough — but simply because they loved Col. Carter and thought him hasty in making the proposition. He was an excellent man & officer — genial, sun shiny — and lovable ... He came back to the pulpit — and said, he would withdraw the order — because he saw how distasteful it was to the men. Then there was an uproar, and shaking of hands, and glad comradeship that was very pleasant to see. After that, Carter was more popular than ever.[26]

George Washington Carter, former president of Chappell Hill's Soule University, a doctor of divinity, had been admirable in stirring the hearts of men to enlist. Whether he would be an able field commander remained to be seen. But there was much time for that. He was a man who could overcome setbacks. As Marmaduke's shattered columns withdrew southward in the late spring of 1863, Carter was making plans for himself.

Marmaduke failed in his attempt to bring Missouri into the Confederacy. Confederate partisans continued to bushwhack Unionists and Federal troops in Missouri. William Quantrill and Bloody Bill Anderson were among the most infamous. They joined together in August 1863 to attack Lawrence, Kansas. The resulting massacre left 150 men dead. Federal forces and outraged Unionists across Missouri forced Quantrill and Anderson to withdraw into north Texas by mid–October 1863.[27] Lt. General Edmund Kirby Smith, commanding the Confederacy's Department of Trans-Mississippi, ordered General Henry McCulloch to use Quantrill to round up deserters and draft dodgers. Chappell Hill resident Lt. John Washington Lockhart was engaged in recruiting during 1863 following the glorious retaking of Galveston at the beginning of the year. The archives of the Chappell Hill Historical Society suggest that Lockhart "rode all day one day with Quantrill's gang."[28] Confederate authorities realized their mistake by early 1864. McCulloch had Quantrill arrested. The partisan escaped and fled north with his men with Confederate troops in pursuit. Neither Quantrill nor Anderson returned to Texas or survived the war. John Lockhart had a story to tell to family and friends. The contrast between the well-respected Lockhart and the infamous Quantrill must have been sufficiently striking to always make the story interesting, no matter how often it was told.

In May of 1861, the same week that Dr. George Washington Carter arrived at Chappell Hill to begin his duties as president of Soule University, Andrew Keller was reporting to the board that the new university building was completed.[29] Keller was a stonemason, who became the subcontractor responsible for the actual execution of the construction at Chappell Hill. The cornerstone had been laid in November 1858[30]

JOHN WASHINGTON LOCKHART. Chappell Hill planter John Washington Lockhart was a close friend of Sam Houston. He raised and led a company of Chappell Hill men for the Twentieth Texas Infantry in the re-taking of Galveston. He moved to Galveston after the war, but kept his land in Chappell Hill. He survived the Galveston Hurricane of 1900, only to die a month later in Chappell Hill after a challenging ordeal to return home. (From *Sixty Years on the Brazos*, 1930.)

and construction on the magnificent structure occupied several years. During this period, Keller petitioned Chappell Hill's Masonic Lodge for admission and was accepted on July 10, 1860, despite noting that Keller had received five black balls at Belton Lodge in Bell County.[31] Keller finished up his work in the summer of 1861and headed to north Texas as the war commenced. He enlisted on September 7, 1861, in the Sixth Texas Cavalry that Warren Stone was raising in Dallas.[32]

Stone's Sixth Cavalry, attached to McIntosh's Brigade, moved north into Indian Territory in the fall of 1861. Albert Pike, Confederate commissioner to the Indian Nations, had signed treaties with all five of the Civilized Nations, but the Creek Nation was split.[33] Opothyleyahalo, a veteran warrior who had led the Upper Creeks for many years, remained loyal to the United States government[34] and was determined to stand by his treaty. He and his 2,000 followers posed a threat to Confederate control of Indian Territory. Confederate authorities directed McIntosh's Brigade against the Upper Creeks. Opothyleyahalo sent an urgent request for military assistance to the U.S. commissioner. Federal General John Fremont had driven Sterling Price's Confederates out of Missouri and was in a position to move west into Indian Territory. Instead, Federal authorities removed Fremont from command and ordered his forces to withdraw 120 miles to the east. Confederate authorities responded as soon as they learned of this development by moving in force back into Missouri, cutting off Opothyleyahalo and the Upper Creeks from any possible support.[35]

Opothyleyahalo and his followers withdrew north across Indian Territory with McIntosh's Brigade in pursuit. On Christmas Day 1861, the Confederates caught up with Opothleyahalo's rear guard, approximately 500 strong, which had taken up a position on a prominent height above Chustenahlah Creek in the Cherokee Nation.[36] McIntosh ordered an assault on the position the following morning. The Sixth Cavalry was on the right in the attack up the steep slope. Trooper George Griscom later wrote: "fight was short but hotly contested & resulted in total rout of the Indians ... the enemy's loss was very heavy."[37] The Texans pursued the Creeks for the remainder of the day and Opothleyahalo's power was broken. Thirteen Confederates died and another 30 were wounded. Andrew Keller was among the wounded. His wound healed quickly and he returned to the campaign.

SARAH ANN ELIZABETH BROWNING LOCKHART. The daughter of prominent Chappell Hill planter William Westcot Browning married John Washington Lockhart and ran his plantation during the war. Her dear brother, Daniel Harvie Browning, was one of several Chappell Hill men who died in the war. (From *Sixty Years on the Brazos*, 1930.)

Confederate authorities held high hopes for Missouri through much of the war. Sterling Price had served Missouri as governor from 1853 to 1857. Price was the presiding officer at the Missouri state convention, which voted in February 1861 to oppose secession, despite Price's efforts to the contrary. The ex-governor had led Missouri volunteers in the Mexican War of 1846–1848 with the rank of brigadier general. When the Civil War began, "Old Pap," as he was affectionately known, assumed command of the pro–Confederate Missouri State Guard. Price combined his force with Ben McCulloch's Confederate Army of the West in northern Arkansas. McIntosh's Brigade with Andrew Keller moved eastward from Indian Territory to join McCulloch and Price. Federal forces defeated this combined Confederate force in the Battle of Pea Ridge in March 1862 and established Federal control in Missouri. Both McIntosh and McCulloch died in the fighting. There was much dissension among Confederates in the West in the aftermath, as Missouri was a key border state and the gateway into the Lower Mississippi River Valley. There was also dissension among the soldiers of the Sixth Cavalry, many of whom had never been happy with Warren Stone's command. In May 1862, Lawrence Sullivan "Sul" Ross replaced the unpopular Stone as the regiment's new commander.

In the aftermath of Pea Ridge, Confederate authorities gave Sterling Price a commission in the Confederate Army as major general in March 1862. Upon hearing of Price's CSA commission, Reverend Dr. Benjamin T. Kavanaugh traveled north to offer his services as assistant surgeon and chaplain. Confederate authorities in July 1862 officially approved Reverend Kavanaugh's appointment as chaplain to Price's army.[38] Benjamin T. Kavanaugh had been at Chappell Hill, his posting as a Methodist minister, since 1860. He was the son of a traveling Methodist circuit rider and one of four sons who became preachers. Kavanaugh studied medicine at Rush Medical College in Chicago in the late 1840s and began practicing medicine in St. Louis in 1850.[39] He ministered to Methodist congregations in Independence and Lexington, Missouri, in the western part of the state near the Kansas border during the mid 1850s, a time of considerable bloodshed. He was also a zealous Mason and it may have been in this role that he came to know Governor Sterling Price.

Sterling Price, following the disappointment at Pea Ridge, attempted to move his army eastward to combine with Braxton Bragg's army in middle Tennessee against Federal forces under Don Carlos Buell. Rosecrans' Federal Army of the Mississippi moved north to block Price. The opposing forces clashed at the major battle of Iuka on September 19, 1862. The fierce fighting ended in a clear Federal victory. Only the dense woods and a brave rear-guard action saved Price's army from a more serious loss.

Vicksburg, Mississippi, remained the only obstacle to Federal control of the Mississippi River. Federal forces converged on this strategic Confederate stronghold in the summer of 1862. The Confederates in the west made every effort to hold Vicksburg. Andrew Keller and the Sixth Texas Cavalry, as part of General Earl Van Dorn's cavalry division, took part in the successful raid on the giant Federal supply base at Holly Springs, Mississippi, in December 1862. The Confederates destroyed vast quantities of war supplies and likely delayed Grant's capture of Vicksburg for more than six months. The daring raid was not without its losses. On December 21, 1862, Keller was among those captured by elements of the 25th Indiana Infantry near Lagrange, Tennessee.[40] He was taken to Memphis and shipped north by train. Andrew Keller's destination was Camp Douglas, the infamous Federal prison camp outside of Chicago. He later wrote:

> We arrived in Camp Douglas, on the last day of January; the weather was exceedingly cold, and some of our men had no blankets, and a few had not so much as a coat. We were thrown in dilapidated old shacks, that were hardly fit to shelter cotton. I had charge of 112 men in one of those barracks. We were without fire for 24 hours. The second night twelve men were frozen to death.[41]

Some of the Arkansas Post prisoners had arrived at Camp Douglas only days before Keller's arrival. The reunion with old friends from Chappell Hill would have offered only temporary joy. The conditions were grim. Keller appealed to the officer commanding the camp for blankets and clothing, later recalling: "Some had not changed their clothes for five or six weeks and their clothes were alive with those loathsome vermin they had caught from Yankee soldiers."[42]

Smallpox was spreading through the camp and taking its toll of lives. Three hundred eighty-seven prisoners died at Camp Douglas in February 1863, Andrew Keller's first month interned there.[43] Keller went to General Jacob Ammen, the commanding officer of the camp, and offered a $10,000 bond for his freedom. Ammen refused, but suggested that an oath of allegiance to the government might help his situation.[44] Amnesty had been reinstituted on February 18, 1863, with the stipulation of the prisoner taking an oath of allegiance. Keller wrote that he answered defiantly: "Sir, I had rather die and be eaten by rats, as many as my fellow-prisoners have been in yonder death house than take an oath to a miserable, corrupt government."[45] Ammen was perhaps referring to Keller when he told the Chicago *Tribune* of February 28, 1863, that Texans "are very hostile and do not wish any terms except to fight it out."[46]

Andrew Keller was a man of action. He could see dead and dying around him and realized that, once his physical situation deteriorated, he would be unable to escape. Keller managed "through the interposition of friends"[47] to escape Camp Douglas. Chicago was full of Southerners and Confederate sympathizers. Although they lacked the numbers and organization to confront Federal troops, the Chicago sympathizers did what they could to aid Confederates who managed to slip out of Camp Douglas. Keller spent one day and a night in Chicago with "friends true as steel, devoted to the Confederate cause."[48] They gave him civilian clothes and a horse. Keller rode south through Springfield and St. Louis. However, he did not head directly back to Texas. He stopped at Belleville, Illinois, and took up residence there for two months.[49] He traveled widely, meeting with Confederate sympathizers and gathering information. It was widely recognized that Bickley's Knights of the Golden Circle had considerable standing in southern Illinois.

Andrew Keller returned home to Texas, determined to do all that he could to spread the word about the extent of Confederate support in Illinois. He wrote and published an extensive article, which the Galveston *Tri-Weekly News* featured on the front page of the July 2, 1863, issue. Keller in his "The North-West ripe for Revolution — Now is the Time for the Confederate Armies to carry the War among the Enemies" urged Texans to understand "the dissatisfaction in the North-western States" and that "they want [General Sterling] Price in Illinois."[50] Keller reported that the U.S. government had used the military to disarm the Democrats and left them powerless for the time being, but that they had organized and were ready "to come out boldly for the South, demand peace upon the principles which governed the South in seceding."[51] He argued that the organized anti-war movement had sufficient strength that Illinois and adjoining states in the Northwest would "refuse any more men or money to support the abolition war."[52] He urged Confederate authorities to "Invade the North-Western States, and I will stake my honor that we get from one to two hundred thousand recruits— they have pledged their word to me it would be so; I believe it."[53]

Keller proposed a scenario for Southern victory. The basis of this outcome was the expiration of the terms of service for 300,000 of the best soldiers in the Federal Army between May 1 and June 17, 1863. He insisted, "Not one in a hundred will re-enlist"[54] and predicted, "If we are successful at Vicksburg, we will have peace in less than four months."[55] Keller's letter, dated June 6, 1863, was published on July 2, 1863. Even as readers in Galveston and Houston followed Andrew Keller's words, Grant was on the verge of finally taking Vicksburg. He did so just two days later.

8

Vicksburg and Gettysburg — The Turning Points

Everyone in the Confederacy realized the seriousness of Grant's siege at Vicksburg in 1863. Texas, Louisiana and Arkansas would be cut off from the rest of the Southern Confederacy once Federal gunboats controlled the Mississippi River. Texans continued to embrace optimism at every opportunity. The June 13, 1863, edition of the *Bellville Countryman* reported:

> We are indebted to James E. Wallis of Chappell Hill, for a late Extra which confirms the most of the news given to-day. Grant and Banks are both whipped; General Wallace is licked; Grant reportedly mortally and Sherman severely wounded; the blockade at Mobile raised...[1]

When that report proved inaccurate, the *Countryman* tried a less definite approach, this time printing a letter in its July 4, 1863, issue that had been posted from Chappell Hill, dated June 1, 1863:

> One of our soldiers ... after a long absence, returned home, very unexpectedly to all his family. His wife was so overcome at his sudden and unexpected appearance that she fainted. After she resuscitated, she went into a swoon and remained in that condition four days. She revived from that and conversed a short time with her friends. Among other things she told them that on the 17th of this month (June) an event would transpire of the greatest importance to this country; but whether this event would be favorable or unfavorable, she would not reveal—said she was not allowed to reveal it; but that we would all see it and know it. The lady

died in a few hours after she made this revelation. I have no doubt that the circumstances transpired as related....

Many people of the North and South recognized that 1863 would be critical as to the outcome of the war. Consequently, everyone anticipated fearful fighting and corresponding casualties. Rufus King Felder of the Fifth Texas Infantry wrote home to Chappell Hill on May 2, 1863, on the eve of the spring fighting:

> Never before has returning spring brought with it such feelings of sorrow & regret. Regret because a winter so suitable for making peace should have passed and nothing done & sorrow at the thoughts of so many bloody battles this coming spring we'll be called upon to witness, and the many family circles that will have to mourn the loss of one or perhaps more of its members.[2]

As Grant's victory at Vicksburg became more certain, 30,000 Confederates under siege pondered their fate. Waul's Texas Legion, including a number from Chappell Hill and nearby towns, was among these. Thomas Waul established a base camp north of Chappell Hill, near Gay Hill at the headwaters of New Year's Creek, in the spring of 1862 and recruited some 2,000 men from Washington County and nearby. He was a wealthy Gonzales County planter selected by the Texas secession convention as a delegate to the Provisional Congress of the Confederate States. When Waul failed in his bid to become one of two senators representing Texas in the Confederate Congress, he returned home in the spring of 1862, determined to go to war.

Waul's Legion was the only true legion formed in Texas—composed of 12 infantry companies, six cavalry companies and two artillery companies. The concept, outdated by the time of the American Civil War, was that a legion could be self-sufficient in terms of military capabilities. The Confederate command broke up Waul's Legion and the units fought in separate campaigns.

Three men from Chappell Hill, Robert Wooding Chappell Jr., Thomas Davidson and Charles T. Kavanaugh, became part of Company E of Waul's Fifth Cavalry Battalion. A number of German immigrants from Washington and Austin counties also enlisted with Waul. Henry Christian Brandt of Chappell Hill was among these. Brandt arrived in Texas in December 1856. He was 18, the youngest of the children of his father's second marriage, his mother having died just a month after his birth.[3] He and five of his six brothers and both of his sisters emigrated to Galveston, Texas, just two years after Henry's half-brother died of yellow fever in that city. Henry Brandt settled at Chappell Hill, working as a carpenter and builder—a trade in which he had apprenticed in Germany. He married Laura Jane Burns on January 24, 1860. A year later, Laura, seven months pregnant, wrote her mother in Oso, Texas.

> I have got good news for you and I know will do you good [to] hear it. Mr. Brandt has prayers night and morning and nothing does my heart more than for us to pray together it was quite a cross to him but he has overcome that now he commenced it the second night of the new year. I think he is greatly revived....[4]

Their time together was soon interrupted by war.

8. Vicksburg and Gettysburg — The Turning Points

A note written by Henry in his native German upon his departure survives to this day. It translates:

> My heart is full of pain because I have to separate, my heart breaks, my dear eyes are filled with tears to look out of the window, she is waving her scarf and sends hundreds of kisses to me and silent she whispers so long, so long, so long. You are so dear to me, so true and so good, so long my dearest girl with your holy look my thought is coming back to you and I silently I said so long, so long, my heart is with you at all times, goodbye my dearest so long, so long, goodbye my dearest so long.[5]

Henry Christian Brandt enrolled on March 22 and was mustered into service on April 4, 1862, as a private in Captain Robert Voight's Company C of Waul's Legion.[6] He was 24 years old. Henry's first cousin, Herman Knolle, son of Ernest, also enlisted and was assigned to Company B. While neither owned slaves, these men, as Texans, saw the war as their fight.

Waul's Texas Legion camped at New Year's Creek on the south edge of Thomas Affleck's 3,500-acre Glenblythe Plantation for most of the summer of 1862. Thomas Affleck wrote of the Fourth of July celebrated that summer at the Legion's encampment:

> Our young folks, aye and old ones too, are resolved to hold on to the 4th of July and the "Star Spangled Banner." As to Yankee Doodle, the doodles are welcome to it.... The La Bahia Rifles, our neighborhood company, gave a barbecue yesterday ... the result of a three days' effort.... The locality is one of the most beautiful in this very lovely country. And the sight was a gay one, I assure you. There were about a thousand persons present; a very large proportion of whom were ladies; and really, I don't know when I have seen so many pretty faces in one crowd! ... the troops again made a display on the prairie; the people turning out en masse, in carriages and on horseback.... The prevailing sentiment, nay the unanimous one, was that of resistance to the death, to Yankee aggression! ... Let us have a full, final and satisfactory settlement before we lay down our arms.[7]

On August 18, 1862, Waul's Texas Legion marched off to war. Although the Legion just missed fighting in the Battle of Corinth that followed bloody Shiloh, they did take part in the "skedaddle" in which the Confederate Army withdrew and fought its way back south.

Waul's Legion became part of the determined Confederate defense to hold Vicksburg. Waul's Legion took part in the determined defense of Fort Pemberton, upriver of Vicksburg. Afterwards, while most of the infantry of Waul's Legion moved into the entrenchments surrounding Vicksburg, three companies from Waul's Legion, including those of Henry Brandt and Herman Knolle, were assigned to defend Yazoo City, northeast of Vicksburg. Brandt had earned the rank of sergeant by this time. Federal troops already had destroyed the important shipyards at Yazoo City and there was little left to defend. Nor was there need for either side to utilize the Yazoo River, as Federal troops were moving down the Mississippi River towards Vicksburg. Herman Knolle wrote in his diary:

> June Fifth made 15 miles reaching Yazoo City by noon. The enemy had destroyed all government property, and had left again. We camped one mile from town ... we were artillery and infantry both. My company had 3 land guns ... the 12th of July when we heard that gun boats were coming up the river. We slept by our guns that night.[8]

Knolle and Brandt and their comrades remained in Yazoo City, relatively undisturbed while the siege of Vicksburg continued. They were spared the agony of the Vicksburg siege, which ended on July 4, 1863, with the surrender by Confederate General John Pemberton of 30,000 starving, shell-shocked soldiers. Just over a week later, Federal forces were directed to cleanup the small Confederate force at Yazoo City. A flotilla of four gunboats with 5,000 soldiers moved upriver. The Confederates were outgunned and out-manned. Herman Knolle wrote:

> July 13th in the afternoon of that day the gunboats came in sight. Our 3 guns and 2 others opened up on them and after hours firing they fell back. They landed a force, as we had no force to meet them we were captured at our guns. We did not have a man that got hurt at the engagement. Although we blew up one of their best gunboats, with a torpedo.[9]

An experiment with a five-gallon container of powder armed with an artillery friction tube proved successful. The assembly was placed in a wooden box and suspended below the surface on a wire. When a ship made contact with the wire, the powder was supposed to explode below water level and rip the boat's hull open. The Union gunboat *DeKalb* went down as she moved in to attack the Confederates. Nonetheless, the overwhelming Union force retook Yazoo City and captured a number of the Confederate soldiers. Herman Knolle, Henry Brandt and some of the men of Voigt's Company were in for a shock.

> My legion had gone through the siege of Vicksburg were all paroled, and had all gone home. Half of my company were sick at the time I was captured. All of those that were sick was also paroled, as I had a great longing to see my dear parents again. I had no fancy for going north as a prisoner but in this I was sadly disappointed, for after keeping us at Yazoo City for two days they put us on a boat....[10]

Knolle, Brandt and the others were taken upriver to St. Louis. Knolle and two others attempted to escape and nearly drowned before being recaptured.

> We reached St. Louis at 10:00 o'clock in the evening. At 3 we were brought into jail where we were first searched and then put into one room as many as could lay on the floor side by side. We had two meals a day. Our breakfast consisted of one cup of coffee and a piece of bread and bacon. Our supper was a spoon full of cabbage, and a piece of beef and a little bread. Coming down [up, actually] the river we had more to eat than we could eat, but now we had hardly enough.[11]

Their journey northward continued.

> Aug. 13th, we left St. Louis for Camp Morton, Indiana ... We reached our camp on the 14th, a little before sundown. Our camp was situated one mile

8. Vicksburg and Gettysburg — The Turning Points

from Indianapolis. It contained 20 acres of enclosed ground, around which was a high fence. Our rations were so that a man could just make out.... The climate of the country was more severe than any I had ever seen before. On the 25th of August it was almost freezing cold.

The situation became even worse. Rations were low. Many men were without shoes and even clothing. Some had only a blanket for clothing. Many slept in their clothes without a blanket for cover.

Camp Morton had been the Indiana State Fair Grounds since 1859. When the original buildings were constructed, there was criticism as to their acceptability for properly sheltering livestock from the elements—and that in the summer. The prison camp, its guards and conditions were not subject to the Federal Commissary General of Prisoners. The commander at Camp Morton was ordered, "so long as a prisoner has clothing upon him, however much torn, you must issue nothing to him, nor must you allow him to receive clothing from any but members of his immediate family, and only when he is in absolute want."[12]

The winter of 1863–64 was a harsh one. The temperature fell to 20 degrees below zero on New Year's Day. Only then were all prisoners provided blankets. Even then, the suffering was unbearable. Even as late as March, there was snow. Herman Knolle wrote:

> Sometimes 15 to 20 died in a day. The hardest blow fell on me Jan. 28, 1864, that day my cousin, Frederick, died of pneumonia at one o'clock in the morning. His death was very sudden, as he had been sick for only 36 hours. Brandt [Henry] was the only kin I had left that was with me and we shared a bed together.

The prison doubled in size from May 1864 to July 1864, by which time Camp Morton held 5,000 prisoners. The heat of summer and the overcrowding led to outbreaks of disease that made the men wish for the winter. There were numerous attempts at escape, even when the men knew there was little chance of success. They were more desperate emotional responses. On November 4, 1864, Knolle noted that he received a package of clothes from his uncle. He gave an extra pair of pants and a pair of boots to cousin Henry. Knolle wrote:

> Shall I ever see my dear parents again ... hardly a night do I sleep but that I am dreaming of those dear ones far away, but which I hope to God I shall soon see again.... Dec. 1 it is cold, wet rainy day with 4 inches of snow on the ground.... Grub is very scarce and I can't help but think of home today ... To be sitting by a blazing chimney fire, to have a loving mother ask whether you are cold ... I am almost despairing of ever getting out of imprisonment.[13]

For the remainder of the war, Herman Knolle and Henry Brandt could only dream of the rolling hills and spring wildflowers of Washington County, Texas.

Robert E. Lee recognized the seriousness of Grant's siege of Vicksburg and knew that the Confederacy would need a major victory in the eastern theater. He seized the initiative on June 26, leading his Army of Northern Virginia across the Potomac

River into Maryland. Meade pursued Lee into Pennsylvania. Rufus King Felder wrote home:

> [S]ince the 10th of May when we took up a line of march from Richmond we have been all the while on the march or lying in line of battle. You cannot imagine the fatigue & hardships we have been exposed to having been on a forced march all the while, making 15 to 25 miles a day ... we reached Gettysburg, Pa. ... met Meade....[14]

Advance elements of both armies made contact at the little town of Gettysburg, Pennsylvania, on July 1, 1863. Additional units moved quickly to support and the situation escalated into one of the major battles of the entire war. The Federals commanded the high ground on Cemetery Ridge. The Confederate officers debated whether to attack or disengage, but Lee chose to attack. Hood's Division, including the Texas Brigade, arrived on the field of battle on the morning of July 2. Lee's plan was to roll up the left flank of the Federal line. But as the Confederates prepared to attack, they realized that the Federal line extended further south than they had expected. Hood requested permission of Longstreet, his corps commander, to shift the attack and move around the Federal flank. When this request was denied, Hood repeated the request, again to no avail. Hood then sent his adjutant general, a man well-known to Longstreet, to repeat the request for a third time and to file a formal protest. Hood later recalled that it was the only time in his entire military career that he lodged a formal protest against an attack order. Longstreet insisted: "We must obey the orders of General Lee."[15]

The Federal artillery found the range even before Hood's attack had begun. One shell killed or wounded 15 men in the Fourth Texas, who were lined up awaiting orders to advance. General Jerome Robertson subsequently ordered his Texas Brigade to assume the prone position. Captain Decimus et Ultimus Barziza of Independence, Texas, commanding Company C of the Fourth Texas Regiment, wrote:

> The enemy's shells screamed and bursted [sic] around us, inflicting considerable damage. It is very trying upon men to remain still and in ranks under a severe cannonading. One has time to reflect upon the danger, and there being no wild excitement as in a charge, he is more reminded of the utter helplessness of his present condition. The men are all flat on the ground, keeping their places in the ranks, and as a shell is heard, generally try to sink themselves into the earth.[16]

Major General John Bell Hood took his place at the head of his vaunted Texas Brigade. He rose up in his stirrups and yelled out: "Fix bayonets, my brave Texans. Forward and take those heights!" Rufus King Felder, James Landes and their comrades surged across the open field towards a jumble of rocks known as Devil's Den. They had advanced only a short distance when an artillery shell exploded above Hood. Shell fragments rendered his arm useless and he was taken to the rear in shock as his Texans moved on. Federal sharpshooters posted behind a stone wall poured a deadly fire into the brigade's ranks as the Texans advanced. The brigade pressed on through

8. Vicksburg and Gettysburg — The Turning Points

thick woods and boulders to the saddle between the Big and Little Round Tops. Little Round Top's rocky slope was defended by well-entrenched Federal troops. Large boulders forced the Texans to break ranks and file through them. On the left, the Fourth Texas went in yelling and whooping. John C. West of the Fourth Texas later wrote, "Round the rude rock the ragged rascal ran."[17] The tactical objective was for the attacking line to reach its objective, despite the horrific loss of life along the way, as so often the attackers were able to break the defensive line by virtue of their momentum. For two long hours on the afternoon of July 2, 1863, the brave men of the Texas Brigade and other units in Longstreet's Corps pressed forward, only to suffer terrible losses, then regroup and advance again. Rufus King Felder wrote home shortly after the battle.

> Meade ... took possession of a high mountain [Round Top] & that night & next day made it impregnable. The evening of the 2nd, Lee attempted to carry the heights by storm.... It seemed like madness in Lee to have attempted to storm such a position. He came very near losing his whole army by it.... The slaughter on both sides was terrible.... I will give you some idea of our brigade in the fight. We were on the extreme right & had the highest portion of the peak [Round Top] to charge. We charged a mile at double quick up an almost perpendicular peak at the top of which the enemy had fortified to make it impossible to take had the enemy only been armed with rocks. Our regiment suffered severely having charged up within thirty yards of the enemy four successful times & having to fall back as many times two hundred yards from the enemy's works. I must close by giving a list of casualties in our company.... All those not able to walk out fell into the hands of the enemy.[18]

The Texas Brigade suffered 600 casualties at Gettysburg. Thomas Bates of Chappell Hill, serving in Captain Tacitus Clay's Company I of the Fifth Texas, was among the dead. It would be some time before word reached his beloved grandmother back home in Chappell Hill. Years later, on the 50th anniversary of the battle, the Galveston *Daily News* would refer to the Devils' Den as "a dismal mausoleum of glory-crowned Texas heroes"[19] and recall of Gettysburg: "there the sunburnt veteran from the verdure clad steppes of the Brazos and the pale faced boy from the frozen lakes of Minnesota make one common funeral pile."[20] General Jerome Robertson was wounded, as were every colonel and lieutenant colonel in the Texas Brigade, but one.[21] Captain Decimus et Ultimus Barziza of the Fourth Texas Infantry was taken prisoner. The Fifth Texas Infantry had 211 total casualties, including 54 killed or mortally wounded. Colonel Robert Powell, commanding the Fifth Texas Infantry, was wounded and captured. Powell recalled years later: "for the first time in its history the Fifth Texas recoiled in the slaughter pen and yielded the field."[22]

Rufus King Felder and James Landes of Chappell Hill survived yet another battle. As the war dragged on with no end in sight, the struggle became less and less one of principle and more one of survival. A man's allegiance became centered on his comrades-in-arms in his regiment. After months in the army and having experienced and survived battles, a man did not run because he owed it to the man next to him to stand with him. Meanwhile, the famed Confederate charge was taking its toll, slowly bleeding the South of a generation of men. Everyone imagined someday going home. But the spring bluebonnets of Chappell Hill were becoming a distant memory for Felder and Landes by the summer of 1863.

The slaughter of the Texas Brigade on the second day at Gettysburg was such that it never recovered. Brigadier General John Gregg, a Texan, assumed command of the shattered remnants of the Texas Brigade that had survived. A full-page feature in the Galveston *Daily News* on the 50th anniversary of the Battle of Gettysburg closed with the following:

> The orator, the poet, the historian must tell how Colonel Powell, obeying General Hood's instructions, saw the banner of the Fifth Texas ... go direct to Great Round Top, penetrate the gorge, drive the enemy from the side of the mountain and fight through the slaughter pen up the side of Great Round Top, where the blood of our brave Texans flowed in rivulets down the mountain side; where every Texan was a hero; where their gallantry erected an indestructible cenotaph to their memory; where the rising sun ever smiles in ecstasy over their renowned deeds; where the pale moon in her moonlight wanderings sheds a halo of glory over the hallowed spot; where the night wind mourns their sad requiem among the rocks where they fought; where their glorious actions have made a page in history imperishable as the granite beneath their crumbling bodies as lasting as the coming and going of the rainbow.[23]

The state of Texas dedicated a monument at Gettysburg 100 years later. The inscription reads:

> TEXAS REMEMBERS THE VALOR AND DEVOTION OF HER SONS WHO SERVED AT GETTYSBURG JULY 2–3, 1863. FROM NEAR THIS SPOT THE TEXAS BRIGADE AT ABOUT 4:30 P.M. ON JULY 2 CROSSED EMMITSBURG ROAD AND ADVANCED WITH HOOD'S DIVISION ACROSS PLUM RUN TOWARD LITTLE ROUND TOP. THE TEXAS BRIGADE AFTER SEVERE FIGHTING ON THE SLOPES OF LITTLE ROUND TOP RETIRED TO A POSITION ON THE SOUTH SIDE OF DEVIL'S DEN. THE BRIGADE HELD THIS POSITION THE NIGHT OF JULY 2 AND DURING THE DAY OF JULY 3. THE BRIGADE THEN FELL BACK TO A POSITION NEAR THIS MEMORIAL ON THE EVENING OF JULY 3. ON THE FIELD AT GETTYSBURG THE TEXAS BRIGADE SUFFERED 597 CASUALTIES.
>
> OF ALL THE GALLANT FIGHTS THEY MADE NONE WAS GRANDER THAN GETTYSBURG.
>
> A MEMORIAL TO TEXANS WHO SERVED THE CONFEDERACY ERECTED BY THE STATE OF TEXAS 1964

Whatever insight the poor dying woman in Chappell Hill had, her timing was off by a mere 20 days. The outcome was all Federal. Federal forces won two major victories and altered the course of the war over the Fourth of July of 1863. Texas, Louisiana and Arkansas would be cut off from the rest of the Confederacy for the remainder of the war and Lee would never again muster the necessary strength to invade the North.

9

The Home Front 1863–1864

Texans feared being cut off from the Confederacy since the beginning of the war. The loss of New Orleans and Memphis in early 1862 drove home that reality, and the loss of Vicksburg in July 1863 sealed off the Mississippi River and split the Confederacy in two. Meade's victory over Lee at Gettysburg in the same week made a bad situation even worse. The war shifted in favor of the Federals in the aftermath of the significant Federal victories in July 1863. The people of the South were beginning to suffer the effects of the Federal blockade and the subsequent loss of trade with the outside world.

Major General Theophilus Holmes, head of the Confederacy's Arkansas-Missouri district, led an attempt to retake the key Mississippi River port of Helena, Arkansas, on July 4, 1863, even as the Federals were winning major victories at Gettysburg and Vicksburg. The Federals had occupied Helena, located 230 miles above Vicksburg, for a year. The Confederates needed a port on the Mississippi to offset the loss of Vicksburg. Helena's defenses were formidable, despite the many Federal troops that had been diverted from Helena to Vicksburg.

Sterling Price was serving under Holmes. Price was much more popular with his men than he was with the Confederate government in Richmond. He was infuriated when Richmond passed him over for the command of the Confederacy's Arkansas-Missouri district and instead promoted Holmes, a North Carolinian. The inspector general of the Trans-Mississippi Department later reported that the dissatisfaction with Major General Theophilus Holmes "both in the army and among the people is very great."[1] There can be little doubt that Price was not helping the situation. The relationship between Price and Holmes worsened when the Confederates' attempt at a coordinated attack on Helena was unsuccessful, due in part to a series of confusing and contradictory orders by Holmes. Price's own command took their assigned objective at Helena, capturing a battery on a key hill with heavy losses on the third assault. Sterling Price's resentment toward Holmes deepened.

There was growing dissatisfaction among Confederates in the West with what was perceived as Jefferson Davis' lack of support for the war effort in the Trans-Mississippi region. Many felt strongly that Missouri and southern Illinois, in particular, were fertile ground with many willing recruits waiting for the Confederacy to establish a presence. Many were frustrated that Richmond seemed to not understand this situation. A conference was held in Marshall, Texas, in August 1863 to discuss the matter.[2] Andrew Keller's essay on the subject had appeared in the Galveston paper only one month earlier.

Texas governor Frank Lubbock chaired the conference. He was accompanied by Pendleton Murrah, the man who had just been elected to succeed Lubbock in that position at the end of the year. When Frank Lubbock declared in the spring of 1863 that he would not seek re-election as governor, most Texans had expected the governor's race in the summer of 1863 to be a wide-open fracas. The contest developed quickly into a two-man race when a number of expected candidates backed off. Little-known attorney Pendleton Murrah of Marshall opposed Thomas Jefferson Chambers of Anahuac, an outspoken critic of Jefferson Davis.[3] The results indicated that Texas voters may not have shared Chambers' feelings about Davis.

The governors of Arkansas and Louisiana were present at the Marshall conference. Thomas Reynolds, who had succeeded to the tenuous post of the Confederate governor of Missouri upon the death of Claiborne Jackson only months earlier, was also in attendance. The conference attendees declared their determination to remain part of the embattled Confederacy. They expressed confidence in General Edmund Kirby-Smith and called upon him to assume greater powers in his role as head of the Trans-Mississippi.[4]

Sterling Price was a proud, even headstrong, man. He was well aware that Edmund Kirby-Smith held him in low regard.[5] When the governors at the conference gave Kirby-Smith their vote of confidence, Price chose to take extended furlough to Washington, Texas, in late 1863.[6] His wife and children had been in Washington since Missouri fell under Federal control. The situation was so tenuous that news of Price's departure led to persistent rumors that he had abandoned the cause. Federal General Frederick Steele wrote in a dispatch:

> Refugees and spies report to me that Price's division is very much demoralized, and that the men deserted in great numbers while crossing the Red River. They say 400 left in one day. Price and some members of his staff went to Texas on sixty days' leave of absence, and it is currently reported here, on good grounds, that they have deserted the sinking ship and gone to Europe. I believe it is true.[7]

Reverend Kavanaugh, Sterling Price's chaplain, accompanied his commanding officer back to Washington County, Texas, to see his own family in Chappell Hill. Kavanaugh appears to have chosen to remain in Chappell Hill amid the controversy and did not return to the front. He resigned from military service on October 16, 1863,[8] and rejoined the faculty of Soule University.

9. The Home Front 1863–1864

Colonel George Washington Carter returned to Texas in September 1863. One might imagine a different outcome in the Texas gubernatorial elections if Carter had been in Texas that summer. His military service record states: "Absent with leave. Sick for sixty days. Aug. 10."[9] However sick Carter may have been, he was addressing "large audiences at Houston, Brenham and Galveston,"[10] among other places. In fact, Carter was suffering from hemorrhoids,[11] a common ailment of men at the front, and obtained medical treatment from Gideon Lincecum of Long Point in Washington County. Carter also had a problem with his ear. Lincecum wrote Carter out a lengthy set of instructions to accompany prescriptions, closing with:

> Accept, dear sir, this prescription with my strongest wishes for your speedy good health and my hope that you may become a terror to our insane foes and survive to participate in the grand jubilation that is to follow our triumphant success a few years hence.[12]

George Washington Carter was a Texas hero in the fall of 1863, still "well remembered"[13] for his speech before the secession convention and having added acclaim with his exploits as a dashing cavalry officer.

Reverend Carter had been engaging crowds since he was a young man. It was written of Carter: "In social life he was fascinating. He was either disliked or loved."[14] Prominent men who knew Carter were on record saying he had few intellectual peers. He was compared to Alexander Hamilton and Jonathan Edwards, the brilliant Colonial Congregational preacher who became president of Princeton College.[15] Professor Richard Smith of Randolph-Macon College and a newspaper editor of some prominence called Carter the foremost intellect in the country.[16] The Galveston paper reported to its readers:

> Col. Carter returned home by an apparent accident, just at the time when the people needed him most. And his addresses will contribute now to elements of strength to the great conflict....

Carter's address in Brenham lasted three hours and the *Galveston Tri-Weekly News* devoted an entire column to relating his major points. Carter, a man known around Chappell Hill, Brenham and Austin for his oratory skills, told the gathering:

> One great encouragement was that our enemies were fighting for expedient, we for principle ... the case was similar to that between the colonies and the mother country.[17]

One of Carter's key points concerned the frightful condition of Confederate currency. The Galveston paper related Carter's argument:

> [S]ome small depreciation was inevitable owing to the sudden and large issue of Confederate money; but this should have been inappreciable in amount and limited in its duration. There was no more Confederate money in reality than the people needed; no more than necessary to represent the exchangeable values of the country. If the people pay their debts and taxes, fund their treasury notes, or

> hold them in reserves, as capital, there would be no more Confederate money than was needed. But speculation, taking advantage of the times, labored to create a panic about the ability of the Confederacy to sustain itself in the war, in order that they might buy up Confederate notes at a low rate in one local market with the view of using them at a higher rate in another.... If the country were too poor to pay its debts, or if it lacked the nerve to fight this war to a successful issue, then Confederate notes would be worth nothing; but as the country is both rich and capable of maintaining its freedom, the unnecessary depreciation of her currency was the work of either the coward or the traitor; and the appreciation of that currency, by all means in his power, active and passive, was the legitimate work of every sensible and determined Southern man.[18]

Colonel George Washington Carter told his audience that they "had never realized the proportions of the struggle." He condensed the struggle to: "Twenty millions of people on one side, against ten million on the other, contending for the most magnificent empire in the world, immense in its extent, varied and rich beyond comparison in its production" and he chided his fellow Southerners for having had "too much confidence in the civilization and decency of our foe ... before the development of his true character and purposes."

The Galveston paper praised Carter:

> The intellectual force which the country possesses in Colonel Carter, regulated as it is by purity of life, and by the most thorough devotion to the cause of the Confederacy, is a treasure which the people are beginning to appreciate, if we may judge from the intense desire manifested in all parts of the State to hear the Colonel's views ... appreciating the importance of a truly useful man....[19]

Word of Abraham Lincoln's Emancipation Proclamation of September 1863 was beginning to filter through the South. Texas, unlike the other states of the Confederacy, did not suffer from invading Federal armies that could spread the news, and effort was taken to prevent the slaves from learning of the revolutionary announcement that threatened the structure of Southern society. Texans discussed the matter privately. Federal armies were invading the South and men were fighting to defend their families and homes. While the commonality of slaveholding had been the basis of the thin thread of nationality that tied the Confederate states together, it was easier to argue the defense of one's homeland as the cause of sacrifice. This became less tenable as people throughout the South, many of them non-slaveholders, suffered more and more as the war progressed. Slaveholding planters remained adamant. Thomas G. Banks, the wealthiest man in Chappell Hill, ran an ad in the *Tri-Weekly News* on October 9, 1863, offering to liberally reward anyone assisting in the return of three runaway slaves believed to be trying to make their way to Louisiana.[20]

The rising demand and, correspondingly, the price for cotton due to the blockade was incentive for many planters to transport their cotton to Mexico. The men who hauled the cotton the long distance by wagon train were also well rewarded, often with 50 percent of the profit on the sale.[21] More than 150,000 bales of cotton passed through Matamoros, Mexico, before Federal troops took Brownsville, Texas, in December 1863. The Texans then moved the trade upriver and continued. The Federals withdrew from the Rio Grande area after eight unsuccessful months attempting to block the cotton trade with Mexico. This, to some degree, was due to concern regarding the potential for clashes with French forces in Mexico, an escalation which Lincoln did not desire. An estimated 320,000 bales were shipped across the Rio Grande by the end of the war. This trade during the war resulted in fortunes for men like Richard King, Mifflin Kenedy and William Marsh Rice.[22]

Chappell Hill residents, as did those of many other cotton centers in Texas, took part in the trade with Mexico during the war. Francis Jarvis Cooke served the Confederacy as the agent for the Cotton Bureau in the Department of Trans-Mississippi during the war. He was a veteran of the Battle of San Jacinto, and was one of the guards for the captured General Santa Anna. He became ill while in Brenham and was nursed back to health by Mr. and Mrs. Hugh McIntyre. He subsequently came to know and on December 28, 1845, married their niece, Emily Stockton.[23] Cooke was a merchant and alderman in Chappell Hill in the 1850s and resided in the region during the war. He died in 1903 at the age of eighty-seven.[24]

FRANCIS JARVIS COOKE. Francis Cooke fought in the Battle of San Jacinto and later served as one of Santa Anna's guards. He was also a Texas Ranger and took part in the Texan campaign against Adrian Woll. Cooke was a merchant and alderman in Chappell Hill in the 1850s and served the Confederacy as the agent for the Cotton Bureau in the Department of Trans-Mississippi during the war. He died in 1903 at the age of 87. (From the Archives of the Chappell Hill Historical Society.)

John Sterling Smith moved to Chappell Hill in the 1850s as a young man. Smith's maternal uncle, Dr. Joseph Routt, helped him buy his first tract of land near Chappell Hill. Smith ran a profitable freighting operation from Chappell Hill during the war, transporting cotton by wagon to Mexico and returning with provisions procured there.[25] He became a wealthy man. His estate at the time of his death consisted of nearly 7,000 acres, mostly in the fertile soil of the Brazos River bottoms.[26]

The townspeople of Chappell Hill were able to follow the course of the war in the numerous letters they received from men at the front. The town soon found itself face-to-face with the realities of war. As casualties and attendant disease mounted quickly in the war, Confederate authorities recognized the need for hospital facilities "as soldier after soldier relapsed from too early exposure after being confined in temporary hospitals." As a result, Confederate authorities established a series of convalescent hospitals across the South. They selected, among other places, Soule University "as a suitable locality for a Convalescent Hospital, being a country abounding in forage, wood and water, high and dry, and having the facility of railroad transportation."[27] The railroad had only just been completed across the Brazos River through Chappell Hill to Brenham in 1861.[28] Chappell Hill subsequently became a Confederate quartermaster depot.[29] The Confederate authorities no doubt also selected Chappell Hill for the hospital by taking into account Soule University's new three-story building. The Galveston *Daily News* noted, "The building is spacious and perhaps the largest in the State."[30]

The board of trustees of Soule University enthusiastically supported the Confederacy from the outset. Nearly all of the board members, men like Gabriel Felder, W. W. Browning and William Chappell, watched younger family members enlist and head off to war. The board resolved to buy Confederate bonds and treasury notes,[31] a decision that would have dire consequences for the financial viability of the school in the future. However, while loyal to the Confederate government, they also recognized a fiduciary responsibility to the new University which meant so much to Chappell Hill. On July 4, 1861, as the conflict began, the board resolved that "the New University Building be not used for any other purpose than that for which it was constructed, that is for Educational purposes."[32] The board, prominent as they were in Washington County, Texas, had little leverage over the government of the Confederate States of America and a Confederate convalescent hospital was subsequently established in the main building on the Soule University campus.

The hospital brought Chappell Hill more closely in contact with the outside world than residents might have liked. In January 1864, a Chappell Hill woman wrote a friend:

> [W]e have a good deal of excitement about small pox. There are six or seven cases at the hospital, some of the girls are very much excited, we have all written home about it, and some I expect will go home, I don't know what I'll do, whether Pa will come for me or not, I told him I was not afraid of it.[33]

Another woman wrote a similar report a week later:

> I presume you have heard the small pox had made its appearance in town ... what a stampede it has produced among the girls.... It is confined wholly to the hospital and as they intend having that quarantined, I don't think I need apprehend much danger.[34]

Confederate authorities did all they could to convince women to work for the war effort. A woman from Chappell Hill fired off a sharp rebuke to the Houston *Tri-Weekly Telegraph* in October 1863 in response to an offer of a pair of cards to any woman delivering 25 pairs of socks to Houston. "Does Maj. Wharton know the cost of these socks to a poor woman? ... if she takes the government price for socks she can earn one day's boarding with five days work ... The government cannot purchase socks at their price."[35] Nonetheless, the frustrated woman encouraged her fellow Texan women "to have a few pair of socks ready for the call that must soon be made for the soldiers."[36]

While some came home to Chappell Hill and never returned to war, others were determined to return to the fight alongside their comrades. Andrew Keller left Chappell Hill in the fall of 1863 to rejoin his regiment. The Sixth Texas Cavalry was in the Yazoo Valley in Mississippi. Sul Ross had risen to brigade commander during Keller's long absence and was making a name for himself among Texans. Keller ran into an old Chappell Hill friend at Shreveport, Louisiana. John Jackson was returning to Terry's Texas Rangers after recovering from his wounds incurred at Woodsonville. The two Chappell Hill men traveled together from Shreveport to Pickensville, Alabama, where they spent two weeks before parting company and heading off in different directions. John asked Andrew to post a letter to his father, as he was heading eastward. Keller wrote Terrell J. Jackson:

> It is in obedience to a promise made to your son John that I now address you ... to drop you a line to let you know where he was and how he was.... I was pleased to meet and renew my acquaintance with him. I never met a pleasanter traveling companion in my life. His heart is in the right place and as large as all-outdoors.[37]

He added at the end of his letter: "John's health is not very good. I do not think he will stand the service well."[38]

Andrew Keller returned to duty and served in Sul Ross's Texas Cavalry Brigade in the Yazoo Valley from autumn 1863 to May 1864. In May the brigade was ordered eastward to Georgia to participate in the fierce defense of Atlanta. John Jackson was already there with Terry's Texas Rangers, as were numerous other Chappell Hill Confederates.

Some of the Chappell Hill men were unable to return. Miers M. Felder, following his serious wounds sustained at Second Manassas, was discharged from the service at Columbia, South Carolina, on February 14, 1863.[39] He returned home for good and married Catherine Felder in Chappell Hill on December 31, 1863.[40]

There were other battles being fought back home. In early 1864, the *Galveston Tri-Weekly News* carried a letter on its front page titled "The Chappell Hill Convalescent Hospital." The anonymous writer addressed "various rumors in circulation derogatory to the good character of this institution."[41] The writer noted that he was "an inmate and close observer," and reported "I find every report unfavorable to this Hospital false, and *know them to be false*."[42] He wrote further that he

> went through the wards among some eighty patients ... and to the question, How are you treated? The reply was, Could not be treated better; his wife is so kind; she gives us delicacies from her own table and purse; I fear she deprives herself;

DR. WILLIAM ROGERS. Dr. William Rogers taught clinical medicine at the Medical Branch of Soule University in Galveston before the war. He enlisted to serve as brigade surgeon for Colonel George Washington Carter's Cavalry Brigade. Dr. Rogers managed to escape capture during the Arkansas Post surrender and made his way back to Chappell Hill. He served for the rest of the war as a doctor in the Confederate military hospital in Chappell Hill. He died in 1887. (From *A History of Texas and Texans*, 1916, vol. IV, courtesy of the Texas State Library.)

she treats us as if we were at home with our mothers and sisters; and the Doctor, he not only does his duty as a surgeon, but is so interested for our comfort, that he watches with unceasing care that others do not neglect to perform their duty. God knows that man could do no more than he does with his limited means.[43]

The author stated, "Every patient in the wards assert that it is but due to the Surgeon in charge."[44] Dr. William Samuel Rogers was the surgeon at the Chappell Hill convalescent hospital.

William Rogers moved to Texas with his parents in 1840 at the age of 18 years. He grew up in Washington County and was a charter member of the Masonic Lodge in Chappell Hill in 1850. He subsequently practiced medicine with R. J. Swearingen in Chappell Hill. Both doctors became part of the medical faculty formed for the medical branch of Soule University to be established at Galveston, Rogers as the chair of "Diseases in Women and Children."[45] Dr. Rogers was 39 years old in 1861 when the war began. He came from a line of fighting men who were also inclined toward medicine. Patrick, William's older brother, had been a captain in the Texas Rangers and brother Edward served in his brother's company for a time before studying medicine. Another brother, John D., a graduate of Tulane University, was practicing medicine at nearby Washington when the war began. John formed a company for Hood's Brigade. William Rogers' own son, Joseph D., a recent graduate of Soule University, enlisted in Dave Terry's Cavalry Regiment — not to be confused with Terry's Texas Rangers.

Dr. William Rogers, at Soule University when the war began, enlisted to serve as brigade surgeon for Colonel George Washington Carter's Cavalry Brigade. When Carter split with Wilkes and Gillespie, it was Rogers' misfortune to accompany the latter. As a result, he found himself at Arkansas Post in January 1863. He somehow managed to avoid the fate of his comrades and to escape capture and imprisonment after the fall of Arkansas Post. Dr. Rogers made his way home to Chappell Hill. He seems to have decided that campaigning was not for him, but he was determined to make himself useful. That opportunity arose in Chappell Hill itself. Rogers assisted

Confederate officials with the establishment of the convalescent hospital in Chappell Hill. Many locals were opposed and Rogers' success was at the expense of local friendships.

The local position never changed with regard to the hospital. Smallpox and other diseases aside, Soule University needed its building. There had been few, if any, meetings of the board in 1863 and early 1864. In August 1864, the board wrote to the hospital surgeon requesting a "formal turning over to the Trustees of the University building."[46] When that failed, the board of trustees authorized its president, Gabriel Felder, at its October 1864 meeting, to

> make all arrangements necessary to place the impressment of the University Building by the Confederate authorities before the Confederate Congress.[47]

While Soule University's president basked in the spotlight as a war hero with a political future, the school was in dire straits. The board resolved to settle its account with Dr. George Carter. It was later written of Carter: "During the contest he lost his religious integrity."[48] In any case, Soule University had little basis without a building.

JOSEPH D. ROGERS. Joseph Rogers enlisted in Dave Terry's Cavalry Regiment in 1863. The regiment served in Louisiana and Rogers was a staff courier for General Gillespie. He returned to Chappell Hill after the war, only to lose his wife and little son during the yellow fever epidemic of 1867. He was a merchant and also engaged in farming in Chappell Hill until becoming a physician in the early 1870s. He was an alderman in Chappell Hill for a time. He died in 1929. (From *A History of Texas and Texans*, 1916, vol. IV, courtesy of the Texas State Library.)

The most pressing threat to Texas came in the spring of 1864. Federal General Nathaniel Banks led a force of 20,000 Federals up Louisiana's Red River, accompanied by a flotilla of ironclad gunboats. Banks's initial objective was Shreveport, but his ultimate goal was to then march west into Texas, shut off Texas' Mexico connection and gain control of the cotton trade for Northern markets. General Richard Taylor, son of President Zachary Taylor, commanded the outnumbered Confederate forces facing Banks's formidable force. Walker's Texas Division was among these Confederate troops. This was the only division in the Confederate Army composed of troops from a single state. Charles Carmer was one of several men from Chappell Hill who served in Walker's Division. Carmer enrolled at Chappell Hill in March 1862. He was 18 years old. The Seventeenth Texas Infantry Regiment promoted Private Carmer to ordnance sergeant for Company A in November.

The second lieutenant, later captain commanding Company A, was Oliver Hazzard Perry (O.H.P.) Garrett. He was of the Garrett family from Jacksonville, Texas. The settlement, three miles north of Chappell Hill, took its name from the three Jackson families, who were members of Stephen F. Austin's Old Three Hundred. This was the site of the earliest sawmill in Washington County and, later, Terrell Jackson's magnificent plantation. The Jacksons were Baptists and Jacksonville became a Baptist center. The Reverend Hosea Garrett constructed a church on the outskirts of town, towards Chappell Hill. Jacksonville declined through the 1850s as many residents moved to Chappell Hill.

General Taylor withdrew his forces northward up the Red River for 150 miles as Banks advanced. Tom Green's cavalry from Texas joined up with Taylor's infantry and set the stage for a Confederate stand on April 8, 1864, at Sabine Cross Roads near Mansfield, Louisiana. An aggressive Confederate attack on both flanks turned Banks's left flank. Banks withdrew with severe losses. This was the decisive battle that destroyed the greatest threat of invasion of Texas soil. The Federals repulsed an assault at Pleasant Hill the next day and kept on withdrawing south.

Taylor was determined to pursue Banks and decisively finish off the invading Federals. Instead, General Edmund Kirby-Smith ordered Walker's and Churchill's infantry divisions northward to attack a Federal column, which was to have converged with Banks further north. The rapid march led to Walker's Division becoming known as Walker's Greyhounds. They marched into Arkansas and slammed into Federal General Frederick Steele's column at Jenkins Ferry on April 30, 1864. The fighting was fierce and bloody. Steele's force escaped across the Sabine River, but the 1864 Federal invasion of Louisiana was over. Texans breathed a sigh of relief.

Samuel C. Littlepage was a Methodist minister at LaGrange in 1864. He later recalled "one of the most glorious revivals I ever saw" at LaGrange. The Confederacy sent out an appeal to ministers during the 1864 invasion "to go as missionaries [chaplains] to the army." Littlepage, a man in his mid–20s,[49] was assigned to Walker's Division. He joined them near Camden, Arkansas, in the aftermath of the Battle of Jenkins' Ferry.[50] He wrote:

> I traveled with the army, visited hospitals, preached to the soldiers at night and on the Sabbath, ministered to the sick and served the boys in every way I could. I organized four army churches in our division. I overtaxed myself and my health gave way.[51]

Littlepage stopped in New Salem, Texas, on his way home. The Baptist congregation asked him to preach the next day, which Littlepage did. The Baptist preacher introduced Rev. Littlepage to his congregation as a missionary to the soldiers in the army. The congregation raised $460 in the collection for the Methodist minister to use for the boys at the front. Reverend Littlepage saw this as "providential indication" and raised $5,000 during his six-week recuperation at home.

The enterprising Littlepage used the money to purchase writing stationery from Texas governor Allen, buying all that the office "would sell to one man at one time." The minister sold the stationery to soldiers at cost so that they could maintain contact with their loved ones back home. One soldier was quoted as saying, "The parson sells it to us at $10 and if the boys have no money he gives it to them just the same." Littlepage returned to Texas when his money ran out and made the circuit to gather more, visiting Galveston, Houston, Chappell Hill and Brenham among others. The minister remained with Walker's Division until the end of the war. He later reminisced, "I think I have never done as much good to my fellow man in the same length of time as I did during my connection with Confederate service."[52]

Samuel Littlepage continued to serve the Lord after the war. He resided at Chappell Hill in 1884, when he petitioned the local Masonic Lodge.[53] When Benjamin, Samuel's son, died in Houston, the family buried the last remains in Chappell Hill's Atkinson Cemetery. It is not known where Reverend Samuel died or where his remains lie.

The first session of the Confederate Congress convened in Richmond on May 2, 1864, just days after the end of the Red River Campaign in Louisiana. Williamson Simpson Oldham was one of two senators from Texas. He previously represented Washington County (State District 51) at the Texas secession congress in early 1861. That body of men appointed Oldham to the Provisional Congress before his election in November 1860 to the regular Confederate Senate.[54] Oldham resided in Chappell Hill during the course of the war[55] when he was not in Richmond. Oldham opposed conscription and any other measures he felt violated states' rights. He was determined to see the war continue, even if Texas fought alone. He even introduced a bill to arm the slaves for military service. Passage came too late.

10

Eastern Tennessee Campaign

Confederate authorities gave Richard Swearingen a commission to raise a company after he returned to Chappell Hill from Rip Ford's Brownsville expedition of February 1861. Swearingen was occupied with this task when he received word that his little brother was sick and in need of assistance. John Thomas Swearingen was four years younger than his brother, Richard. He had enlisted at the outbreak of the war and headed east with his regiment to Virginia, only to be discharged in Tennessee for being underage. He was determined to be in the fight, and subsequently enlisted in a local unit, Brazelton's Third Tennessee Cavalry Battalion. However, the younger Swearingen became very ill and sent an urgent request home for help.

Dick Swearingen, upon hearing from his younger brother, left Chappell Hill quickly and made the long journey to eastern Tennessee. "Reached Cumberland Gap on the 15th of Nov., substituted myself in Tommie's place, started him homewards and embarked for the second time on the stormy waters of the revolution."[1] The older Swearingen found himself in Company K. On the following day, the troopers moved out. Dick himself was ill from the long journey, but he was determined to more than adequately fill his brother's role. His narrative of the war included this reflection:

> It was a cold bleak day and colder at night. I rested on the frozen ground with nothing over me but a frozen blanket — gazed at the chilly jewels and the icy moon above, thought of a warm room in a far off western home and realized for the first time that war was not a romance.[2]

Dick Swearingen would discover soon enough that he had pneumonia. The battalion surgeon, upon seeing that Swearingen's fever was rising, ordered him to find shelter.

10. Eastern Tennessee Campaign

The weak trooper rode into the nearby hamlet of Sneedville, Tennessee. The hotel was full. Swearingen recalled years later that, while standing in the street, numb with the cold and racked with pain, he heard a piano. "Believing where music was, there must be soul," he knocked on the door, introduced himself and explained that he was sick. The man gave him a room and allowed him to remain there for a month. Swearingen wrote of these days as "the most delightful ones of my life."

The kind-hearted gentleman was Mr. Lea Jesse. Dick Swearingen of Chappell Hill, Texas, came to know the Jesses and their five children. Jennie was the Jesses' second oldest daughter of whom Swearingen wrote:

> [A] brunette with graceful figure, a proud queenly step, dark spiritual eyes with a voice as soft as ... a heart constant to the last and a face as beautiful as ever rose o'er fairy dreamland. I loved her. It was she who dressed the frozen world in blooming flowers, filled the air with music and transformed cheerless winter into violet-eyed Spring.[3]

Dick Swearingen fell in love. But duty called and on January 1, 1862, Dick Swearingen kissed Jennie goodbye and bid her family farewell to return to his regiment. He wrote: "Time flew on leaden wings through a murky sky, was a dreary scene."

Swearingen's commanding officer was killed in action later that same month and Alex Goforth became captain of Company K. Swearingen described Goforth as "a gallant soldier and accomplished gentleman ... for three years he was my constant companion. I loved him as I have loved few men on earth."[4] Brazelton's Third Tennessee Cavalry Battalion supported Rains's small Confederate force that was assigned responsibility of guarding Cumberland Gap. The Gap was a strategic pathway east and west. It was easily defendable by virtue of the steep cliffs and narrow road that worked its way up the slope. "The federals were guarding the passes into Kentucky while we were defending the frontiers of Tennessee and Virginia, for all three of these states corner in the Gap."[5] Most of 1862 was spent with the Gap as the focus. Swearingen wrote of the period:

> Now and then, each army would advance but made it convenient to alternate so that no serious collision could possible [sic] occur. A few rounds of musketry, the war of half dozen shells, would never fail to restore the amicability of our warriors. Our commanders gave these hostile demonstrations the elegant name of "reconnaissance in force" but the soldiers, unskilled in dainty expressions, honored them with the less-dignified appellation of "failure."[6]

The situation changed dramatically when General George Morgan assumed command of Federal forces in the Cumberland Gap region. Morgan, upon receiving substantial reinforcements, subsequently feigned engagement at Cumberland Gap then crossed the divide 16 miles to the south at Roger's Gap. Confederate Colonel James Carter was ordered to take his cavalry battalion to Roger's Gap with haste. Dick Swearingen, by this time a lieutenant, was ordered by Carter to lead the advance guard. He had six men accompanying him. Thomas Milton Keesee of Chappell Hill, Texas, was one.

Tom Keesee had originally enlisted in the Fifth Texas Infantry of Hood's Texas

RICHARD SWEARINGEN. Swearingen, the son of wealthy Chappell Hill planter R. J. Swearingen, served with distinction in the Tennessee cavalry. He became a doctor after the war and tirelessly cared for the people of Chappell Hill during the yellow fever epidemic of 1867. He became a renowned authority on yellow fever, served as state health officer, and was appointed to the National Board of Health when it was created. (From *Types of Successful Men of Texas*, 1890.)

Brigade. He came down with dysentery and was admitted to St. Charles Hospital in Richmond on Sept. 29, 1861. He was discharged on February 24, 1862, with a medical disability citing "chronic dysentery" and labeling him "unfit for duty."[7] The Fifth had yet to see action. Instead of heading home to Chappell Hill, Tom Keesee made his way to his friend Dick Swearingen at the Cumberland Gap. Swearingen wrote of Keesee:

> He had left the Virginia army in order to be with me. We were raised together and I can say with pride that nature never created a truer friend, nor a more courageous and daring soldier.

Lt. Swearingen wrote of "riding leisurely along enjoying the witticisms of Thomas M. Keesee" when they rounded a bend in the road and found themselves before a vast Union army encampment "not more than a mile from us ... The sand in the road was covered by a thousand new-made tracks! A profound silence reigned, which told in its quiet vernacular that we were recklessly treading on the brink of a volcano."[8]

Swearingen's orders were to proceed until he engaged the enemy. Despite the obvious signs, the advance guard had yet to encounter a sentry or posted picket. Then eight mounted soldiers appeared about 200 yards in front of them.

> I was riding a fiery, impetuous horse and could not fire with much accuracy without dismounting; I in consequence called to one of my men, threw my reins to him, leaped on the ground and commenced firing from a Colts revolving rifle. My shots were well-aimed and created great excitement in front—but not near so as that produced in our rear. A soldier called to me "For God's sake, look behind

you." I glanced back and beheld a cloud, a wall of blue moving rapidly from the timber on the left down the road.

My position was critical and no time could be spared to discuss it. I saw my only chance was to run the gauntlet! The command "about face, gallop march" was instantly given and away we flew, swift as the wind ... the most tremendous roar that has ever been sounded on my ears. The air seemed filled with flying splinters and whizzing bullets. My spirited horse made a lofty plunge and fell to his knees. Then as if conscious that life and death depended on his efforts, the noble animal struggled to his feet and dashed onward with wilder speed. For six hundred yards we were exposed to the fire of two thousand muskets but God in his mercy carried us safely through the storm ... only one of the six men was wounded. I believe that was the most concentrated fire that I ever saw a few men exposed to.[9]

Swearingen and his men returned with word of the large Federal force. The Confederate Army withdrew from its position three days later on June 15, 1862. The Federals occupied Cumberland Gap. Confederate General Kirby-Smith moved quickly with his army to regain control of Tennessee and Kentucky. At one point, Swearingen carried dispatches from Colonel Carter to General Kirby-Smith. He rode with 28 men through dangerous, unknown territory, for the mountaineers of eastern Tennessee were fiercely loyal to the Union. Swearingen and his men posed as Yankee scouts and even used locals to guide them. One man led them for a considerable distance, "entertaining in the meantime by unmercifully abusing Rebels."[10] When Swearingen learned that the guide knew the whereabouts of a wounded Confederate soldier, he asked the man to lead him to the man. The mountaineer obliged, expecting the soldiers to finish off the man. Swearingen recalled of the wounded and frightened soldier, a Virginian, "He was alarmed when I first came to him but a little whisper brought tears to his eyes and smiles to his cheek." Arrangements were made and the wounded soldier was successfully returned home. Swearingen wrote that he later visited the man after the war.[11]

After Captain Goforth was promoted to major, the three successive men who replaced him to lead Company K were killed in action between April and August 1862. Dick Swearingen succeeded to that command in August 1862 and led Company K for the remainder of the war. Goforth himself died in battle in December 1863. On September 18, 1862, following a significant Confederate victory at Richmond, Kentucky, the Union Army withdrew from Cumberland Gap. The strategic pass was again in Confederate control.

Brazelton's Third Tennessee Cavalry Battalion became the nucleus for the First Tennessee Cavalry, which the Confederate command formed in November 1862. The First Tennessee was assigned to Joseph Wheeler's Cavalry Brigade. At this point, Brazelton's men were fighting alongside Terry's Texas Rangers and there likely was a Chappell Hill reunion. Both regiments participated in Wheeler's celebrated cavalry ride at Murfreesboro/Stones River. They fought constantly for 10 days, their efforts effectively delaying the Federal Army. Wheeler's troopers repeatedly raided the army's rear and engaged in numerous fierce fights with the enemy. They routed several hundred Federal soldiers and captured a wagon supply train in an action at LaVergne. A Confederate officer wrote:

> At LaVergne the turnpike as far as the eye could reach was filled with burning wagons. The country was overspread with disarmed men and broken-down horses and mules. The streets were covered with empty valises and trunks, knapsacks, broken guns, and the indescribable debris of a captured and rifled army train.[12]

The scene was repeated at Nolensville and again later outside Nolensville. Wheeler's cavalry also provided cavalry support to the Confederate infantry in a major battle of epic proportions, then acted as rear guard to prevent pursuit.

The year 1863 was spent campaigning in Kentucky and Tennessee. On September 9, 1863, the Union Army re-took Cumberland Gap. Dick Swearingen and the First Tennessee Cavalry were involved in numerous engagements and escaped up the valley. The Federal Army advanced southward across Tennessee into Georgia. Confederate General Braxton Bragg withdrew, awaiting an opportunity to strike the overconfident Federals, who had dispersed their forces across a wide swath.

As Confederate authorities concentrated their forces in Tennessee, other men from Chappell Hill moved into that strategic battleground. A prisoner exchange resulted in the Arkansas Post prisoners, including the Chappell Hill men in the Twenty-Fourth Texas Cavalry, returning south in the spring of 1863. The Federals released the prisoners in Virginia, where Confederate authorities reorganized them into Deshler's Brigade of Major General Patrick Cleburne's Division. The surrender at Arkansas Post remained their only experience in battle and, unfortunately, the basis for much talk in the Confederate Army. Some went so far as to suggest that only Cleburne agreed to accept them under his command. The former prisoners of war were anxious to redeem themselves in battle.

Rufus King Felder of Hood's Texas Brigade was excited to hear that the men of the Twenty-Fourth Texas Cavalry were in Virginia. He had written his sister, Emma, in Chappell Hill on May 2, 1863, of his hopes of seeing her husband Thomas Elliott:

> The Arkansas Post prisoners are at Petersburg ... I will try to stop and see Thomas and the rest of my acquaintances if they are living. They suffered very much while in prison and I understand that they lost three hundred by death. I have not heard about Thomas, but I feel confident that the many fervent prayers of his pious wife will not be unheeded by a just God & that he will eventually be returned to the bosom of his devoted family.... And now dear sister I must close praying that our lives may be spared & we may all be permitted to meet once more & enjoy the pleasure of a happy peace. I remain your affectionate brother, Rufus.[13]

However, before Felder could see Tom Elliott, the Texas Brigade moved out on May 4 and marched north with the Army of Northern Virginia toward the battlefield at Gettysburg. In the aftermath of that colossal clash, Lee withdrew into Virginia. But there would be no rest for the Texas Brigade. General Robert E. Lee recognized that, while Meade seemed to have no intention of advancing on Richmond, the

Federal capture of Chattanooga threatened Atlanta and the heart of the South. Lee agreed to a bold plan to shift Longstreet's entire corps, including the Texas Brigade, by train to Georgia to augment Bragg's force outside Chattanooga and stop the Federal drive.

On September 8, Longstreet's Corps moved out. The train passed through the Carolinas enroute to Georgia. Rufus King Felder obtained a pass to visit family and friends at the old Felder hometown of Orangeburg, South Carolina, while his comrades moved on. Among those Rufus saw was Dr. Elliott, the father of his brother-in-law, Thomas Elliott. Rufus reported to his mother from a camp near Chattanooga:

> I was proud to see the reception given us by the ladies as the cars stopped. They had gathered at the depot in numbers & showered the potatoes and bread in the cars which was very acceptable to our hungry boys. They all say if they ever get wounded they will go to Orangeburg. The first one I met after getting off the car was Joe Pooser. He carried me to town and the first one I saw there was Dr. Elliott. I recognized him as soon as I saw him across the street. He has grown grayer and his health is quite feeble, but he still keeps up a large practice.

Rufus King Felder discovered that the war had ravaged Orangeburg and its townspeople, as it had so many other hamlets across America. His letter continued:

> Things had changed so much in the family it did not seem natural. Cousins John and Sam are no more and cousins Eugene and Adella have moved off, and Ed is in the service. I did not see any of the family except cousin Lou ... I saw a great many of your old acquaintances who made numerous inquiries of you & yours.... I did not forget to pay our old place a visit. Mrs. Love, the lady living there was very kind & offered to take me all over the place & show me everything. I went to the back door & looked out. Everything looked so natural. I did not wish to carry my inspection any farther.[14]

While Rufus King Felder was visiting family and friends in Orangeburg, his regiment was charging into an inferno in the woods along Chickamauga Creek. Federal General Rosecrans had deployed his army along a 50-mile front as it advanced into Georgia. Bragg attempted to take advantage of this situation, attacking the vanguard of Thomas' Corps on September 19, 1863. Rosecrans rushed reinforcements to Thomas and a major battle ensued. The Battle of Chickamauga was mayhem. Men became lost in the thick woods and treacherous ravines and confusion reigned amid the thick smoke from thousands of weapons discharging.

The men taken prisoner at Arkansas Post, serving in Brigadier General James Deshler's Brigade, endured ridicule from some of the other troops as they moved up into position to fight. The brigade moved past wounded men, stragglers and prisoners toward the sound of battle on the afternoon of September 19. The woods were thick and the smoke from thousands of muskets added to the confusion. One man in the division wrote: "bullets fly like the wind you can hear them zip zip — zip but you can't see them. You know they are passing very thick."[15] Colonel Franklin Wilkes's regiment moved forward in the confusion and surprised elements of the enemy. They unleashed a volley and charged, killing and wounding many, taking over 100 prisoners and capturing two regimental battle flags.[16] It was their much-needed first taste of victory. Wilkes, wounded in the shoulder, remained with his regiment, but turned command of it over to his junior officer. Darkness set in and the fighting ceased. The men who endured the Arkansas Post ordeal, numerous Chappell Hill men among the Texans, proved themselves worthy of being soldiers. There was a sense of relief for them, despite the terrible carnage.

Both sides maneuvered for the next day's action and dug in. Deshler's brigade advanced against heavy artillery and small arms fire on the next morning at 10:00. Colonel Franklin Wilkes of the Twenty-Fourth Texas Cavalry wrote in his battle report:

> After advancing about 600 yards through the timber, we came upon an open field completely commanded by the enemy's battery and we made our way at a double-quick across this field under a most terrific fire of shot and shell, grape and canister.[17]

The men of Deshler's Division were pinned down by heavy fire and were unable to take the Federal breastworks before them. Valor was useless in the face of entrenched and well-armed soldiers. Losses mounted while ammunition ran low. Brigadier General Deshler was among the casualties, killed by an artillery shell through his chest at about noon.[18] Colonel Wilkes received "a contused wound upon the right leg which completely disabled"[19] him and was relieved of command.

Longstreet's Corps arrived at Chickamauga early on the morning of September 20. While Cleburne's and Breckinridge's Divisions were hurling themselves into the Federal left with little success all morning, Longstreet prepared to attack the Federal right. At about noon, over 20,000 Confederate soldiers rushed through the woods, screaming the Rebel yell. They moved in closely arrayed columns, as opposed to the thin, broad lines usually employed in advancing. The shock effect on the Federal defenders was overwhelming. The impact of the attack was even more successful than Bragg and Longstreet might have imagined. In a major blunder, the Federal forces had rearranged their forces just prior to Longstreet's attack. Ironically, in trying to close a gap, the Federals opened one in their line right where Longstreet struck. Confusion reigned in the thick smoke-filled underbrush. The attackers poured through the opening and struck at the flank of the arrayed Federal divisions. The Federal line broke and thousands of men scattered. The Confederates nearly captured Rosecrans himself. The entire right side of the Federal line collapsed.

The Federal left in front of Deshler and Breckenridge held. Some scattered Federal divisions consolidated with Thomas. Longstreet's men swung around to crush the Federal left but it held, conforming into a tight "horseshoe" position. Fierce fighting continued until dark, when the battle finally ended. The losses on both sides were horrific. The Confederates suffered over 18,000 casualties, the Federals over 16,000.

Rufus King Felder had missed one of the great battles of the war. He wrote home to Chappell Hill:

> After I left Orangeburg I heard of the battle that was raging at Chicamauga [Chickamauga]. Having seen that our division was seriously engaged, my

curiosity was excited to the highest pitch to know who of our devoted band were made victims to the ruthless invaders. I met thousands of wounded between Atlanta & Ringold....[20]

Cleburne's Division lost over 1,300 men of 4,700 in his division.[21] Deshler's Brigade, which included the men of Chappell Hill in the Twenty-Fourth Texas Cavalry, went into battle with nearly 1,800 men. The brigade lost 52 men killed and 366 wounded.[22] Thomas Elliott, Rufus King Felder's brother-in-law in the Twenty-Fourth Texas Cavalry, was among the dead. Rufus wrote his mother:

Memorial marker to Thomas Elliott of Chappell Hill, killed in action at Chickamagua.

> I received a letter from Dr. Elliott saying he would come or send in a few days for the remains of Thomas. He seems to take his death very hard. How did poor Sister E. [Emma] take his death? It must have been a terrible blow to her, she was so loving and devoted. You must all stay with her as much as possible & try to divert her mind & keep her naturally quiet mind from becoming too disponding [despondent]. Would to God that he could have spared her, but in His all wise power He has decreed otherwise, & it is for us to subject to his command.[23]

The dense woods along Chickamauga Creek hid bodies for years, some forever. Thomas Elliott's body was never recovered, certainly not identified. His family honored his memory with a cenotaph in the cemetery at Chappell Hill.

Lafayette Routt was another Chappell Hill man who lost his life near Chattanooga. Lafayette, one of three Routts from Chappell Hill serving with Terry's Texas Rangers, was killed by a mule. Many men died in the War Between the States in ways other than from enemy fire on the field of battle. Sunstroke claimed many lives. The sheer numbers of men and weapons led to countless deaths from accidental shootings. The danger posed by the hind legs of the ever-present mule was very real.

F. M. Williamson of Chappell Hill served with the Fifth Texas Infantry, Hood's Brigade, since enlisting in July 1861. He saw action at Second Manassas, bloody Antietam and Fredericksburg during 1862. In late 1863, Williamson fought at Chickamauga and Knoxville. It is likely that Williamson made contact with his old friends from home, Dick Swearingen and Tom Keesee, during the Knoxville Siege in November–December 1863. All three were nearly the same age, Williamson being a year older than Swearingen, and Keesee a year and a half younger than Swearingen. Williamson apparently missed his good friends and liked what he heard about cavalry service. He transferred from the infantry and became a second lieutenant in

Company E of the First Tennessee Cavalry. Muster rolls show Williamson present and accounted for with the First Tennessee Cavalry in 1865 and through the end of the war.

Rosecrans, in the aftermath of the battle of Chickamauga and the near total annihilation of his Federal Army, regrouped in Chattanooga. The Confederates under Bragg controlled Lookout Mountain and Missionary Ridge overlooking Chattanooga. The Federals were desperate and starving. Bragg, confident in his entrenched heights, detached Longstreet's Corps with 5,000 cavalrymen into eastern Tennessee towards Knoxville. Major General Joseph Wheeler commanded the Confederate cavalry advancing with Longstreet into eastern Tennessee. The First Tennessee Cavalry with Dick Swearingen and Tom Keesee and Terry's Texas Rangers with Daniel Harvie Browning, James Fiske Matthews, John Jackson and many others from Chappell Hill were among the cavalry regiments in Wheeler's command.

Ambrose Burnside, the Federal commander at Knoxville, moved to consolidate his forces inside the fortifications and hold out until reinforcements arrived. A race ensued with Longstreet and Burnside vying for the vital road junction that would allow one to beat the other to the fortified city of Knoxville. Longstreet ordered Wheeler to attack the Federal forces south of Knoxville with his cavalry and, in so doing, create a diversion. Longstreet also reasoned that, if Wheeler was able to seize the heights on the south bank of the Tennessee River overlooking Knoxville, Confederate artillery from this vantage point could destroy the city. The destructive firepower would force Burnside out into the countryside, where Longstreet could engage the Federal forces on more even terms. Wheeler received these orders on November 12 and noted later that his cavalry was "much worn and depleted by the arduous service they had undergone during the preceding two months."[24]

Several thousand Confederate cavalrymen, advancing from the south, surprised a smaller Union force, a single regiment, at Little River Ford at Maryville on November 14. A Confederate after-action report read:

> [W]e ran down and captured 151 men, the remainder of the regiment being dispersed over the country.... [T]he Federal Colonel Wolford, with his brigade, came to the assistance of the Eleventh Kentucky and attacked my command. He was met and repulsed by the Eight and Eleventh Texas and Third Arkansas Regiments ... charged the enemy and drove him over Little River in the wildest confusion, capturing 85 prisoners.[25]

Wheeler's cavalry crossed over Little River on the morning of November 15 and drove the enemy back three miles to Stock Creek. The Union forces regrouped and took a strong position on elevated ground behind the creek, which was not fordable by horses. It was not possible to turn the flank and the Confederates were compelled to fight on ground advantageous to the defenders. The Confederate report continued:

> I dismounted nearly half my command, crossed the creek under cover of a fire from my battery and drove the left wing of the enemy from its strong position. This enabled a detail to repair the bridge while I pressed on with the dismounted

10. Eastern Tennessee Campaign

men, compelling the entire line of the enemy to retreat.... we continued to push the enemy with dismounted men, driving him from several strong positions.... we charged the enemy with.... The Eight Texas Regiment in advance.... The lines of the enemy were broken and the entire mass of the enemy swept toward Knoxville in the wildest confusion. The charge was continued successfully for 3 miles to within less than half a mile of the river opposite the city.... One hundred and forty prisoners were taken in the charge and a considerable number killed and wounded.[26]

Wheeler's force, upon approaching the river, found themselves facing Union fortifications bristling with artillery and infantry. Fort Dickerson and Fort Stanley defended the heights, which Longstreet wanted Wheeler to occupy. The crest of the ridge stood nearly 200 feet up a steep slope. The only approach for the attacking Confederate cavalry was across open ground. The river behind the fortifications prevented encirclement of the position. It was apparent to the Confederate officers, as well as the rank and file, that a frontal assault would be suicidal. Darkness set in as Wheeler considered his options.

The price of victory for the Confederates at Stock Creek that day was high. Their dead and wounded were strewn out over the countryside. Private Daniel Harvie Browning of Terry's Texas Rangers was among the Confederate losses of November 15, 1863.[27] He would never again see the ladies of Chappell Hill, nor the Texas bluebonnets cover the hills in spring. James "Doc" Matthews, Daniel's buddy from Chappell Hill, was alongside 22-year-old Daniel when he was shot. Doc went back after the fighting ended that day and found Daniel's body. He managed somehow to dig a grave in the frozen Tennessee dirt and mark the grave with stones and a wooden marker on which he carved Daniel's name. That the Confederates had won the field of battle that day was fortunate. The side that remained on the field of battle took much better care in identifying and burying their own in individual graves. Those of the enemy were usually buried in trenches converted to mass graves.

Wheeler, while counting casualties and studying the fortifications before him, received a message from General Longstreet: "Unless you are doing better service by moving along the enemy's flank than you could do here, I would rather you should join us and cooperate."[28] Longstreet lost the race to the critical road junction that would have allowed him to beat Burnside to Knoxville. Wheeler rejoined Longstreet on the north side of the river before Knoxville. Time was on the Federal side, as considerable reinforcements were on the way. Longstreet hesitated for several days and then ordered an all-out assault of Knoxville. Rufus King Felder, James Landes and the men of the Texas Brigade charged bravely up the icy slopes in front of the massive fortifications of Knoxville. The Confederate infantry were slaughtered in repeated assaults. There was no hope of victory. Longstreet was forced to withdraw without having achieved his objective. Knoxville and eastern Tennessee remained in Union control for the remainder of the war. It was a serious blow to the Confederacy.

Confederate General Braxton Bragg's gamble in diverting Longstreet's veteran corps from Chattanooga to Knoxville was a grave error. Federal forces overran Bragg's seemingly impregnable position on Missionary Ridge overlooking Chattanooga on November 25, 1863. Bragg later remarked that a panic set in among his fighting men that he had never before witnessed. It is possible that the Confederates' vantage point on the ridge allowed them to view a spectacle like few had ever seen, that of the vast Federal Army deploying in formation in the valley below them.

In fact, Bragg also ordered Cleburne's Division to Knoxville, but realized his mistake and ordered them back just as they were beginning to board the train. The division was barely back in position when the assault from Sherman's command commenced.

Cleburne's Division was positioned on the eastern end of the ridge and threw back with heavy losses repeated assaults by Federals under William Tecumseh Sherman's command. Colonel James Smith ably led Deshler's Brigade in the action and again the Twenty-Fourth Texas Cavalry and the Tenth Texas Infantry and the men of Chappell Hill fought bravely. While Cleburne's Division held off Sherman's army, the Federals achieved the seemingly impossible along the center of the ridge, sweeping the entrenched Confederates from the crest and routing them. One might argue the ridge might have been held had Longstreet's veteran corps been on Missionary Ridge when the Federals attacked. Instead, the Federal troops won what many consider to be the decisive battle of the war, opening the way for Sherman's march to Atlanta with Chattanooga as the major supply base.

News of the outcome in Tennessee and the corresponding casualties traveled slowly back to Chappell Hill. The December 28, 1863, issue of the *Galveston Tri-Weekly News* carried a report of the fighting in the first column of the first page:

> By Express from Shreveport, December 21, 1863. Dear News, – We have nothing yet upon which we can rely with certainty as to the situation at Knoxville. We have a renewal of reports this morning and apparently from a correct source of the surrender of [Federal General] Burnside, but I must acknowledge that these reports need confirmation.

The same issue in the next column carried the following update:

> Later by Express from Shreveport! December 23, 1863 ... Knoxville has not been taken and Longstreet has retired towards Virginia.[29]

The local Texas papers, as elsewhere in the South, did their best to portray Missionary Ridge in a positive light. The *Galveston Tri-Weekly News* editorialized:

> I do not regard the late fight at Missionary Ridge as a defeat ... the panic of one of our brigades enabled the enemy to gain a position of great strength.... Our loss was insignificant — only about three thousand killed, wounded and prisoners, whilst the loss of the enemy is put down as high as 35,000.[30]

Word reached Daniel Browning's parents of his death on the battlefield. Some would say that the war was a poor man's fight. William and Elizabeth Browning of Chappell Hill, among the wealthiest plantation owners in Washington County, Texas, paid the ultimate price with their son's life in November 1863.

A poem written at Chappell Hill after the war was submitted many years later to the Center for American History in Austin. It seems likely that the author of the anonymous poem entitled "In Memory of My Brother" was Mattie Browning, Daniel's sister:

> Young as the youngest who donned Gray,
> True as the Truest who wore it,
> Brave as the brave when he marched away,
> (Hot tears on the cheeks of his Mother lay)
> Triumphant waved our flag one day,
> He fell in the front before it.
>
> Firm as the firmest where duty led,
> He hurried without a falter;
> Bold as the boldest who fought and bled,
> And the day was won — but the field was red —
> And the blood of his fresh young heart was shed
> On his country's hallowed altar.
>
> O'er the trampled breast of the battle plain
> Where the foremost ranks had wrestled,
> On his pure pale face, not a mark of pain
> (His Mother's dreams they will meet again)
> The fairest form amid the slain,
> Like a child asleep and nestled.
>
> In the solemn shade of the wood that swept
> The field where his comrades found him,
> They buried him there — and the big tears crept
> Into strong men's eyes that had seldom wept,
> (His Mother — God pity her — smiled and slept,
> Dreaming her arms were around him).
>
> A grave in the woods with the grass o'ergrown,
> A grave in the heart of his Mother —
> There is not a name, there is not a stone,
> And only the voice of the winds maketh moan
> O'er the grave where never a flower is strewn,
> But — his memory lives in the other.[31]

11

The Defense of Atlanta

The year 1864 began as a difficult and trying one for the people of the South. They struggled to hold on, but began to recognize that their hope of a clear military victory was slipping away. The *Galveston Tri-Weekly News* published a poem from Chappell Hill:

Is This a Time for Revelry and Mirth?

Is this a time for revelry and mirth?
While Southern blood flows freely o'er the earth
Where every breeze comes freighted with the sighs
Of men who die in mortal agonies

Is this a time for banqueting and balls?
For giddy throngs in brilliant lighted balls
While starving thousands cry aloud for bread
And carnage holds her festal o'er the dead

Is this a time for barbecue and wine?
While Southern sons in Northern prisons pine
While wounded soldiers gasp their lives away
No "loved one" by to cheer the lonely day

Is this a time to dance? When our fair land
Is desecrated by a Northern band
More ruthless than a Goth or vandal horde
Or savage Indians so much abhorred

11. The Defense of Atlanta

> Throw off your gala dress and dare be free!
> Fight to the death, maintain your liberty!
> "God and my right!" be still the battle cry,
> We'll live forever free and free we'll die!
>
> CHAPPELL HILL Feb. 19, 1864 H. J. H.[1]

Georgia was open to invasion in the spring of 1864 following the Federal victory at Missionary Ridge. Atlanta was second only to Richmond in terms of importance to the Confederacy. The city was a vital industrial center, as well as the heart of the South's aristocratic culture. It was apparent to all that the loss of Atlanta would be devastating to the Confederacy. Optimists in the Confederacy maintained that there might still be hope if Atlanta could be held and the war sufficiently stalemated. If Northern voters felt that the bloody conflict could drain the country indefinitely, they might turn to a peace candidate in the November 1864 presidential elections. To be sure, many on both sides were beginning to question the continuing slaughter by 1864. The *Galveston Tri-Weekly News* presented a front of optimism in March 1864 as a new season of fighting approached:

> [T]he Confederate armies are at this moment better able to meet the enemy's forces than they ever have been before ... now their lines have been extended far into our own territory, and their own supplies can only be obtained at vast expense and with great delay, while a large portion of their troops will be required to defend those lines.[2]

All eyes were on Federal General William Tecumseh Sherman to whom had been given responsibility for taking Atlanta. Sherman had more than 100,000 well-equipped men under his command. General Joseph E. Johnston, a widely respected general, replaced Bragg and assumed command of a Confederate army of 65,000 men facing Sherman. The Atlanta campaign began in early May 1864 and lasted five months. Tens of thousands of men gave their lives in the desperate struggle, which both sides realized held the key to the final outcome of the war.

Numerous men from Chappell Hill took part in the desperate defense of Atlanta. These included the men of Terry's Texas Rangers and the Twenty-Fourth Texas Cavalry (Dismounted). Dick Swearingen and the First Tennessee Cavalry were in the fight. Andrew Keller and Ross's Cavalry Brigade was in the fight. There was also the Tenth Texas Infantry, a regiment that had been captured along with the Twenty-Fourth at Arkansas Post. Numerous other men who later moved west to Chappell Hill after the war were also involved.

Hosea Garrett of Chappell Hill was a first lieutenant with the Tenth Texas Infantry. He moved to Texas from his home in South Carolina to be with his favorite uncle for whom he had been named. Hosea's uncle, the Reverend Hosea Garrett, was an early Chappell Hill pioneer. The Garretts were Baptists and Rev. Garrett was among the founders of Baylor University at Independence, just north of Chappell Hill. Young Hosea enlisted to fight for the Confederacy on October 25, 1861, at Houston. He was given the rank of fifth sergeant. in Company G of the Tenth Texas Infantry. The Tenth was composed of men from Washington, Houston, Tyler, Grimes, Freestone and St. Augustine Counties and led by Colonel Roger Mills. These men endured imprisonment at Camp Douglas in Illinois after their capture at Arkansas Post. Hosea Garrett and the men of the Tenth served in the Army of Tennessee after their exchange and release. They fought well at Chickamauga and Missionary Ridge. Hosea Garrett was the color sergeant for his regiment, a position of honor bestowed on men who had proved their bravery in battle. The 32-year-old Garrett was promoted to first lieutenant on April 10, 1864, at Dalton, Georgia, on the eve of the Atlanta campaign.

When Sherman took the offensive, Johnston began a series of delaying tactics. Johnston desired to slow the Federals' advance, but also avoid battle with their superior numbers unless he was on ground of his own choosing. Johnston maneuvered for three months across northwest Georgia using the mountains and the key passes. He took advantage of the terrain and made every attempt to convince Sherman to attack each of selected positions. The Confederates were forced to retire each time, as Sherman maneuvered around their flank. Confederate casualties mounted with each action, depleting the already-thin ranks. There was also a gradual wearing down of the ill-equipped and poorly fed soldiers.

Johnston covered strategic Allatoona Pass on May 19–20. When Sherman attempted to slip around Johnston's left flank, Johnston anticipated the move and was waiting for the Federals at New Hope Church. There was fierce fighting there on May 25 and then again on May 26 at Pickett's Mill. The Confederates were victorious in both battles, repulsing the Federals with severe losses. Hosea Garrett wrote his uncle in Chappell Hill about the fighting:

> J. L. Clark fell, pierced through the head on the 27th of May [Pickett's Mill]. John Gary fell on the same day, shot through the body, but was carried to the Field Hospital and died in a day or two. He said to me that he wished me to tell his uncle John Walker know that he died an honorable death. He was shot near me while the battle was raging the hottest. He is gone, I trust, to heaven. He was a member of the Baptist Church. He made one of the best of soldiers. Let his uncle know this. Tom Barton of our Co. [G] is dead. His brother William wounded in some hospital. George Hill that lived with [Rev.] Kavanaugh is also killed. I could mention numbers of others, but not of your acquaintance. H. D. Malone of our Co. was also killed, not far from Marietta. He was a son-in-law of the Widow Lockridge that lives in the upper part of W. [Washington] Co. Col. Wilkes' [Franklin Wilkes of Chappell Hill] son killed not far from the same place. All the bravest men in our Co. have been killed. J. V. Buster [of Chappell Hill and in the Tenth Infantry's Co. G] has been complaining for the last few days. I hope nothing serious will take him, for he has been a strong stake in this war. He is beliked by all that know him. If it is the will of God, we would like to come [home] this coming winter.[3]

Sherman moved east after his defeats at New Hope and Pickett's Mill to concentrate on capturing the city of Marietta. William H. Harmon had been working as a clerk and living in Tom Chappell's house in Chappell Hill when he had enlisted in Terry's Texas Rangers at the age of 18. In June 1864, Harmon and his fellow Rangers were in the lines outside Marietta. Harmon wrote home to Miss Mollie Jackson, sister of John, his comrade-in-arms:

11. The Defense of Atlanta

> Having a few leisure moments I know of no way I could better employ them than in writing to my lady friends in The Lone Star State. But as my time for writing is short you must not expect a long or interesting letter. We are now in the neighborhood of Marietta and awaiting the advance of the Enemy. We are well fortified and feel able to disconcert any movement on the part of the foe to dislodge us from our stronghold. The Army is in the best of spirits and feel that they are able to cope with the overwhelming forces of the Enemy.

In fact, the purpose of Harmon's letter was not to report the war to friends in Chappell Hill.

> But enough of this war. You probably think that I am rather late in writing, but the excuses rendered by myself are these, thinking we would return soon, not having opportunities and no materials, and lastly I did not think myself competent to correspond with any young Lady, but as I see the probabilities are that there will never be any chances of improvement, and going so upon the old adage "That it is better late than never," I make my first attempt, knowing you to be of a generous nature.... I will close I hope the day is not far distant when I with the rest of my Companions will be permitted to return to our peaceful homes and enjoy the society of our Lady friends. I had no idea how much I esteemed the Ladies until I joined the Army.

Harmon closed by telling Miss Jackson:

> John [her brother] is well also all the Boys with whom you are acquainted but all desirous of seeing home.... your earliest convenience would be kindly received by your friend.[4]

Sherman's determined advance on Atlanta continued. Sherman's movement forced Johnston to withdraw toward Kennesaw Mountain. Sherman attempted to move around Kennesaw Mountain, only to find his soldiers confronted by Confederates led by John Bell Hood. In October 1863 after Chickamauga, Rufus King Felder had written home to Chappell Hill telling family: "Our three Texas reg. are raising money to buy Hood a calk leg. We intend raising $3000."[5] A wound that shattered a limb often led to gangrene, necessitating amputation. That was enough to earn a man a trip home. John Bell Hood, former commander of the Texas Brigade, was no ordinary man. Rufus King Felder and his Texas Brigade comrades raised the money and presented Hood with an artificial leg. Hood defiantly returned to battle strapped to his horse with one good arm and one good leg, the epitome of the resolute warrior. Hood, as a division commander under Johnston, continued his aggressive fighting style. Hood attacked Sherman on his own initiative on June 22 at Kolb's Farm. Although the Federals won the engagement and Confederate losses were three times those of the Federals, Sherman's attempt to bypass Kennesaw Mountain was blocked. The Federals were severely bloodied in a frontal assault at Kennesaw Mountain five days later. Yet, even as Johnston was able to inflict significant losses upon the Federals, Sherman again turned Johnston's flank and forced the Confederate Army to withdraw. Johnston's army was on the outskirts of Atlanta by July 10. President Jefferson Davis, who rejected Johnston's repeated requests for more troops, wanted

Sherman stopped. He subsequently determined that Johnston was not the man to do it. Davis replaced Johnston with Gen. John Bell Hood, midway through July, as Sherman neared Atlanta.

George Kerby passed through Atlanta was on his way back to Richmond from a visit to Chappell Hill. He wrote Chappell Hill on July 20:

> When I got to Atlanta I found that place in a ferment in consequence of the retreat of Gen. Johnston's Army to the neighborhood of that city, and the people were moving out with their household furniture and negroes to places of greater Security. Gen. Johnston has just been removed from the command of the Army of Georgia and Gen. Hood placed over it. This was done as a censure upon Johnston for not standing his ground and fighting the enemy a long way north of Atlanta. Public opinion is divided as to the propriety of the President's course in this matter; for myself, I have no opinion in this regard. I fear however that the change just on the eve of a great battle may have an injurious effect upon the troops.[6]

Hood proceeded to take the offensive at Davis' urging. He attacked at Peachtree Creek on July 20. The bloodbath cost the Confederates 5,000 casualties. Hood attacked again on July 22 and again was repulsed with heavy losses. Lt. Hosea Garrett of the Tenth Texas Infantry had a definite opinion about Hood within days. Garrett wrote home to Chappell Hill:

> I suppose that you have heard, or will before this reaches you, that Gen. Hood is in command of this Army. For what reason Johnston was released it is more than any of us know. The army had the utmost confidence in Genl. Johnston, and I well say that I have not heard a man say anything about it but what regretted his being released. All that I hear say anything about Genl. Hood say that he is too fond of charging the enemy's works. We had rather not charge them, but would rather be charged by them, until our number equals theirs. And then we would be willing to meet them in an open field. We are all quite tired of this war but will stay as long as life last of see the end of this cruel War.[7]

Garrett described the action of July 22. Hood sent Hardee's Corps on a 15-mile route to attack the Federal left flank, commanded by McPherson, on the eastern outskirts of Atlanta:

> We have had three fights with them, beginning on the 18th of July and lasting to the 22nd of the same. It seems that our Brigade is quite lucky to get into fights. We worsted them every time, but the last one, and I supposed did then. I understand that our Genl claims a victory even then. I will give you rather a detailed account of the fight of the 22nd. The enemy was flanking us on our right as usual. Our corps [Hardee's] was sent round to flank them and rout and drive them from their positions. We moved all night, and next day we came on them about noon and found them strongly fortified. We charged their works and carried some two lines of works. The enemy abandoned their artillery and wagons in our front. The Brigade on our right and left failed to come up; so did our support, and we had to fall back. The Brigade on our left met with stubborn resistance but carried two short lines of works (rather, the enemy's front works), and captured all that was

11. The Defense of Atlanta

in them. They said that our Brigade captured some 15 or 16 pieces of artillery, two 20 pound Parrots among them by not having support at the right time. Late in the evening of the same day, we were sent on another charge, pretty much over the same ground. But the enemy fought with great courage and no doubt but what they had masked their forces; at all events, we failed to carry their works. I suppose I got in 10 paces of their works with the colors of the Tenth Texas Regt. but could not stay there, from the fact that the men did not come up.

I suppose that there was not more than half a dozen men with me. The men were badly scattered and many exhausted from the loss of sleep and warm weather and long marching. This is the first time that the Tenth Regt. ever failed to accomplish anything of the kind since they have been on this side of River. Had it not been from Genl. [William H. T.] Walker killed in the early part of the engagement while leading his Division in the charge, we would have completely routed the entire flank, but he and his Senior Brig. Genl. were both shot before they could get their men in position. His Brigadier was not killed but wounded, and consequently that noble Division on our right did not accomplish anything scarcely, but lost quite a number of men.

Some estimates of Confederate casualties exceeded 10,000, one quarter of the total men engaged, far exceeding the Federal losses. Federal General James McPherson lost his life in the action.

Sherman approached Atlanta from the east and north. He sent Howard's Federal Army of Tennessee to attack from the west and cut the railroad supply line. Hood, not one to await an attack, made the first move. The Federals entrenched and met the oncoming Confederates at Ezra Church on July 28. Three thousand additional Confederates were added to the casualty list. Sherman was slowly encircling Atlanta, setting the stage for the month-long siege of Atlanta. Garrett wrote on August 1 from his position just outside Atlanta. The Confederate position was becoming desperate and the Texans, far from home, were feeling forsaken:

> Elder H. Garrett, My Dear Uncle, I avail myself of the present opportunity for writing you another letter, notwithstanding I have but poor encouragement to write to any of my relatives in Texas. I have written repeatedly to one or the other of you but have received but one letter since my release from prison, and that one came from Perry [Oliver Hazard Perry Garrett]. I am anxious to hear from you all but cannot.
>
> We have been lying in the ditches near the City [Atlanta] for something like a week. The enemy has almost quit shelling this portion of our lines. It is said they are concentrating their forces on our center; for what purpose I cannot say. I hardly think that they will charge our works. I have heard repeatedly that they Yankee Gents can't get their men to charge rebel works, and I believe it from what I have seen. I have heard them blow their forward calls but could not get their men in advance.

The fighting continued to drain Confederate manpower:

> Our Brigade is quite small. I suppose that it will number some 6 to 700 men. There are 10 Regt. in it: 9 from Texas and the 5 Confederate. Our Regt. numbered, after the fight, between 90 to 100 men, but some have come from the Hospital and I suppose we will number 125 at this time.

Lt. Garrett remained optimistic and determined:

> There is a heavy cannonading on our left today [August 1], in fact has been ever since we have been here, with but short intervals between. We on this end of the line know but little or nothing about what is goin' on on the other. It is thought that the enemy has an overwhelming force in our front, and I don't doubt it, for we may stretch our lines as far as we can, and they have plenty of men to go around us. Our brigade is strung out in our rank, and so is one more on our right at this time, and there may be others for all I know, and yet it seems that they still outreach us. Report says that Genl Forrest & Lee from Miss. are coming to our relief, and the militia is being sent forward as fast as the trains can bring them, and we also have a rumor that Lt. Genl. Smith is coming over with his force from the Trans-Miss. Department. If we can get all the help that we hear is coming, we will give this army such a beating as no other has had. We have retreated from Middle Tenn. to Atlanta, fighting the enemy hard in several instances, and always whipping them when we had anything like an equal chance.... We have heard of another victory in Miss. Forrest is the man in the right place. This army seems to be in good spirits and looking forward to the day when we will gain a victory over Sherman and Thomas.

An inflamed Garrett wrote about family:

> Father [John Garrett] is in [within] the enemy's lines. How they have treated him I cannot say, as I have not heard from him in more than a month. I suppose that they have taken all that he had, for I understand that they take even the ladies' wearing apparel, also that of helpless children. I can't believe that God will let such a people go unpunished. I believe that the day for their overthrow is not far distant. I have heard that they cut the throat of a very wounded man that they came across in Miss ... this is the treatment that our brave soldiers, wounded at that, received at their hands. And I heard that some of our men found some of their wives tied to stakes and dead from the cruel treatment that they received from their foul hands. If such as this will not make men desperate, what will? We are not what we should be in a religious point of view, but I am certain that we have no soldier that would commit such outrageous acts on helpless women and children as theirs has been guilty of. I would to God that our entire Amy were true Christians. I have been spared this far, for which I thank God, for, both by day and night, I desire and entrust in the prayers of all relatives and friends in Texas. Pray the Lord to spare me though this cruel war, and that I may do some good in the name of my master's cause. I have tried to make a Christian soldier as well as a soldier for my country's rights. In this I pray to be sustained. Uncle Isaac [Garrett] is also in the enemy's lines, if he has not move out. Uncle Joe Owens was completely broken up by them last winter. There are thousands of families that were in fine circumstances that have been broken up by the enemy, and I do not see anything but starvation for such opportunities. God can and may provide for all such. Oh, that I had the means and power to relieve them. My heart seems to reach after all such, and, if I had it, none should want for the necessities of life. Vengeance is mine, saith the Lord.

Hosea Garrett had seen friends fall around him in combat since the war began. That only had increased during the Atlanta campaign and Hosea began to feel his mortality. He wrote his uncle as to disposing of his earthly remains:

11. The Defense of Atlanta

> I have been thinking for some time that I would like for you to preach my funeral at Old Providence Church, if I should fall in our struggle for liberty. I often think of the very spot in the Church where God forgave me for Christ's sake for all I had ever done in sinning against his righteous laws. I thought then that my troubles were all over. But I find since that even the Christian has many trials in this life. But, blessed be God, there is a promise to those that hold our faithful to that end. And I am determined to be one of that number, by the help of the Lord. I have selected the 2 chapter of Paul to the Ephesians and 8 verse. It reads "For by grace are us saved through faith and that not of yourselves: it is the gift of God." This looks to me like it is a very appropriate text. However, I will leave you to judge.... Remember me to all my friends & relatives. I have hope that I will be spared to meet you all in days of peace again. I have promised myself many things, if I should, in the kind of life that I will live, etc. My kindest regards and best wishes to yourself and family and all relatives. My compliments to those that may inquire after my welfare.

Lt. Hosea Garrett, like everyone else, knew that the final clash was looming in the near future. Sherman turned his focus in late August on the two key rail lines that supplied Atlanta. His objectives were the Macon & Western and the Atlanta & West Point Railroad. Sherman shifted his army 15 miles south of Atlanta towards Jonesboro for this purpose. Hood, not realizing that Sherman had deployed nearly his entire army, sent two corps to oppose the Federals at Jonesboro. Lt. Hosea Garrett and John Vaughn Buster of the Tenth Infantry were under Patrick Cleburne's command. Cleburne attacked the Federal forces on August 31.

Private Ben Seaton of Garrett's company wrote in his diary:

> 31 August 1864. Wendsday 31st — formed in line ... I think from all appearances that we are going to advance our line untell we meat the foe. Moved our line into the timber and are waiting fer orders— it is now 12 o'clock and the order is from General Hood to drive the enemy across the creak (Muncus) some haff mile. Now we are in fer a change let it cost what it will — we made a brilent charge and drove the enemy one mile out of thar line of breastworks— our loss was small but few killed or wouned and perhaps the enemy loss was not much grater.[8]

Cleburne was to have supported Stephen Lee's Corps. However, Cleburne's own left was exposed to six Federal corps when Lee's Corps was repulsed and withdrew. Confederate casualties again were serious. One entire brigade was lost. The Confederates managed to escape only with the fall of darkness. In any case, the outcome of Jonesboro was inevitable from the onset of the fighting. Seaton's diary entry continued:

> I went to the division hospital that nite with Lt. H. Garrett who was mortally wouned as wer several others of the regiment. Shermon move have develop itself on the left by flanking and hard fighting — in all probbilityu [probability] by this move he may reach Atlanta as it now bids fare to fall — I hope not but it is possible.[9]

Jonesboro was the last effort to save Atlanta. Supplies ceased flowing into Atlanta with the railroad lines cut. Hood ordered the evacuation of Atlanta on September 1, even as Cleburne's command was desperately fighting to survive at Jonesboro. The Confederates destroyed the ammunition supplies and withdrew, leaving a burning Atlanta to the victors. The Confederate soldiers, for all their courage and élan and their determination to protect their homeland, were facing superior forces of veteran Federal troops, who also could fight.

Litter bearers managed to remove Hosea Garrett from the battlefield and take him to Floyd House and Ocmulgee Hospitals, Macon, Georgia. The official records list him still there on September 26, 1864. "Ball entered pectoralis major muscle. Not extracted."[10] Chest wounds often were not fatal, as long as they were not too close to the heart. Head wounds, in contrast, unless superficial, and wounds in the abdomen were nearly always fatal. Ensign Hosea Garrett recovered and by November of the same year was back with John Bell Hood and the Army of Tennessee, serving on the staff of Major General Benjamin Cheatham, Corps Commander over Cleburne's Division.[11]

Sherman's capture of Atlanta in September sealed Lincoln's re-election in November 1864. Sherman, in order to make the point that Federal victory was imminent, advanced from Atlanta in his infamous March to the Sea. There was little reason for anyone, Northerner or Southerner, to doubt that the end was near. The announcement of Lincoln's victory in the presidential election confirmed that reality.

The *Galveston Tri-Weekly News* of November 9, 1864, while awaiting the results, told its readers:

> Yesterday the great contest between the Abolition and Democratic parties was to be decided.... This is the sacrifice which the wisdom of our constitution has devised in order to conciliate that spirit of anarchy and revolution.... The election of Mr. Lincoln would be a solemn decision on the part of the American people that war be continued until one or the other of the belligerent parties be destroyed. It would banish all hope of peace from the minds of men.[12]

Captain Dick Swearingen, far from his family in Chappell Hill and serving in the First Tennessee Cavalry, saw considerable action in the campaign for Atlanta in the spring and summer of 1864. Eleven days after the Confederate forces conceded Atlanta to Sherman, Captain Richard Swearingen slipped off on leave and married Miss Jennie Jesse. Miss Jennie and her sister Sallie made the perilous journey from Sneedville over the mountains and through enemy lines to Jonesville, Virginia, where the marriage was performed.

Jennie returned home. Ten days later, Captain Swearingen slipped through the lines to Sneedville to see his wife, only to be surrounded and captured by mountain bushwackers. Eastern Tennessee was home to many Union loyalists, who fought against the Confederates as irregulars. Swearingen's captors were led by Joab Buttry, who was said to have begun a reign of terror after seeing his brother shot down in cold blood by Confederate soldiers. Swearingen suffered at the hands of Buttry's men for two weeks. Buttry himself may have prevented Swearingen's outright execution — his men certainly had killed their share of Confederate soldiers.

11. The Defense of Atlanta

Eastern Tennessee was a particularly bloody scene of partisan fighting. There were many hostages taken by both sides. By November 1863, the Confederate and Union authorities began to work together to exchange prisoners on an informal basis.[13] When Captain Swearingen was captured, Jennie contacted Confederate authorities. John C. Breckenridge, commanding the Department for the Confederacy, sent a letter to Buttry stating "that he would give the bushmen any three men that they might name, then in Confederate prisons, in exchange for their prisoner."[14] Buttry, as the story goes, took Swearingen to the north bank of the Clinch River and released him. Dick Swearingen would continue the fight to the end. His mission at this point in the war, as with so many other soldiers, was to survive and return home to his loved ones.

There was little that the Confederates could do to stop Sherman's army from ravaging South Carolina. Hood took his shattered Confederate force into northern Georgia after the loss of Atlanta, hoping to cut Sherman's railroad supply line. Sherman's army lived off the land instead and Hood's strategy failed. The Confederacy desperately sought victory. Hood moved his Army of Tennessee into northern Alabama to re-supply. He then moved northward towards Nashville in the hope of diverting Sherman. The exhausted men marched through bitterly cold weather in thin, worn-out clothes and remnants of shoes. The long march was too much for Confederate soldiers in need of rest after the long Atlanta campaign. Meanwhile, fresh Federal forces awaited them in Tennessee. Chappell Hill men in the Twenty-Fourth Texas and Twenty-Fifth Texas Cavalry (Dismounted) and Tenth Texas Infantry marched along in Granbury's Brigade, Cleburne's Division.

The Army of Tennessee engaged Federal forces under Major General John Schofield near Spring Hill, Tennessee, on November 29, 1864. The Federals repulsed an afternoon attack and withdrew to the north that night. Hood caught up with Schofield at Franklin, just south of Nashville. The Federals awaited the attack in strong entrenchments. Hood deployed his troops before the Federals' formidable position at four o'clock in the afternoon. Their alignment was a military spectacle. A single line spread in open view across more than two miles. Six Confederate divisions were arrayed as if on dress parade with 125 regimental battle flags flapping in the breeze. The brass band began playing when the order to advance was given. One soldier later recalled that it was the first and only time he heard the bands playing on the battlefield.[15] The music was a collection of Confederate martial pieces and lasted for nearly 20 minutes as the vast line surged across the valley towards the Federal lines.

> O, I wish I was in the land of cotton
> Old times there are not forgotten
> Look away! Look away!
> Look away! Dixie Land.
>
> In Dixie Land where I was born in
> Early on one frosty mornin'
> Look away! Look away!
> Look away! Dixie Land.

> O, I wish I was in Dixie!
> Hooray! Hooray!
> In Dixie Land I'll take my stand
> To live and die in Dixie
> Away, away,
> Away down south in Dixie!

The Federal bands responded with their own music.[16] Then the artillery of both began to pick up the action.

The Confederate attack surged through two Federal brigades holding an advance position in front of the main entrenchments, but the main Federal line held. The frontal assault had little hope of success. Men later described the hand-to-hand fighting as some of the bloodiest in which they had ever been involved. Those Confederates who penetrated the Federal lines paid with their lives. General Patrick Cleburne was killed in the assault, as was General Hiram Granbury. Granbury's last words were said to have been, "Forward, men; never let it be said that Texans lagged in the fight."[17] Four other Confederate generals also died in the fighting. Scores of officers were lost and the ground in front of the entrenchments was covered with piles of Confederate dead.

Schofield withdrew his victorious Federal forces to Nashville the following day, leaving the Confederates to dispose of the bodies of their dead heroes. Never before in a single day had so many Confederates died. Granbury's Brigade was reduced to only 500 men, commanded by a captain. They carefully set up grave markers for their own and dumped the enemy dead en masse into ditches, as was the usual fashion in that war. Most of Franklin became a hospital complex for the wounded and dying. Hood persisted in continuing towards Nashville. The advance, after the horrific slaughter at Franklin, seemed to be sheer insanity. Perhaps Hood felt he needed to make one final, desperate attempt at achieving the much-needed victory. Nonetheless, one can imagine that even the most aggressive soldier in the aftermath of Franklin would have considered it prudent to withdraw. But not John Bell Hood. The shattered remnants of the Army of Tennessee moved to the outskirts of Nashville and set up their lines. They remained in camp for two weeks, extending their suffering in the bitter cold.

Federal troops from Nashville attacked Hood's Confederates on December 15. They were fresh, well-equipped and possessed far superior numbers. Granbury's Brigade was in the thick of the fighting.[18] The Confederates withdrew after two days of bloody fighting. Fewer than 350 men remained to answer roll in Granbury's Brigade. Andrew Keller and Sul Ross's Cavalry Brigade covered the retreat as the rear guard. The Army of Tennessee was no more.

As 1864 ended, the outlook for the Confederacy was bleak and many began to wonder what hope remained. William Westcoat Browning of Chappell Hill remained a defiant Confederate to the end, never wavering from his cause. The Confederacy desperately needed money to continue the fight. William Browning bought a considerable number of Confederate war bonds in late 1864. No one thought it to be a sensible investment. It is unlikely that Browning did either. Nonetheless, the man had already lost his only son Daniel and could not imagine quitting the fight to defend his way of life.

12

The Wilderness and Petersburg

The Texas Brigade returned to the Army of Northern Virginia after the defeat at Knoxville. General Robert E. Lee reviewed the brigade on April 29, 1864. There was a clear sense that both Lee and the brigade were glad to be reunited. The Texas Brigade would fight tenaciously for Lee less than a week later and the bond between the general and his shock troops would grow even stronger.

There were repercussions in the aftermath of the disastrous Knoxville campaign. General Longstreet filed court-martial charges against the Texas Brigade's Brigadier General Jerome Robertson. Micah Jenkins had ordered Robertson to advance the Texas Brigade to attack during the futile assault on the fortifications at Knoxville. Robertson was upset about the lack of promised food and shoes. Instead of advancing, he called together his regimental commanders and expressed his lack of confidence in the campaign. He pointed out that whether or not the Confederate forces before Knoxville won the engagement, they would be compelled to retreat with larger forces moving toward them.[1] The fighting was over by the time the Texas Brigade began its advance. Perhaps Robertson's resisting saved the lives of men such as Rufus King Felder and James Landes of Chappell Hill, but it was not becoming an officer. A seven-member court heard testimony and sent Robertson home to Independence, Texas. He commanded the Texas State Militia until the end of the war.

Lincoln and many other powerful men in the Federal government felt that Meade should have crushed Lee's Army of Northern Virginia in the aftermath of the victory at Gettysburg. President Lincoln made Ulysses Grant general-in-chief of the Federal armies in March 1864 on the basis of his success in the West, stressing to his new commander the importance of relentlessly engaging Lee and his army. Grant subsequently left Washington and went to the field to join Meade and the Army of the Potomac. As Sherman was preparing to move on Atlanta, Grant pressed Meade to commence the Overland Campaign with the intention of capturing Richmond. Grant and Sherman were determined to either resolve the war or, at least, cinch the outcome of the November 1864 election.

Grant's Overland Campaign of May and June 1864 involved a series of battles across Virginia leading up to the siege of Petersburg. The opening battle in this campaign was the Battle of the Wilderness on May 5–7, 1864. The battle represented the first time that Grant and Lee faced one another in battle. It was said by some to be the finest hour for the Texas Brigade and Rufus King Felder wrote home:

> I am sorry to say that I was not in the great fight of the wilderness. I was quite sick with the fever at the time in the hospital at Lynchburg.[2]

Lee knew the Wilderness well. His victory at the Battle of Chancellorsville the previous year was a result of Lee's recognition that the thickly wooded terrain of the Wilderness was an ideal ground for his smaller Army of Northern Virginia to engage Grant's larger forces. He attempted a maneuver similar to the one that worked at Chancellorsville, separating his own force to execute a turning movement and hit Grant's exposed flank. The fighting was fierce.

On May 6, 1864, the second day of fighting at the Wilderness, the fate of the Army of Northern Virginia hung in the balance. General Robert E. Lee's right flank was crumbling under pressure from a five-division Union attack. Lee watched the routed troops of Lieutenant General A.P. Hill's III Corps run west along the Orange Plank Road, away from the approaching enemy. Lee quickly took action to avert disaster. He sent an aide to hurry Lt. Gen. James Longstreet's advancing First Corps into the fight. Longstreet brought his two divisions the last mile and a half at the double-quick, moving in parallel columns on the road.

At the head of the two columns were Brig. Gen. B.G. Humphrey's Mississippi Brigade and Gregg's Texas Brigade with only 800 effective fighting men. They moved forward through the confused mass of demoralized men from Hill's Corps. Longstreet ordered General John Gregg to form his Texas Brigade north of Orange Plank Road. The Brigade's regiments, once formed into battle line, began moving forward under fire. The Fifth Texas Regiment was on the far right. Lee rode up to Gregg and asked him what unit he commanded. Gregg was standing near the color bearer for the Fifth Texas. Bullets were whizzing all around. Gregg answered, "The Texas Brigade," to which Lee responded, "I am glad to see it. When you go in there I want you to give those men the cold steel." Gregg saluted Lee and spurred his horse to the front of his command. Standing up in his stirrups, he yelled out: "Attention, Texas Brigade! The eyes… of General Lee… are upon you! Forward march!"

Lee, at the rear of the Brigade, rose in his saddle, raised his hat over his head and shouted out, "Texas always moves them!" Those troops within hearing range raised a cheer and word passed quickly through the ranks. There was a tremendous uproar of cheering and emotion. General Lee himself became caught up in the

12. The Wilderness and Petersburg

emotional surge and spurred his horse Traveler toward the front. Leonard Groce Gee of Independence, Texas, was standing nearby, serving as a courier to General Gregg. He was a member of Company E of the Fifth Regiment, the same unit as Rufus King Felder. Most accounts support Gee as being the one who first grabbed Traveler's bridle reins. Men began crying out, "General Lee to the rear." The emotion built to a frenzy with Texans surrounding Lee, shouting, "To the rear! General Lee to the rear! We won't move until you go back!" Lee finally relented and allowed adjutant John Kerr to lead him away from the front.[3] By this time, the Texans were in a state of near frenzy. The Texas Brigade charged forward with a fierce Rebel yell.

The Federals were formed in two lines of battle, the first line being 300 yards across an open field. The Texas Brigade advanced without hesitation into heavy fire and took losses every step of the way. Each time a man fell, another stepped into his place to fill the gap. The Texans overran one line and then a second line, 200 yards beyond the first. The Texans would not be stopped. They routed veteran Federal soldiers, Maj. Gen. Winfield Scott Hancock's II Corps, and pursued them with a vengeance. The men of the Texas Brigade, after advancing another 200 yards through heavy fire, found themselves facing a formidable line of log breastworks while Federal fire swept their right flank. Gregg ordered a charge. The Texans came under fire from two artillery batteries. Federal artillery swept the ranks with canister shot. One survivor later wrote:

> The storm of battle became terrific. The Texas Brigade was alone; no support on our right, and not only none on our left, but a terrible enfilading fire poured on us from that direction.

Amid withering fire, the Brigade formed a line within 20 yards of the main Union line. Another soldier in the brigade wrote:

> For twenty five minutes we held them steady and at the expiration of that time more than of our brave fellows lay around us dead, dying and wounded, and the few survivors could stand it no longer.[4]

General Gregg finally ordered the remains of his devastated Texas Brigade to withdraw. They reoccupied the positions lost earlier in the day by Hill's Corps. The Brigade's unsupported charge had stopped the attack of two Federal corps and restored Lee's right flank. The price paid was high. Of the 800 Texans who charged under Lee, 565 were dead or wounded. General James Longstreet, the Corps commander, was seriously wounded. The Fifth Texas Infantry Regiment lost its commanding officer, all of his officers and nearly two-thirds of its infantrymen.[5] The Texans had saved Lee's army, but would never again be the same. Rufus King Felder's illness may have saved his life. James Edward Landes, Rufus King's comrade-in-arms from Chappell Hill, lost a finger in the action. Landes was admitted to the General Hospital, Howard's Grove, Richmond, three days later.[6] The warrior returned to the regiment, with whom he finished out the war to the bitter end.

Federal casualties at the Wilderness totaled 18,000 killed and wounded. Confederate forces lost 11,000 — 11,000 they could ill afford to lose. Grant showed his determination in the aftermath of the battle by pressing on toward Richmond, despite the loss. No Federal general had done that in the war. Robert E. Lee would never again have the chance to reorganize his Army of Northern Virginia and allow his men to rest.

The Battle of Spotsylvania followed and again Lee blocked Grant's progress. Grant blundered at Cold Harbor, losing over 7,000 men in 20 minutes in an all-out assault on Lee's entrenched army. Cold Harbor was Grant's worst defeat and a great victory for the Confederacy, but it would be Lee's final victory of the war. Grant swung south in an attempt to take Petersburg, below Richmond. The gamble failed and Grant proceeded to dig in before Petersburg. The enthusiasm of Federal soldiers to assault Lee's entrenched troops greatly diminished after the slaughter at Cold Harbor. A 10-month siege commenced that would cost thousands of lives on both sides.

Rufus King Felder was in good spirits when he wrote home on July 14, as the Army of Northern Virginia entrenched around Petersburg :

> We are in strong entrenchments here. The breastworks of the enemy are in 75 yards of ours in some places. Our brigade was relieved last night to rest two days. We have been in entrenchments six days without relief, sharpshooting with the enemy.... There were only eight or ten killed or wounded. McPherson of our company was wounded in the waist.... The news is incouraging. Rebels in two miles of Baltimore. Grant defeated & the Dixie Blues in fine spirits.[7]

George Kerby wrote from Richmond to his Aunt Elizabeth (Cocke) McRee on July 20, 1864, in the aftermath of Grant's bloody Overland Campaign. Chappell Hill's Cocke clan had pondered George's fate for some time. George Kerby, who studied at Georgetown and Princeton in the 1850s, was in Maryland when the war began and then disappeared. Federal authorities arrested George and his brothers on suspicion of being spies and imprisoned them in Washington, D. C. George waited two months for an opportunity to slip away after his release on parole. He obtained work in the Confederate Treasury Office in Richmond. He had only just returned from a visit home to Chappell Hill and reported, "I came near being caught by the Yankees after I crossed the Miss. River." Kerby's letter conveyed the same confidence as had Felder's:

> Gen. Lee still holds the enemy at bay around Richmond and Petersburgh ... a feeling of most complete security seems to privail [sic].... A part of Gen. Lee's Army under Gen. Early has just returned from Maryland ... frightening the Yankees of Baltimore and Washington out of their wits [The Battle of Monocacy, July 9, 1864].[8]

Kerby commented on the high cost of living in Richmond but added, "I think everything will be cheaper when the Yankees are driven from around Richmond." In fact, Richmond had survived previous Federal thrusts.

The Texas soldiers, despite feeling secure in their ability to hold off Grant's Federals, were homesick. Rufus King Felder wrote on August 13, 1864:

> The carrier came in a few minutes ago with a large Texas mail. Everyone was anxious to get a letter & read the news from home & none more so than your

12. The Wilderness and Petersburg

> worthy brother. You can imagine the surprise & merriment it created when we all opened our letters & read the news ... one nearly fourteen months on the way. I suppose the mail was sent to us while we were lost in the wilderness of East Tenn. & being cut of from all communication it was stopped in Georgia. It matters not how old your letters are ... though a year old gave me the greatest deal of pleasure. It carried my mind back to my dear home (which I almost forgot I had) & the memory of its dear loved ones always produce within me feelings of the most pleasant nature.[9]

There was a deeply sad part to Rufus' letter. His sister Emma was still grieving over the loss less than a year earlier of her husband Thomas Elliott. Tom's brother George had suffered the same fate.

> I suppose you have heard of the death of George Elliott. He was killed in one of the battles before Petersburg. I understand that Dr. Elliott takes his death very hard. The old man's recent bereavements must be almost unsupportable in his declining years. OH! When will this dreadful contest end & put a stop to our troubles & suffering.[10]

The Texas Brigade moved from their entrenched position, east of Petersburg, south to New Market Heights on July 29. Rufus Felder wrote on September 18:

> We are still on the north side of the James.... We have only three skeleton brigades on this side of the river. The consequence is our picket duty is very hard. We are on duty every other night & some times every day.[11]

The long travail of the war with its ongoing carnage had not calloused Felder, who related an incident that made an indelible impression upon him:

> I witnessed quite an affecting scene the other day. While we were sharpshooting with the enemy, one of the regiment at my side received a fatal shot through the breast. He seemed to not think of himself or the agony he suffered, but prayed to God to spare his life that he may defend his beloved country & avenge himself on dastard foe. Such exhibitions of patriotism from an humble private is of daily occurance & makes one proud to know he belongs to such an army & feels confident that when he goes into battle he has comrades that will not desert him. You have perhaps wondered why your brother has not obtained some position of rank & honor, which so many are so eagerly seeking after. I acknowledge that some positions afford a great many advantages for ease & pleasure than a private has, but it will be to the private that the honor will be given, so if our independence is achieved.... All that I want on this earth to make me happy is independence & a safe return to our once happy home, but this faint hope grows still more glowing.[12]

The Texas Brigade was facing emancipated African Americans, who had enlisted to serve in the Federal Army. They were designated United States Colored Troops and often bore the brunt of the battles in which they took part. Felder shared his perceptions:

> Rutters Negro division is on our front. There is scarcely a day but some of them come over & ask to be sent back to their masters. The slaughter pen they were forced into at Petersburg quite demoralized them. They say they don't think they have anything to do with this fuss. This white folks fight. The white soldier are also deserting in large numbers & claiming protection.... It is very humiliating to know that we have to fight & expose our lives to this mixed horde of black & white demons. Autumn is upon us, but still the campaign goes on, nor do I see any probability of its ever coming to an end until the friendly snows of winter shall come & drop its shroud on the thousand of departed heroes, whose bones & bodys yet scarced decayed are still exposed to the gaze of man & at the sight of which the very angels weep.[13]

The Texas Brigade was part of a small force of 2,000 Confederate soldiers spread from the James River to New Market Heights. Rufus King Felder was about to find himself facing a determined assault by the United States Colored Troops, just 10 days after writing his letter. Grant conceived a surprise attack against the Richmond defenses in the hopes of weakening Lee's position around Petersburg. Major General Benjamin Butler led 20,000 Federal soldiers on a 12-hour forced march across the James River to the north bank on the night of September 28–29. The assault on the Texas Brigade's New Market Heights position commenced at 5:30 the next morning. The Texas Brigade was entrenched on a rise overlooking a 300-yard field of fire that the Federals would have to cross. The final 150 yards consisted of an elaborate defensive network of sharpened stakes and felled trees with sharpened limbs. Duncan's Brigade, U.S. Colored Troops, made the initial advance and sustained over 50 percent casualties before withdrawing. Three USCT regiments spearheaded the second assault, which commenced at 6 A.M., just after sunrise. They suffered under intense fire before pushing near the Confederate line over an hour later. Lee ordered the withdrawal of the Texas Brigade to support the more critical position at Fort Harrison and the USCT took the position as the Confederates withdrew. They suffered over 1,300 casualties in just over an hour. The United States Army awarded 14 African American enlisted men with the Medal of Honor for their bravery that day.[14]

Lee attempted a major offensive against the Union right flank to offset the increasing threat against Richmond. There was fierce fighting on October 7, 1864, at Darbytown. The attack was unsuccessful and losses were heavy. The Texas Brigade was in the heart of the action. Confederate General John Gregg, commanding the Texas Brigade, was among the dead. Captain Tacitus Clay of Independence was another casualty at Darbytown. He had survived wounds at Gaines' Mill and Wilderness. He wrote his wife Bettie on October 24, 1864:

> I wrote you a few days ago—that in a fight with the enemy on the 7th I was wounded and that my right leg was taken off just above the knee, and that I was doing fine. I am glad to say that I am still doing well with a prospect of speedy recovery. I cannot well expect to get home under four months. This looks like a terrible calamity, but I can bear the loss without repining. I hope the time will not be long before I am with you, and then for a little house, and the dear ones around us.... Kiss the children for me and retain an embrace for yourself. God bless you my dear is the prayer of your Affectionate Husband.[15]

12. The Wilderness and Petersburg

Clay's magnificent Greek Revival mansion in Independence, known as Clay's Castle, was renowned for its glassed-in ballroom on the third floor overlooking his fields.[16] The ballroom had been the scene of numerous dances in antebellum days. Tacitus Clay would never again dance as he once did.

Rufus Felder wrote on December 18 of two fighting comrades, wounded at Darbytown, who were heading home:

> Capt. Baber & Frank Eldridge have both been retired & will start home tomorrow. They will be the bearers of many letters from absent & loved ones to anxious & expectant friends & relatives…. whenever any of you write, you are sure to say that the last time you heard from me, was in the hospital…. As a general thing my health has been much better since I have been in the service than at home. It is true I have been unfortunate in having several very sick spells, but during the long periods that I have been in the army, I have not been absent from the front more than three or four months out of forty one…. My chances are good to live at least until the grass rises. We have been using every exertion in our power to have the brigade transferred or furloughed to Texas this winter. We have drawn up a memorial to that effect, signed by all the officers & men of the brigade and presented it to the President. Many are confident that we will go home this winter, but I must confess that I think our chances are very slim. I could conceive of no event (except the establishment of our independence) that would create so much joy in the brigade than such a change.[17]

Private Felder could not have imagined that the stubborn Confederate Army of Northern Virginia would hold out in the Richmond-Petersburg environs for nearly another year before surrendering.

13

The End of the War

Rufus King Felder wrote from a defensive position near Richmond on February 23, 1865:

> You are aware by this time all communication south cut & the man who carries this will have to walk a long ways to get around Shearman's [Sherman's] army. Yes, my dear sister, the insolvent foe have dared to march through the very heart of South Carolina & I have no doubt committed depridations on the property, if not on the persons of our dear, but unfortunate relatives. God grant that they may have been spared and that the scenes of our childhood of our noble ancesters not desecrated by the _____ of our brutal enemy. Our cause looks gloomy indeed.[1]

While Grant was tightening the siege around Petersburg in Virginia, William Tecumseh Sherman was in Savannah, Georgia, preparing to begin his Carolinas Campaign. The *Galveston Tri-Weekly* published a letter from Colonel Gustave Cook, commanding Terry's Texas Rangers, "29 miles above Savannah ... immediately in front of the enemy on outpost duty." Cook wrote that he and his Rangers "have been fighting for about four weeks almost daily. My regiment has lost a great many." Cook, like many Texans away in the eastern theater of the war, expressed false optimism that their regiment would be furloughed for Texas soon. His final remark, a more realistic one, added, "as soon as all is quiet, we will be allowed to come home."[2]

Sherman headed northward from Savannah, Georgia, on January 19, 1865. Meanwhile, Federal forces under Schofield and Terry closed Lee's last major supply line by capturing the port of Wilmington, North Carolina, in February 1865. Grant ordered this force to march inland with Goldsboro, North Carolina, as its objective. Goldsboro was the junction of the Wilmington & Weldon and Atlantic & North

13. The End of the War

Carolina railroads. Sherman's army moved through South Carolina to converge with Schofield and Terry's force at the junction of Bentonville, North Carolina. Bentonville was a strategic crossroads where the roads from Smithfield, Fayetteville and Goldsboro intersected. Sherman's ultimate objective was to combine forces with Grant outside Petersburg and overwhelm Lee's extended line of exhausted soldiers.

Confederate authorities recognized that they had to block the Federals in North Carolina and prevent Sherman from uniting with Grant in Virginia. Confederate President Jefferson Davis, after much reluctance, gave in to Robert E. Lee's pressure to recall Joseph E. Johnston from retirement to command an army in North Carolina. Johnston collected various scattered Confederate units on short notice and formed what became known as the Army of the South. This was a consolidation of the remnants of Hood's Army of Tennessee, forces under Braxton Bragg and those under General William Hardee. Johnston, once again, faced a superior force under Sherman.

Sherman's Army ravaged the land at will as it advanced. Confederate cavalry under Joe Wheeler and Wade Hampton did their best to strike back and slow the advance. The troopers struck back with a vengeance at Federal raiders and foragers in an attempt to minimize the extent of destruction. The Eighth Texas Cavalry was in the midst of the fierce reprisals. General Hugh Judson Kilpatrick, commanding a Federal cavalry division, sent a dispatch to Sherman's headquarters on February 22, 1865:

> An infantry lieutenant and seven men were murdered yesterday by the Eight Texas Cavalry after they had surrendered. We found their bodies all together and mutilated, with paper on their breasts, saying, "Death to foragers." Eighteen of my men were killed yesterday and some had their throats cut. There is no doubt of this, general, and I have sent Wheeler word that I intend to hang eighteen of his men, and if the cowardly act is repeated, will burn every house along my line of march, and that can be reached by my scouting parties. I have a number of prisoners and shall take a fearful revenge. My people were deliberately murdered by a scouting party of 300 men commanded by a lieutenant colonel.[3]

Joseph Johnston and his Army of the South chose to fight Sherman's Federal Army at Bentonville. Johnston knew that his enemy far outnumbered him and that his only hope was to set a trap for the confident Federals. He organized his force of 16,000 infantry and 4,000 cavalry into a hook-shaped line, blocking the Goldsboro Road. Sherman's left wing marched right into the trap on the morning of March 19, 1865. The Confederates launched a massive attack that drove the Federals back with serious losses. However, Federal heroics prevented Johnston from delivering the decisive blow to attain the victory so desperately needed. When Sherman moved his entire army into position by midway through the next day, he had 60,000 men in place, far outnumbering the Confederates. Johnston refused to leave the field of battle, hoping to lure Sherman into a costly frontal assault that never came. The two armies fought for the next two days with little change.

Federal General Joseph Mower's division moved against the Confederate left toward Mill Creek Bridge on the afternoon of March 21. Mill Creek was out of its

JAMES FISKE "DOC" MATTHEWS AND JOSEPH WIER MATTHEWS. Three of five brothers, James Fiske "Doc" Matthews, John Fletcher Matthews and Joseph Wier Matthews, enlisted together in the Eighth Texas Cavalry. "Doc" is on the right and Joseph is on the left. Captain "Doc" Matthews was the senior officer on the field at the Battle of Bentonville, North Carolina, on March 21, 1865. He led what is generally regarded as the last great cavalry charge of the war. "Doc" Matthews married Mattie Browning. They inherited the Browning Plantation Manor House from her parents and lived out their lives in Chappell Hill. (From the Archives of the Chappell Hill Historical Society.)

banks from spring rains and the bridge was the only escape route for Johnston's army. The Confederates faced complete destruction if the bridge was lost. Confederate General Wade Hampton later described what transpired:

> On the 21st ... my pickets reported that the enemy seemed to be moving in force on our left.... I immediately rode down to report this fact to General Johnston, and I told him that there was no force present able to resist an attack, and that if the enemy broke through at that point, which was near the bridge across the main stream, our only life line of retreat would be cut off ... rendered our position extremely dangerous.... I then sent a courier to bring up all the mounted men I could find, and in a few minutes a portion of the 8th Texas Cavalry — sixty or eighty men — responded to my call. All of these troops were hurried up to meet the enemy, who were then within a few hundred yards of the road, and just as I had put them in position General Hardee arrived on the ground ... he at once ordered a charge, and our small force was hurled against the advancing enemy. The attack was so sudden and so impetuous that it carried everything before it, and the enemy hastily retreated across the branch.[4]

General Joseph Johnston later reported in his own report to Robert E. Lee on the action at Mill Creek Bridge that "the Eighth Texas Cavalry distinguished themselves."[5]

Twenty-four-year-old James Fiske "Doc" Matthews of Chappell Hill, who attained the rank of captain in October 1864, led the famous charge of the Eighth Texas Cavalry. Matthews, who was wounded seven times in the course of the war,[6] had commanded a company of Rangers since December 1863, shortly after the disastrous Knoxville Campaign. The loss of Colonels Cook and Jarmon in the preceding 10-day campaign leading up to the Battle of Bentonville left Captain Matthews as the highest-ranking officer in the decimated ranks of the Rangers. When General Hardee rode up and asked for the commanding officer, young Doc Matthews stepped forward. An observer noted that the expression on Hardee's face seemed to indicate his surprise at the officer's youth. Wheeler told him, "Captain, mount your men as fast as you can and charge whatever you find at the bridge." Matthews advanced with 150 troopers, which was all that remained of Terry's Texas Rangers. They paused on high ground overlooking the strategic bridge and saw a sea of blue infantry advancing. This was Mower's Division. General William Hardee rode up and reportedly asked the young officer, "Can you hold these people in check until I can bring up the infantry and artillery?" Matthews replied, "General, we are the boys that can try!" Hardee's response was "Then execute your orders." One of the Rangers who participated described the action:

> [T]here was a laying of spurs to horses' sides and once more Terry's Rangers were sweeping over a battlefield. It was like the old days: Rose the clatter of horses' feet on the evening air, rang the Rebel yell in its purity. The men crossed the five hundred yards, their shotguns bellowing. The Federals could not stand it. The first line broke and fell back on the second, causing confusion in their ranks and presently the second, too, gave way.[7]

Captain "Doc" Matthews of Chappell Hill had led the last great cavalry charge of the war. It perhaps was fitting that the Eighth Texas Calvary, Terry's Texas Rangers, made the charge. Confederate cavalry clashed sharply at the bridge again with the Union advance guard on the morning of March 22 and again held. Johnston achieved his objective of impeding Sherman's advance. There was a brief period of increased morale in the Confederate ranks. Johnston slipped away from Bentonville with his Army of the South intact as an effective force.

While Johnston and Sherman clashed in North Carolina, Grant prepared to deliver the final blow at Petersburg in Virginia. The men of Lee's Army of Northern Virginia were exhausted and hungry. The Federal victory at the Battle of Five Forks on April 1 sealed Grant's victory. Lee reluctantly evacuated Richmond and marched his army to the west. The once-mighty Army of Northern Virginia consisted of fewer than 30,000 exhausted men. Grant followed in hot pursuit with far greater numbers of well-supplied troops. The Texas Brigade, so often looked to by Lee as his shock troops in the attack, served as Lee's rear guard in retreat. It was a role to which they were unaccustomed.

An article in the *Galveston Tri-Weekly News* of April 7 cited an extract from the *Philadelphia Press*:

> The time is swiftly coming when this great struggle is to be determined on the issue of a single field.

Yet, business was as usual for some. An ad in the same issue announced "Four No. 1 Negroes" were among the property to be auctioned off that Friday by J. S. & J. B. Sydnor of Houston.

Units of Grant's army blocked the further retreat of the Army of Northern Virginia by April 9 and the Texas Brigade took up its final combat position as rear guard. The men were "ragged, starved and exhausted," not having eaten for three days.[8] They built breastworks across the road, but there was to be no more fighting. Lee rode to meet Grant at Appomattox on the afternoon of April 9. They reached agreement in two hours.

Longstreet and others wanted to fight their way out. The men of the Texas Brigade were ready, as well. A committee of representatives from all four regiments met just a few months earlier and resolved to fight to the end.[9] Many of the men of the Fifth Texas Infantry bent the barrels of their muskets in the fork of a tree or smashed them on rocks, when word came of Lee's surrender. They were determined that they would not surrender a workable weapon. Captain Hill, commanding the Fifth, cautioned the men, noting that the terms of parole required a "good gun."

The formal surrender for the soldiers was held early on the morning of April 12. It was a cloudy day with a mist of rain. The Confederate veterans marched to the site shortly after 9 A.M. General John Gordon rode at the head of the long procession. Many of the veteran soldiers were hobbled by sickness and injuries. All were weak with hunger. Brigadier General Joshua Chamberlain accepted the surrender on behalf of the Federal Army. His infantry division formed a double line at order arms along the road down which the Confederates marched. Chamberlain gave the command "Carry arms" as a show of respect as the Confederate column approached. Commands were shouted out as each Confederate unit marched forward to the assigned spot. "Halt!" "Close up!" "Front face!" "Stack arms!" "Unsling cartridge boxes!" "Hang on stacks!"[10] General John Gordon wrote:

> The veterans ... could no longer control their emotions, and tears ran like water down their shrunken faces. The flags which they still carried were objects of undisguised affection.... as we reached the designated point, the arms were stacked and the battle flags were folded. Those sad and suffering men, many of them weeping as they saw the old banners laid down upon the stacked guns ... began to tear the flags from the staffs and hide them in their shirts.[11]

General Chamberlain described the emotional scene from his perspective:

> As each successive division masks our own, it halts, the men face inward towards us across the road, twelve feet away; then carefully 'dress' their line, each captain taking pains for the good appearance of the company, worn and half starved as they were.... They fix bayonets, stack arms; then, hesitatingly, remove cartridge

13. The End of the War

boxes and lay them down. Lastly, — reluctantly, with agony of expression, — they tenderly fold their flags, battle-worn and torn, blood-stained, heart-holding colors, and lay them down; some frenziedly rushing from the ranks, kneeling over them, clinging to them, pressing them to their lips with burning tears.[12]

It was nearly 4 o'clock before the laying down of the arms and battle flags was completed.

Of the estimated 5,300 men who served, only 617 remained to represent the Texas Brigade at Appomattox.[13] Thirteen officers and 148 enlisted men of the Fifth Texas were present. Rufus King Felder and James Landes of Chappell Hill were among them. They received their official paroles on April 12 and prepared to head home.

Some 300 men of the Texas Brigade set out together to head home on the afternoon of April 12. Captain Hill of the Fifth Texas led them. Major George, Hood's old quartermaster, led his cow, which provided milk to the men along the way. The journey home was long and tedious. The rail lines were crowded with Union soldiers, who took priority. The Texas Brigade veterans arrived at Houston on June 3.[14] The band split up in Houston to go off their separate ways.

These men formed special relationships with one another through the experience of war. They marched together through the choking clouds of dust for months. They shared countless meals and experienced hunger together. They slept together, often huddled against one another in the cold winter nights. They stood side by side to face death many times. The veterans of the Texas Brigade embraced and bid farewell at the train station in Houston, not knowing if they would ever again see their comrades with whom they had shared so much.

It was a relatively short walk home for Rufus King Felder and James Landes from Houston to Chappell Hill after all the marching they had done. They likely shared company with other veterans heading to Brenham, Independence and Washington. They missed that spring's bluebonnets, but there would be many more springs for at least some of them. These veterans returned to a quiet life, which paled in comparison to the adrenaline rush of battle. They had thrilled in the camaraderie, the excitement of battle and the euphoria of victory, despite the carnage and horror of war. Shopkeepers, farmers, schoolteachers and others could never again experience these emotions.

News of Lee's surrender caused great anguish in the ranks. The Federals under Sherman took Raleigh on April 13, 1865, just days after Appomattox. Confederate General Joseph E. Johnston opened negotiations with Sherman on that day. Johnston surrendered near Durham, North Carolina, on April 26. Sherman was magnanimous in victory, allowing the Confederates to retain some sense of honor. As a result, Edwin Stanton, Lincoln's Secretary of War, as well as others seething with vindictiveness against the South, launched a vicious campaign in Washington against Sherman.

One of Terry's Texas Rangers wrote later of the general feeling in camp the night before the surrender: "they could not bear the idea of giving up their arms to the Yankees."[15] The regiment was opposed to the idea of surrender. They had fought

MR. AND MRS. RUFUS KING FELDER. The Felders are shown here with a six-foot tarpon caught in the Gulf. Rufus King Felder married Margaret Matthews after the war. She was the daughter of Rev. Jacob and Mary Ann Matthews and the sister of James Fiske "Doc" Matthews. Margaret died in 1884 at the age of 37. Rufus King remarried the following year and lived nearly another 40 years. (From the Archives of the Chappell Hill Historical Society.)

together for over three years, nearly always on the offensive and in a particularly aggressive style. It was written, "There is no record of where — on a *bona fide* charge against either cavalry or infantry, on anything like favorable ground — they failed to break the enemy line. And in cavalry fights against anything like equal numbers, they invariably won the day."[16]

"Doc" Matthews of Chappell Hill found himself in a difficult situation. He sought General Hardee's advice as to how to proceed in regard to surrender. Hardee encouraged Matthews to lead the men west to join forces with General Richard Taylor at Mobile, Alabama. Matthews returned to his regiment and had the bugler sound the assembly. He stood before the men whom he had fought alongside for four years and addressed them. He explained the situation and told them what General Hardee had urged him to convince them to do. "Doc" Matthews, who had led them in the last great cavalry charge of the war at Bentonville, told his comrades-in-arms that he was too young to assume the responsibility of convincing them to continue the fight. The 24 year old told his command to return to their respective companies and within that council to discuss the matter and decide. One Ranger wrote, "two small parties, one of eighteen and the other of thirty, did break out that night.... There is not a pen scratch available that shows, for certain, that one of Terry's Rangers gave up."[17]

Gen. Joe Wheeler offered a farewell address to the men who served so gallantly under him:

> HEADQUARTERS CAVALRY CORPS, Concord, N. C., April 28, 1865.
> Gallant Comrades: You have fought your fight. During four years' struggle for liberty you have exhibited courage, fortitude, and devotion. You are victors of more than two hundred sternly contested fields; you have participated in more than a thousand conflicts of arms. You are heroes, veterans, patriots. The bones of your comrades mark the battlefields on the soil of Kentucky, Tennessee, Virginia, North Carolina, South Carolina, Georgia, Alabama, and Mississippi. You have done all that human exertion could accomplish. In bidding you adieu I desire to tender my thanks for your gallantry in battle, your fortitude under suffering, and your devotion at all times to the holy cause you have done so much to maintain. I desire also to express my gratitude for the kind feeling you have seen fit to extend toward myself, and invoke upon you the blessings of our Heavenly Father, to whom we must always look in the hour of distress. Brethren in the cause of freedom, comrades in arms, I bid you farewell. Signed, JOSEPH WHEELER, Major-General.[18]

14

Texas at the Close of the War

Colonel Franklin Wilkes had more of his share of ups and downs than most of the Chappell Hill men who went off to war to serve the Confederacy. Wilkes, after being captured at Arkansas Post and suffering imprisonment, faced charges by the Confederate Government upon his release. At issue was the surrender of the Twenty-Fourth Texas Cavalry at Arkansas Post. The authorities charged Wilkes with:

> compelling his command to surrender the post under his command to the enemy ... that the accused did permit several white flags to be raised in his Regiment thereby signifying to the enemy his willingness to surrender the place when positive orders had been given to hold the place till the last extremity.[1]

There was also a second charge related to an incident in May 1863 in Richmond in which Wilkes allegedly incited his officers to not march per the command of Colonel Garland. A general court-martial ruled on August 5, 1863, that Wilkes was "Not Guilty" on all charges and declared him "released from arrest and restored to duty."[2] An officer who served under Wilkes wrote in regard to the first charge pertaining to the surrender of Arkansas Post: "They came very near finding where it started; but not who started it. Nor will it ever be known in this world."[3]

Wilkes fought at Chickamauga after his acquittal and was wounded in action. He again was arrested by his commanding officer, Colonel Garland, in early June 1864 during the Atlanta campaign. Wilkes then preferred charges against Garland, who was also put under arrest. The combatants were sent to Atlanta. Neither the cause nor the outcome is known, but Wilkes was retired on July 30, 1864.[4] He retained his commission and was placed in the Invalid Corps. Confederate authorities assigned Wilkes to post duty in the District of Texas with orders to report to General Magruder.⁵

A notice was published during this period in the *Galveston Tri-Weekly News*, posted by a man in Walker County:

> Last fall ... caught a Negro Boy, who calls his name Henry, dark complexion, about 28 years old .... sold him to a Dr. Wilkes since the war, who moved out to the neighborhood of Chappell Hill, Washington County, Texas, and that he ran away about June 1863. The dogs bit him severely in catching him ... In December last he made his escape ... In February following he returned ... asked that he might stay til he could hear from his master ... the owner is requested to call and identify his property, pay expenses and get his Negro.⁶

Franklin Wilkes had more serious problems at the time. A Federal patrol captured Wilkes on September 27, 1864, as he was traveling across Tenshaw Parish, Louisiana, on his way home to Texas. He spent three weeks in prison at Natchez, Mississippi, before being moved to New Orleans and then shipped to New York City. After a month in the prison at Fort Lafayette, Wilkes was transferred to Fort Warren in Boston Harbor,⁷ arriving there December 21.⁸ Fort Warren was the Federal prison for Confederate officers. The conditions were grim and there was little protection offered from the cold. The prison was extremely overcrowded. The commanding Federal officer of the prison protested so vehemently about the conditions that he was officially retired for doing so.⁹ The prison, designed to accommodate 175, was at an all-time occupancy of nearly 400 prisoners during Wilkes's incarceration during early 1865.¹⁰

COLONEL FRANKLIN C. WILKES. Tennessee-born Wilkes was a Methodist preacher from the age of 19. He was said to have been a gifted man and a powerful preacher. Wilkes went to Texas in 1854 and served in various positions with the Methodist Texas Conference until war broke out. He served with distinction as a colonel with the Twenty-Fourth Texas Cavalry (dismounted) during the Civil War. He returned to the ministry after the war and also served as agent for an orphans' home until his health failed him in 1879. He was chaplain of the Texas Senate in 1881, but resigned because of further complications in his health. Wilkes died in Lampasas, Texas, in December 1891. (From the Harold B. Simpson Research Center, Hill College, Hillsboro, Texas.)

Wilkes, in a letter dated February 13, 1865, beseeched the commissary-general of prisoners in Washington:

> Through various sources of information we have learned that the Confederate prisoners captured west of the Mississippi River have been sent down that river for exchange. We beg to call your attention to the fact that a few officers belonging to that department are at this place and we respectfully request that we may not be made an exception to the general exchange in that department. A speedy reply is respectfully requested. We have the honor to be, very respectfully...[11]

A later note read:

> If it be impracticable to make this exchange I then respectfully request to know upon what terms, if any, I can be paroled. My disability is of such a character that imprisonment must necessarily be more than ordinarily burdensome.[12]

Wilkes and some fellow officers were removed on March 5, 1865, and sent to City Point, Virginia, where they were exchanged. Wilkes was fortunate in the sense that Grant ordered at the beginning of April that no more prisoners be passed through City Point in light of the serious fighting around Petersburg and Richmond. Those prisoners remaining languished several more months in prison after the war ended.[13] Wilkes was finally given leave on March 14 to go home to Texas. Franklin Wilkes, as did so many other Chappell Hill men heading home, traveled down through Danville, Virginia, then to Greensboro and on to Salisbury, North Carolina, by train. Sherman and Johnston were still fighting to the east. The train from Salisbury, on which Wilkes was traveling, headed due west toward Texas and left the fighting behind.

Franklin Wilkes was only one of number of Confederate officers facing charges as the rebellion faltered. Major-General Sterling Price led a disastrous invasion of his home state of Missouri in the fall of 1864. Price led 12,000 men in the hopes that tens of thousands of Missouri men would take up arms and join him. The reality was that the outcome of the war was becoming clear and there was little interest among the populace toward embracing a defeated Confederacy. Price's primary support came from notorious guerrillas, including "Bloody Bill" Anderson's gang, who carried scalps from a recent massacre. Price's invasion began with a tactical error in an attack against a well-fortified Federal garrison near Pilot Knob that cost him well over 1,000 men. Price moved westward, pursued by a superior force of Federal regulars augmented by militia. A second Federal force from Kansas City awaited Price in the west, even as his pursuers closed in from the east. The Federal pincers closed at Westport, just south of Kansas City, on October 23, 1864. Price's entire army was severely defeated and nearly all captured, only escaping at the cost of severe losses to Shelby's division serving as rear guard. By the time that Price and his self-proclaimed Army of Missouri limped back into Texas in December, his command numbered less than a third of its original number.

Thomas G. Reynolds, whom the Confederate government had hoped to install as their governor of Missouri, accompanied Price on his raid. He wrote a scathing open letter published by the *Texas Republican* in Marshall on December 23, 1864, that constituted a personal attack on Major-General Price. There was some basis for some of Reynolds' charges. Price had become an obese man, weighing nearly 300 pounds,[14] and Reynolds' charge that "His regular course was to sit in his ambulance at the head of his train of march, rarely mounting his horse" was not surprising. There also was support for the charge: "His outfit was on the scale that even Federal generals dare not adopt. Three vehicles with fourteen mules carried him and the personal effects and camp equipage of his mess."[15] Price's tactical decisions also seem to have been wanting and discipline was lacking. The general's association with guerrillas and the corresponding wholesale plundering by stragglers and camp followers was hardly consistent with the campaign's aim to win local support. Price replied in the January 10, 1865, edition of the *Shreveport News*, referring to Reynolds as "who pretends to be, and styles himself, Governor of the State of Missouri."[16] This was followed by another retort by Reynolds days later in the *Texas Republican*.[17]

Reverend Dr. Benjamin Kavanaugh of Chappell Hill's Soule University had served as chaplain under Price in 1862–1863. Price's association with guerillas may have caused Kavanaugh to resign from military service on October 16, 1863,[18] and rejoin the faculty of Soule University. This was the man who later wrote to his Masonic brothers:

> Let us never forget that the chief glory of our institution lies ... in an exalted and perfected manhood; in those unseen temples of the human heart garnished with the solid splendor of divine virtues, and lighted and warmed with unquenchable and unconquerable love.[19]

Reverend Kavanuagh of Chappell Hill nonetheless published his own letter in Price's defense. He took the offensive, referring to Reynolds as a "dead-head" that remained with the train "and therefore knew nothing of the campaign."[20] Kavanaugh's attack on Reynolds, in turn, caused General Shelby to publish a letter praising Reynolds' conduct in the campaign. While the debate raged, the Confederacy slipped away.

General Edmund Kirby-Smith, commanding the Department of Trans-Mississippi, had low regard for Price.[21] He only reluctantly agreed to Price's Missouri campaign in the unlikely event that it might distract some Federal forces from the onslaught upon Atlanta and Richmond. There was also the faint hope that Price's assertions that thousands would flock to his standard would prove accurate. Kirby-Smith called for a court of inquiry. Price insisted on a court-martial proceeding so as to allow a full airing of the charges, but Kirby-Smith denied the request.[22] The date for the final hearing was set for April 21, 1865. The capitulation of the Confederacy pre-empted Price's hearing.

Diehard Confederates after Lee's surrender on April 9, 1865, still hoped that Johnston's Army might join with that of Kirby-Smith in the West. That hope vanished with Johnston's surrender on April 26. Yet, the outcome in the West in the Confederacy's Trans-Mississippi Department was undecided. Texas had resisted invasion throughout the conflict and northern Louisiana also remained in Confederate hands. There was talk in both states of continuing the fight. Some Confederate soldiers from Lee and Johnston's armies refused parole and headed West of their own accord in the hopes of joining up with General Edmund Kirby-Smith.

General Edmund Kirby-Smith was a veteran of the Mexican War and also warfare against the Comanche on the Texas frontier. He was a brigadier general at Bull Run and inflicted a stunning defeat upon Federal forces at Richmond, Kentucky, in 1862. He commanded and held together the Trans-Mississippi Department from early 1863 on, most of which time the Department was cut off from the rest of the Confederacy. Kirby-Smith defeated Banks's Red River Campaign into North Louisiana and intended to lead to the invasion of East Texas. All this is to say that Kirby-Smith had a record of success. Many felt that an army of stalwart Texans and Louisianans, led by Kirby-Smith, could stave off defeat.

The *Galveston Daily News* of April 8, 1865, carried a front-page article entitled "Washington County Mass Meeting," which described a gathering at the Courthouse in Brenham on April 3. The paper reported that the people resolved:

> That the only alternative presented to us in the struggle in which we are engaged are perfect independence or complete subjugation; and in that form we accept the issue.... we can look with calmness upon the disasters of the present hour ... we find nothing to repeat or regret in the course we then pursued ... we count nothing as lost.... confident of the justness of our cause ... That the indomitable spirit which animates the soldiers in the field and in the trenches, as manifested in their resolutions recently adopted in Virginia and at Mobile, is shared by the people at home.[23]

General Lee met with General Grant at Appomattox on April 9, the day after the article appeared in the *Galveston Daily News*, to discuss the terms of surrender of his Army of Northern Virginia.

If Texas was to hold out against the Federals, unity was a necessity. But Texas was in a terrible state. While Lee's Army of Northern Virginia and Hood's Army of Tennessee fought bloody battle after bloody battle hoping to stave off defeat, the Confederates in the West fought one another. Officers bickered, feuded and even dueled.

All acknowledged that Texas had not yet surrendered. Some still doubted the news of Lee's surrender, while others insisted on continuing the fighting. The debate raged among civilians and military.

Waller's Cavalry had been back in Texas since November 1864.[24] Captain W. A. McDade was in command by this time. The Houston *Tri-Weekly Telegraph* referred to the Chappell Hill man as "a much respected, though young officer."[25] Dunn's Company was assigned to Waller's Battalion in December 1864. Private Thomas T. Shapard of Chappell Hill, who had enlisted in 1861 at the age of 16, was among Dunn's soldiers. Confederate authorities in Texas sent Waller's Thirteenth and Brown's Thirty-Fifth Texas Cavalry to north Texas on April 13, 1865. Captain Robert Hargrove of Chappell Hill commanded Company B of Brown's Battalion. He left Hood's Brigade to recruit the unit in 1862. There were several Chappell Hill boys in Hargrove's command, including his brother John, George Chappell and George Keesee. These men and their comrades-in-arms were under orders to arrest the men of the Fourth Texas Regiment of the so-called Arizona Brigade, C. S. A.

The Arizona Brigade originally was raised for the capture of Arizona, but never

14. Texas at the Close of the War

fought in that theater. Sibley's ill-fated expedition was the last Confederate threat to Federal control over the American Southwest. Many of the men recruited for the Arizona Brigade were draft evaders and deserters from the "no-man's land" between Texas and New Mexico. Discipline was lax from the beginning, but the situation became serious when the Fourth was assigned to north Texas along the Red River in late 1864. The Confederacy was no longer able to provide sufficient provisions for its armies or pay them. Good men overlooked the hardships and fought on, but gangs of men from the Fourth responded by looting and murdering.[26] The last action of McDade's and Waller's Cavalry, as a result, was against fellow Confederate soldiers, albeit bad ones.

Waller's and Brown's Cavalry covered as many as 30 miles a day. Only the commanding officers knew the purpose of the expedition and there was much speculation among the men under their command. When the objective was presented to the regiment, the Houston *Tri-Weekly Telegraph* opined:

> This was not a work so agreeable as fighting Yankees. The faces of some of Waller's veterans became a little soured at the intelligence. It would have suited them better to be on a campaign into Missouri.[27]

There would be no more daring invasions of Missouri. The days of Sterling Price's glorious visions were long past. The *Tri-Weekly Telegraph* proudly reported that the soldiers "prompted by duty, that noble and indispensable quality of a soldier, they did their part well."[28] The veteran troopers rode nearly 300 miles to confront the Arizona Brigade. There was no forage over more than half of that distance, but the horses managed on grass. The Arizona Brigade had some sense of pending confrontation, but had no idea that the cavalry sent to return them were upon them. They awoke on the morning of May 3 to find their camp surrounded with no chance of escape. One of their captors wrote sympathetically of them:

> These heavy clouds of war had not quenched all love of country. They therefore gave up almost without a murmur.... Their declaration was that they would have preferred marching to Houston without a guard. The general opinion among our boys is that these men have been censured for many things of which they were ignorant to this day.... The mistake committed, if any there be, is in granting permission to raise a regiment for any special purpose.... It is hardly thought that the capture of Baird's command was the best work of the campaign.[29]

Waller's and Brown's Cavalry escorted the captured renegades to Houston. Much had happened by the time they arrived in Houston,.

The Houston *Tri-Weekly Telegraph* on April 22, 1865, reported Lee's surrender to Grant at Appomattox. The editor of the paper had acknowledged one week earlier that the report of Lee's evacuation of Richmond and Petersburg "is most likely true."[30] The paper printed the following on April 24: "Disaster more fatal than our worst apprehension has fallen upon the army of Virginia. Its great and noble commander and all its officers and soldiers have yielded to the adverse fate of war and surrendered."[31] The adjacent column reported on the "Great War Meeting in Houston."

The *Telegraph* reported "a spirit of resistance."³² The citizens of Houston and the surrounding region gathered at the courthouse. The facility could not handle one-tenth of the crowd and the speakers addressed the vast crowd from the outside balcony of the post office.

Colonel George Washington Carter was among the speakers at the Houston gathering. He retained his stature among Texans. A petition by the Citizens of Washington County published in the March 20, 1865, *Galveston Tri-Weekly News* reported:

> [M]any gentlemen of different counties have determined to propose COL. G. W. CARTER for the next Governor of the State. No man should be proposed, except with a single eye to the good of the State and the Confederacy in the present crisis. We must have a man of large mental capacity, of undoubted patriotism and who will not and cannot be overcome by the vicissitudes, actual or possible, of these perilous times. Col. Carter possesses these qualifications in an eminent degree. He has devoted his whole life to the Southern cause.³³

However, not everyone agreed. The Houston *Telegraph* ran a column on April 24, 1865, criticizing the "Col. Carter for Governor" movement and suggesting, "the good colonel has thousands of equals in Texas."³⁴

The eloquent Carter stirred the crowd gathered that day in Houston. He reminded them that the Confederacy still had several hundred thousand more soldiers in the field and asked, "Are we whipped with all these troops?" He urged Texans to "stick fast to our principles—to stand by our colors and our cause. Hold in readiness all the troops in the Department until we get an honorable peace."³⁵ Carter reminded the people, "We can't be whipped unless we whip ourselves!"³⁶

Colonel Clayton Gillespie, a colleague of Carter at Chappell Hill before the war, spoke to the crowd next. Gillespie cautioned the people, "Upon the impulse given now may hang the turning point."³⁷ He assured his listeners that he would never change his sentiment about the war and would live under Yankee rule only by force. Gillespie told the crowd with dramatic flourish that he would rather share a common grave with his family than submit. He pleaded that they consider, "The loss of an army is not the loss of a nation. This is our first great disaster."³⁸ Gillespie did his best to convince the people gathered that, "Johnston, Hardee, Taylor and our other Generals will all become greater now."³⁹ He chided those on medical disability and other exceptions and urged all men to fight.

Rumors began to circulate that General Johnston had surrendered. There was disbelief among Texans, as they recognized that without Johnston there was little realistic hope for continuing the fight. Men reasoned that surely Johnston would not pass up this opportunity to finally eclipse Lee.⁴⁰ The *Tri-Weekly Telegraph* was speculating by May 11 that perhaps Lee and Johnston had not surrendered the heart of their armies. The editor argued that, despite the loss of Lee's and Johnston's armies,

> the great bulk of our forces east of the Chattahoochie have not been surrendered, have refused to surrender and are yet available for the defence of the cause.⁴¹

Edmund Kirby-Smith, commanding Confederate forces in the Trans-Mississippi Department, was offered on May 8 the same terms as Grant gave Lee at Appomattox.

14. Texas at the Close of the War

He outright rejected the offer. Kirby-Smith had the support of several of his top officers, who wanted to continue the fight. He left his headquarters at Shreveport to meet with the various Trans-Mississippi Confederate Governors in Marshall, Texas. Kirby-Smith decided with their support and encouragement to continue the fight. The *Telegraph* of May 16 declared:

> In union there is strength and the union of the people and soldiers is now of the utmost importance. If all we are united, if all we stand firm, there will be no trouble.[42]

General Edmund Kirby-Smith announced on May 18 his plans to move to Houston, headquarters for the Texas department of the Trans-Mississippi, to gather his core following. He left Shreveport two days later. It seemed that the war was not yet over for Texas. Meanwhile, Federal troops began to gather for the invasion of Texas as the final episode of the war.

Colonel Franklin Wilkes made his way from New Orleans in the midst of this tense setting and entered Federal Army lines at Rodney, Mississippi, on April 20, 1865. He wrote a most interesting letter, dated April 27, in New Orleans to Colonel F. A. Starring, the provost marshal:

> I have the honour to state that I am a Confederate Officer (on parole) with the rank of Colonel of Cavalry. I came into the lines of the United States forces at Rodney, Miss. on the 20th under the flag of truce. My object in coming within your lines was to have a consultation with Major Genl. Banks, Comdg. Dept. of the Gulf, on questions involving the interests of the State of Texas of which I am a citizen. It is proper that in this communication I should state that I am not an accredited agent of either the Civil authorities of the State or of the military authorities of the Confederate States. I represent the views of quite a large number of influential gentlemen who have held high civil and military positions in the State and army — and in the Congress & Senate of the Confederacy. The specific object of my interview with the Maj. Genl. Commdg. was to learn from him the probable policy of the U. States Government towards the State of Texas in the event of that State's giving satisfactory assurances that her citizens were no longer in arms against the authority or government of the U. States and such other evidences of loyalty to the General Government as are shown by States sustaining their "proper relations" to the National Authority.... She ceases her opposition to the Genl. Government. That State Government loyal to the General Government will be respected and that under these circumstances the Military forces of the United States would not be a hostile power to the State of Texas. I have now to ask that you grant me a permit and such facilities as may be convenient to pop out of your lines into the State of Texas so that this matter may be fairly presented to the authorities and citizens of Texas. Being unaccredited I can of course make no pledges as to the final decisions of the State; but on my responsibility and in behalf of those whose views I represent I pledge that a fair and rigorous (and I think successful) effort shall be made at once for peace on the terms offered by the U. States; And that the responsibility of further bloodshed shall be with the State of Texas.

Wilkes ended his direct proposal with:

> One word of personal interest must be left on record here. It is this; It was my intention to come within your lines and apply for the Amnesty Oath but late events and consultations induces me to forego that personal privilege in the hopes of securing my state against the desolations of invasion, believing that as a Confederate I can be more successful in my efforts that I could be if I were to accept the Amnesty at present. I am your obd. Servt. F. Wilkes.[43]

Wilkes was not alone in such efforts to avert further bloodshed. Various Confederate civil and military authorities were making similar overtures to representatives of the Federal government as Kirby-Smith was heading to Houston. However, as Federal authorities had no interest in piecemeal surrender, they did not pay serious attention to either Wilkes or the others.

The Houston *Tri-Weekly Telegraph* printed a number of rousing letters supporting a continuation of the fighting. The edition of May 24 printed a resolution from Sul Ross's Cavalry Brigade:

> determined to continue battling for our rights until we have achieved that independence for which we are striving ... this brigade will never be subjugated so long as there is room to load a gun or face a foe ... and claim as a soldier's right, to say when this war shall cease.[44]

There were other similar resolutions printed, including one by the Twentieth Texas Infantry.[45]

Major General Thomas C. Hindman commanded a division in Polk's corps at Chickamauga and Chattanooga. He was invalided after an eye injury at the Battle of Atlanta. Hindman wrote from San Antonio, urging Texans to consider:

> the circumstances to which Lee and Johnston succumbed do not touch the Trans-Mississippi country. It is in itself an imperial dominion, worthy of a distinct nationality, and possessed of the elements with which to achieve it.[46]

He closed his long letter, "With the blessing of Stonewall Jackson's God, we can and will make our homes and kindred free."[47]

Most realized, beneath the surface of the patriotism and courageous calls to rally, that to fight on was fruitless and would only lead to unnecessary further bloodshed. The *Tri-Weekly Telegraph* of May 24 acknowledged:

> The confused, disorderly division of Government property among the soldiers, that has been going on for several weeks all over the country, from Hempstead to Shreveport, commenced here yesterday morning.[48]

More disciplined soldiers in camps began to debate with their officers the practicality of continuing the fight. Many men just wanted to put an end to the killing and return to their families. Texas troops from Louisiana gathered at Camp Groce near Hempstead, not far from Chappell Hill. Walker's Texas Division arrived there on April 15 and awaited orders into May. When word reached of Lee's, Johnston's and Taylor's surrenders and then of Kirby-Smith's capitulation,

14. Texas at the Close of the War

> They commenced leaving their camps, not furtively in the night, but openly in the daytime. It was not with a disaffected spirit in mutiny against their superior officers; but ... the manning of the boat any longer was seen to be hopeless, and the personal safety of each one ... was the common concern.[49]

One veteran of many fights with Walker's Texas Division remembered:

> Curse, deep and bitter, fell from lips not accustomed to such language; while numbers, both officers and men, swore fearful oaths never to surrender. It was such a scene as one seldom cares to witness.[50]

He wrote of unbearable humiliation and the dead left behind. Most of the soldiers left or were preparing to leave on May 19. Those remaining were formally discharged on May 20, 1865.

> Many put their arms around each other's necks, and sobbed like children; others gave the strong grasp of the hand, and silently went away with hearts too full for utterance; while still others would mutter a huskily-spoken "Good-bye" or deep oath. ... their hearts were linked together in bands of steel, with ties unspeakable, inexpressible ... the parting—perhaps for years, perhaps forever—wrong their souls with tortured agony.[51]

Kirby-Smith's generals, who had remained in Shreveport when he headed to Houston, went to New Orleans on May 25. They agreed, subject to Kirby-Smith's approval, to surrender by the Appomattox terms. Kirby-Smith for his part found Houston in chaos. Confederate soldiers were on a rampage, ransacking Confederate stores. Large numbers of men were deserting and heading home. These events convinced Kirby-Smith that the end had come. He no longer had control of his command, either the officers or the men, such that he could concentrate them. Kirby-Smith went aboard a U.S. navy vessel off Galveston on June 2 and formally surrendered the Trans-Mississippi Army. The war was finally over for everyone. He made clear in his farewell address, published in the *Galveston Tri-Weekly News* three days later, that, "I intended to struggle to the last; and with an army united in purpose, firm in resolve, and battling for the right, I believe God would yet give us victory." He expressed his disappointment that, "I reached here to find the Texas troops disbanded and hastening to their homes." And he bitterly reprimanded the soldiers and populace who had "forsaken their colors and ... abandoned the cause.... You have made your choice. It was unwise and unpatriotic."[52]

Word of the end of the hostilities traveled slowly. Brigadier General James E. Slaughter, commanding the Western Sub-District of Texas, and Colonel "Rip" Ford met with Federal Major General Lew Wallace in southernmost Texas at Port Isabel on March 11, 1865, to arrange an end to the fighting. Although tentative agreement was reached, Major General John Walker in Houston sharply rebuked Slaughter for meeting with the Federals.[53] Consequently, despite developments further up the coast of which they were unaware, these soldiers prepared to continue the fight, as ordered.

The Confederate command sent Ford to the Rio Grande in mid–1864. The sale of Texas cotton in Mexico was critical to the obtaining desperately needed weapons and other military supplies. Ford's "Cavalry of the West"[54] was made of older men and young boys, as well as deserters and outlaws. Terrell A. Jackson of Chappell Hill was among them. The veteran of the Mexican War was already 38 years of age when the War Between the States broke out in 1861. He was a man of some prominence in the community. The older Jackson stayed behind when the young men went off to fight. Jackson became embroiled in a legal dispute with the Confederate government in mid–1863. The threat of a Federal advance caused Confederate military authorities to order the burning of the steamboat *Wave*, owned by Jackson, in May 1863 to prevent it from falling into enemy hands. Jackson requested payment of $30,000 for the loss of his boat, to which Major-General Richard Taylor replied that the steamboat was not removed after receiving notice to do so.

Terrell Jackson overcome his anger and signed up when George H. Giddings, who operated the San Antonio-Santa Fe mail line before the war, organized a battalion of Texas Cavalry to serve under Ford. He and W. G. Keesee were among the Chappell Hill men who signed up with Giddings. Giddings' Battalion proceeded south to the Rio Grande Valley and was involved in its first action at Rancho Las Rinas in June 1864. The Federals subsequently withdrew most of their force from the Rio Grande Valley in July 1864, leaving only a small contingent at Brazos Santiago on Brazos Island to blockade the mouth of the Rio Grande. The Confederates transported cotton into and out of Mexico through Brownsville, which they controlled, and through the Mexican port of Bagdad with no further Federal interference.

The Federal force at Brazos Santiago crossed to the mainland and moved towards Brownsville when word of Lee's surrender reached the Rio Grande Valley in May 1865. The Federals were not expecting resistance, having understood that the Confederates were evacuating Brownsville. While some Confederates left and headed home, most stayed to continue the fight. A skirmish ensued when the Federals encountered a company of Confederate cavalry on May 12, 1865, at Palmito Ranch. Both sides rushed troops to support and the fighting escalated. Ford ordered an assault. Giddings' Battalion attacked the Federal left flank. The Confederates routed the Federal troops, who fell back toward the coast. The fighting lasted four hours until the Federals finally stabilized their line with the help of reinforcements. Even as this, the last land engagement of the war, was being fought, the Confederate governors of Trans-Mississippi were agreeing to end resistance. A few days later, a truce was arranged and the war was over in Texas. Terrell Jackson and W. G. Keesee headed home to Chappell Hill to join their family and friends and fellow townspeople, who had been gone for so long.

The war was over for the boys of Chappell Hill.

15

Texas Homecomings

The men of Chappell Hill headed home from the war. They had left the plow and the classroom, the store and the plantation, as young men dreaming of glory. Their enthusiasm and swagger faded over time, as they became veteran soldiers, accustomed to the rigors and the horror of war. The various reasons that motivated men to enlist had become distant memories in the final months of the war. Many men on either side simply wanted to survive and be able to return home to loved ones. Dick Swearingen expressed his feelings in his narrative written after the war:

> [O]ur Bonnie Blue flag … the joyful emotions which thrilled my heart and swelled my soul that lovely morning when my eyes rested upon that silken emblem of a noble people. Dear fallen but still glorious banner, never, never will you dance from those grand old cliffs with mountain breeze. No more will you stream above blazing ranks and reeling columns. Your stars, all fringed with silver clouds and gilded sorrows, have gone to a night that will have no dewy morn nor radiant East.[1]

The returning Confederates could hold their heads high, knowing they had not shirked their duty. Still, the agony of defeat was oppressive. Many could not imagine that their own sacrifices and the lives of so many dear friends had been in vain. The emotions of lost youth and dead friends mixed with the sweet joy of reunion with family.

The small bands of soldiers returning home became smaller as each man reached the turn for his hometown and, ultimately, for his home. Comrades-in-arms bid sad goodbyes to one another and moved on. Their mood generally was sober, if not sad.

The war ended for Captain Richard Swearingen when General Joseph E. Johnston surrendered to General William T. Sherman at Bennett Place, North Carolina, in April 1865. His Company K "did not possess a tent or wagon, or anything in the shape of a cooking vessel"[2] for the last year of the conflict. They dreamed of the hearth back home. Captain Swearingen, in abiding by the terms of the parole, led his company back to Tennessee before disbanding. The last muster was held on the banks of the French Broad River. The farewell was described as follows:

> For three years those men had shared each other's dangers, and under the shadow of a common sorrow, the humiliation of a hopeless defeat, they were to look for the last time upon each other. The commanding officer [Captain Swearingen], whose route at that point diverged from the one to be taken by the company, fronted them into line and tried to call the roll, but failed to do so. He then moved around by the roadside and they filed by, one at a time, and shook his hand. There was a profound silence; no one attempted to speak a word, and every eye was filled with tears, as the curtain rolled slowly upon the saddest act in that long and well-played drama of war.[3]

Dick and Jennie Swearingen tried to begin a new life. They recognized that eastern Tennessee would be dangerous for them after the war so they settled in Lee County, Virginia. Their new home was a distance of only 20 miles from Jennie's family home in Sneedville, Tennessee. Dick found work teaching in a country school. Their new life did not last. Word reached Swearingen before the year was out that Governor Brownlow of Tennessee had requested of Governor Pierpont of Virginia the arrest and transfer of Captain Richard Swearingen, formerly of the C.S.A. Dick Swearingen had no idea for what offense he was being indicted. He was certain that there would be no due process in eastern Tennessee.

Word of his desperate situation reached Texas. John Thomas Swearingen had a debt to pay to his older brother. He returned to Texas after older brother Richard took his place in the Tennessee Cavalry and joined brother Patrick in the Twenty-Fourth Texas Cavalry. John Thomas, along with brother Patrick, was captured at Arkansas Post and was a prisoner for a time at Camp Butler in Springfield, Illinois. John Thomas, after being paroled, rose to the rank of sergeant and saw considerable action.[4] It was a battle-hardened fighting man who rode to the aid of his older brother, Richard. Richard Swearingen wrote in his narrative of the war:

> About 10 o'clock the first night after closing the school, while the husband and wife were discussing the situation, a rap upon the door and an unforgotten voice announced the arrival of the young brother, who four years before had been found at Cumberland Gap, only a few miles from the place of their second meeting. J. T. Swearingen had heard of his brother's dangerous surroundings, and selling about all of his earthly possessions to get funds for the trip, went to his relief. The next morning R. M. Swearingen left his wife in safe hands and started for Texas. At Huntsville, Alabama, he waited (as had been previously planned) the arrival of those left in Virginia, and with bright faces, they journeyed on to Alta Vista where the best of all good sisters, Mrs. Helen M. Kirby, received them with open arms.[5]

15. Texas Homecomings

Dick Swearingen, having returned to the relative safety of Washington County, Texas, could see that a legal career would be difficult, at least for a time, for a paroled Confederate officer in the occupied South. He and Jennie went to New Orleans, where he enrolled in the school of medicine. He graduated in March 1867 and delivered the valedictory address.[6] Then he and Jennie headed home to Chappell Hill.

Henry Brandt, Herman Knolle and many other Texans were held prisoner at Camp Morton in Indianapolis, Indiana, ever since their capture at Vicksburg in mid–1863. The winter of 1864–1865 was less harsh than the previous one. Yet, 117 prisoners died in January and another 133 in February. Federal authorities began to make arrangements for exchanges to relieve the suffering of prisoners from both sides by late 1864. The end of the war was imminent. Grant was tightening his siege around Petersburg and Richmond. There was a general realization that enough Americans had already died. Two thousand prisoners were led out of Camp Morton during February and March 1865. Henry Brandt was going home. Herman Knolle spoke for many when he described his reactions:

HENRY C. BRANDT. Henry Brandt arrived in Galveston, Texas, from Germany in December 1856 at the age of 18. Brandt settled inland at Chappell Hill, where he worked as a carpenter and builder — a trade in which he had apprenticed in Germany. He married Laura Jane Burns in 1860. Henry Christian Brandt enlisted in Waul's Legion on April 4, 1862. He was taken prisoner in the Vicksburg Campaign and spent the duration of the war in a prisoner of war camp. (Courtesy of Fred and Mary Brandt of Chappell Hill, Texas.)

> Feb. 2 — it rained very hard and in the hardest kind of rain 500 of us were searched, we were then put under guard and were sent away on Feb. 26 on an exchange. Words cannot express the joy I felt as I walked out of the gate and was at last once more on the road to be free.[7]

The war was over by the beginning of April and Camp Morton ceased to exist by June 1865. Approximately 26,000, or 12 percent of the 214,000 Confederates that were imprisoned during the War Between the States, died. While none of the men from Chappell Hill lost their lives during imprisonment, they would never forget the experience.

Knolle marched out of Camp Morton on February 26, 1865. He wrote of near-starvation on the trip from Indiana. There were so many men being moved that there was never more than just enough room for a man to sit down in the boxcars, from the beginning of the trip to the end. Knolle's journey home from Richmond, Virginia, involved traversing 1,600 miles. Men caught rides on trains when they could. They had no choice but to walk, more often than not. Herman Knolle did not arrive home in Texas until September 4, 1865.

Henry Brandt left Camp Morton just before his cousin Herman Knolle, departing on February 19, 1865. Brandt had been married to his wife Laura just over a year when he went off to war with Waul's Legion. Their son, Frederick Dennis, was born on March 19, 1861, just days before Henry went off to war,[8] and had grown into a sturdy young boy, nearly four years of age, when his father started home from Camp Morton in Indiana. Brandt and his traveling comrades traveled through Baltimore, Maryland, to Point Lookout, Maryland, where the prisoners were exchanged.[9] Brandt arrived at Richmond, Virginia, on March 2. The Federal siege of Richmond and Petersburg was in its ninth month. Brandt passed through Fortress Monroe on Virginia's eastern shore and then the vast Union supply depot at City Point on the James River. The massive Union buildup must have convinced Brandt that the end was near. Henry Brandt, having just endured and survived a horrific prison stay, was thinking only of seeing his wife Laura in the flower-covered rolling hills around Chappell Hill, Texas.

Brandt left Richmond on the evening of March 5, 1865, by train, even as Grant was tightening his siege lines around the Confederate capital. One of the main lifelines for supplies into Richmond and Petersburg was up from Greensboro, North Carolina, through Danville. The train on which Henry Brandt was traveling arrived at Danville, 100-plus miles to the southwest, on the following morning. Brandt was on a train to Greensboro two hours later and arrived there that evening. He had escaped the gauntlet. Johnston and Sherman were fighting off to the east and Brandt's way home was clear.

Henry traveled to Charlotte from Greensboro, then to Chester, South Carolina. Brandt's journey became more difficult after Chester. Brandt set off on foot for Newberry, South Carolina, on March 12. He was in the company of three men, P. B. K. Thompson, Robert Drane and John Moore. Moore may have served in Voight's Company with Brandt and all four may have been released from Camp Morton. Day after day, the men moved westward.

> March 16th started this morning at 6 o'clock ... walked to Savannah river by 12 ½ o'clock, are waiting now to get across the river ... crossed the river at 3 p.m. ... walked till dark and took supper and then went on again and walked til 11 p.m. went to a house and sleped till 4 a.m. next morning[10]

15. Texas Homecomings

HENRY BRANDT HOME. Henry Christian Brandt purchased this house in 1860. His wife Laura lived here during the war, awaiting his safe return from prisoner of war camp. Henry and Laura lived in the house until 1893 when they sold it to Providence Baptist Church. The structure, located on Chappell Hill's Main Street, is now the Visitor Reception Center. (Photograph by Thomas G. Stevens of Chappell Hill.)

The four traveling companions reached Macon, Georgia, on March 19. The group parted company. Thompson and Moore went one way, Brandt and Drane the other. Brandt and Drane reached the home of a cousin of Drane's on the next night. They spent the next two days resting. They moved on and arrived at the home of Judge Drane on March 22, where they remained for four days before continuing their journey home. Henry Brandt and Robert Drane made their way to Jackson, Mississippi, by the end of March. They spent the night of the April 1 "with Mr. McNair, free of charge." The night of April 2 "with a Mr. Clark were splendetly treated free of charge." The two soldiers "got Breakfast at Miss Debenport House free of charge ... stayed all night with Mrs. Valentine free of charge" on April 3, 1865. Brandt and Drane had no idea that General Lee evacuated Richmond on April 2 and was retreating towards Appomattox.

Henry Brandt and his friend covered 20 to 25 miles on a good day of walking. They walked all day in the rain on some days, slogging through the mud, and made much less progress. Brandt and Drane parted ways at Port Gibson. Robert Drane took a turn for home and Henry Brandt continued on to Texas on his own.

Henry Brandt arose from his bed at 5:30 on the morning of April 10 in Alexandria, Louisiana. Lee was surrendering to Grant at Appomattox, back east. Brandt walked 20 miles, slipping and sliding and sticking in the mud. He finally crossed the Sabine River at Burr's Ferry at 6 A.M. on April 14. The far bank was Texas soil.

Henry Brandt arrived home at Chappell Hill at 3 P.M. on April 24, 1865. The bluebonnets likely were past their peak, but Henry must have been excited to see even a single bluebonnet along the road. He had traveled over 1,600 miles, the trip taking the better part of two months. Henry Brandt was joyfully reunited with his wife, Laura, and their four-year-old son Dennis. He received a discharge, signed by Confederate General John Magruder in Houston on May 26, 1865.[11] The Brandt house remains standing on Chappell Hill's Main Street to this day.

Hosea Garrett survived Hood's disastrous Tennessee campaign and turned home toward Chappell Hill. He had no way of expecting what happened. As he had expressed to his Uncle Hosea from Atlanta, there had been little word from family since he had left home for war. Consequently, no one heard from him and some began to wonder if he had survived the bloody ordeal at Franklin where so many good men had died. What further confused the family was one Milton Bell, also of Chappell Hill. Bell returned home and related how Lt. Hosea Garrett had died on the battlefield in his arms. He went so far as to describe how he laid the hero to rest in his grave and buried him. A Garrett family member wrote:

> This made us all feel very kindly to Milton Bell, to think he had been with your father in his dying moments, trying to relive his sufferings. Bell was looked upon by all the neighborhood as well as by the relatives as a hero.[12]

As a result, when Hosea Garrett did return home some time later, no one expected him. Further, the war had sufficiently changed Garrett such that none recognized their beloved family member. A cousin wrote that Hosea

> came to Grandpa's on foot in the night, a little after supper-time, and shouted "Hello!" When Grandpa came to the door, he asked permission to stay all night. His request was granted, and he sat around the fire for an hour, talking to Grandpa and Grandma without being recognized. Finally, he got to joking and teasing, and Grandma recognized him and nearly hugged him to death. Although it was bedtime, the news of his return spread like wildfire, and all the kinfolks were soon on hand to welcome him.[13]

Four years of exposure to the elements, as well as the camp smoke and black powder, changed a young man's face. The marches and many hardships had worn their bodies. Those who left Chappell Hill for the war returned home aged beyond their years. Their eyes were never again the same. They had seen so much suffering and death, the gruesome contortions of the dead across a field of battle. These experiences tended to remove the bright-eyed optimism of young men. Men grieved for longtime friends, who had died alongside them. The sadness which the survivors carried never completely left them.

15. Texas Homecomings

John Jackson of Terry's Texas Rangers started home for Chappell Hill after Johnston's surrender to Sherman. He spent time in Alabama with distant relatives on his way home. As a result, it was not until November 1865 that Jackson set out for Chappell Hill.

> When he rode up to his father's gate he asked if he could stay all night. His father, not recognizing him, said he could if he had the money to pay his bill, although as a matter of fact Terrell J. Jackson had never charged a man for such accommodations in all his life. His family thought the boy was dead and were not expecting even his ghost to appear. But when the family dog recognized him and jumped the fence and leaped to greet him, all the strangeness was dispelled, and the young man was received with joy and thanksgiving and figuratively at least dined upon the fatted calf.[14]

John Jackson found his father's business affairs in near ruin. The Washington County Railroad Company, in which his father had invested so much, had collapsed during the long war. "Terrell J. Jackson was very despondent, saying that all his property would be confiscated by the Yankees and it was no use to make further effort."[15] John worked hard and settled his family debts. He built up his own estate and returned to raising horses: "at one time he had a fine race track and he himself was the owner of some very fast horses."[16] His farm became one of the first on which experiments were carried out with regard to truck growing in the area.[17]

The homecoming was not so joyous for all of the Chappell Hill families. James Fiske "Doc" Matthews of Terry's Texas Rangers had a mission at the end of the war. He had been with his best friend, Daniel Harvie Browning, when Browning died at Knoxville in 1863. Matthews and Browning's manservant had buried the body and carefully marked the grave before withdrawing from the field a year and a half earlier. Matthews was determined to bring his friend back home to Chappell Hill.

Locating a grave was challenge enough. Transporting the remains home was another matter. James Matthews located a local man near the battlefield and engaged his services to disinfect the remains. The process was more involved and more expensive than embalming, but the Brownings spared no expense. After the body was cleaned and disinfected, it was set into a disinfecting case for the long ride home.[18] James Fiske Matthews accomplished his objective. Daniel Harvie Browning was reburied in Chappell Hill's Atkinson Cemetery at the western edge of the Browning Plantation. The inscription on Daniel's tombstone reads "brief and glorious was his career." James Fiske Matthews, having completed his journey home with Daniel's body, married Daniel's sister, Mattie Browning, on the Fourth of July, 1867. They inherited and moved into the Browning manor home. Annie Matthews married Martin Kenney, formerly a captain in George Washington Carter's Twenty-First Texas Cavalry.[19] The Confederates of Chappell Hill began a new life.

A. J. Robinson and his comrades from the famed Val Verde Battery headed back to Texas when the war ended. They served proudly in Louisiana during the war, preventing Federal intentions of advancing overland into Texas. The group planned to disband in San Antonio. However, when several men from Fairfield reached home and decided to not go any further, the battery disbanded in that Texas town. The men buried their four artillery pieces in the dirt floor of a buggy house in Fairfield. They would retrieve the pieces long after Reconstruction. One three-inch ordnance rifle survives to this day, resting on the lawn of the Fairfield County Courthouse. A second for many years stood at the Confederate reunion ground near Mexia. A. J. Robinson rode on home to Chappell Hill alone, proud of his accomplishment of having served in such a famous unit.

The transition to civilian life was a difficult one after the Confederate soldiers returned home to Chappell Hill. Most endeavored to live a good life, having survived a war that had claimed the lives of 600,000 soldiers, among them neighbors, friends and beloved family members. The daily routine of the farm, the workshop, the schoolroom or even the courtroom could never compare to the rush of combat and the camaraderie formed under fire. One of Terry's Texas Rangers wrote of his comrades, "some of them would never be quite tame again."[20] One imagines the men had grown in wisdom. It is unlikely any of them ever again took for granted the sheer joy of a family picnic by the creek or the beauty of a field of Texas bluebonnets in the spring. Men who had suffered so much, lost so many friends and seen so much death and destruction could recognize the gift that a quiet day was.

The *Galveston Daily News* reported to its readers on September 21, 1865, that Robert E. Lee, in accepting the presidency at Washington College in Virginia, wrote a letter

> in which he says that it is the duty of every citizen, in the present condition of the country, to do all in his power to aid in the restoration of harmony and peace, and in no way to oppose the policy of either the State Government, or of the general government, which is directed to that object.[21]

Many agreed with Robert E. Lee. There was much work to be done. John Hargrove was with Elmore's Twentieth Texas Infantry when they were paroled at Richmond, Texas, on May 25, 1865. Hargrove moved back home and wrote in his memoirs, "I did not have a horse, cow, hog, nor any chickens."[22]

Alexander Thompson owned a dry goods store in Chappell Hill with his brother Charles before the war. Both served with Elmore's Twentieth Texas Infantry at Galveston. Charles moved to Wheelock after the war's end. Alexander expanded his business to Galveston as A. B. Thompson & Co., Commission Merchants. They took consignments of shipments unloaded from steamships.

William S. Oldham, Jr., wrote Alexander Thompson in November 1865, seeking employment. Oldham was a student at Chappell Hill's Soule University before the war. He enlisted in Terry's Texas Rangers, but was later promoted to first lieutenant on General Sam Bell Maxey's staff. The Oldham family had influence. Judge William S. Oldham, Sr., represented Washington County at the secession convention and was later one of the signers of the Confederate Constitution and one of Texas' two senators to the Confederate Congress. He made his home in Chappell Hill and traveled between Chappell Hill and Richmond between sessions.[23]

15. Texas Homecomings

Young Oldham wrote Thompson:

> Since the grand discharge of our unfortunate army I have been doing nothing, could find nothing to do that would bring me a decent support, like a great many others of the unfortunate Confederate band. I have been blown about upon the waters of adversity like a storm beaten bark, with no rudder by which to stem the fierce and angry winds of destiny, and they have certainly driven me about without mercy.[24]

Oldham told how he had been in Houston that summer and found it impossible to obtain employment of any kind, "as the City was filled with persons in my own situation and seeking employment similar to myself."[25] He remarked that some were content to accept employment that allowed them board and clothes, but that he felt his services were worth a little more than that. Oldham wrote how he "buried myself for a few months in the solitudes of Brazos bottom where I obtained money enough on the cotton fields to bring me here to the gay capital of the Lone Star State."[26] In fact, conditions in Austin were little different than those in Houston and Oldham remarked, "Dame Fortune frowned grimly upon me with a clouded brow."[27]

Oldham reminded Thompson that he had known him as a schoolboy at Chappell Hill and could judge his merit. As with so many veterans through time, he had no other experience but military to offer his prospective employer, putting forward "the only place I have ever done any business was in the Adjutant Genls. Office, and I think I did my duty to the satisfaction of the Generals I was with."[28] He sent a copy of the general's endorsement. Oldham appealed for whatever help Thompson could offer, adding, "I hope fate may now place you in my condition."[29]

Confederates relied on old comrades and family friends to get themselves back on their feet. One by one, they helped each other and restored their lives to some semblance of comfort. Many never lived to see the return of the prosperity from before the war. For the most part, they were simply happy to be alive and among loved ones.

Some of the defeated Confederates could not surrender, nor would they accept occupation. The homecoming for these men was delayed for as many as 10 years or more. Columns of men moved southward across the border into Mexico as Federal forces moved into Texas at the close of the war. These men included governors and generals, sergeants and privates. Texas governor Pendleton Murrah, Henry Allen of Louisiana and Thomas Reynolds of Missouri were among them. Top-ranking military officers included Sterling Price, Cadmus Wilcox, Thomas Hindman, William Hardeman and John Magruder. General Jo Shelby of Missouri was among the most prominent.

John Millican Buchanan was among the Confederates-in-exile in Mexico. He was a South Carolinian. The Felders were among his neighbors near Orangeburg before moving to Chappell Hill, Texas. Buchanan married Eugenia Mary Felder before the family's move westward to Texas. Buchanan moved his family to Alabama in the second year of the war and joined a Confederate guerrilla band under the command of John Gatewood. The Buchanans lost nearly everything to the soldiers when

Sherman's Army passed through northeastern Alabama on its drive to Atlanta. Andrew, John's son, recalled many years later, "The Yankeys didn't leave us enough corn to make big homeny, but they couldn't use all the pumpins. So we lived on pumkin bread for a month.... You never got so tired of anything in my life."[30]

When Gatewood's band grew to 100 men, they split into two groups, one under Gatewood and the other under Buchanan. They were "all armed with six shooters, one in each boot, one in each sadel [saddle] pocket, 2 in a belt on their wast [waist]."[31] They harassed Sherman's army and dealt harshly with any Yankee foragers they came upon. The killing of four foragers near the Buchanan property led to retribution. Eugenia Mary and the children just escaped a Federal raiding party that surrounded her home that same night and subsequently burned it to the ground.[32] Eugenia took her family west and settled in Mississippi until the end of the war. John Millican was able to rejoin his family only briefly. Sherman was offering a reward for the heads of both Buchanan and Gatewood. The two wanted men headed to safety in Mexico, while Eugenia and her six children continued their journey westward. Their destination was Chappell Hill, Texas, where Eugenia's Felder clan had settled before the war.[33] Eugenia arrived in Chappell Hill, having lost three brothers in the course of the war, one at Second Manassas and two to typhoid fever,[34] as well as her property and her home.

The many Confederates who entered Mexico were permitted to pass after selling their heavy weaponry to Benito Juarez' rebel forces. They presented themselves to French Emperor Maximilian in Mexico City in August 1865. Many subsequently offered their military experience, but only a few were granted commissions. Most moved to settle one of two areas. John Millican Buchanan secured a place for his family in Mexico in the Tuxpan Valley, north of Vera Cruz along the coast. The region was renowned for its sugar cane. He then traveled to Chappell Hill for his family. The Buchanans left Galveston on a 20-ton vessel bound for Tuxpan. The 500 mile voyage lasted 10 days in the course of which the travelers were pounded at sea by three severe storms. The vessel spent three days at the mouth of the Tuxpan River in a hard norther, awaiting a pilot to guide them across the sandbar into the main channel. The captain, having lost his centerboard days earlier, was concerned about drifting in the storm. He chose to navigate blindly rather than wait. Waves swept over the boat time and time again, pounding the boat on the sandbar, but the storm finally thrust the vessel across the bar into safer waters. The party managed to make it upriver and ashore safely. Eugenia Felder sold a gold watch given her by an uncle and with the proceeds, supported her family for the first two months. The entire family set to clearing the land to grow sugar cane from which they would make sugar.[35]

As many as 500 colonists, including Jo Shelby, Sterling Price and William Hardeman, settled in the Cordova District in the state of Vera Cruz, 150 miles south of the Tuxpan Valley. Problems developed from the beginning with the locals, who opposed Maximilian's regime. There were frequent raids and all-out assaults on the settlements. The colonists abandoned their lands by 1867. Some, like Shelby, returned to the United States. Others made their way north to Tuxpan.[36]

The Tuxpan settlements fared better. There were 500 families at Tuxpan in 1869, three years after the first arrival.[37] Physician Gideon Lincecum arrived at Tuxpan in the summer of 1868 and remained until 1873. He wrote in the spring of 1869: "the people are as gay and cheerful as can be ... there are a number of substantial families in the valley who are doing very well."[38] Indications are that the Buchanans were not among them. Eugenia Felder Buchanan wrote her sister in Chappell Hill in April 1869:

> [Y]our letter made us all so happy. I read them out to all and as usual I'd read and then cry a little bit and read ... if you knew what glad hearts we all have when the boat comes and brings us letters you would write often.... We are all getting on very well ... clearing land to plant corn and cane ... will have 8 acres cleared.... The cane yields a great deal of sugar here.

John Millican worked for hire on a farm upriver to support his family, while his sons cleared the family land. The work was hard and progress was slow. It was an isolated existence. There were no roads—a half-hour boat trip was required to visit neighbors. Someone always had to stay behind to watch the property. Eugenia wrote that she was not sure anyone would take anything "but we are not able to lose an old rag yet."[39]

Her most exciting bit of news was in regard to a barrel of flour that had been sent to them from Texas. "We are all so proud of it, just to think we can have biscuits, a rare occurrence here to poor Americans. I am sick and tired of this everlasting corn brad and homony."[40] The letter conveyed resolved determination—"we will have a flourishing colony yet"—but also a plea for family: "I do want Dr. F. to come out and see the country so much.... Do for God sake Lou come to see us. Tell Dr. F. to come out. It will be charity and charity is a great thing."[41]

The settlement struggled on. It became apparent over time that the subsistence existence was not justifiable. Young men began to leave for the United States for formal education. The Buchanan boys returned to Chappell Hill, one by one.[42] John Millican Buchanan remained in Mexico until sometime after 1875. His descendants hold a certificate attesting to his being appointed a Deputy of the National Grange for the State of Vera Cruz, Mexico.[43] The sons of John Millican Buchanan and Eugenia Felder married into the families of Chappell Hill. Samuel Rice Buchanan married Laura Jackson, daughter of John Andrew Jackson, formerly of Terry's Texas Rangers, and Nannie Perkins. John Felder Buchanan married Emma Elliott, daughter of Thomas Elliott, deceased of the Twenty-Fourth Texas Cavalry, and Emma Felder.[44] The last of the families finally returned to Chappell Hill.

16

Occupation and Reconstruction

No state of the late Confederacy was found by the close of the war in such a condition as Texas. Hostile hosts had not invaded her soil. Her society and her industry were intact. Her plantations were conducted as of old, and the black laborers on them were not demoralized, as in other States, by the presence of invading armies.[1]

So wrote Colonel Clayton Crawford Gillespie. All of that changed soon after the hostilities ended.

Encounters with Federal soldiers in Texas were insignificant until the war's end. President Johnson appointed Andrew Jackson Hamilton, a Texan who had served as an officer in the Federal Army, to be governor of Texas on June 17, 1865. The occupation of Texas began two days later when Federal troops landed at Galveston.[2] Federal authorities announced on that day, June 19, 1865, that the slaves had been emancipated. Word spread inland and there was great celebration among the former slaves. The U.S. Army gave notice that all Confederate military and civil officers were to report to be paroled. The Federal soldiers moved into Houston on June 20.[3] George Washington Carter obtained his parole in Houston on June 29.[4] Companies of Federals subsequently moved out from Houston to Hempstead, Brenham and other cities during late June and early July. Lt. Colonel Patrick Henry Swearingen received his parole, signed by Major General Gordon Granger, at Millican, Texas, in southern Brazos County on July 3, 1865.[5] Five companies of the Ninety-Ninth Illinois Regiment made Camp Groce their base.[6] Routine patrols from Hempstead and Brenham passed through Chappell Hill. George Armstrong Custer marched overland into Texas from Louisiana at the head of several thousand Yankee cavalrymen. They foraged at Hempstead during September and October before moving to Austin.[7] This formidable force passed through Chappell Hill and Brenham at the end of October 1865 on their way to Austin. Many Texans remained defiant, even in the face of the soldiers who marched down the main streets of their towns. There was little in the way of Texas hospitality. Thomas Cogley of the Seventh Indiana Cavalry wrote of Texas: "it is a very mean state."[8] Elizabeth Custer, wife of the famed general, wrote that the locals were insulting, ready to fight and well armed.[9] General Phil Sheridan, who assumed command of the Military Division of the Southwest on May 30, 1865,[10] wrote to General Grant, "Texas has not yet suffered from the war and will require some intimidation."[11] He was not far from wrong.

E. H. Cushing had been a staunch advocate of states' rights and Southern nationalism since first becoming editor and publisher of the Houston *Telegraph* in 1856. He overcame numerous obstacles to continue to publish his tri-weekly (later daily) paper through the entire course of the war. Cushing advocated near the end of the war that Texans resist Federal occupation by guerrilla warfare. When Cushing went north to purchase new equipment for his newspaper in the summer of 1865, his careful observations in the course of this trip caused him to change his views. He reversed his stance, advising his readers that acquiescence to the victorious Federal government was advisable. Texans, it seems, were not yet ready to concede defeat. The resulting backlash against Cushing's new position was so strong that he sold his paper in the spring of the following year. The new owners of the *Telegraph* hired Colonel Clayton Crawford Gillespie as their editor. The unreconstructed Confederate used the *Telegraph*'s editorial page to blast radical Republican plans to revolutionize Texan society during the occupation.

A constitutional convention to gain readmission to the Union met in Austin in February and March 1866. Secessionist Texans, who never lost their economic power, quickly recovered political power in the statewide elections of January 8, 1866. They were present in force at the constitutional convention and took a defiant stance, refusing to repudiate the ordinance of secession of 1861, arguing that it was null and void. The members took a similar position on the adoption of the Thirteenth Amendment to the United States Constitution, which concerned the abolition of slavery. They argued that the people of Texas had taken an oath to support the Constitution and that that act sufficed for acquiescence. They intended no formal ratification. Clayton C. Gillespie wrote on June 19, six days before the statewide vote to ratify the convention's proposed changes:

> The people of Texas will never ratify these amendments—we may have to submit to them but it will be the act of others.[12]

Meanwhile, Gillespie blasted the Republican-controlled Congress and told his fellow Texans:

> We are indulging the hope that the mass of the Northern people will, at the next elections, disavow the ultra Radical policy of the Congressional majority.[13]

Clayton C. Gillespie noted the first anniversary of the emancipation of the slaves on June 19, 1866, writing:

We earnestly trust that nothing will be done by the inconsiderate or ill-disposed to interrupt or mar the merry-making of the freedmen. Throughout the war, up to the last hour, the negroes were faithful and dutiful to their masters. That they are now freedmen is not their act, and whatever may be thought of emancipation, it is none of their doing. Let them enjoy its celebration unmolested.... Generosity and kindness to inferiors is a Southern virtue.[14]

He kept up the barrage as the vote of June 25 approached:

Among the changes ... is the conferring on freedmen the right of suffrage. We need not repeat our former declaration that the people of Texas will never ratify an amendment to the Constitution conferring this right on the freedmen. But even supposing the worst, the Radical enemies of the South would take nothing by the motion...[15]

and added:

Nothing that we can do will facilitate our "reconstruction," so as to admit us to a representation in Congress.... We wait in silence with dignity until it be the pleasure of the parties having authority to open Congress to our representatives.[16]

COLONEL CLAYTON C. GILLESPIE. Clayton Gillespie, a veteran of the Battle of San Jacinto, was a prison superintendent, a Methodist minister and a newspaper editor before the Civil War. He commanded the Twenty-Fifth Texas Cavalry (Dismounted) during the war. Clayton C. Gillespie escaped charges of war crimes after the war for his role as the commanding officer at Camp Groce in the latter part of the war. He was an outspoken opponent of Reconstruction as editor of the Houston *Telegraph* just after the war's end. Gillespie became superintendent of the state penitentiary at Huntsville, the construction of which he had supervised in 1846. Neither he nor any of the guards fled their charges when yellow fever began to take its toll in 1867. Guards and inmates nursed one another as they came down with the dreaded disease. Colonel Gillespie, his wife and young son were among the many who died. (From the Harold B. Simpson Research Center, Hill College, Hillsboro, Texas.)

Gillespie did caution his readers that any "demonstrations of respect for the Confederacy" would not be wise, given the situation. He promoted the sense that it was in the interest of both white and black Texans to focus on the year's crop.

That Gillespie was publicly delivering his opinions was one measure of the pos-

16. Occupation and Reconstruction

ture assumed by Federal authorities in the aftermath of the war. Most Confederate leaders and officers were allowed to resume their lives after the war, other than Jefferson Davis, whom the Federal government imprisoned until May 1867. Texan Frank Lubbock, who had been an aide to Davis, spent eight months in solitary confinement at Fort Delaware before being paroled. There was an investigation of war crimes. Federal authorities hung Captain Henry Wirz, who had been commandant of the Confederacy's Andersonville prison, on November 10, 1865. Clayton Gillespie was among others investigated by a Federal commission for possible war crimes. John Read, who had been a prisoner in Camp Groce at Hempstead, which Clayton Gillespie commanded, testified before the commission:

> The camp was under the command of a Colonel Gillespie, a clergyman, who openly avowed his intention to maltreat prisoners, as proved by the confessions of his own subordinate officers, who stated that they would alleviate the sufferings on several occasions, but that the colonel wished to retaliate upon us for alleged maltreatment of confederates in northern prisons.[17]

The prominent writer A. J. H. Duganne was another prisoner at Camp Groce. Duganne rushed into publication a 400-page indictment entitled "Camps and prisons: Twenty months in the Department of the Gulf" after his release from prison in 1865. Despite the earnest efforts of these men and others, Clayton Gillespie escaped punishment and was allowed to return to civilian life.

The reality was that, however bitter the defeat for the Confederates, the Federal occupation at the end of the war was not particularly harsh. There were no mass imprisonments, much less executions, of former rebels. Plantations were not repatriated from owners. The Federal government did not force reparation payments from the devastated Southern states to pay for the cost of the war. Yet, for some Southerners, the emancipation of the slaves and their suffrage was so revolutionary and difficult to accept that they began the legend of the harsh Reconstruction. Clayton Gillespie, writing in the *Telegraph*, blasted the heavy taxation while being excluded from the government and warned, "This state of things cannot always endure."[18]

Texans were intent on governing themselves. The local level mirrored the state level with former Confederates returning to positions of power and authority. William Campbell, who ran a factory in Fairfield, Texas, during the war making Colt-style revolvers for the Confederates,[19] was elected alderman in Chappell Hill in November 1865.[20] Captain Oliver Hazard Perry Garrett became chief justice of Washington County and in that capacity authorized ex–Confederate W. R. D. Crockett of Chappell Hill in December 1865 to raise a company of 50 men to serve as the police force of Washington County.[21] Colonel Franklin C. Wilkes, who had returned home from the war to open a pharmacy, became mayor of Chappell Hill in December 1866, replacing John McDonald. He would be re-elected in 1867.

That the spirit of the Confederacy remained in the hearts of many was quite clear. Chappell Hill reinstated the tradition of the annual spring jousting tournament. A tournament was held in June 1866 "for contributing to the noble object, the raising [of] a suitable monument to the fallen Texas soldiery."[22] Captain Richard

Swearingen was the orator of the day and a reporter wrote, "Every sentence thrilled the soul, and every sentence moved the heart of Knight and lady, patriot and citizen."[23] Southern and Texan pride remained in evidence. The jousting tournament was witnessed by thousands of onlookers. The competitors were known as "The Knighthood of the Lamented Dead." Alex Hammond, formerly of Terry's Texas Rangers, became "The Knight of Chickamauga." He led the parade, mounted on a white steed. Other former Terry's Texas Rangers included Albert Iankes as "Knight of Shiloh," Robert Elgin as "Knight of the Sable Plume" and John Jackson as "Terry's Rangers." Walter Keesee, who served with the Twenty-Fourth Texas Cavalry, was "Knight of the Shivered Lance." Dell Perkins of the Twentieth Texas Infantry tried to look ahead rather than behind and rode under the name "Better Day Coming."[24] The Galveston paper noted that the riders rode 80 yards down the track in four and one-half to five seconds while taking the ring. A. D. Gee of Washington, the "Knight of the Golden Circle," won the competition, beating out 30 other young men for the right to crown Miss Ella Holland of Independence as queen.

The memorial to Texas soldiery in Chappell Hill was never built. The Reconstruction administration forbade such monuments at the time. Some men ignored the mandates of the Reconstruction administration. The same spirit that made Terry's Texas Rangers such a formidable fighting unit caused them to form the Terry's Texas Rangers Association in nearby Austin in 1867 for the express purpose of erecting a monument. Numerous Rangers from Chappell Hill joined. Although economics likely prevented the monument — it would be 40 years before the Rangers Association raised enough money — the Rangers began gathering annually somewhere in Texas as early as 1868.[25] Confederate veterans turned to their comrades-in-arms for brotherhood.

Texans ratified the new constitution and elected James Throckmorton governor in statewide elections held in June 1866. Throckmorton, who opposed secession in the days before the war, served the Confederacy as an officer. He was inaugurated on August 13, 1866.[26] The Texas Eleventh Legislature reaffirmed in 1866 the inferior position that slaves and free blacks had held in antebellum Texas. The codes reflected the continued unwillingness of white Texans to accept blacks as equals and continued legal discrimination. The legislature defined all individuals with one-eighth or more African blood as persons of color and, thus, subject to special provisions in the law.[27] President Andrew Johnson declared the rebellion in Texas over and Throckmorton undertook to restore civilian rule in lieu of the military administration. The new governor suggested within the week of his inauguration that the U.S. Army remove its occupation force from the interior of Texas and relocate to the frontier, where the Comanche were a very real threat.[28]

The U.S. Army began to replace the volunteer troops in Texas with regular army during the spring of 1866. The Seventeenth U.S. Infantry landed at Galveston on April 24, 1866.[29] They were a rowdy bunch and there were severe problems with fighting and drinking. The 24 companies[30] of the Seventeenth were scattered along the Texas Coast by the summer of 1866.[31] Company B of the Seventeenth passed through Chappell Hill to Brenham, where they set up camp near the center of town. The site is called Camptown to this day.[32] This unit under the command of Major

16. Occupation and Reconstruction

G. W. Smith assumed responsibility for Washington County. Routine patrols made their appearance in Chappell Hill and the other surrounding towns. The rugged fighters of the Seventeenth and the determined Texans of the Washington County would prove to be a volatile mixture.

Former Confederate Dan McGary moved to Brenham and established a daily newspaper, the *Brenham Banner*. McGary, as editor, poured forth a steady stream of anti–Reconstruction editorials, including personal attacks on local authorities. A clash was evident. There were rumors of volunteers being organized in the countryside around Brenham to challenge the Federal military control.[33] Some of the Confederates of Chappell Hill, no doubt, were among them, bristling for one last fight. McGary contacted Clayton Gillespie at the *Telegraph* in Houston in mid–June, alerting him to the fact that "General Grant is about to order the Banner to be suppressed."[34] Gillespie lent support and editorialized the situation in his paper: "No danger, brother M'Gary, no danger.... Moreover, we have never seen anything of a treasonable tendency in the Banner."[35]

The situation was tense all summer. A fight between Federal soldiers and local men broke out in Brenham on the evening of September 7, 1866. Two Federal soldiers died and several others were wounded. Their comrades, a company strong, responded by marching into town and burning a building. The fire spread and an entire city block went up in smoke. The soldiers proceeded to arrest newspaper editor Dan McGary for his fiery columns denouncing the soldiers. He remained in their custody for 14 days.[36] Still, Federal authorities did not prosecute McGary or anyone directly involved in the clash. They seemed to sense a potential for much greater violence waiting if emotions exploded. Texans, meanwhile, proceeded to regain control of the state.

The Eleventh Texas Legislature resolved on October 3, 1866, to exhume the remains of Albert Sidney Johnston, the distinguished Confederate general killed at the Battle of Shiloh, and return them to Texas. He had been a favorite son of Texas, who in death became revered. General Sheridan became convinced after the Brenham incident that he needed a tougher officer over Texas. He found that individual in Brevet Major General Charles Griffin. Texas found itself under the control of a severe and uncompromising occupying force from December 1866 onward. Griffin's response, when the Texan committee brought Albert Sidney Johnston's remains back from New Orleans in January 1867, was to prohibit any formal ceremony. The Texans brought Johnston's remains to Galveston by steamer on January 24. D. C. Farmer, who had commanded James E. Landes in Company A of the Fifth Texas Infantry, was among the pallbearers. Johnston's body lay in state all that day and thousands passed by to pay respects. A special train took the remains to Houston on January 25. Many businesses in Houston shut down and many buildings were shrouded in respect. Church bells tolled throughout the city on Sunday, January 27, and thousands of people marched quietly in the streets. That afternoon, a train carrying the body left Houston and passed through Hempstead, Chappell Hill and Brenham on its way to Austin.[37] Governor Throckmorton presided over the final services in Austin. He attacked the Federal administration for denying them the "sacred and blessed privilege"[38] of having a memorial service. Throckmorton took the opportunity to tell the crowd, "May the purity of his private life be an exemplar for the young men in all time to come."[39] No monument was allowed over the gravesite. It would be another 25 years before that happened.[40]

Reconstruction was far from complete and Texas' problems were just beginning. Men like Clayton Gillespie at the *Telegraph* would learn that the reconstruction that Texas faced in 1865–6 had not been so bad after all. The Radical Republicans swept the national elections in the fall of 1866. They were unhappy with what they considered the lenient policies of President Andrew Johnson in dealing with the defeated Southern states. The Radical Republican-controlled U.S. Congress passed the Reconstruction Act over the president's veto on March 2, 1867. The act declared the governments of the Southern states to be illegal. It more clearly defined the precise steps necessary for any state of the former Confederacy to qualify for readmission. These included specific repudiation of the ordinance of secession, ratification of the Thirteenth and Fourteenth amendments to the U.S. Constitution and incorporation of these into a new state constitution that must be approved by the U.S. Congress. The Thirteenth Amendment to the U.S. Constitution abolished slavery. The Constitutional Convention of 1866 had sidestepped ratifying this amendment. Congress became specific, adding the Fourteenth Amendment, which forbade any state to deny to any person "life, liberty, or property, without due process of law" in June 1866 and insisting that both be ratified before readmission. Congress recognized the unrepentant attitudes and further moved to divide the former Confederacy into five military districts with full authority to the military administration. The act also specifically authorized the military administration to remove any official considered "an impediment to Reconstruction." The right to participate in political office was restricted to only those individuals who could swear that they had not taken part in the secession effort. Congressional Reconstruction was intent upon breaking Southern will.

The citizens of Washington County held a mass meeting at the courthouse in Brenham on June 8, 1867, in the midst of this new adversity.[41] The tone was conciliatory, rather than belligerent. Most recognized that any sense of renewing rebellion was beyond reason. The Honorable John Stamps, an early settler who had represented the area in the Congress of the republic, presided. He would die three months later. Noted attorney John Sayles told the crowd that they were gathered "for the purpose of considering the proper course to be pursued by our people in reference to the reconstruction measures proposed."[42] All listening knew well that Sayles had lost his own right to vote by virtue of having been a brigadier general in the state militia during the war. Sayles quoted former Confederate General James Longstreet in saying that the Reconstruction Acts were "an olive branch held forth to the South by Congress." He reminded the crowd that if they accepted the terms, Texas would be restored to the Union. He declared his opposition to the government ended and urged all to bury their past differences with "the dead issues." Sayles warned that harsher and more rigorous terms might be forthcoming if Texans resisted.[43]

The situation worsened when General Sheridan replaced Texas governor Throckmorton at the end of July 1867 with a Republican appointee. Throckmorton was the first Southern casualty of Congress' Reconstruction Act and many more would

16. Occupation and Reconstruction

follow. Special Order No. 195 on November 1, 1867, removed hundreds of local officials across Texas. Reverend Franklin Wilkes, former colonel with the Twenty-Fourth Texas Cavalry, who had been serving Chappell Hill as mayor since his election in July 1866, was among the casualties.[44] Chappell Hill would not have another mayor for several years. Sheridan also removed Hugh McIntyre, the Brenham planter who had insisted that Sam Houston be allowed to speak in 1861, from his position as mayor of Brenham. McIntyre, like Wilkes, had been elected in 1866.[45] All of the city officials of Austin and San Antonio were removed. No one was allowed to assume office unless they could swear under oath that they had never taken up arms against the United States government.

The struggle for power was at all levels. Congress impeached President Johnson in February 1868 for violating the tenure of his office and removing Edwin Stanton as secretary of war. Johnson's trial in the Senate lasted through all of April and May, before he was acquitted. President Johnson removed General Sheridan from his position as administrator of the Fifth Military District for removing Texas governor Throckmorton. There was a national struggle going on of colossal proportions.

The U.S. Congress passed into law in February 1869 the Fifteenth Amendment, which gave the right to vote to persons of all race and color. Many conservative Texans preferred military rule to the reality of blacks being enfranchised. Section Two of the Fourteenth Amendment, ratified in 1868, disenfranchised those who had taken part in the rebellion. Consequently, Republicans carried the state in the December 1869 election, in which Ulysses S. Grant became president of the United States and Edmund J. Davis became governor of Texas. Both were former Federal Army officers, who benefited from the African American vote. This election also sent 14 African Americans to the Twelfth Legislature of Texas.

A powerful Republican Party emerged in Washington County.[46] Matthew Gaines, a former slave who had settled after emancipation in nearby Burton in Washington County, was among them. The Baptist preacher-turned-politician became state senator representing the Sixteenth Senate District. Gaines was considered by many to be the most charismatic and most militant African American leader in Texas during this period. One of Gaines's major issues involved mobilizing the black vote; i.e., the protection of blacks who went to the polls and the election of blacks to public office. He worked on prison reform and the protection of blacks from mob violence. Gaines recognized that unscrupulous landlords were able to effectively keep freedmen as slaves through tenant farming and he subsequently pushed for tenant-farming reform. He unsuccessfully voiced opposition to the Landlord and Tenant Act of 1872. Gaines was relentless in his efforts to establish a system of public education. Gaines, who taught himself to read as a slave through books smuggled to him by a young white friend, believed that only public education would allow blacks to better themselves economically.[47]

Texas was a lawless state and violence often went unpunished. The famous outlaw Bill Longley shot and killed Green Evans as he and several other African Americans were passing down the road in Washington County on December 20, 1868. He later claimed to have killed another African American earlier. Longley disappeared when a search warrant was issued for his arrest. Speculation was that he never left

Washington County.⁴⁸ The law did not catch up with Longley until 1877 after a long string of murders.⁴⁹ However, it was the Ku Klux Klan, not homicidal individuals like Longley, that posed the main problem in securing law and order. The Klan was active in Washington County, as elsewhere in the state.⁵⁰ The Twelfth Legislature created the State Police in an attempt to contain the lawlessness and violence that was rampant in Texas. The Police Act of July 1870 authorized the recruitment of over 200 men. Most of the men were Republicans and an estimated 40 percent were African Americans.⁵¹ One of the eight State Police district headquarters was in Brenham.⁵² While the force filled a dire need, the general populace hated the State Police. The Democrats replaced the State Police with Texas Rangers when they regained control of the legislature in 1873.⁵³

Public education was perhaps the greatest legacy of the Twelfth Legislature. The United States Congress passed the Land Grant College Act, better known as the Morrill Act for its sponsor, in 1862. This act provided for the funding of public institutions of higher learning for agricultural and mechanical arts. Any state providing the school (the land, buildings and facilities) would receive 30,000 acres of federal lands for each congressional representative. This land could then be sold to establish an endowment to fund the school. The debate on federal involvement in higher education through land grants began before the Civil War and was quite heated. Many in Texas and throughout the South opposed the concept as a move by the federal government in violation of states' rights. There was grave concern that further federal intervention might eventually lead to the issue of slavery itself. The Twelfth Texas Legislature addressed the issue of public education after the Civil War.

The Twelfth Texas Legislature under the leadership of State Senator Matthew Gaines passed Senate Bill 276, which established a college for the agricultural and mechanical arts. The House passed the bill and sent it to Governor Edmund Davis, who signed the bill into law on April 17, 1871. The Agricultural and Mechanical College of Texas opened its doors near Bryan, Texas, 35 miles north of Chappell Hill, on October 4, 1876. The Texas Constitution of 1869, which created in Texas the first statewide public school system financed by public lands and taxation, stated that schools would be provided for both black and white students. The black legislatures understood that the bill obligated the state to build a separate school for blacks if Texas A&M was to be segregated. The result was the corresponding Agricultural and Mechanical College for Colored Youth.

A commission purchased the Alta Vista plantation from Chappell Hill native Helen Marr Swearingen Kirby. Helen was the daughter of prominent planter R. J. Swearingen and the sister of Colonel Patrick Henry Swearingen and Captain Richard M. Swearingen. She married Colonel Jared E. Kirby, the wealthiest man in Austin County, in 1858 and moved to his Alta Vista plantation near Hempstead. She ran a girls' school at the manor house from Kirby's death in 1865 until moving to Austin in 1875. Helen Marr Swearingen Kirby later became the first dean of women at the University of Texas. The Agricultural and Mechanical College for Colored Youth opened in 1878 in the manor house of the Alta Vista plantation. The college ultimately became what is today known as Prairie View A & M University, the second oldest public university in Texas.

The Twelfth Legislature of Texas assembled at Austin on February 18, 1870, and proceeded to ratify the Thirteenth, Fourteenth and Fifteenth amendments to the U.S. Constitution and also a new state constitution. President Grant signed the act that re-admitted Texas to the Union on March 30, 1870, after five long years of occupation. Republicans remained in power throughout the state. The 14 African American members of the Twelfth Texas Legislature faced threats and the reality of violent deaths through their tenure serving the state. A Democrat in the legislature denounced Gaines from the Senate floor as a "flat-footer [sic] nigger."[54] A grand jury at La Grange in Fayette County indicted Matthew Gaines on a charge of bigamy in 1871. Gaines was convicted and relinquished his seat. Even though the Texas Supreme Court overturned the ruling and Gaines was re-elected, the Democrat-controlled Thirteenth Legislature refused Gaines his seat. He died in 1900, fighting to the end for the rights of his fellow African Americans.

The attitude of former Confederate chaplain Rev. Dr. Benjamin Kavanaugh was perhaps representative of unrepentant Texans. He returned to Chappell Hill after the war and edited the *Texas Masonic Mirror*, the official journal of the Grand Lodge of Texas. Reverend Kavanaugh reported to his readers on the front page of the February 28, 1872, issue:

> Negro Masons. Many efforts have been made to incorporate the sons of Ham into the Masonic Fraternity in this country.... no man, or body of men, has a right to introduce the elements of discord and confusion to the body of an Order which has for its object the union and happiness of all who are qualified to enter and enjoy the universal Brotherhood.... We had hoped that we had seen the end of the fanaticism of Northern innovators ... such mischief-makers. They will soon find there is a fortress.[55]

Reverend Kavanaugh alerted the membership in November 1872 to an attack on Freemasonry by the Western Tract Society:

> organized before the extinction of slavery, on ultra anti-slavery principles. That enemy demolished and out of the field, its restless, aggressive spirits have turned their attention to the great evil of Freemasonry.[56]

Kavanaugh's perspective was not unique. The U.S. Congress established the Freedmen's Bureau in March 1865 as a branch of the U.S. Army to supervise affairs related to African Americans in the former Confederate states. The main emphasis was on establishing a free agricultural system and on securing education for the freedmen. The Bureau operated in Texas from September 1865 until July 1870.[57] Nearly 8,000 slaves made up more than half of the population of Washington County in 1860. That number increased by 1864 to 8,700 as Southerners fled west to Texas during the war. The Freedmen's Bureau, as a result, established an agency in Brenham. Many whites took a hostile stance.[58] General William E. Strong noted, "It is the same old story of cruelty, only there is more of it in Texas than any other southern State."[59] Strong further wrote of "the most intense hatred shown by Texas whites toward Northerners, soldiers and the Federal government."[60] Washington County was no exception.

One indication of interaction between black and white in Chappell Hill is recorded in the minutes of Providence Baptist Church. Chappell Hill was predominately Methodist but also had a considerable Episcopal congregation. The arrival of new settlers led to Presbyterians and Baptists. The Presbyterians erected a church on the west side of Main Street in 1859 and allowed the Baptists to use the facility in town. The Baptists met in an old church north of Chappell Hill twice a month and in the Presbyterian Church twice a month. A violent storm in April 1866 destroyed the Baptist Church. The Baptist congregation offered the wreck of the old church to the African American members of the congregation. The African Americans of Chappell Hill accepted and built a new structure on the site. Consequently, approximately 100 African Americans went off to form their own church in 1870. Providence Baptist was left with only 79 White members. They then built their own white church in Chappell Hill in 1873.[61]

President Grant's return of the vote to previously disenfranchised Confederates in 1871 set the stage for the return to power of unreconstructed Southerners. The impact in Texas became clear in the 1873 gubernatorial election. Confederate veteran Richard Coke, a Democrat who served as a captain in Louisiana with the Fifteenth Texas Infantry, defeated the incumbent Republican governor, Edmund Davis, a Texan who had been a high-ranking Federal cavalry officer during the war. The election, which was "characterized by fraud and intimidation on both sides," became known as the Coke-Davis Controversy. The Democrats disregarded a court decision that the election was illegal and managed to gain physical possession of the Capitol. Davis' appeal to President Grant for intercession was denied and Coke became governor. A 102-gun salute in Austin in January 1874 marked Coke's inauguration. Democratic control in Austin spread throughout the state. Chappell Hill elected Confederate veteran Thomas J. Scurry its mayor in October 1876. Scurry was quartermaster under Brigadier General William Read Scurry,[62] who died in 1864 at the Battle of Jenkins Ferry in Louisiana and was buried with honors in the Texas State Cemetery. General Scurry's brother Thomas died in 1879 and is buried in Chappell Hill's Atkinson Cemetery.[63]

Texas Democrats, once back in power, repealed most of the legislation enacted by the Radical Republicans. The Democrat-controlled Texas Legislature held a constitutional convention in 1875. Texas voters adopted a new constitution in 1876, replacing the Constitution of 1869. This was a prelude to the presidential election of 1876, in which Republican Rutherford B. Hayes became president with the promise of withdrawing Federal troops from the South and formally ending Reconstruction. The grim reality of the Constitution of 1876 dashed the hopes and dreams of Texas' emancipated African Americans. The active role of freedmen on Washington County juries ended in 1876.[64] Many freedmen from Washington County and the surrounding region migrated north to Kansas with their families over the next several years in search of a better life. The mass movement caused such a labor shortage for white landowners in Washington County that, in desperation, they began to offer better terms to African Americans sharecropping on their farmlands.[65] Stephen Hackworth of the Brenham Union League made such an effort to stem the migration to Kansas that black leaders in Texas passed as resolution thanking him.[66]

16. Occupation and Reconstruction

George Washington Carter, former president of Chappell Hill's Soule University, was in need of a future after the war. Though there had been discussion of his becoming governor of Texas before the Confederacy capitulated, nothing happened after the Federal occupation. George Washington Carter remained in Texas for a time, but he did not return to his former position as president of Chappell Hill's Soule University after the war. However, he did retain business dealings with Chappell Hill, as evidenced in a letter from Colonel Carter to William Westcoat Browning of Chappell Hill, dated September 4, 1865:

> Col. Dr. Lockhart requested me to see you relative to some business in which you and himself were interested — viz. some cotton and special application for amnesty. I will go to Austin in few days and then to Washington city and will attend to those matters for you upon reasonable terms. My friend Lt. Fauntelroy who is a lawyer will prepare the papers and bring them to me. I send him because the sickness of my family prevents my coming in person.[67]

Carter's future changed in 1867 when he represented a man from New Orleans charged in Galveston with embezzlement.[68] Henry Clay Warmoth, a former brigadier general in the Federal army, made New Orleans his home in 1865 at the end of the war. His personal connections included General and, later, President Ulysses S. Grant. He was what Southerners referred to as a "carpetbagger." Carter obtained an acquittal for Warmoth and apparently made a strong impression on his client. Warmoth later wrote of Carter:

> He was ... a man of exceptional education and polish, and was gifted with a remarkable ability to state and illustrate a proposition. He was a fine speaker, and I was attracted to him at once.[69]

The Radical Republicans' control of the U.S. Congress and the subsequent Reconstruction Act of 1867 formed the defeated Southern states into military districts and placed their administration under the U.S. Army. Grant ordered the appointment of 26-year-old Warmoth as military governor of Louisiana in June 1868.[70] George Washington Carter recognized that he had little future in Reconstruction Texas as a former Confederate officer and soon thereafter moved to Louisiana to take advantage of his connection with Warmoth.[71] Louisiana's experience in the War Between the States contrasted greatly with that of Texas. Federal forces occupied much of Louisiana, but particularly New Orleans, its most important city, for three years of the war. Northern connections were well established in that city by the end of the war.

Warmoth rapidly assimilated almost despotic power in his adopted state of Louisiana. He correspondingly gained considerable wealth, as did his friends. The governor signed a bill on March 16, 1870, creating Cameron Parish in the extreme southwestern-most corner of the state. Cameron Parish, which Warmoth carved out of Calcasieu Parish, was a thinly populated region of swamps between Sabine and Calcasieu Lakes. Governor Warmoth then appointed his friend George Washington Carter as the parish judge. Carter's complete power in "his" parish led to his being elected soon thereafter as the parish's representative to the Louisiana House of Representatives. Carter was later said to have boasted that he had been "elected to the Legislature as a Republican on his Confederate record."[72] His switching of parties was no laughing matter to his former comrades-in-arms. They referred Carter and others like him as a "scalawag," a term used for Southerners who became members of the Republican Party after the war.

George Washington Carter proceeded to New Orleans, then the capital of Louisiana, when the new legislature convened in January 1871. The first motion of the Louisiana House was to remove Mortimer Carr as speaker of the House. While Carter had no prior experience in government service, he was very much attuned to politics. He also was an impressive man with a fine mind and exceptional speaking ability. He also had a circle of influential friends, which included the governor himself. All of these factors clearly played a role in the Louisiana House electing George Washington Carter, former president of Chappell Hill's Soule University, as the new speaker of the House on January 31, 1871.[73]

Carter became "an influential factor in the reconstruction days in the South in Louisiana."[74] Stories abounded about the man. It was generally acknowledged that Carter refused to sign a bill in favor of the Chattanooga Railroad until that line retained him as one of its attorneys for $10,000 dollars a year.[75] One story told how Carter, in the middle of a consultation with his railroad clients, pulled out a jew's-harp and began playing. The businessmen adjourned at which time one suggested to another that Carter was a madman. The colleague was said to have responded, "That may be but he only can deliver our lines to us."[76]

Carter, an unreconstructed Confederate, used his considerable influence to expand his support. The trustees of Centenary College expressed their gratitude to Congressman Carter in July 1871. The Methodist institution had been closed during the war and reopened in October 1865. The law obligated Centenary to accept 22 indigent students on state scholarship covering their tuition and expenses. There was grave concern among the trustees that one or more of these scholarships might be given to a black man. Congressman George Washington Carter managed to get the scholarships abolished so as to eliminate the threat.[77]

Carter already was re-aligning himself politically by July 1871. He told a Republican gathering that Governor Warmoth had too much patronage and urged that limits be placed on the governor's powers.[78] Warmoth, in fact, had become a wealthy man. He told a newspaper reporter, "I don't pretend to be honest ... only as honest as anybody in politics ... everybody is demoralized down here. Corruption is the fashion."[79] Warmoth responded to Carter's charges by referring to him as "once a saint but is now a blackguard ... a liar, a drunkard and a gambler."[80] The war had changed George Washington Carter, as it had so many others. Carter divorced from his wife, who had come with him to Texas from Virginia. He began drinking heavily and carousing. The errant minister later told close friends that he never ceased to believe in the faith of his religion and that he prayed by his bed every night. A man reported passing through the French Quarter early one morning and hearing a familiar Methodist camp-ground hymn on the accordion. At the top of a staircase, his eyes closed, humming as he played the instrument "was George Carter, a politician, lawyer, duelist, sinner.... He alone of the carousing crowd had so early left his bed in this garish seat of vice."[81]

Carter's new lifestyle apparently weighed heavily on his mind. He attended the General Conference of the Methodist Church in New Orleans, but insisted on sitting in the back. Friends attempted to convince the well-known and influential figure to move to his rightful place at the front to which he responded "I am unworthy — a poor sinner."[82] Yet, Carter was quick to fight and was known to challenge to a duel anyone who called into question his sincerity in his days as a minister. He earned a reputation of being a man of calm nerves with an accurate shot.[83] This reputation served Carter well in rough-and-tumble New Orleans, particularly as Southern white Republicans were often threatened, harassed and even terrorized by the Knights of the White Camellia.[84]

There was a major power struggle going on in Louisiana. A mixture of antagonism, revenge and personal gain pulled together powerful forces against Governor Warmoth. Warmoth refused to support James Casey, the Federal Custom House collector for the port of New Orleans, for U.S. Senate. Casey was a powerful man and brother-in-law to President Grant's wife.[85] Casey allied with Warmoth's many enemies, including Lieutenant Governor Oscar Dunn (a black man), U.S. Marshall Stephen Packard and others. The Republican Party subsequently split at the state convention of August 1871.[86] It was Warmoth's faction against the Custom House Gang, as they were known. George Washington Carter aligned himself with the Republicans seeking to remove Warmoth. The fight was limited to name-calling for a time. Carter attacked Warmoth in the newspaper, "as a Republican, a practical Lie, as a politician, a fraud."[87] The stakes were high and the fighting escalated. There were rumors of poisonings when Carter's ally, the lieutenant governor, died unexpectedly in November and Carter himself fell ill during the same period. There was talk of impeaching the governor as the legislature reconvened in January 1872.

The opening of the 1872 session of the Louisiana Legislature was tumultuous with both sides attempting to eliminate the opposition. The Packard-Carter faction attempted to impeach Governor Warmoth. They planned to suspend the governor from office while he awaited trial. Carter, as house speaker, seemed the likely replacement as governor. The Warmoth forces in the legislature attempted to call for the election of a new speaker. Carter refused to acknowledge them. The opposition then rushed Carter, who had expected as much, and called upon a well-armed crowd of hired guns to protect him. The house adjourned with no one clear as to what might follow. Federal troops moved into the street and the militia, commanded by former Confederate General James Longstreet, was called out.

U.S. Marshall Packard sent out his men to arrest the governor, the chief of police and other leaders of the Warmoth faction. While the Republicans met at the capitol protected by the militia, Carter reconvened his faction at the Gem Saloon on Royal Street. He sent out sergeants-at-arms to locate and escort other legislators to the establishment in order to have a quorum. Some zealous underlings engaged in this activity killed a state legislator.[88] The police chief ordered Carter's arrest for the death. The situation was on the verge of open warfare in the streets and both sides requested Federal protection from Washington, each side confident that they could rely on their connections with Grant.

George Washington Carter decided to act on January 14. He gathered an excited mob of several thousand men and advanced to attack the legislative hall.[89] Only the firm presence of federal troops and their unyielding officer prevented a pitched battle between the two factions. When the federal soldiers returned to their barracks and the commanding officer advised both sides that he would not order his men back into the city without approval from Grant in Washington, Carter was certain that he was about to take control through violence. He and his faction circulated inflammatory fliers around town advising the people that without the troops they could have their way with the Warmoth faction. Federal authorities reluctantly moved the troops back into the city streets.[90]

George Washington Carter again rallied his forces to gather on January 22 to seize control of the state house by force. One handbill read: "To Arms! To Arms! To Arms! Colored Men to the Front!"[91] All indications were that the long-anticipated battle would finally occur. The military set up Gatling guns behind barricades in the streets and officially advised both sides that it had authority from President Grant to use whatever force necessary to restore order. Warmoth was secure for the moment and the opposing faction melted away. A New Orleans editor noted: "Warmoth's strength at Washington was evidently underrated by Carter and his followers."[92] The reality was that, however corrupt Warmoth may have been, he held office and physically occupied the state office buildings, while his opposition was mounting an attack on both. The federal troops had little choice but to protect Warmoth.

Carter challenged General A. G. Badger of the Metropolitan Police to a duel in February. The two went across the border into Mississippi to fight. The choice of weapons was rifles at 60 paces. Amazingly, neither hit the other at that range. They considered the score settled and returned to town. The duel was publicized in the New Orleans *Picayune*, which wrote that neither "could hit a barn unless they were to go inside and shut the door."[93] Warmoth, despite having been saved by Grant, broke ranks with the president in May 1872.

The election at the end of 1872 was controversial and both sides challenged the results. Both Democrats and Republicans claimed victory. The State representatives impeached Warmoth in December and President Grant declared Republican William Kellogg the new governor — despite the fact that Warmouth, the Democratic candidate, received the most votes. The unsettled and sometimes bloody state of affairs in Louisiana state politics continued for several years. It perhaps was too much even for an old fighter like George Washington Carter. He left Louisiana by August 1874 and returned to his native Virginia.[94]

Southern resistance over time began to convince the Federal government that Reconstruction was only building up hatred and preventing a reuniting of the nation. The whites of the nation began a slow evolution back towards unity with the end of Reconstruction. Meanwhile, many of the gains made by freed blacks were lost. The Louisiana State Constitution of 1868, which extended voting rights to black males, established an integrated, public school system and guaranteed blacks equal access to public institutions, slipped away into history as soon as the Democrats returned to power.

17

Yellow Fever

Yellow fever is a most horrific way to die. The disease takes its name from the jaundice that is an early symptom and the deep yellow color that sets in after death. Victims suffer internal bleeding with kidney and liver failure. In its most severe form, the disease degenerates the walls of the stomach and intestines. The result is "black vomit." There was no known cure for yellow fever in 1867. Medical authorities did not even understand how the disease was transmitted. It was generally understood that personal contact did not increase the risk. Their best guess was that the fog rolling in across low, wet ground at night somehow spread the disease. People knew that warm summer and autumn nights in low-lying regions could be deadly. They also had deduced that sleeping on a second story was safer. All of this was true, but the perpetrator was the *Aedes aegypti* mosquito. Marshy ground is ideal for the propagation of mosquitoes. The insect is nocturnal and generally low flying. And the cold weather of winter ends the mosquitoes' cycle for the year. The identification of the *Aedes aegypti* mosquito as the carrier was not made until 1881 and it was many more years before effective treatment was available.[1]

Yellow fever had claimed victims in Chappell Hill every summer and fall since the founding of the settlement. However, the disease was never epidemic in proportion until 1867. Chappell Hill was considered too far from the coast, where the vast expanses of low-lying areas made yellow fever an annual threat. Yet, the broad floodplain of the Brazos River, adjacent to Chappell Hill, provided vast acreage in which mosquitoes could proliferate. Further, New Year's Creek was just to the north of Chappell Hill and Caney Creek just to the south. The very reason for the success of cotton growing around Chappell Hill made it susceptible to yellow fever.

The disease made its first 1867 appearance in Texas in early July at Indianola on the coast. Yellow fever appeared at Galveston by the latter part of the month. Medical authorities reported the disease in a number of inland towns, including Victoria, Goliad, Hempstead and Navasota, by middle to late August.[2] There was some question for several weeks as to whether yellow fever was the cause. Reverend Dr. Benjamin Kavanaugh, editor of the *Texas Masonic Mirror* in Houston, wrote on September 17, 1873:

> If our opinion is worth anything, we again repeat that we do not believe that we have any real cases of yellow fever in Houston; and there is no just cause for the fearful alarm that is kept up here and in the surrounding county.[3]

Richard Swearingen had been attending medical school in New Orleans when the War Between the States broke out. He returned to school after the war and graduated from the New Orleans School of Medicine in March 1867, at which time he delivered the valedictory address. Dr. Swearingen returned home to be faced with perhaps the greatest challenge of his life. The first death to yellow fever in Chappell Hill was on September 7, 1867. Many more followed within days. Dr. Swearingen urged his wife Jennie to leave with their infant daughter, less than a year old. Jennie refused and worked tirelessly alongside her husband. The Swearingens subsequently lost little Helen Jessie to the fever.[4]

Mary Presler waited three years for her husband, Captain James Presler of the Cavalry Battalion of Waul's Legion, to return home to Chappell Hill from the war. James Presler did return home from the war, but the reunion was short-lived. Mary wrote a friend in Brenham on September 18:

> I know you have reason to think hard of my long silence.... For the last two or three months you might call our house a hospital. We have from two to three sick all the time. Mr. P has had three attacks, has been sick for the last two weeks, not confined to his bed all the time, but every day has a little fever. Mollie has been sick nearly all summer, looks worse that I ever saw her. Milton has had three or four spells of fever.... Some of the doctors say we have yellow fever in Town. I do not know what kind of fever it is but they had black vomit with it. Miss Jennie Crawford died with it last week and Mary Glass this week ... I think we are living in a sickly place, I would not be willing to risk it another year & such a wet season we have had. Every family in the whole community that I have heard of has been sick.... I am anxious to see cold weather come.[5]

Alex Thompson wrote a letter to J. W. Thompson in Galveston, dated September 20, 1867:

> I expect you were astonished to hear that yellow fever had become epidemic in Chappell Hill, I never thought it would spread here. Dr. Wm. Rogers et al contended it was not yellow fever until a couple of days since. Mr. P. G. Smith was the first case, and death; since then thirteen (white) deaths ... Col. Atkinson lost his youngest daughter yesterday with black vomit, most have died with black vomit. F. M. Williamson thought to be dying this morning. T. W. Chappell much better, his wife not expecting to live, both children sick.... If it does not spread in the country, it will soon run its course in Chappell Hill as the place is nearly deserted, stores closed &c.[6]

17. Yellow Fever

Thomas Chappell did live, but Mrs. Chappell and F. M. Williamson did not. Williamson had survived numerous actions during the war with the Fifth Texas Cavalry and later the First Tennessee Cavalry, only to lose his life to yellow fever. A. B. Thompson, who had distinguished himself as a lieutenant with the Twentieth Texas Infantry that recaptured Galveston, himself died of yellow fever less than two weeks after writing the letter.

P. A. Smith, a quartermaster clerk with Parson's Brigade, died at Chappell Hill on September 20, 1867, and was buried in the Masonic Graveyard.[7] John E. Crockett, formerly a lieutenant with Elmore's Twentieth Texas Infantry at Galveston, died on September 22, 1867. His wife Sallie also died of the fever.[8] John's sister raised the two small boys left orphaned, William Davie Crockett, who became a State legislator in the early 1900s,[9] and John Jesse Crockett. John E. Crockett's brother, W. R. D. Crockett, died of the fever in November.[10] The number of deaths reported in Chappell Hill by September 29 was 49 with two of every five cases resulting in death.[11]

Mary Presler again wrote her friend in Brenham on October 20:

> When I received your letter several days ago I was sick. Mr. Presler and Ma thought I would die for a day and a night. I was taken with a chill directly after breakfast and it lasted me until about dinner time, then such a fever as I had, burning hot.... Mrs. Iankes moved out the day we did and camped near Mrs. Miller's place. Mary [Iankes] was taken with the fever there, she of course died. Charles [Co. K, Terry's Texas Rangers, C.S.A] took it shortly afterwards and died.... There have been between eighty and ninety deaths.... Gansello & Bob Elgin [Co. A, Terry's Texas Rangers, C.S.A] were considered well but they were so imprudent they relapsed. Bob Elgin moved up to the Hotel the evening that Gansello died that night. Bob relapsed and soon died. Mary [Elgin] then took it, lived about two days. She had a babe about a month old, it died a few days after her, then Mrs. Stanchfield [Mary's mother] took it & Olivia. Mrs. Stanchfield was unmanageable from the first. The nurse could do nothing with her. She soon followed them.[12]

Bob Elgin and Charles Iankes, who survived four years of combat with Terry's Texas Rangers, died on October 1 and October 5, 1867, respectively. Their wives died within days, as did Bob's small child. There were others who had survived the bloody war, only to die within two years to yellow fever. Dr. Edward W. Rogers, also of Terry's Texas Rangers, died on October 16.[13] Charles Carmer, who had been a sergeant with the Seventeenth Texas Infantry, died October 3. Thomas Davidson, who served under Captain Presler in the Cavalry Battalion of Waul's Legion, lost an infant. Franklin Wilkes, former colonel commanding the Twenty-Fourth Cavalry, lost his eight-year-old daughter Josie.[14]

The disease did not spare men of wealth and power, any more than it did gallant veterans of the Confederacy. Terrell J. Jackson, one of the wealthiest and most influential men in Chappell Hill, died on October 21. Dr. John P. Perkins of Chappell Hill died while helping victims of the disease.[15] Reverend Dr. Benjamin T. Kavanaugh survived, only to lose a grown son, also a doctor, and a daughter on October 8 and 9, respectively.[16] A Texas history book published in 1875 stated, "The year 1867 will long be remembered as the most disastrous ever known.... About thirty interior towns and villages have suffered a most appalling mortality, such as has scarcely ever been known in cities subject to the same visitation almost annually."[17]

James Carlisle, a relatively new resident of Chappell Hill, died on November 1, 1867, of the fever. His move to Chappell Hill was an unfortunate decision. He was 21 years old when the war ended in 1865. He served with his twin brother, John,[18] and his neighbors in Company G of the Forty-Second North Carolina Infantry. He fought against Grant at Cold Harbor in June 1864. When Grant made his thrust around Richmond to capture Petersburg, the Forty-Second was among those who marched hard to secure that strategic rail center until Lee could bring in reinforcements. Federal soldiers captured Carlisle on April 2, 1865, the day Grant's forces broke the siege at Petersburg and sent Lee retreating toward Appomattox.[19] Carlisle, like so many of the veterans of the Deep South, left a devastated home in the South and headed west to seek his future in Texas. Texas for him was a short-lived experience and James Carlisle became one more tragic casualty.

The yellow fever that devastated Chappell Hill in 1867 also struck other communities along the Gulf Coast. Nearly one-third of the inhabitants of Huntsville in Walker County died. Many veterans of the Twenty-First Texas Cavalry Regiment that had served under George Washington Carter were among these victims.[20] The state penitentiary, or "the Walls," as it was known locally,[21] was the only Confederate prison still standing at the end of the War Between the States.[22] It was on higher ground than other parts of the town and was not affected at first. Clayton C. Gillespie, who escaped charges of war crimes after the war for his role as the commanding officer at Camp Groce, became superintendent of the state penitentiary at Huntsville after his year as editor of the *Houston Telegraph*. Gillespie had supervised the construction of the Huntsville prison in 1846. Neither he nor any of the guards fled their charges when yellow fever began to take its toll. Guards and inmates nursed one another as they came down with the dreaded disease. Many died. Colonel Gillespie, his wife and young son were among those who died.[23]

The yellow fever epidemic of 1867 was a setback from which Chappell Hill never recovered. That was not the last year of the fever. Henry Brandt lost his wife Laura in the epidemic of 1871. His marriage to Laura had been less than two years old when he went off to war with Waul's Legion, was captured at Vicksburg and imprisoned in Indiana for the remainder of the war. Laura died only six years after Henry's long journey home at the end of the war. Henry Brandt remarried in February 1872, only to lose his new wife Emma the following November.

Henry A. Landes, formerly of the Twentieth Texas Infantry, lost his wife, Elmina "Pickie" Lockhart, on March 9, 1871. Their son, John Lockhart Landes, was less than two months old when his mother passed away. Young John died in August before his first birthday. Chappell Hill began to gain a reputation for being an unhealthy place to live. Henry married Pickie's sister, Mary Elizabeth Lockhart, in the following year. They moved away to Galveston,[24] where Henry later served two terms as mayor.

Reverend Robert Taliaferro, who served as chaplain of Flournoy's Sixteenth Texas Infantry Regiment, was in Chappell Hill in 1873. He was a Baptist missionary for many years, an editor for *Texas Baptist Herald* and chaplain for the Texas Senate. The distinguished gentleman contracted yellow fever in Chappell Hill and went to Austin, where his health declined and he died.[25]

Dr. Richard M. Swearingen moved from Chappell Hill to Austin in 1875. The medical field recognized him as an expert of sorts on yellow fever. When a yellow fever epidemic swept through the Mississippi River Valley in 1878, Doc Swearingen responded to an appeal for help. He arrived at Memphis on September 3, accompanied by his close friend and colleague, Doctor T. D. Manning. They were assigned to Holly Springs, Mississippi, and worked tirelessly there serving the sick. Manning himself died of the disease, one of 20,000 to do so. Dr. Swearingen eulogized his colleague, of whom he said, "I perhaps knew him better than any man," and to whom he referred as "a man, in the broadest and grandest sense."[26] President Rutherford B. Hayes appointed Doc Swearingen, the old Confederate, to a national commission of experts to investigate yellow fever in the aftermath of the epidemic. The report by this commission resulted in the establishment of the National Board of Health.[27]

HENRY LANDES. Washington County native Henry Landes was a 17-year-old student at Soule University when he enlisted in John Wallis' Company of the Twentieth Texas Infantry. He rose to the rank of orderly sergeant by the end of the war. Landes went into business after the war with John and Joseph Wallis. The firm they established became a prominent commercial house in Galveston and Landes ultimately became mayor of Galveston. (From *Indian Wars and Pioneers of Texas*, 1890.)

Yellow fever originated in West Africa. Ironically, scientists believe the disease may have been carried to the Americas on the same ships that brought slaves from Africa. The larvae of the disease's carrier, the *Aedes aegypti* mosquito, were likely in the water casks aboard ship.[28] Confederate veterans and their families, the African American men, women and children who had only just been freed from the bondage of slavery, and the soldiers of the Federal occupation force were all impacted by the epidemic. General Charles Griffin, the Federal officer commanding Texas, was among those who lost his life to the fever.

Yellow fever was a terrible tragedy to strike just two years after the relief to all of the end of the bloodshed of the Civil War. While many cities were hit hard by the epidemic, Chappell Hill gained the undesirable reputation of being an unhealthy place to live. The town would never recover.

18

National Reconciliation

Stephen Crane wrote in his classic novel of the war, *The Red Badge of Courage*, of

> the subtle battle brotherhood more potent even than the cause for which they were fighting ... a mysterious fraternity born of the smoke and danger of death.[1]

The Confederate veterans bore the painful memory of defeat, even as their dead comrades rested in peace. They sought solace in their lives, but often turned to their former comrades-in-arms as the only ones who truly understood. Unknowingly, these men added a new facet to the American character, the Southern experience of defeat.

There was little sign of any reconciliation between North and South in the early years after the war. When the government held the first official observance of Memorial Day at Arlington National Cemetery on May 30, 1868, guards did not allow Virginia families to decorate with flowers the graves of Confederates.[2] The process of reconciliation was a slow one that took time. That it ultimately did take place remains one of the greatest stories of our nation's history and offers perhaps one of the most compelling reasons to study the war. While Federal officials moved to care for the widows, orphans and indigent soldiers who fought to defend the Union, Confederate soldiers had no one to turn to for support.

Members of Hood's Brigade began discussing the formation of a relief association for maimed and indigent members, as well as widows and orphans, as early as mid–1866.[3] A group in Houston proposed the formation of the Hood's Texas Brigade Relief Association of Harris County. The *Houston Telegraph* encouraged readers in regard to the effort and the founding members thanked editor Clayton Gillespie for his support. A general convention was to have been held in December. Somehow, the matter never quite got underway. A few veterans of the Fourth Texas Infantry, Hood's Brigade, met outside Austin at Barton Springs on June 27, 1871. It was the anniversary of the brigade's first victory, the Battle of Gaines' Mill. The Confederates had buried their tattered battle flag in 1865 to keep it from falling into the hands of the occupying Federal troops. They felt such emotion upon digging up the old flag that they resolved to approach General Jerome Robertson in Independence about organizing a reunion. Robertson commanded the Texas Brigade longer than anyone else (14 months), including through Gettysburg and Chickamauga. He agreed and Hood's Texas Brigade Association was formed on May 14, 1872.[4] The association elected Robertson president in 1875 and re-elected him eleven times between 1875 and 1889.[5]

The association met every year after that for 61 years, except for the war years of 1898 and 1918. The reunion was always held on or around the anniversary date of the Battle of Gaines' Mill, June 27. Texas towns vied for the right to host the event. Twenty-nine did so at least one time. The silk battle flag, presented to the Fifth Texas Infantry by Mrs. Maude Young of Galveston in 1862, was on hand for the first reunion of the Hood's Texas Brigade Association and every reunion thereafter.[6] Fourteen men of the regiment had died as the color bearer of the torn and tattered flag,[7] which saw the Fifth Texas through all of its many battles until after Gettysburg.[8] John Bell Hood made his one and only appearance at the sixth annual reunion held at Waco in June 1877. He told his comrades that he was hopeful for the future, but admitted that he had only recently been able to look forward.[9] When John Bell Hood was dying of yellow fever in New Orleans two years later, he asked that the Texas Brigade take care of his children.[10]

Confederates organized throughout Texas to assist their own. Franklin C. Wilkes, formerly colonel with the Twenty-Fourth Texas Cavalry, was serving as general agent for the Bayland Confederate Orphans' Home in July 1872.[11] Wilkes had been mayor of Chappell Hill in 1866 and 1867. When Reconstruction set in, Wilkes went to Austin and served as pastor of First United Methodist Church for several years.[12] A group of gentlemen from Houston and Galveston, led by Rev. C. C. Preston, organized the Bayland Home not long after the war.[13] Up to 250 orphans lived on a 200-acre farm on Galveston Bay (near present-day Baytown, Texas) and attended school. This location was "easily accessible by steamboats, and so isolated as to be free from all sources of dissipation and ruin."[14] Wilkes became general agent for the home and traveled across the state seeking funds to maintain it.

An article in the July 20, 1872, *Dallas Herald* announced that the Rev. F. C. Wilkes, the general agent for the Bayland Orphans' Home, had arrived in town the previous morning and would remain for a few days. The editor noted:

> [W]e hope to have the further pleasure of hearing him preach at the Methodist church. As he was a gallant Colonel in the Confederate Army, so we believe him to be a faithful soldier of the cross.[15]

One writer later described Wilkes as "a peculiarly gifted man, eminently original, natural, practical and powerful as a preacher."[16] The Dallas paper explained to its readers that Wilkes was "traveling over the State looking for the destitute children, soliciting funds and making known the plans and aims of the board of managers of the Bayland Orphan Home."[17]

Wilkes's health in the fall of 1873 made it impossible for him to continue his itinerant ministry and he transferred to the Tennessee Conference. He was partially paralyzed by 1879 and returned to Texas to spend his last days with his three sons. Rev. Dr. Franklin Wilkes, despite his poor health, became chaplain of the Texas Senate in 1881. Although unable to stand, the old minister spoke "with trembling limbs, but with a clear and well modulated voice flashing volumes of thought with wonderful effect upon his audience."[18] His health continued to deteriorate and soon forced his resignation. Still, the stubborn old Confederate persisted. A church in Lampasas asked Wilkes to fill the term of a departing pastor. He moved there at the beginning of October and "though unusually feeble, his sermons were rich."[19] Franklin Collett Wilkes was on his deathbed at the beginning of December 1881. This man, who made a profession of religion at age 16 and became licensed to preach at age 19, expressed regret to a friend that he had not been more spiritual in his life. His devoted wife and his three sons were with him when he passed on December 8, 1881.[20] His final words were "Lord Jesus, be with me to the end!"[21]

Many of the Confederate veterans of Chappell Hill died off as early as the 1870s. Spelman Routt died in 1872. Green Bouldin died in 1874. Amos Allen and Thomas Davidson died in 1875 and R. W. "Curly Bob" Chappell, Jr., died in January 1876. James Norfolk Cocke died in June 1876. The 36-year-old Cocke left his 27-year-old wife Mattie McDade with four children, ranging in age from six months to seven years. He asked his sister Margaret from his deathbed to help Mattie raise the children. She did so faithfully until they were grown, at which time she went to live with her son and raise his seven children after his wife died.[22] Thomas J. Scurry died in 1879, as did Thomas Milton Keesee. Hosea Garrett, Jr., proud color-bearer for the Tenth Texas Infantry, died in October 1880.

The District Court of Washington County paused to honor Patrick Henry Swearingen when the Confederate colonel passed away on March 15, 1880. He had only a week earlier tried a case before the court. Swearingen suffered a stroke but a few hours after returning home and soon thereafter died. His colleagues agreed: "To us, members of the Bar to whom he was best known, with whom and of whom he has been one for nearly twenty-five years, the loss is well nigh irreparable,"[23] fondly recalled his rare talent as a public speaker and noted: "He was the soul of honor ... manly and candid ... eloquent, learned and polished in debate." The bar paid tribute to Swearingen's contributions, noting: "The community of which he was a leader in all lofty aspirations and worthy enterprises, the Religious and Educational institutions, to which so much of his time and attention were cheerfully given are bowed in grief."[24] His son and namesake grew up to become a prominent attorney and judge in San Antonio and the name is still carried proudly in the family.[25]

Rufus King Felder, James Landes and John D. Rogers attended the 1874 meeting of Hood's Texas Brigade Association in Galveston. Major F. C. Harme in the welcoming address told his comrades, "Standing in the sunshine and peace of the present, we welcome you, soldiers of the stormy past."[26] Harme went on to remember the dead: "we can love them just as much and cherish their memories just as tenderly, as if their names had never been associated with the canting reproach of disloyalty and treason."[27] The attendees greeted the appearance of the brigade's tattered old battle flag "with a torrent of applause that lasted for some minutes." General Thomas Waul echoed Harme's theme, when he delivered the main address, saying:

> [N]o such cause as that which was lost at Appomattox was odious. Such self-sacrifice as that displayed during the four long years of strife could not have odium attached to it. The men who fought the battles of the South would have the veneration and respect of the good and brave of all nations.[28]

Some Federal veterans were in attendance at Brenham in June 1881 when Hood's Texas Brigade Association gathered for its annual reunion. The Honorable D. C. Giddings addressed the gathering. The former cavalry officer, who served under George Washington Carter in the Twenty-First Texas Cavalry, by this time had become the first Southern Democrat to gain a seat in the U.S. Congress after the war.[29] He told the crowd:

> [Y]our presence will tend to dissipate the error that the reunion of the two armies will tend to keep alive the animosities of the late war. Had the matter of issue in that war been left to a vote of the soldiers of the two parties, or even of the Union soldiers, a peaceful solution would have followed and much bloodshed been saved.... All honor to the men who fought on both sides, whether they wore blue or gray. Their blood and their ashes mingle in the same soil.... Washington County welcomes to her borders the soldiers of the Lost Cause and just as warmly welcomes the honest soldiers of the Union.[30]

John C. Justice, who served in Company F of Terry's Texas Rangers, died at Chappell Hill in 1885. He had returned to Chappell Hill after the war and opened a general store that he ran for many years. Justice, along with Solomon Carter, Riley Condron and Austin Baker among others, were members of the Traveling Masonic Lodge of the Eighth Texas Cavalry during the war. He was active in the Chappell Hill lodge after the war, as well as an alderman in the city government. He lost an infant daughter in 1874 and his wife Emma Toland just three months later.[31] His second wife, Mary, daughter of Terrell J. Jackson, outlived him.

Many Confederates moved west to Texas after the end of the war. There was a sense that Texas was not only undestroyed, but even perhaps "unreconstructed." The letters "G T T" scrawled on doors throughout the South stood for "Gone To Texas." While the Confederacy had struggled to evolve a clear nationalism of its own, the Lone Star State had always had a distinct sense of Texan nationalism. People across the South recognized that and sought refuge in Texas. They also recognized opportunity in the open spaces of Texas. Numerous Confederates moved into Chappell Hill and vicinity after the war.

West Pointer John Creed Moore commanded the Second Texas Infantry at Shiloh. He was commended for gallantry and promoted to brigadier general. He led his brigade at Corinth, Vicksburg, Chattanooga and in the Atlanta campaign. Moore taught school in Texas for many years.[32] He was in Chappell Hill with Soule University in the early 1870s.[33]

18. National Reconciliation

Augustus David Sadler was among the Confederates from the east who took up residence in Chappell Hill. He served during the war as a sergeant with the Twenty-First Mississippi Infantry, Barksdale's Mississippi Brigade. These Mississippians distinguished themselves with Robert E. Lee's Army of Northern Virginia.[34] Augustus David Sadler fought his last fight in December 1862 at Fredericksburg. Barksdale's Mississippians were stationed in the town, as Confederate artillery on the heights was ineffective against the Federal engineers building pontoons across the Rappahannock River.[35] Sadler wrote:

> [W]e were descending the hill onto the plain ... the flash from at least 100 of the 170 cannon mounted on Stafford Heights and more than half-encircling Fredericksburg on the north and east. The shells came shrieking and bursting in the city, over the city, seemingly everywhere, as we double-quicked now to get into position on the river bank. ... From daylight to afternoon we remained in this position, firing not a gun but receiving the fire of batteries and sharpshooters all the time. The ranks were lying in the street-gutter, heads to pavement for protection ... there was a terrific explosion almost in my face and a powerful shock as a heavy galvanic battery, and turning my eyes towards my feet which seemed benumbed, I saw that I had no feet.... Just behind me lay two of my company, killed dead by fragments of the same shell and two others seriously wounded.... I crawled on my hands and knees ... four of my company ran to me and began to pick me up.[36]

Barksdale's Mississippians suffered severe losses, but held out and delayed the Federal crossing "longer than anyone might have expected or even hoped"[37] and their Southern comrades-in-arms held the heights against repeated Federal assaults that day. Fredericksburg was a major victory for the Confederates as 1862 ended. Augustus David Sadler lived to tell of the victory to the young people of Chappell Hill. His daughter Eva married State Representative William David Crockett.

There were others. James P. Thompson fought with the Eighteenth Alabama Infantry before moving to Chappell Hill after the war. The Eighteenth Alabama fought at Shiloh and Chickamauga, faced Sherman as he marched on Atlanta and suffered through the bloody defeats at Franklin and Nashville. They took part in one of the final battles of the war at Spanish Fort near Mobile and were paroled at Meridian. Thompson died at Chappell Hill in 1884 and is buried in the town's Atkinson Cemetery. William Haley saw the war with the Fifty-Seventh Alabama Infantry. The Fifty-Seventh suffered 48 percent casualties at the Battle of Peach Tree Creek in the Atlanta Campaign and similar losses at Franklin and Nashville, two of the worst debacles of the war.[38] Six Confederate generals, including Hiram Granbury of Waco, were killed in the slaughter at Franklin. Bill Haley was severely wounded by a shell at Nashville "from which he suffered greatly during his life and was partly the cause of his death."[39] Bill Haley farmed in Chappell Hill until his death in 1898. Charles Askew fought with the Eufaula (Alabama) Light Artillery and saw action at Chickamauga and Atlanta and Tennessee.[40] He moved to Chappell Hill after the war and lived there until his death in 1909.[41]

As early as 1875 at their annual reunion at Huntsville, the Hood's Texas Brigade Association resolved:

> That all soldiers now present whether Confederate or Federal who were true to his command colors during the war are cordially invited to participate with us in the association and hospitalities of the day.[42]

The group further also unanimously adopted the proposal of General Jerome Robertson that a reunion of the veterans of both sides "would be productive of much good."[43] The association went so far as to appoint a committee to begin arrangements for such a gathering. But nothing came of the idea. The 1876 reunion at Bryan, Texas, officially recognized the bravery of their former adversary, General George Custer, and extended its sympathies to his family just months after his death at the Battle of Little Bighorn.[44] James Landes and John D. Rogers were among the participants.[45] The association did invite President Rutherford B. Hayes to their 1877 reunion in Waco, although he graciously declined.[46] Instead, John Bell Hood appeared. "Cheer after cheer greeted him ... while the tears were streaming down the faces of his old comrades."[47] Only 100 of the remaining 400 still living attended. James Landes was among these. The Texas warrior pride remained. The Brenham Grays, composed of former troopers of Terry's Texas Rangers and Tom Green's Brigade, issued invitations to a grand military ball at the Brenham Opera House in November 1877.

Efforts at national reconciliation gained momentum in the 1880s. The attendance of several distinguished Confederate generals at Ulysses Grant's funeral in New York City in August 1885 made a significant statement to the nation. A number of Blue-Gray reunions were held in this period. While men from both sides sought to heal the rift, emotions still ran high. These men faced attacks from some of their former comrades-in-arms for their attempts at extending overtures to former enemies. These conflicts prevented early Blue-Gray encounters in the 1880s from being at the battlefields where they had first met. Instead, individual veterans groups from North or South invited groups from the opposing side to their hometown. These events were major commercial successes. A breakthrough occurred in 1887 when veterans of Pickett's Brigade met with Pennsylvania veterans on the battlefield at Gettysburg. One observer called this first ever Blue and Gray gathering on a battlefield the most remarkable reunion ever held by opposing forces.[48] The press in both North and South embraced the occasion and furthered the effort toward national reconciliation. Photographs of men from either side embracing emphasized that these men were not Northern or Southern, but simply American heroes.

Washington County seems not to have been too concerned with the important reunion that later took place at Gettysburg in 1887. The *Brenham Banner* made no mention of the event. Instead, the focus in Brenham, Chappell Hill and the surrounding communities was on the threat of the prohibition of alcohol. A prohibition club had been organized at Chappell Hill.[49] Five hundred people attended a barbecue and debate on the subject of prohibition between Harry Haynes and D. C. Giddings. Both were active members of the Washington Camp of United Confederate Veterans and were well known to all. Giddings argued: "The true function of the government was to simply prevent the trespassing by one man on the rights of another," and added, "no question ever presented to the people, except that of secession in 1860,

18. National Reconciliation

was in his opinion so important."[50] Giddings declared, "In that fight Washington county sent forth her sons to battle for what they thought was a constitutional right given them by their fathers ... this was one of no less importance."[51]

While the strained relations between North and South continued to fade, some things could not be forgotten. It was rumored that General Phil Sheridan, formerly in command of Texas during Reconstruction, might run for president. Many Texans could not forgive Sheridan for his harsh rule. The April 15, 1887, issue of the *Brenham Banner* carried the following on the top of the page:

> It is said that Phil Sheridan is being urged for president. Phew![52]

Sheridan died on June 1, 1888, and saved Texas any further concern in that regard.

Jefferson Davis and William Tecumseh Sherman carried on a fierce battle of angry dialogue long after the war was over. Sherman, commanding general of the U.S. Army until 1884, found intolerable Davis' firm stand as to his belief in his cause and his corresponding refusal to feel a need to apologize. The *Brenham Banner*, in discussing the contempt these two men expressed publicly for one another, wrote:

> While the animosities growing out of the war may be said to be over, the feeling of the people toward the two gentleman named is influenced to a great extent by the section of country in which they were raised.[53]

Brigadier General Sullivan "Sul" Ross, who had led Andrew Keller and others in his famed Cavalry Brigade during the war, became governor of Texas in 1886. The Adjutant General's Office of the U.S. War Department advised Governor Ross in 1887 that President Grover Cleveland had delivered an executive order to return all Texas Confederate battle flags captured in battle. Governor Ross responded enthusiastically and Texas prepared to receive the flags at the UCV reunion in Dallas that summer. While plans were being made, the Grand Army of the Republic, an association of Federal veterans, raised such a furor that President Cleveland rescinded the order.[54] A disappointed Governor Ross told the Hood's Brigade Association that summer:

> Those whose hatred had remained implacable through all these years of peace, are men who ... seek to make amends for their lack of deeds of valor by preaching a crusade of bitterness.[55]

The Confederate veterans continued to age. Rev. Dr. Benjamin T. Kavanaugh, who had served as chaplain of Sterling Price's Army, remained in Chappell Hill until 1871. He continued to actively minister throughout the Houston-Austin region, including editing and contributing to a number of journals, until he lost his eyesight in 1881 at the age of 76. His wife, Margaret, had passed on in October 1880[56] and was buried in Chappell Hill's Masonic Cemetery alongside the two children they lost in the 1873 yellow fever epidemic. The old Confederate, "her venerable companion" of 53 years of marriage, returned home to his native Kentucky to be cared for. He lived another seven years and died in 1888 at the age of 83 years.[57]

The veterans, even as they addressed their own needs, became more active in their communities by the late 1880s. Veterans of Hood's Texas Brigade raised money for a Texas Confederate Veterans Home in Austin. A major fund raiser for the benefit of the Confederate Home was held in Austin on December 27, 1886. *The Philomathean*, a monthly literary newspaper published in Chappell Hill in connection with the Chappell Hill Female College, ran an ad for the benefit on its front page for four months. The ad highlighted "1500 PRIZES ranging in value from One Dollar in Silver to a One Thousand Dollar Piano." Among the mid-range prizes were a tract of land near Austin, 320 acres in Harris County and 70 acres of land in Travis County, as well as two farm wagons and a tea set.[58] John Day Jackson was the agent for the Home in Chappell Hill. The November 1886 issue of *The Philomathean* reported:

> Mr. Jackson deserves much commendation for the straightforward, energetic manner in which he has conducted the interests of the Home; and we predict no one will bring up a longer list of names in proportion to the territory.[59]

The paper also announced that Jackson had offered a medal to the student of Chappell Hill Female College who wrote "the best essay on any subject bearing on the Confederate cause."[60]

I. M. Onins, formerly a private in Company B of Terry's Texas Rangers, served as the president of Chappell Hill Female College in 1880 and 1881.[61] Soule University had numerous presidents after the war. Among these was Reverend Edward W. Tarrant, who was employed to teach and later served as president in 1884–1885. The native Alabaman raised and led an artillery battalion during the war. Captain Tarrant led his men in the Atlanta campaign and afterwards with Hood into Tennessee. Tarrant's Battery lost most of its men and horses and all of its guns at the disastrous Battle of Nashville in December 1864, whereupon Tarrant and his few remaining men were reassigned to Fort Blakeley on Mobile Bay.[62] It was there that the last major battle of the war was fought on April 9, 1865, and Tarrant achieved a certain amount of fame among Southerners for having fired the last cannon fired by the Confederates at the end of that fight.[63]

There was spirited competition among the students of Chappell Hill Female College for the best Confederate essay. The judging committee included Miss Irene Toland, Captain J. W. McNeely and Dr. Peter Raysor. *The Philomathean* published the winning essay in the December issue. Miss Lulu Thompson's essay, "All Lost, and Nothing Won," reiterated the argument that the compact between the states was voluntary but added, "Since this Union was equally dear to every heart, the Confederation was not formed to destroy it, but to secure the blessings of liberty under it."[64] Miss Thompson lamented the loss of "many noble lives" and expressed horror at the conduct of Sherman and Sheridan. The theme of Miss Thompson's essay expressed the mindset that perhaps still existed for many in Chappell Hill in 1886:

> I think that in the heart of every true Southern woman, to the end of time, "Gray will be Gray, and Blue will be Blue."[65]

Miss Thompson closed her essay with:

18. National Reconciliation

> Time, the magic healer, has cured the wounds, but the scars are with us still, they will be with us forever, and forever will be with us the consciousness, that, though our Cause was defeated, the nobleness and glory of it are recorded in unfading letters of Truth.[66]

The fund raising was successful and the home, which became known as The Old Confederates Home, was completed in 1887. The construction and the early years of operation were entirely financed by private funds. The state of Texas gradually became more involved, assuming management of institution in 1891 and instituting a special tax in 1894 to help cover the cost of supporting the veterans, their widows and the Home.

Confederate literature was not restricted to the Chappell Hills across Texas and the South. A literary critic wrote in 1888:

> Not only is the epoch of the war the favorite field of American fiction to-day, but the Confederate soldier is the popular hero. Our literature has become not only Southern in type but distinctly Confederate in sympathy.[67]

New Orleans became the center of Southern culture and politics in the post-war period by virtue of having survived the war relatively intact. New Orleans, having been occupied by the Federals since 1862, was in sharp contrast to the ruins that were Atlanta and Richmond. Numerous Confederates relocated to New Orleans after the war, including such leaders as James Longstreet, John Bell Hood and Jefferson Davis. The various veterans groups across the South, which joined in 1889 to form the United Confederate Veterans, were in place when Jeff Davis died in New Orleans in December 1889.

The leaders of United Confederate Veterans organized an immense show of Confederate solidarity for their former president. Jeff Davis' body lay in state for one and a half days. Tens of thousands traveled to New Orleans to pay their respects and to join together. The city honored Davis with the greatest funeral the South has ever known and a large delegation from Texas attended. Memorial services also were held throughout Texas "at nearly every city, town, and hamlet in the State"[68] in honor of Jefferson Davis. Dr. Richard M. Swearingen made an eloquent address at a large gathering held in Austin.[69] Dr. Swearingen asked that his "Memorial Address" of that day be appended to his biography, "not on account of any special merit claimed for it, but to perpetuate, and, if possible, to make imperishable some evidence of his love and admiration for a pure, a good and great man."[70] The address read in part:

> Jefferson Davis was the ideal Southerner—the highest type of American manhood ... when his official light went out forever, he won the glory of a martyr. ... Farewell my peerless, unconquered old chief. Your fame will go down the ages as the purest and grandest of mortals; and I do pray that your mighty spirit has found some beautiful spot on the ever shining river, where no beat of a drum nor clank of chains shall mar the melody of golden harps when swept by angel fingers; where no prison walls can hide the light of the throne, and where the smile of a loving God will fall around you forever.[71]

Noah Whitten died at Chappell Hill in 1890. The *Brenham Banner* reported that he "died in poverty and almost indigent."[72] The 80-year-old enlisted in the Seventeenth Alabama Infantry at the age of 46 and served in the Atlanta campaign and the bloody disasters at Franklin and Nashville and was among the shattered remnants that surrendered to Sherman at Greensboro in April 1865. Whitten, as did many Confederates of the Deep South, moved to Texas after the war. He never found the success he had imagined. More Confederate veterans lived in Texas than any other state of the Confederacy by 1890. The Fourteenth Amendment to the Constitution prohibited Confederate veterans from receiving any federal benefits, so the states did what they could. The state of Texas handed out nearly 2 million acres to surviving disabled and indigent veterans between 1881 and 1883, each man receiving two sections of land, 1,240 acres. In 1889 the state began granting pensions to indigent Confederate veterans or their widows. Widows of the Chappell Hill Confederates who applied for and received pensions included Mrs. Henry Brandt, Mrs. James Landes (Kate), Mrs. Rufus King Felder (Lula), as well as Mrs. Gideon Keesee, Mrs. John McDade and Mrs. R. C. Tapscott.[73]

The push toward national reconciliation between North and South continued to gain momentum, even as the South became more and more focused on the "Lost Cause." *Century Magazine* assumed a significant role in the reconciliation movement. This well-regarded publication of its day published hundreds of articles on the Civil War between 1884 and 1887. The magazine's editors worked tirelessly to engage high-ranking officers, Federal and Confederate, as authors. The emphasis was on the Federal soldier as savior of the Union and also the Confederate as the noble defender of his home, his heritage and states' rights. While there was merit to recounting American valor, this perspective tended to obscure race as the cause of the war, the emancipation of the African Americans and the liberation of the democratic republic from the hypocrisy of slavery. The magazine ultimately combined these articles into a much celebrated, four-volume series, *Battles and Leaders of the Civil War*, published in 1888. The editors intentionally played an important role in the matter of "reconciliation through battle recollection."[74]

Century Magazine continued such articles after the publication of its landmark series. Some of these articles led to harsh debates on issues beyond what really happened and what better command decision might have been made. The treatment of prisoners of war by each side was one such issue. *Century Magazine* published an article in March 1891 by Dr. John Wyeth entitled "Cold Cheer in Camp Morton" in which the former Confederate soldier described his experiences as a Federal prisoner during the war. Wyeth was sensitive to the fact that the exploitation of the experience of Northern prisoners in Southern prisons had damaged the reputation of the South. He argued that this was able to take place only because the Confederate experience in Federal prisons had not been told. Wyeth presented horrific details relating to imprisonment in Camp Morton and concluded that there was "little cause for death had humane and reasonable care of the prisoners been exercised."[75] The former secretary to Oliver Morton, Indiana's war governor, fired off a sharp response in *Century* that September, accompanied by an endorsement by the Indiana Grand Army of the Republic. He wrote that the treatment of the Confederate prisoners at

18. National Reconciliation

Camp Morton had "long been a matter of pride to the people of Indiana."[76] The condescending rebuttal suggested: "Young Wyeth seemed to forget that he was a prisoner of war and apparently was surprised to find that Camp Morton was not a hotel upholstered in modern style."[77] Wyeth was allowed a response, in which he provided numerous letters of support. Dr. W. E. Shelton of Austin wrote: "The treatment of prisoners in a great many instances was brutal and inhuman,"[78] and Congressman C. B. Kilgore of Texas wrote: "You have drawn a very moderate picture of the horrors of that horrible pen."[79]

Henry Christian Brandt of Chappell Hill never spoke of the horrors of Camp Morton. He took his personal stories to the grave with him. Brandt wanted no reminders in 1891 to resurrect the nightmares he had buried within his psyche. He was a devout Christian and this may have given him the insight to understand the need for personal reconciliation. Brandt's own experience at Camp Morton included a friendship with another German American. Frederick Fouts, a lieutenant in the Fifteenth Indiana Artillery, was captured when Harper's Ferry fell to the Confederates in September 1862. He was released on parole and subsequently assigned guard duty at the prisoner of war camp at Camp Morton in Indianapolis. Fouts and Brandt likely met as a result of their common first language, as well as their shared love of carpentry.[80] Frederick Fouts returned to action in April 1863. Fouts and Brandt would have known each other for only a couple of months. The United States government awarded Frederick Fouts the Medal of Honor in 1896 for his bravery under fire at Harper's Ferry. Fouts wrote a book about the Civil War, which was published (in German) in 1902. He gave a signed copy to his friend, Henry Brandt, with whom he kept in touch after the war. The book remains in the Brandt family to this day and is on display at the Chappell Hill Historical Society.

Racial reconciliation between white and black remained a barrier to sectional reconciliation between Northern and Southern whites. The withdrawal of Federal troops from the South following the election of Rutherford B. Hayes to President in 1876 led to the return of white Democratic control throughout the former Confederacy. The voting rights of African Americans in the South disappeared with the absence of Federal supervision of elections. Republicans attempted over for over a decade to pass a "force bill," so named because it proposed authorizing the use of military strength to enforce Federal law and protect African Americans in the South. President Benjamin Harrison, elected in 1888, promised voters his support of such legislation. Many Federal veterans of the war, members of the Grand Army of the Republic (GAR), had strong views about the bloody sacrifice made by their comrades and the emancipation of the African Americans. The GAR lost control of the party to the new generation, led by the corporate capitalist elite. The Republican-controlled House passed the Federal Elections Bill of 1890, but Democrats, allied with pro-business Republicans, defeated the bill in the Senate. The Democrats gained control of Congress in the elections of 1892 and blocked any further such efforts. Federal influence on civil rights in the South essentially disappeared for the next 60 to 70 years.[81]

The 1891 reunion of Hood's Texas Brigade Association was held in Livingston, Texas. E. C. Dwyer of Houston, who fought in the war as a Federal soldier, was among the speakers. He told the gathered Confederates:

> With us the war is over, and its only existence is upon the tongues of politicians and demagogues, the half of whom never smelt powder.... Among the old soldiers there is a spirit of fraternity that mantles our country ... a spirit that binds us closer together in bonds that let us trust.[82]

Dr. John Washington Lockhart spoke at the unveiling in Galveston of a monument to General Sidney Sherman and David Burnet in 1894. He had moved from Chappell Hill to Galveston in his later years, although he kept his land in Chappell Hill and returned each year for harvest. Dr. Lockhart included the following among his remarks:

> Now all this took place scarcely thirty years since, yet the recuperative power of humanity is so great that one rarely ever hears the great civil war spoken of except by the old participants in their annual conclaves.... The north and the south have long since shaken hands over the bloody chasm, which was filled with the best blood of both parties and now the proud flag of our fathers floats as of yore over the south as well as the north.[83]

The dedication of Chickamauga and Chattanooga Military Park in 1895 was the occasion for a gathering of 40,000 veterans from both sides and there was a sense that America was coming come back together. The 1895 reunion of the United Confederate Veterans was held in Houston on May 22–24 in the new Winnie Davis Auditorium. The auditorium was named for the youngest daughter of Jefferson Davis, who made an appearance and received a one-minute standing ovation. The Texas A&M Corps of Cadets traveled from College Station to Houston to attend. Washington Camp No. 239 of the United Confederate Veterans met the week before. The *Brenham Banner* reported Rufus King Felder of Chappell Hill and Bolling Eldridge of Brenham, both formerly of the Fifth Texas Infantry, were among 10 delegates elected by the Washington Camp to the Texas Division.[84] Felder's signature appears on the sign-up sheet of members of Hood's Texas Brigade Association who attended the Houston event.[85] Once the meeting began, the *Brenham Banner* noted: "Houston is entertaining the largest crowd ever assembled in Texas, if not the South."[86]

Seven of the Confederacy's lieutenant generals were still living at the time of the Houston UCV gathering. These included James Longstreet, Wade Hampton, John Gordon, Stephen Lee, Alexander Stewart and Joseph Wheeler. General "Fightin' Joe" Wheeler, under whom Terry's Texas Rangers served, attended. The souvenir album noted that one of the biggest events was a reception given by Terry's Texas Rangers at the Light Guard Armory in honor of General Wheeler and his daughter, Miss Annie. The souvenir album for the event noted:

> The "Old Bee Hunter," as the boys used to call him, felt his condition and appreciated the demonstration of kindness shown by the survivors of his "old guard." ... For two long hours, to the strains of martial music, cordial greetings were exchanged and a happy time was had. It is estimated that at least five thousand of the leading gentlemen of Houston graced the occasion by their presence.[87]

RUFUS KING FELDER and friends with a catch on the coast. (From the Archives of the Chappell Hill Historical Society.)

The album made light of the past, noting of Wheeler that for the second time in his life he was compelled to strike his colors and surrender to the force of superior numbers.

Even while the wounds seemingly were being healed, a new battle was brewing. Ex-Confederate General Stephen D. Lee of Mississippi, as chairman of the UCV's Historical Committee, warned the Houston attendees of the need to defend the history being written of the war they had fought.[88] General Patrick Cleburne had said:

> Surrender means that the history of this heroic struggle will be written by the enemy, that our youth will be trained by Northern school teachers; learn from Northern school books THEIR version of the war; and taught to regard our gallant dead as traitors and our maimed veterans as fit subjects of derision.

The United Confederate Veterans took these words to heart. Texas Confederate societies became active in monitoring libraries and schools throughout Texas. Children of the Confederacy chapters were formed. The "Lost Cause" became an active effort. Texas passed a uniform textbook law in 1897 that mandated books "shall not contain anything of a partisan or sectarian character"[89] and gave preference to textbooks by Texas authors and publishers.[90] Some authors thereupon proceeded to glorify the brave Texan Confederate veterans as knights of a crusade.

Meanwhile, others worked hard to offset sectionalism. Henry Cabot Lodge began publishing his classic *Hero Tales from American History* in 1895. By 1902, he coauthored the latest version with Theodore Roosevelt and continued to do so for several years after that. The book included heroes from both sides of the War Between the States among its stories, noting: "Countless deeds of heroism were performed by Northerner and by Southerner, by officer and by private, in every year of the great struggle." Men like Jackson and Lee received as much reverence from Lodge, a Massachusetts Yankee, as they did in any "Lost Cause" volumes published in the South.

Confederates joined in the effort to begin to more aggressively promote national unity. One Confederate discovered that Federal veterans of two Chicago Grand Army of the Republic posts had been decorating Confederate graves in Oakwoods Cemetery in Chicago since 1876! John Underwood obtained permission from the Federal government to erect a monument to the 6,000 Confederate soldiers who died and were buried at Camp Douglas in Chicago. That the government would admit to such loss of life in a Federal prison was a breakthrough. A large number of Federal and Confederate veterans attended the dedication on Memorial Day 1895. An aged General James Longstreet, who had advocated reconciliation not long after the end of the war, was among those present.[91]

Former Confederate officer and Texas senator Scott Field told the participants at the 1895 Hood's Brigade reunion at Calvert, Texas, that he would leave no heritage of hate to his children, insisting, "We are all together in the house of our fathers."[92] Field also did expressed a desire that there be "justice to the dead and the noble cause for which they died," and that "the true southern sentiment should live forever," remarks which one reporter noted were wildly applauded.[93] Two years later, a speaker at the annual reunion in Floresville reminded the crowd:

18. National Reconciliation

> What a feeling of loyalty and patriotism pervades the air at these Reunions! It is a false impression that these gatherings have a tendency to engender strife and malice; on the contrary ... they have for their object a more lofty patriotic and praiseworthy aim, that is to perpetuate and instill in the minds of the younger generation those sacred, inherent, constitutional principles involved in the late war.[94]

One member made public his intention to advertise and return the sword of a colonel in the Fifth New York Zouaves, which he had taken at Second Manassas.[95]

Dr. Richard Swearingen returned to Chappell Hill to address a graduating class at Soule University in his final years. Swearingen served as state health officer for Texas in 1881 and again in 1883, as well as on the Austin School Board of Trustees for many years. The former Confederate officer told the young men:

> A great destiny is awaiting some of you. Your country will soon demand your services. The last century is but the first page of that immense volume that must tell her story. The hopes of the patriot now repose in the rising generation. The presence race of men is so embittered ... that they can never revive the lost love [of country]. But I beg you to cherish none of their passions, none of their animosities.[96]

Dr. Richard Swearingen died in Austin on August 7, 1898. He witnessed a remarkable upwelling of patriotic sentiment across the nation in his last months of life.

It was war that gave the nation the greatest opportunity to heal and the South to show its renewed dedication to the nation. The battleship *Maine* blew up in Havana harbor on February 15, 1898. Newspapers across America had been calling for the nation to invade Cuba and free it from Spain. The United States government declared war on Spain on April 21. Texan men rushed to enlist, just as they had 35 years earlier to fight the North. This time, the men of North and South found common cause. Men across the South, including Confederate veterans, seized the opportunity to prove their patriotism to the Stars and Stripes. Fightin' Joe Wheeler, under whom a large number of Chappell Hill men had fought in Terry's Texas Rangers, was a U.S. congressman representing Alabama. The 62-year-old man accepted command of the U.S. Cavalry at the request of President McKinley. McKinley had told a gathering of Confederate veterans during his campaign for the presidency in 1896, "Let us remember now and in all the future that we are Americans and what is good for Ohio is good for Virginia."[97] Crack Regular Army troops, composed entirely of African Americans, were among those who fought under Wheeler. There were also Teddy Roosevelt's Rough Riders, organized in San Antonio. The Rough Riders caused a great local fanfare. The Stars and Stripes may never before have been waved so wildly in Texas. When the hostilities began, the first American to die in the Spanish-American War was a Southerner.[98] There was a sense across the country that the surge of nationalism that accompanied the Spanish-American War was bringing together North and South. African Americans, even as some distinguished themselves in the same war, were forgotten in the euphoria of this healing.

Well over a thousand American women went to Cuba during the Spanish-American War to serve with Clara Barton as nurses. Miss Annie Wheeler, daughter of General Fightin' Joe, became known as "The Angel of Santiago" for the role she played.⁹⁹ Dr. Irene Toland of the Toland planter family of Chappell Hill went to Santiago as an army nurse under the auspices of the Daughters of the American Revolution. Dr. Toland had a successful medical practice in St. Louis, Missouri. She contacted the government and offered her services upon learning that yellow fever had broken out among the American troops in Cuba. Irene considered herself immune to the disease, having contracted yellow fever in Chappell Hill years earlier and survived. She received her commission on July 19 and was assigned to Siboney, Cuba. Dr. Toland ministered to the sick and wounded for a month. Malaria and dysentery were widespread. She became ill with malarial fever on August 23 and died on September 25 aboard a hospital ship off Santiago. The St. Louis *Post-Dispatch* ran a full-page feature in her honor on Sunday, October 2, 1898, headlined "Dr. Irene Toland of St. Louis Gave Her Life To Save Suffering Santiago Soldiers."¹⁰⁰ Numerous tributes by prominent citizens who knew her well were included. Dr. Irene Toland's remains were returned to Chappell Hill and interred in Atkinson Cemetery.

M. M. FELDER.

MIERS FELDER. Miers Felder served in the Fifth Texas Infantry during the war. He was promoted to the rank of corporal, but sustained severe wounds at Second Manassas and was discharged and sent home. Miers lost his hand in a cotton gin accident in 1876. He persevered and was elected representative in the Texas Legislature in 1889 and 1891. He was an alderman in Chappell Hill for many years and served as president of the Board of Trustees of Chappell Hill Female College. He passed away in 1899. (From *Personnel of the Texas State Government, with Sketches of Distinguished Texans*, 1889.)

Rebecca Toland, Irene's sister, attended seminary in Texas from 1883 to 1890. She moved to San Luis Potosi, Mexico, upon graduation and ran a mission school there for 12 years. A school in Matanzas, Cuba, was named for Irene Toland. Rebecca Toland transferred to Matanzas in 1902 and served that school for the next 23 years until her retirement in 1925.¹⁰¹ Such links served to deepen the ties between the Southern states and Cuba, far more so than any attempts by filibusters or Bickley's Knights of the Golden Circle before the Civil War.

Meanwhile, the Confederate veterans continued to die out. William Haley had been among the many Confederate veterans who moved west and began a new life for himself in Chappell Hill after the war. He fought in the Atlanta campaign and

Hood's Tennessee campaign with the Fifty-Seventh Alabama Infantry.[102] Haley passed away on his farm in Chappell Hill in November 1898. Other veterans and family friends took care of the aging Confederates. Charles W. Thompson, formerly of Chappell Hill, wrote his daughter in 1895:

> I am looking every day for Mr. [John] Grissett. He is an old friend of the Thompson family at Chappell Hill. He will live with us. He is the best old man in the state. He is the son-in-law of Travis who fell at the Alamo."[103]

Grissett, a Chappell Hill farmer before and after the war, was a private in Company K of Terry's Texas Rangers with so many other men from Chappell Hill.

Horace Shattuck died at Chappell Hill in February 1899 at the age of 83. He left New Hampshire as a young man and settled at Velasco on the Texas coast near modern-day Freeport. Shattuck fought in the Texas Revolution, most

RUFUS KING FELDER. Rufus King Felder of Chappell Hill was one of Washington County's most distinguished Civil War veterans until his death in 1922. He served the entire war with Hood's Texas Brigade, being present at the surrender at Appomattox in April 1865. (From the Harold B. Simpson Research Center, Hill College, Hillsboro, Texas.)

notably in the Battle of Velasco in 1832. He served the Confederacy as a sergeant with Waller's Texas Cavalry and returned to Velasco after the war. He moved to Chappell Hill to be among his former comrades-in-arms after he lost three daughters in the hurricane that completely destroyed Velasco on June 25, 1875, and lost his wife three months later.

Miers M. Felder died at Chappell Hill on March 11, 1899. The Hood's Brigade veteran lived with a disabled arm and foot from wounds received at Second Manassas. In 1876, he lost his hand to a cotton gin saw.[104] He was an alderman in Chappell Hill for many years, president of the Board of Trustees of Chappell Hill Female College

and a representative for Washington County in the Texas Legislature in 1889 and 1891.[105] Miers's cousin, Rufus King Felder, was present at the annual Hood's Texas Brigade Association reunion in Austin on May 2, 1899, that acknowledged Miers as one of "our heroes who have crossed over the river...."[106] The 1899 Hood's Brigade reunion also elected Rev. Henry M. Haynie of Chappell Hill as chaplain of the association.[107] Haynie, who grew up in Washington County and served in the Fourth Texas Infantry, settled in Mississippi after the war. He returned to Texas in 1884 after entering the ministry, and the Methodist Conference sent Haynie to Chappell Hill in 1897.[108] It was written, "No preacher in the conference was more universally loved than he ... he never failed to get into the hearts of all the people, both saints and sinners."[109] He died in 1901 at the age of 64 years.[110]

Dr. John Washington Lockhart, a prominent Confederate veteran spokesman, was living in Galveston at the time of the great hurricane that destroyed that city on Sunday, September 8, 1900. He was 76 years old. The Lockharts weathered the storm on the island. They managed to gain passage from Galveston on a steamer the following Thursday. When the ship ran aground at nearby Texas City, the passengers were forced to row ashore in lifeboats. They walked two miles along a railroad track to find transportation into Houston late that night. From there they made their way to the Lockhart plantation at Chappell Hill. The entire experience was too much for a man of Dr. Lockhart's advanced years.[111] He expired within the month and was buried in Chappell Hill's Masonic Cemetery alongside so many other Confederates. The *Galveston News* cited a dispatch from Brenham on the day following the death of Dr. Lockhart, which read:

> No man ever lived in Washington County who stood higher as a physician and a man than Dr. J. W. Lockhart and no man ever died in the county enjoying higher esteem and whose death was more universally and sincerely deplored.[112]

The Great Galveston Storm of 1900 did much damage inland, as well. Huge oaks, pecans and elms were uprooted in Chappell Hill and Brenham.[113] The storm destroyed Chappell Hill's beautiful Methodist Church. Henry Christian Brandt responded. He designed and supervised the construction of a new church using East Texas pine. The woodwork within the church, which still stands to this day, is beautiful.

Annual gatherings of the United Confederate Veterans regularly attracted tens of thousands of veterans and an even larger number of non-veteran participants throughout the 1890s. The membership of the United Confederate Veterans peaked in 1903. Some 80,000 members represented nearly a third of all living veterans. The group could boast 1,565 camps in 75 percent of the counties of the states of the former Confederacy. There were more in UCV camps in Texas than in any other state.

Opposite: 1900 REUNION OF HOOD'S TEXAS BRIGADE. The Hood's Brigade Association was organized on May 14, 1872. Sixty-three reunions were held between that date and 1933. The association was responsible for erecting a monument in memory of the brigade on the grounds of the state capitol in Austin in 1910. (From the Harold B. Simpson Research Center, Hill College, Hillsboro, Texas.)

Dan Winston of Washington County was introduced at the 1902 meeting of Hood's Texas Brigade Association at Bryan.[114] It was noted at the 1904 reunion in Ennis that Winston, "the only negro in the association,"[115] had never missed a reunion since the organization of the association in 1872. Winston went off to war as the body (personal) servant of Tom Baber of Bryan. Baber was a first lieutenant with Company E of the Fifth Texas Infantry, the Dixie Blues to which the Felder boys of Chappell Hill belonged. Baber was promoted to captain on July 22, 1862, after John D. Rogers resigned and led the company until being wounded in October 1864 at Darbytown.[116] Winston remained with Company E through the course of the war as the cook.[117]

Cities, states and organizations became active in erecting Confederate monuments across the South as the turn of the century neared. The monuments honored the dead, but also helped the South hold on to its legacy. These monuments to the dead perhaps did become shrines to the "Lost Cause," just as the Reconstruction government after the war had feared. The monuments also served to remind people to honor the living veterans, who had fought so bravely and were advancing in years. The federal government realized and acknowledged that the South needed its heroes as part of the healing process.

When veterans from across Texas gathered at Livingston in 1901 to dedicate a Confederate monument, they heard an address by the Honorable James E. Hill, who served with Walker's Texas Division during the war. Hill reminded the gathering, "The Yanks invaded us," and he called the Northerners "traitors to the Constitution."[118] But Hill understood the federal government's gesture of conciliation in allowing such monuments and made the clear statement to all gathered: "we buried our passions in pathos as we buried our heroes in love. This dedication of this monument is not a revival of the war spirit."[119]

The Confederates retained their fierce pride, but insisted that their fighting spirit was no longer directed against the federal government. Captain T. W. Hill, addressing the Hood's Brigade Association at Jacksonville in 1903, insisted, "This Association is purely a social one.... We meet not with malice to our Government, as we even doff our hats to old 'Glory', but in so doing our love to our little reg [regimental] flag is in no way abated, for it never looked more beautiful than when dancing over the field of battle in pursuit of its large enemy."[120] Yet, Augustus David Sadler in Chappell Hill spoke for many of his comrades when he wrote in his memoirs in 1901 of

> that piercing cry from Southern throats that spoke the heart's resolve on Victory or Death! Ah, how my old heart throbs now as I recall and try to tell of that war-cry of the South![121]

The Texas Division of the United Daughters of the Confederacy met in Bryan, Texas, in December 1906. One of the memoriams was to the passing of Mrs. James F. Matthews of Chappell Hill.[122] The original muster roll of Company B of Elmore's regiment, donated by Mrs. J. A. Jackson of Chappell Hill, was among the contributions acknowledged for the local UDC historical collection. Mrs. R. M. Swearingen contributed an original order issued by General Peters to General Joseph Johnston

18. National Reconciliation

on April 27, 1865, just before the surrender.[123] The Texas Daughters had only just unveiled the monument over General Albert Sidney Johnston's grave in the Austin State Cemetery in September 1906. Their leader, speaking at the dedication ceremony, reminded the audience that the Federal commander of Texas had not allowed a ceremony at the time of Johnston's reburial in Austin and remarked, "I see the Daughters of the Confederacy making yearly pilgrimages to this tomb, with their children and children's children."[124]

The efforts of the Daughters of the Confederacy since 1895 had been successful, the textbook committee reporting "with pleasure a marked increase of school literature by Southern authors."[125] The committee highlighted a number of textbooks that were favorable to the South, in particular a series of school readers prepared by G. G. Hill, son of General Hill and nephew of Stonewall Jackson. Another book given high praise was *The Legends of King Arthur and His Court*, "so that teachers may point out to our children historical Southern examples of its ideals of honor and chivalry."[126] Though some critics challenged "loving faith in a chivalry which perhaps never existed,"[127] the Daughters of the Confederacy stuck to their ideals. The Galveston chapter of UDC published in 1904 the *UDC Catechism*, written by Mrs. Cornelia Branch Stone of Galveston, the tireless leader of the Texan United Daughters of the Confederacy. John D. Rogers, formerly of Chappell Hill, had offered the name of Mrs. Stone as an honorary member at the annual meeting of Hood's Texas Brigade Association in Galveston in 1901.[128] James E. Landes was in the crowd that elected Mrs. Stone to that status.[129] The *UDC Catechism* began by reiterating that disregard on the part of the North for the rights of the South had caused the war and near the end reminded all readers that the Confederate Army was not defeated, only overpowered by numbers.[130]

The John Bell Hood Camp of the United Confederate Veterans in Austin discovered a math textbook being used that violated the state's uniform textbook law. The book used math problems such as, "Gen. Grant was born April 27, 1822 and was 41 years 2 months and 7 days old when Vicksburg, Miss. was captured. When did he capture Vicksburg?" It is not known what Henry Brandt, the old Chappell Hill veteran of the Vicksburg siege, thought of the Myers-Brook Elementary Arithmetic controversy of 1908. Other questions incorporated Phil Sheridan, the generally disliked military governor of Texas during Reconstruction, and William Tecumseh Sherman. A well-financed effort among Texans forced the Chicago publisher to rush to the governor's office to make amends and replace the textbooks.[131]

George Washington Carter, formerly president of Soule University and colonel with the Twenty-First Texas Cavalry, died in May 1901 at the Old Confederates' Home in Maryland. An obituary in the New Orleans *Times-Democrat* referred to him as "one of the most picturesque and remarkable characters in the South ... probably had the most varied career of any man in the ministry of this country."[132] Carter's old friends in the church had prayed fervently for him for years. Carter gave up liquor and became a champion of temperance. His mental capacity and oratory skills allowed him to reach out to many. After a year of being so engaged, George Washington Carter declared his reconciliation with God.[133] He moved back to his native Virginia by 1874, although he continued to do business with friends in Chappell

Hill.[134] President James Garfield, the former Federal general during the war, appointed Carter as U.S. ambassador to Venezuela in 1881, a position Carter held for a year.[135] Gone were the fears of a Southern conspiracy encompassing the Caribbean shores. Carter returned home to his ministry. He joined the Virginia Conference of the Methodist Church in 1889, preached at his old church in Lynchburg, Virginia, and served a couple of stations. His reputation was as "one of the most brilliant pulpit orators in the country."[136] Even late in life, restored to his position as a prominent minister, Carter could not avoid controversy. He married for a third time in 1895 to "Virginia Statham, a beautiful and highly connected girl of twenty, of Lynchburg."[137] Some church officials shunned Carter, as he had left his second wife (as he had his first) in Louisiana when he left the state and she was still living. Carter, never one to back down from a fight, insisted on a complete airing of the charges, delivered his own defense and managed to survive.

Colonel Carter gave lectures in his later years, as did many former officers of the war. He remained in the ministry until the end, although his hearing and sight were failing him. Carter moved to the Washington, D.C., area in his later years to be close to his daughter Mary.[138] He requested admission into the Maryland Confederate Soldiers' Home in November 1900, stating that he was unable to provide for himself because of deafness and age.[139] George Washington Carter was 74 years old and gave his occupation as lecturer. Carter applied for membership in the Society of the Army and the Navy of the Confederate States in the state of Maryland at about the same time. His endorsement, written by a man who served with Mosby, read: "I know that Col. G. W. Carter was a brave and efficient officer in the Confederate Army."[140] George Washington Carter died at the Maryland Confederate Soldiers' Home on May 11, 1901.[141] His life, like that of so many thousands and thousands of others, was altered irrevocably by the war.

Peter Raysor, who had fought with the Fourteenth South Carolina Cavalry Battalion at the Wilderness and against Sherman during his campaign in the Carolinas,[142] died at Chappell Hill in September 1903. Dr. Hammond Bouldin passed away in 1905. His obituary in *Confederate Veteran* read in part:

> exemplified the love of God, of country and of his fellow-man. ... through the successes and failures of succeeding years his love and loyalty to the South and the principles for which he fought never faltered. He was a Confederate to the last.[143]

Henry Meyer died in June 1907. John Edmund Wallis died in October 1907. John D. Rogers, who raised Company E of the Fifth Texas Infantry, died in October 1908. Charles Askew of the Eufaula Alabama Light Artillery died in March 1909.

John F. W. Toland, who had never returned to the ranks of the Fifth Texas Infantry after coming home to Chappell Hill upon his father's death, died in April 1909. Toland left Chappell Hill, no doubt as Confederate authorities were looking for soldiers who had not returned to their units. He married in 1870, was in Lampasas County in the 1870 federal census and in McLennan County (Waco region) in the 1880 federal census. A daughter, Euna Pearl, was born at Jonesboro, 40 miles west

18. National Reconciliation

of Waco, in 1886. He returned to Washington County after the turn of the century. He and his wife Carrie died at Brenham on the same day, April 20, 1909.

Some deaths were never recorded, particularly for those Texans who headed south after the war, crossing into Mexico rather than surrender to Federal authorities. John Hargrove, whose sister and mother founded Chappell Hill, wrote in his unpublished memoir in 1903 of his brother "Robert W, who is, if still alive, in Ceralue [Cerralvo], Mexico."[144] Hargrove, originally with Hood's Texas Brigade, organized a cavalry company he led as a captain and served in Brown's Thirty-Fifth Texas Cavalry.

The U.S. Congress allowed for the remains of Confederates to be interred in a special Confederate section of Arlington National Cemetery in 1900.[145] The old Confederate cavalryman Fightin' Joe Wheeler was buried at Arlington National Cemetery in 1906 with full military honors. Both the Stars and Stripes and the Confederate Stars and Bars decorated the caisson carrying his casket. Wheeler's comrade-in-arms in both the War Between the States and the Spanish-American War, General Fitzhugh Lee, was buried in his U.S. Army uniform in 1905. A Confederate reportedly joked, "What'll Stonewall think when Fitz turns up in heaven wearing that!"[146] The nation clearly had turned a corner.

The Hood's Texas Brigade Association Reunion in Ennis is 1904 noted:

> This is a meeting of old comrades, in which there is no politics, and the members give themselves over to reminiscences.[147]

Yet, the Confederate spirit remained in the old veterans. The veterans gathered that year passed a resolution to press the state legislature to make Jefferson Davis' birthday a state holiday.[148] The men were not too old to still gave a rousing rebel yell when the band would strike up "Dixie."

Confederate veterans made inroads into the federal government. President Theodore Roosevelt made Seth Shepard chief justice of the U.S. Court of Appeals in 1905. Shepard, a Brenham boy, had served alongside Gideon Keesee of Chappell Hill in Company F of Tom Green's Fifth Texas Cavalry. He lost a brother at the Battle of Mansfield in 1864. Shepard graduated in law from Washington College after the war (later named Washington and Lee after Robert E. Lee, the university president) and became a noted Brenham attorney, before moving to the nation's capital.[149]

Sectionalism continued to play a role in national politics, despite reconciliation. The August 12, 1904, edition of the *Bellville Times* printed an editorial in response to a comment in the *Chicago Chronicle* which had stated, "Democracy is identified in the minds of the Southern white men with the 'lost cause' and the hope of regaining it. The 'lost cause' is essentially the cause of slavery."[150] The *Times* lashed out at the *Chronicle* editor, calling him "a long distance prevaricator and a witful slanderer of American citizens."[151] Two weeks later, the *Times* deplored a lynching in Georgia as an act that "operates incalculable injury to the entire South, and to put argument against it upon the lowest plane, it will intensify a sentiment at the North which may cost the democratic party a national election."[152] One indication of waning sensitivity

as to the "lost cause" was an ad campaign by Hostetter's Stomach Bitters, which appeared in the *Bellville Times*. The advertisement noted that the success of its product paralleled the glorious record of victory of the Stars and Stripes, including in the Civil War.[153]

President Theodore Roosevelt, who raised and trained his Rough Riders in San Antonio for the Spanish-American War, sent his regrets at declining an invitation to attend a Blue-Gray reunion at Gettysburg in July 1906:

> May I, through you, extend to all who are there present, absolutely without regard to whether they fought under Meade, or under Lee, the heartiest goodwill, and an expression of my abiding faith in their devotion to our Common Country?[154]

The Confederate veterans of Terry's Texas Rangers in 1907 finally realized their dream to erect a monument to their comrades and distinguished regiment. A life-size bronze statue, depicting a Ranger astride a spirited horse, was dedicated on the Capitol grounds in Austin. The comrades and friends of Hood's Texas Brigade erected a monument to their celebrated unit on the Capitol grounds in 1910. Two men from Chappell Hill, Rufus King Felder and James E. Landes, were among those surviving comrades who contributed money.[155] Rufus King Felder made the short trip to Austin for the dedication on October 26–27, joining 125 former comrades. The occasion was the Brigade's 39th annual reunion. William Hamby, president of the Hood's Texas Brigade Association, delivered an address in which he acknowledged to all:

> I feel that I voice the sentiment of every Confederate soldier when I salute the Stars and Stripes as the flag of our country; the only flag and the only country to which we owe allegiance, but that does not mean that we fought for a "lost cause." The soldiers of the Confederacy rebelled against Federal power, but they were not traitors.[156]

Hamby, who had fought with the Fourth Texas Infantry before being severely wounded at Second Manassas,[157] reminded the audience that only one-tenth of Confederate soldiers owned a slave and maintained:

> The men of the North fought to preserve the Union; the men of the South fought to preserve the principles upon which the Union was formed.[158]

The 35-foot marble shaft of the monument to Hood's Texas Brigade is topped by the bronze figure of a Confederate infantryman. Among the inscriptions on the base of the monument are quotes from Jefferson Davis, the president of the

Opposite: 1913 REUNION OF TERRY'S TEXAS RANGERS. The Eighth Texas Cavalry was perhaps second only to Hood's Texas Brigade among the best-known Texas units in the Civil War. Terry's Texas Rangers Association was formed in Austin in 1867 for the express purpose of erecting a monument. John Jackson of Chappell Hill, third from the left in the back row, was one of the original members. The Rangers gathered annually in various sites across Texas beginning in 1868. Jackson regularly attended Rangers reunions until his health failed in the later 1920s. (Courtesy of Ruth and Rice Buchanan of Navasota, Texas.)

RUFUS KING FELDER, JAMES LANDES AND HENRY BRANDT at the opening of the cornerstone of the old main building of Soule University. Felder, Landes and Brandt were the "big three" of Chappell Hill's remaining Confederate veterans in the early twentieth century. (From the Archives of the Chappell Hill Historical Society.)

Confederacy: "Hood's Texas Brigade shall retain its original formation as long as there is a man left to wave its flag," and "They have shown on many battlefields their willingness to die for Dixie and have a right to wear on their banners the motto of Hampden 'No Steps Backward.'" Quotes from other prominent Confederates were also set into the stone, including Robert E. Lee's: "No Brigade has done nobler service or gained more honor for its State than Hood's Texas Brigade."

The 1910 publication for the Fourteenth Annual Convention of the United Daughters of the Confederacy listed an active chapter in Chappell Hill with Mrs. W. D. Crockett as president, Mrs. J. B. Matthews as first vice president, Mrs. Bettie Chappell as secretary-treasurer and Mrs. J. E. Landes as historian. Mrs. Rufus King Felder and Miss Florence Bouldin were among the members.[159] Walstein Keesee, formerly of the Twenty-Fourth Texas Cavalry, passed away about this time. He entered the service as a 19 year old, survived the capture at Arkansas Post, and fought well at Chickamauga, in the Atlanta Campaign and in the Carolinas. He rose to the rank of sergeant and received his parole at the surrender to Sherman on April 26, 1865.[160]

W. D. Crockett, who purchased the land that formerly had been the campus of

Chappell Hill's Soule University, organized a gathering to pay respects to the ruins before they were removed. The school closed in the late 1880s after struggling for 15 years.[161] Henry Christian Brandt served as the last president of the Board of Trustees.[162] The event that took place on June 14, 1911, became a reunion "reviving memories of Chappell Hill in the halcyon days when it was not only the center of Methodism in Texas but of population and influence in that section of the state." The host prepared barbecued pig with all the fixings. A crew tore down all that remained standing, the northeast corner of the old three-story building. The participants opened the cornerstone prior to the dinner. Rufus King Felder, James Landes and Henry Brandt were all present for the opening of the cornerstone.[163] All three also had been present when the cornerstone was laid on November 2, 1858. Each of the old Confederate veterans rose and made a brief speech in which he recalled the event 53 years earlier. There is no record of their remarks. This was a major Masonic event and all three Confederates were members of the local lodge. The officials opened the copper box within the cornerstone to find that the papers inside had disintegrated into dust. A piece of the Atlantic cable, a three-cent piece, a quarter, a half dollar and a gold dollar were all that remained. J. D. Campbell of Beaumont, who attended Soule University as a young man, also spoke at the gathering. He later wrote:

> the building from that time was simply a magnificent and impressive ruin, a monument of what "might have been," a milestone along the great highway of Christian education ... Thus passed a great university. The distinguished and honored in Methodism have raised their voices inside those sacred walls. Men who helped to make Texas gathered inspiration and wisdom in her halls."[164]

Chappell Hill Female College closed its doors in 1912. The college thrived after the war, even as Soule University faded away.[165] Rufus King Felder's second wife, Lula, was the last president of Chappell Hill Female College.

While Rufus King Felder and James Landes both survived the brutal assault of the second day at Gettysburg, neither made it to the golden anniversary of that epic struggle, which was commemorated on July 4, 1913. Rufus King's son, Rufie, passed away on June 26, just a week before the event. Rufie was only 35 years of age and had been in a hospital in Austin for some time.[166] James Landes had been unable to leave his bed since shortly after the opening of the Soule University cornerstone. He died on January 6, 1914, at the age of 73, having spent his last two years as an invalid. Landes' obituary acknowledged that he had been a Confederate soldier who served through the entire course of the war with Hood's Brigade. The obituary closed with the remarks:

> Mr. Landes was a gentleman of the old school, devoted to his family, and faithful to his friends and in his passing the county loses an exemplary citizen.[167]

Kate Landes filed "A Widow's Application for a Pension" with the State of Texas in 1925. The county assessor noted that she had no homestead and no personal property. One affidavit in the file was by a Dr. S. O. Young of Harris County. He wrote:

> I served in the Confederate Army in Company A of Hood's Brigade. I knew James Edward Landes during the Civil War. He was a member of my company all through the war. He was a fine man and served honorably during the entire period of the war. He never deserted but rendered valuable services to the Cause of the Confederacy. He was one of the finest soldiers in Hood's Brigade.[168]

That summer of 1914, the Camp Ground Association met in July for a single day at the site midway between Chappell Hill and Bellville. The Methodist organization had been meeting the first Thursday in May since 1885. On Sunday, July 9, 1914, a memorial service was held for James E. Landes, who had been an officer since the association was founded, and Mrs. Nannie Collins.[169]

Many did attend the 1913 Gettysburg reunion and numerous Texans were among them. The *Galveston Daily News* ran a full-page feature highlighting the role played by Texans in "the grandest, greatest and most important battle in history."[170] The Gettysburg event was perhaps the crowning moment of the Blue-Gray reunions. Fifty thousand veterans from both sides attended. The *Brenham Banner* published several front-page articles, which portrayed the event in a positive light.[171] There was a sense in America that the rift had been healed. Even the conservative *Confederate Veterans* magazine, which refused to call the gathering a reunion, admitted, "How complete the Nation has become."[172] There was no mention of the nation's abandonment of racial reconciliation, much less the numerous lynchings of African Americans in the South.

Part of the reason for the positive Confederate outlook was the election in November 1912 of Woodrow Wilson as president. The *Bellville Times*, just prior to Election Day, had published a list of a dozen reasons for Texans to vote for Wilson. The *Times* noted the election of the Virginian as the first Southerner to become president after the Civil War. The paper also wrote, "He stands for tariff revision downward in the interest of lower prices and the elimination of monopoly."[173] Long-standing issues that went well back into the previous century remained unsettled. Wilson's election to the presidency, in addition to having Confederate veterans as chief justice and an associate justice of the United States Supreme Court,[174] was another reason for Texas Confederates to feel their place in America was being restored.[175] President Woodrow Wilson, who would re-segregate federal agencies under his administration, told the crowd at Gettysburg:

> We have found one another again as brothers and comrades in arms, enemies no longer, generous friends rather, our battles long past, the quarrel forgotten.... How complete the Union has become.... We are made by these tragic, epic things to know what it costs to make a nation.... There are no more patriotic people than the Confederate veterans.[176]

Yet, amid the solidarity, the editors of *Confederate Veteran* magazine refused to call the gathering at Gettysburg a reunion and suggested of the gathering, "the best soldier-veterans are repulsed by it on each side."[177]

The Confederate veterans' world was changing. The nostalgic image of the courageous Confederate hero began to fade away, even as the old men passed on in death. Texas assumed a new image after the turn of the century, that of big oil and corre-

18. National Reconciliation

sponding great wealth. The Spindletop discovery near Beaumont in 1900 changed forever the face of Texas. Other major oil discoveries along the Gulf Coast followed in rapid succession and continued year after year. Houston grew rapidly into a leading commercial center, dominating the Texas Gulf Coast. That position of dominance was further solidified in 1914 with the opening of the Houston Ship Channel. Washington County had been the most populous county in the state until the 1880s. Chappell Hill gradually slipped into oblivion as Texas industry began to dominate the agrarian economy of Washington County and many other counties. Chappell Hill's Confederate veterans remained quiet reminders of the town's glory in a not-so-distant past. They too would be gone before long

The United Confederate Veterans remained an important organization in the South in the 1900s, even as its membership died off. President Woodrow Wilson reviewed the UCV parade held in conjunction with their 1917 annual gathering. The Twenty-Seventh Annual Reunion of the UCV was held in Washington, D. C.— the first time ever to hold the UCV reunion north of the Potomac River. The United States was on the verge of war with Germany. The Grand Marshall of the UCV parade "testified to the perfect union that now exists between all sections of the country."[178] Senator John Bankhead from Alabama wore a Confederate uniform to submit a motion that the United States Senate adjourn in honor of the reunion

> as a tribute to the patriotism of the Confederate veteran and his son, who stand ready and willing to offer their lives and their means for the perpetuation of the Union which they so desperately and at such great sacrifice attempted to dissolve.[179]

The Senate approved the motion and the UCV adopted a resolution approving the action of the president and Congress in declaring the existence of a state of war between the United States and Germany. There was strong sentiment to demonstrate to America and to the world that the country was united.

Master Sergeant Joe Toland,[180] whose ancestor had served with Hood's Texas Brigade, was among those who went off from Chappell Hill to fight the Kaiser. Toland's remains lie in rest among those of the many Confederates of Chappell Hill in the town's Masonic Cemetery. Robert Wallis Knox of Houston, grandson of Private John E. Wallis of the Twentieth Texas Infantry, was a career military man. He trained at Virginia Military Institute, was commissioned a first lieutenant in the Fifty-Fifth Artillery and served in France during World War I with the Allied Expeditionary Force. John Vaughn Buster was named for his grandfather, who had proudly served in the Tenth Texas Infantry. Jack, as John was called, grew up in the Texas Panhandle after his father moved away from Washington County. He enlisted in the United States Army in 1917 at age 17 and saw action in France.[181] Clifton Estes' grandfather was Claudius Buster. Clifton fought with the Third Division in the colossal battles at the Marne, St. Michel and Meuse-Argonne.[182] Edward Benjamin Cushing, the son of Houston *Telegraph* editor and publisher E. H. Cushing, was a member of the Texas A&M graduating class of 1880. He served with the American Expeditionary Force on the staff of General John J. Pershing during World War I. He later became president of the A&M Board of Regents and it is for him that Cushing Memorial Library on the campus of Texas A&M is named.[183]

A man who was 20 years old when he enlisted to serve the Confederacy in 1861 was 76 years old in 1917 when America declared war on Germany. Age continued to take its toll on the Chappell Hill Confederates. Augustus Sadler, veteran of Gettysburg, died on July 10, 1916. James W. Thompson died on June 23, 1917. Henry Landes died on February 6, 1919. on May 4, 1919, Texas A&M University unveiled a 10-foot bronze statue of Sul Ross on campus in honor of the former Confederate general, senator, governor and college president.[184] Sul Ross was the last Confederate veteran to serve Texas as governor. (Freshman cadets at Texas A&M to this day "wash Sully down," i.e. polish the statue, each year.)

Chappell Hill could boast only four living Confederate veterans by 1922, well over 50 years after the end of the war. That spring, the paved highway through Chappell Hill was completed by the state. It was part of the longest stretch of concrete in the state at the time.[185] Two of the Confederates passed away in that year. Thomas Shapard, who was a private in Waller's Texas Cavalry, died on April 4, 1922, at Chappell Hill. He was 76 years old and, no doubt, was buried amid blossoming bluebonnets. Rufus King Felder, one of Chappell Hill's true warriors, also died in that same year. He had served proudly in the Fifth Texas Infantry, Hood's Texas Brigade, one of the most celebrated fighting units in the Confederate Army. He had seen action at the major battles, Antietam, Gettysburg, Spotsylvania, Wilderness and more — and lived to tell of them. He was there until the end and stacked his musket at Appomattox after Lee surrendered to Grant. His remains rest in Atkinson Cemetery just outside the town of Chappell Hill. He fought the fight for what he believed. He was a gallant man, like all of them. They held their heads high in defeat and rejoined to make a better nation than before.

John A. Jackson, veteran of Terry's Texas Rangers and a long-time resident of Chappell Hill, moved to Sealy in 1899. He died there in 1927. Henry Brandt, who survived the siege of Vicksburg and imprisonment for the duration of the war, was the last surviving Confederate veteran of Chappell Hill. Brandt died at Chappell Hill on January 8, 1929, at the age of 93 years. The *Brenham Banner* referred to Brandt as "one of the staunch pioneers of Methodism in this section." Henry Brandt was a member of Chappell Hill's Methodist Church for 73 years and a steward in the church for 55 of those years. Old-timers of Chappell Hill later remembered Brandt for his "twinkly blue eyes" and the perfect pitch with which he led the Methodist choir for so many years.[186] The Brenham paper stated, "Many Brenham friends will go to Chappell Hill to attend the obsequies of this splendid old generation, one of the best citizens of this section for so many years."[187] His obituary referred to Brandt as "a veteran of the Confederacy, having served the South gallantly in the great struggle between the states."[188] A friend wrote the following that was printed in the obituary:

> His day has come, not gone.
> His sun is risen, not set
> His life is now beyond
> The reach of death or change
> Not ended, but begun
> Oh noble soul; oh, gentle heart,
> Hail, and farewell[189]

18. National Reconciliation

METHODIST CHURCH. Chappell Hill for a time was the center of Methodism in Texas. Robert Alexander organized the Chappell Hill Methodist Church in 1847, the same year in which Mary Haller established a post office in Chappell Hill. The Texas Conference established Chappell Hill Male and Female Institute in 1852 and Soule University in 1856. The Methodists of Chappell Hill built a permanent structure for their church in 1853. The storm of 1900, which devastated Galveston, also destroyed Chappell Hill Methodist Church. Henry Brandt designed and supervised the construction of a new church, built of pine in 1901, which still stands to this day. The church is particularly noteworthy for the woodwork on the interior. (Photograph by Thomas G. Stevens of Chappell Hill.)

The beautiful wooden Methodist church in Chappell Hill, which Brandt designed and supervised the building of in 1901, stands today as testimony to his carpentry skills, his faith and his dedication to the church. The building is on the National Register of Historic Places and serves as a silent memorial to the last Confederate veteran of Chappell Hill.

Lt. Bolling Eldridge, Rufus King Felder's lieutenant in Company E of the Fifth Texas Infantry, managed to become the last surviving member of Hood's Texas Brigade. He signed an Affidavit of Witness for the "Widow's Application for a Pension," which Rufus King's widow, Lula, filed in 1931.[190] Elridge passed away in Brenham on October 28, 1938.[191] The last Confederate veteran in America died in 1959. Walter Washington Williams of Houston, who served in Company C of the Fifth

Texas Infantry, was said to be 117 years old when he died. He was among the last.[192] All that remained was the memory of their gallantry and heroism.

Perhaps in the absence of the firebrands and hotheads, the politicians and the preachers, one can imagine that it might have been possible to preserve the Union and even abolish slavery without the tremendous loss of life that ensued. Instead, the nation was born again on the blood of 600,000 American dead. That rebirth was only the beginning of a long process. But it was and is that process that led to America's rise to the position of the greatest nation on earth.

Epilogue

The wildflowers explode with color across central Texas in late March and early April. Texas bluebonnets and Indian paintbrush carpet the rolling hills with brilliant blues and reds. The quiet hamlet of Chappell Hill in Washington County lies in the midst of this profusion of color and the attendant excitement each spring. The Bluebonnet Festival held in Chappell Hill each spring honors the Texas state flower. Thousands converge on Chappell Hill from Houston and the state capital of Austin, two major population centers in Texas.

The Civil War, or the War Between the States, forever changed things. Chappell Hill is no longer a center of wealth and influence. Nor is cotton the dominating crop, the last cotton gin in Chappell Hill having shut down in the 1970s.[1] Houston once existed to serve the wealthy cotton plantations of the Brazos and Colorado river valleys. A network of roads along the Texas coast converged at Houston, from where steamboats laden with cotton headed to Galveston. Galveston's Strand was the commercial center of Texas. Seagoing vessels took Texas cotton from the port of Galveston to New England mills and across the ocean to Europe. Today, Houston has far eclipsed not only the Brazos and Colorado valleys, but also Galveston. Chappell Hill is simply one of many small towns along the highway that stretches from Houston to the state capital of Austin.

The changes made for a better nation and a better people. Dr. John Washington Lockhart, the Confederate veteran and a Chappell Hill planter who had once owned more than 50 slaves, reflected in his later years:

> [I]n the liberation of the slaves they also received their own liberty. After these many years since the terrible conflict, when we can look back over the fields of battle, where so many precious lives were sacrificed, the only regret is that we did

JOHN STERLING SMITH HOUSE. The original house was built as a one-story "dog-trot" structure. John Sterling Smith, Sr., and his wife Claytonia bought the house in 1873. Their son, John Sterling Smith, a prominent cotton farmer and business leader, remodeled the house to its Queen Anne style in 1910. It is the last remaining house of its style in Chappell Hill. The house is now the Mulberry Inn Bed & Breakfast. (Photograph by Thomas G. Stevens of Chappell Hill.)

> not know of the good in store; know of it before the flower of the youth of the country both North and South, had been made victims to our ignorance and passions. There is no doubt that the liberation of the slaves wrought a great hardship to some, but to the majority of the South it was a great benefit. There is also no doubt that the negro was inhumanely treated by some owners ... I will say in behalf of the negro, that it is a wonder that he behaved as well as he did.[2]

The immediate impact on the South was devastating. The wealthy planters, who once made Chappell Hill the aristocratic center of Texas, suffered severe setbacks when their plantation economy disappeared. Some recovered economically, while others did not. Disease finished what war had left untouched. The 1867 yellow fever epidemic was fatal not only to the residents of Chappell Hill whose lives it claimed, but also to the reputation of the town itself. Recurring epidemics and scares led to Chappell Hill becoming known as an unhealthy place to live. Chappell Hill lost an important part of its identity when the Texas Methodist Conference, on the advice of the president of Soule University, opened a new college in Georgetown, "outside the fever belt."[3] There were financial considerations as well. The planters, who supported Soule University, lost much of their wealth after the war and could not come up with the necessary funds to pay the university's debts. Much of Washington County, the heart of Stephen Austin's old Texas colony, went into further decline around the turn of the century as the new industrial economy displaced the agrarian economy. Washington-on-the-Brazos, the former capital of the Texas republic, disappeared. The railroad bypassed the town of Independence, immediately north of Chappell Hill, and the Baylor University administration moved their school to Waco.

Approximately 30 antebellum homes in Chappell Hill are a quiet reminder of the town's past prosperity and influence. The Browning Plantation Manor is perhaps the most magnificent of those remaining. The Stagecoach Inn, once Jacob Haller's home and later Charlotte Hargrove's, and the Lockhart home, restored in 1970–1971, are also impressive. The many graves of Confederates veterans in four cemeteries in and around Chappell Hill are a reminder of the blood shed defending the Southern

HAYNIE-GUNN HOUSE. The Haynie House was built in 1853 by John A. and Permelia Haynie (sister of Mary Haller). The framework of the house is hand-hewn native cedar held with wooden pegs and square nails. The house originally had a "dog-run" porch. (Photograph by Thomas G. Stevens of Chappell Hill.)

WAVERLY PLANTATION MANOR HOUSE. Dr. William Tunstall build his Waverly Plantation Manor House in 1850 of native cedar, heart of pine and stone. The sills are hand-hewn cedar. Wooden pegs and square nails are used throughout. The house features three fireplaces of native stone and handmade brick. Colonel William Sledge, who with W. W. Browning organized the Washington County Railroad, bought the home in 1854. (Photograph by Thomas G. Stevens of Chappell Hill.)

way of life and the Southern homeland and honor. Charles Carmer of Walker's Texas Division, Thomas Chappell, Del Perkins, J. W. Thompson and Jacob Umland of Elmore's Twentieth Infantry Regiment, Thomas Elliott of Wilkes' Twenty-Fourth Texas Cavalry, Robert Elgin of Terry's Texas Rangers, J. Norfolk Cocke of Carter's Cavalry, and Gideon Keesee of Green's Cavalry are among the many Confederates whose remains are interred in Chappell Hill's Masonic Cemetery. Green Bouldin, Alex Hammond and the Routt boys are among the Terry's Texas Rangers laid to rest in the old Routt Family Cemetery. The remains of Dr. John Washington Lockhart along with Rufus King Felder, Daniel Harvie Browning, James Fiske Matthews and others lie in Atkinson Cemetery, on the western edge of what was once the Browning Plantation. The inscription on Daniel Harvie Browning's tombstone reads: "brief, brave & glorious was his career."

Generations that followed, even after the last Confederate had passed away, continued to carry on the tradition of Texan valor. Texans enthusiastically rushed to answer President Franklin Roosevelt's call to arms at the beginning of World War II, joining up as quickly as they had in the spring of 1861. Fred Brandt, Henry Christian Brandt's grandson, served overseas during World War II in the Twentieth Air Force. He was an aerial photographer in Asia and flew many hazardous missions,

The entrance to the Masonic Cemetery, where the remains of many of Chappell Hill's Confederates rest.

including over the Hump. Fred Brandt was on Okinawa, preparing for the invasion of mainland Japan, when World War II ended.[4]

Colonel Harvie Matthews is buried near his Confederate grandfather, "Doc" Matthews, and great-uncle, Daniel Harvie Browning, in Chappell Hill's Atkinson Cemetery. Harvie grew up in the antebellum Browning Plantation home,[5] hearing stories of Terry's Texas Rangers. Colonel Matthews was involved with the early formation of Armored Infantry and was with the headquarters of the Third Armored Division at the beginning of World War II. He was later promoted to headquarters of the Army Ground Forces (AGF), in which capacity he served at the Pentagon in Washington through the course of the Normandy invasion and the drive across France,

The grave marker of James Fiske Matthews, who led the last great cavalry charge of the war.

Four grave markers, four Confederate graves — a view of Chappell Hill's Masonic Cemetery.

the ferocious German counter-attack known as the Battle of the Bulge, the invasion of Germany and, ultimately, victory in Europe.[6]

At least seven direct descendants of Claudius Buster, the old warrior who led the men from Chappell Hill to help re-take Galveston, saw action in World War II. Four of these lost their lives overseas in the conflict. First Lieutenant William Buster served with the famed Thirty-Sixth "Texas" Division, the Texas National Guardsmen who wore the T-patch (for Texas) on their shoulders and referred to themselves as the Texas Army. The Thirty-Sixth had the honor of being the first American division to step ashore on Nazi-occupied Europe when they landed at Salerno on September 9, 1943.[7] Two months later, Lt. Buster, upon losing communications with his forward observation post, exposed himself to enemy fire when he went forward to assess the situation and was mortally wounded by an artillery shell. The United States government posthumously awarded Lt. William Buster the Silver Star for gallantry.[8] Clifford Estes, another descendant of Claudius Buster, was wounded in action during the Normandy invasion. Yet another descendant, Greer Estes, was a captain with the Three Hundred and Thirteenth Infantry Regiment of the U.S. Seventy-Ninth Division. He came ashore at Utah Beach in June 1944 and was involved in heavy

Munyon-Crockett Home. The Munyon House was built in 1853 by Marcus Munyon, a carpenter and sawmill owner. Munyon was a captain in the Texas State Troops (the home guard) during the Civil War. The house was originally a small four-room house. J. R. Routt purchased the house in 1898, enlarged it and added Victorian trim. Routt descendants live in the house to this day. (Photograph by Thomas G. Stevens of Chappell Hill.)

combat as the U.S. forces fought their way out of Normandy's Cotentin Peninsula. Captain Estes was killed in action on July 8, 1944, during heavy fighting capturing hill 84, near the town of Montgardon after the 313th took La Haye-du-Puits.[9] Sergeant Malcolm McInnis, great-grandson of Claudius Buster and a tail gunner on a B-17 bomber, was shot down during a mission over Germany in late November 1944. He was posthumously awarded the Presidential Citation for his sacrifice.[10] Staff Sergeant John Thomas Estes, another great-grandson, survived 30 combat missions over Europe, including the loss of one plane. The Air Medal, which he earned, cited "meritorious achievement" reflecting "great credit upon himself and the armed forces of the United States."[11]

There were many others. Robert Wallis Knox, grandson of Private John E. Wallis of the Twentieth Texas Infantry, served in World War I and spent the next 20 years in the Reserve Corps studying the evolution of artillery and tactics. Knox also served in World War II, as did his nephew Thomas Stark, Junior. Four grandsons of "Billy Dick" Thompson of Elmore's Twentieth Texas Infantry served in the U.S. Armed

Forces during World War II. Joe Eugene Routt was the best known. Routt, born in Chappell Hill in 1914, was the first ever Texas A&M football All-American. Captain Routt was in Holland in December 1944 with the 405th Infantry Regiment when hit by machine gun fire.[12] The authorities returned Routt's remains home in 1949, at which time an estimated 1,000 people attended his service.[13]

Another legacy of World War II stands not far from Chappell Hill. The U.S. Army created Fort Hood in central Texas in 1942 to prepare American soldiers for fighting German panzer divisions in the rolling terrain of Europe. The base, named for Confederate General John Bell Hood, remains the largest Army post in the United States.

These descendants of Chappell Hill's Confederates fought to defend the Stars and Stripes of the United States of America in faraway places such as France, Italy and the Pacific theater. Later descendants served in Korea and Vietnam. The Stars and Stripes flutters in the warm breeze over their graves, just as it does over the graves of their proud Confederate ancestors. The Confederate soldiers of Chappell Hill, Texas, and their comrades-in-arms from across Texas fought as hard as any Americans ever fought and suffered through as much adversity as any American fighting men ever faced.

Perhaps in the final analysis, the lack of a truly distinct homogenous identity made it difficult for the Confederates to continue the fight. The nationalism of the United States of America, buoyed by the emotional crusade of emancipating the slaves, prevailed. Today, men, women and children across the nation, white and black, North and South, share the same loyalty to the flag and service to God and country. The Houston *Daily Telegraph* published an editorial on July 4, 1866, which read:

> The Fourth of July has come. It would be absurd to expect that it should excite any emotion of rejoicing in us.[14]

A long, slow reconciliation changed that sentiment. A visitor to Chappell Hill today on the Fourth will be delighted to discover an old-time Fourth of July parade, complete with floats. Most noticeable are the many horsemen in the parade, a clear sign that Chappell Hill remains agrarian to this day. More important, African American and white ride together, all celebrating the birthday of the greatest nation on earth. There is racial reconciliation yet to be completed in Chappell Hill, as there is across the nation. The Civil War redirected the nation and the evolution continues to the present day. God Bless America.

Notes

Introduction

1. Maxwell, L. C., "Warren," *The Handbook of Texas Online.*
2. Winfield, Judy, "Forgotten Towns Along the Brazos, Part One: Warren," *The Chappell Hill Historical Society Review,* 1996, vol. 2, p. 9.
3. Cloud, Guy M., "John Wurts Cloud Sr.," *The Handbook of Texas Online,* http://www.tsha.utexas.edu/handbook/online/articles/view/CC/fcl34.html.
4. Archives of the Chappell Hill Historical Society. Also, marker of the Texas Historical Commission in Chappell Hill's Masonic Cemetery.
5. Cutrer, Thomas W., "Williams Jones Elliot Heard," *The Handbook of Texas Online,* http://www.tsha.utexas.edu/handbook/online/articles/view/HH/fhe4.html.
6. Pilcher, Walter F., "Francis Jarvis Cooke," *The Handbook of Texas Online,* http://www.tsha.utexas.edu/handbook/online/articles/view/CC/fcoeg.html.
7. Winfield, Nath, "Hubert Masonic Lodge #67," *The Chappell Hill Historical Society Review,* 1999, vol. 5, p. 15. Also, Hyman, Caroline, "Benjamin Thomas," *The Handbook of Texas Online,* http://www.tsha.utexas.edu/handbook/online/articles/view/TT/fth5.html.
8. Winfield, Judy and Nath, "The Stagecoach Inn," *The Chappell Hill Historical Society Review,* 2000, vol. 6, pp. 5, 7.
9. Winfield, Judy and Nath, *Cemetery Records of Washington County, Texas* (1974), p. 31.
10. Baker, T. Lindsay, *Ghost Towns of Texas* (Norman: University of Oklahoma Press, 1986), p. 61.
11. Archives of Chappell Hill Historical Society. Also, Winfield, Nath, "Hubert Masonic Lodge #67," *The Chappell Hill Historical Society Review,* 1999, vol. 5, p. 15.
12. Campbell, Randolph, *An Empire for Slavery: The Peculiar Institution in Texas 1821–1865* (Baton Rouge: LSU Press, 1989), p. 68.
13. Archives of the Chappell Hill Historical Society.
14. Winfield, Nath, "A Letter From Texas," *Southwestern Historical Quarterly,* vol. LXXI, p. 427.
15. Winfield, Nath, *All Our Yesteryears: A Brief History of Chappell Hill* (Waco: Texian Press, 1969), p. 3.
16. Hesterley, Wayne, "Huisache—The Real Villain," unidentified newspaper article dated February 8, 1984, Archives of the Chappell Hill Historical Society.
17. United States Census for Texas, 1860.
18. Winfield, *All Our Yesteryears,* p. 3.
19. *Galveston Weekly News,* Tuesday, Feb. 19, 1861.
20. *Brenham Enquirer,* 1861, cited in *Galveston Weekly News* (February 19, 1861).
21. Christian, Carole, "Chappell Hill Female College," Handbook of Texas Online, http://www.tsha.utexas.edu/handbook/online/articles/view/CC/kbc15.html.
22. *Ibid.*
23. Archives of the Chappell Hill Historical Society.
24. *Galveston Daily News* (Houston), July 19, 1865.
25. Wooster, Ralph, "Wealthy Texans, 1860," *Southwestern Historical Quarterly* (October 1967, vol. LXXI, no. 2).
26. *Bellville Countryman,* July 25, 1863, Houston Public Library Texas Room.
27. Wallis, Mrs. J. L., *Sixty Years on the Brazos: the*

Life and Letters of Dr. John Washington Lockhart (Waco: Texian Press, 1967), p. 14.
28. Wallis, p. 15.
29. *Texana 3* (Summer 1965), 110 (from *The Chappell Hill Historical Society Review*, 1996, vol. 2, p. 15) and *Galveston Daily News*, June 10, 1866, 2 (from *The Chappell Hill Historical Society Review*, 1996, vol. 2, p. 17).

1. Texas Secedes

1. Ford, p. 137.
2. May, Robert E., p. 11.
3. Williams, John Hoyt, *Sam Houston* (New York: Promontory Press, 1998), p. 301.
4. McCutchan, Joseph D., *Mier Expedition Diary*, (Austin: University of Texas Press, 1978), p. 44.
5. Winfield, Judy and Nath, *Cemetery Records of Washington County, Texas* (Chappell Hill: Winfield, 1974), p. 32.
6. Winders, p. 70.
7. White, V. D., *Index to Mexican War Pension Files* (Waynesboro, TN: National Historical Publishing, 1989), p. 270.
8. Seward, W., "The Irrepressible Conflict," speech delivered 25 October 1858 at Rochester, New York.
9. Chappell Hill Historical Society.
10. Walker, D. L., *The Boys of '98*, (New York: Forge, 1998), pp. 24–25.
11. Burns, E. B., *Patriarch and Folk: The Emergence of Nicaragua 1798–1858* (Cambridge: Harvard University Press, 1991), p. 186.
12. Burns, p. 187.
13. Zemler, J. A., "The Texas Press and the Filibusters of the 1850's: Lopez, Carvajal and Walker" (North Texas State University, M. A. Thesis, 1983), p. 158.
14. Fornell, Earl W., "Texans and Filibusters in the 1850's," *Southwestern Historical Quarterly* 59 (April 1956), p. 415.
15. *Texas State Gazette*, May 17, 1856.
16. Fornell, p. 415.
17. May, p. 112.
18. Williams, p. 310.
19. *Ibid.*, p. 310.
20. *Confederate Military History: A Library of Confederate States History* (Wilmington: Broadfoot, 1987–1989), vol. 15, p. 10.
21. Scott, O., *The Secret Six: John Brown and the Abolitionist Movement* (New York: Times Books, 1979), pp. 309–310.
22. Spaw, P. M. (ed.), *The Texas Senate* (College Station: Texas A&M University Press, volume 1, 1990), p. 310.
23. Spaw, P. M., pp. 309–310.
24. White, W. W., "The Texas Slave Insurrection of 1860," in: *Southwestern Historical Quarterly* 52 (Jan. 1949): 278.
25. Reynolds, D., "Texas Troubles," in: *The Handbook of Texas Online*.
26. Gallagher, Gary W., *The Confederate War* (Cambridge: Harvard University Press, 1997), p. 148.
27. Reynolds, D., "Texas Troubles," in: *The Handbook of Texas Online*.
28. Reynolds, Donald E., *Editors Make War: Southern Newspapers in the Secession Crisis* (Nashville: Vanderbilt University Press, 1970), pp. 97–101.
29. Reynolds, D. E., "Vigilante Law During the Texas Slave Panic of 1860" in: *Locus* (Denton: University of North Texas Press, Spring 1990), p. 176.
30. Reynolds, D., "Texas Troubles," in: *The Handbook of Texas Online*.
31. Reynolds, D. E., "Vigilante Law During the Texas Slave Panic of 1860" in: *Locus* (University of North Texas Press, Spring 1990), p. 182.
32. White, William A., "The Texas Slave Insurrection of 1860," *Southwestern Historical Quarterly*, 52 (Jan. 1949), p. 275.
33. Norwood, Frederick A., *The Story of American Methodism* (Nashville: Abingdon Press, 1974). Nevin, D., *The Texans* (New York: Time-Life Books, Old West Series, 1975), p. 171.
34. Reagan, John H., "State of the Union Speech ... Delivered in the House of Representatives, Jan. 15, 1861," in: Wakelyn, J. L., *Southern Pamphlets on Secession, November 1860– April 1861* (Chapel Hill: University of North Carolina Press, 1996), p. 156.
35. Young, Kevin, *To the Tyrants Never Yield: A Texas Civil War Sampler* (Plano: Wordware Publishing, 1992), p. 31.
36. Williams, p. 320.
37. Hicks, Jimmie, "Some Letters Concerning the Knights of the Golden Circle in Texas, 1860–1861," *Southwestern Historical Quarterly* (July 1961, vol. 65), p. 81.
38. *Ibid.*, p. 82.
39. *Ibid.*
40. Hicks, p. 81.
41. Cutrer, Thomas W., "George M. Flournoy," *The Handbook of Texas Online*.
42. *Confederate Military History: A Library of Confederate States History* (Wilmington: Broadfoot Publishing, 1987–1989), vol. 15, p. 11.
43. *Tri-Weekly Telegraph* (Houston, Texas), December 20, 1860.
44. Bains, R. S., letter to A. L. Bains, dated Dec. 3, 1860, Chappell Hill Historical Society Archives.
45. *The Texas Ranger* (Brenham), Dec. 17, 1860, from the Center for American History, University of Texas. Austin.
46. *Ibid.*
47. "Soule University, Minutes of Board of Trustees 1856–1887," Bridwell Library, Southern Methodist University, entry dated May 3, 1860, p. 58.
48. Zuber, William P., *My Eighty Years in Texas* (Austin: University of Texas Press, 1971), p. 188.
49. "Death of Rev. George W. Carter," obituary in: *Texas Christian Advocate*, June 6, 1901.
50. "Death of Rev. George W. Carter," obituary in: *Texas Christian Advocate*, June 6, 1901.
51. Bailey, Anne J., "George Washington Carter," *The Handbook of Texas Online*.
52. *Ibid.*
53. *Journal of the Secession Convention of Texas, 1861. Ed. From the original in the Department of State by Ernest William Winkler* (Austin, 1912), p. 19. "Death of Rev. George W. Carter," obituary in: *Texas Christian Advocate*, June 6, 1901.
54. *Journal of the Secession Convention of Texas, 1861*, p. 65.

55. *Ibid.*
56. Personal communication with Donnie Roberts, owner of the old B. B. Hutchinson plantation.
57. *Journal of the Secession Convention of Texas, 1861*, p. 90.
58. *Ibid.*, p. 91.
59. Hicks, p. 81.
60. Oates, Stephen B., "Recruiting Confederate Cavalry in Texas," *Southwestern Historical Quarterly*, p. 463.
61. Swearingen, Richard M., "Four Year in the Confederate Army or My Part in the Great Rebellion," unpublished manuscript, p. 1, Call Number 2G450, Swearingen Narrative, Center for American History, University of Texas.
62. *Ibid.*, p. 3.
63. *Ibid.*
64. Doegey, L. M., "Sam Houston: Southern Spokesman for the Cause of the Union," Ph.D. dissertation, Southern Illinois University, 1968, p. 161.
65. Wallis, Jonnie Lockhart, *Sixty Years on the Brazos, The Life and Letters of Dr. John Washington Lockhart* (New York: Argonaut Press, 1966, orig. 1930), p. 25.
66. *Ibid.*, p. 99.
67. Houston, Sam, *The Writings of Sam Houston 1813–1863*, 8 (Austin: Pemberton Press, 1970), p. 299.
68. *Ibid.*, p. 296.
69. *Ibid.*
70. *Ibid.*
71. *Ibid.*, p. 297.
72. *Ibid.*, pp. 298–99.
73. *The Brenham Enquirer* (Apr. 18, 1861), The Center for American History, University of Texas, Austin.
74. *Ibid.*
75. *Soule University, Minutes of Board of Trustees 1856–1887* (Bridwell Library, Southern Methodist University), June 25, 1861, pp. 75–76.
76. *Ibid.*
77. *Ibid.*
78. Gracy, A. D., "Edmund Duggan," *Handbook of Texas Online.*
79. Houston, Sam, p. 304.
80. Letter of J. B. Wheeler, dated April 1, 1864, Archives of Chappell Hill Historical Society.

2. Terry's Texas Rangers' First Blood

1. Giles, Leonidas B., *Terry's Texas Rangers* (Austin: Pemberton Press, 1967, originally published 1911), p. 100.
2. Fitzhugh, L. N., "Terry's Texas Rangers: An Address before the Houston Civil War Round Table" (Houston Civil War Round Table, 1958), p. 1.
3. Wallis, Jonnie Lockhart, *Sixty Years on the Brazos: The Life and Letters of Dr. John Washington Lockhart* (New York: Argonaut Press, 1966, orig. 1930), p. 22.
4. "The Browning Family," unpublished notes from the Browning Plantation.
5. McCorkle, Joyce Matthews, personal communication.
6. "The Browning Family," unpublished notes from the Browning Plantation.
7. Personal communication with John Bouldin.
8. Bouldin, J. W., *The Bouldin Family: A Genealogy* (Texas City, Texas: J. W. Bouldin, 1994), p. 19.
9. Chappell Hill Historical Society.
10. *Ibid.*
11. Cutrer, T. W. "We are Stern and Resolved: The Civil War Letters of John Wesley Rabb, Terry's Texas Rangers," *Southwestern Historical Quarterly* (vol. 91, July 87–April 88), p. 198.
12. Browning, Daniel H., letter dated September 29, 1861, Archives of Chappell Hill Historical Society.
13. Jackson, John A., letter dated November 11, 1861, Archives of Chappell Hill Historical Society.
14. *Ibid.*
15. Cutrer, T. W., p. 195.
16. Harcourt, A. P., "Terry's Texas Rangers," *The Southern Bivouac* (November 1882).
17. "Terry's Texas Rangers," *Confederate Veteran* 5 (June 1897, no. 6).
18. Johnson, Frank W., *A History of Texas and Texans* (Chicago: American Historical Society, 1916), p. 1829.
19. Browning, Daniel H., letter dated January 10, 1862, John Lockhart file, Special Collections, Rosenberg Library, Galveston, Texas.
20. *Ibid.*
21. *Ibid.*
22. Browning, Daniel H., letter dated January 22, 1862, John W. Lockhart file, Special Collections, Rosenberg Library, Galveston, Texas.
23. *Ibid*
24. Browning, Daniel H., letter dated March 1862, John W. Lockhart file, Special Collections, Rosenberg Library, Galveston, Texas.
25. "Maberry, R. Jr., "John Austin Wharton," *The Handbook of Texas Online.*
26. *Ibid.*
27. Cutrer, Thomas W., "Thomas Harrison," *The Handbook of Texas Online.*
28. Browning, Daniel H., letter dated March 1862, John W. Lockhart file, Special Collections, Rosenberg Library, Galveston, Texas.
29. Browning, Daniel H., letter dated April 10, 1862, Archives of Chappell Hill Historical Society.
30. *Ibid.*
31. *Ibid.*

3. Sibley's Brigade and Waller's Regiment

1. Thompson, Jerry, *Westward the Texans* (El Paso: Texas Western Press, 1990), p. 143.
2. "Keesee, Gideon," National Archives, Record Group 109, Microfilm Series M323, Military Service Records for Confederate Volunteers, Roll 32.
3. Oates, Stephen B., "Recruiting Confederate Cavalry in Texas," *Southwestern Historical Quarterly*, pp. 471–72.
4. Seat, Benton Bell, "Memoirs," University of Arkansas Library Special Collections in: Frazier, Donald S., *Blood & Treasure: Confederate Empire in the*

South (College Station: Texas A&M University Press, 1995), pp. 119–120.
5. Josephy, Alvin M., *The Civil War in the American West* (New York: Alfred Knopf, 1991), p. 70.
6. Frazier, p. 175.
7. Frazier, p. 180.
8. *Texas Republican* (Marshall, Texas), May 17, 1862.
9. "The Battle of Glorieta," *Houston Tri-Weekly Telegraph*, June 2, 1862.
10. Young, B. H., *Confederate Wizards of the Saddle* (Kennesaw, Ga: Continental Book Co., 1958), p. 314.
11. Spurlin, Charles, *West of the Mississippi with Waller's 13th Texas Cavalry Battalion CSA* (Hillsboro, TX: Hill Junior College, 1971), p. 2.
12. Spurlin, p. 1.
13. Winfield, p. 17.
14. Winfield, p. 18.
15. Spurlin, p. 49.
16. "McDade," National Archives, Record Group 109, Microfilm Series M323, Military Service Records for Confederate Volunteers, Roll 216.
17. Cox, C. C., "Reminiscences of C. C. Cox," *Southwestern Historical Quarterly*, vol. VI, p. 222.
18. Spurlin, Charles D., "James B. P. January," *The Handbook of Texas Online*.
19. Cox, C. C., "Reminiscences of C. C. Cox," *Southwestern Historical Quarterly*, vol. VI, p. 221.
20. *Houston Tri-Weekly Telegraph*, July 6, 1863.
21. Spurlin, p. 6.

4. Hood's Texas Brigade Moves into Action

1. From the memorial statue honoring the Brigade on the State Capitol grounds in Austin.
2. Oldham, W. S., "Colonel John Marshall," *The Southwestern Historical Quarterly*, October 1916, volume 20, p. 137.
3. Simpson, H. B., *Hood's Texas Brigade: Lee's Grenadier Guard* (Waco: Texian Press, 1970), p. 12.
4. "Edmund Duggan," *The Handbook of Texas Online*.
5. Maberry, R. Jr., "Jerome Bonaparte Robertson," *Handbook of Texas Online*
6. Hailey, J. L., "Clay Castle," *Handbook of Texas Online*
7. Daniell, L. E., *Personnel of the Texas State Government, with sketches of distinguished Texans ...*," (Austin, 1889), p. 338.
8. Johnson, Barker, Winkler et al., *Texas and Texans* 4 (American Historical Society, 1914), p. 1617.
9. Felder, Rufus K., letter dated August 5, 1861, The Hood's Texas Brigade Letters Collection, Harold B. Simpson History Center, Hill College, Hillsboro, TX.
10. Felder, Rufus K., letter dated September 12, 1861, The Hood's Texas Brigade Letters Collection, Harold B. Simpson History Center, Hill College, Hillsboro, TX.
11. *Ibid.*
12. *Ibid.*
13. Simpson, H., *Hood's Texas Brigade: A Compendium* (Hillsboro, Tx: Hill Junior College Press, 1977), p. 558.
14. Died of disease, November 1861 (Simpson, *Hood's Brigade: A Compendium*), p. 208.
15. *Ibid.*
16. Felder, Rufus K., letter dated November 17, 1861, in: The Hood's Texas Brigade Letters Collection, Harold B. Simpson History Center, Hill College, Hillsboro, TX.
17. *Ibid.*
18. *Ibid.*
19. *Ibid.*
20. *Ibid.*
21. *Ibid.*
22. Thomas Bates to Eliz. McRee, December 6, 1861, The Archives of the Chappell Hill Historical Society.
23. *Ibid.*
24. *Ibid.*
25. "Del Perkins," National Archives, Record Group 109, Microfilm Series M323, Military Service Records for Confederate Volunteers, Roll 303.
26. Thomas Bates to Eliz. McRee, December 6, 1861, Archives of Chappell Hill Historical Society.
27. Simpson, H. B., *Hood's Texas Brigade: A Compendium* (Hillsboro, Tx: Hill Junior College Press, 1977), p. 240.
28. Felder, Rufus K., letter dated February 20, 1862, The Hood's Texas Brigade Letters Collection, Harold B. Simpson History Center, Hill College, Hillsboro, TX.
29. *Ibid.*
30. Wood, W. J., *Civil War Generalship: The Art of Command* (Westport: Praeger, 1997), p. 198.
31. Boritt, Gabor S. (ed.), *Jefferson Davis's Generals* (Oxford University Press, 1999), p. 86.
32. Felder, Rufus K., letter dated March 3, 1862, The Hood's Texas Brigade Letters Collection, Harold B. Simpson History Center, Hill College, Hillsboro, TX.
33. Sears, Stephen, *To the Gates of Richmond: The Peninsula Campaign* (New York: Ticknor & Fields, 1992), p. 85.
34. Felder, Rufus K., letter dated July 14, 1862, The Hood's Texas Brigade Letters Collection, Harold B. Simpson History Center, Hill College, Hillsboro, TX.
35. U.S. War Department, The War of the Rebellion: A Compilation of the Official Records of the Union and Confederate Armies (Washington, 1881–1900), vol. 11, p. 568.
36. Krick, Robert, "Robert E. Lee's First Victory at Gaines' Mill," talk presented to Houston Civil War Round Table, January 20, 2000.
37. Hennessey, J. J., *Return to Bull Run: The Campaign and Battle of Second Manassas* (Simon & Schuster, 1993), p. 364.
38. Hennessey, p. 368.
39. *Ibid.*, p. 407.
40. Simpson, H. B., *Hood's Texas Brigade: Lee's Grenadier Guards* (Waco: Texian Press, 1970), p. 152.
41. Hennessey, p. 373.
42. Polley, J. B., *Hood's Texas Brigade* (New York: Neale Publishing, 1910), p. 124.
43. Felder, Rufus K., letter dated October 1, 1862, The Hood's Texas Brigade Letters Collection, Harold

B. Simpson History Center, Hill College, Hillsboro, TX.
44. Polley, *A Soldier's Letters to Charming Nellie* (New York: Neale Publishing, 1908), p. 75.
45. *Houston Tri-Weekly Telegraph*, September 29, 1862.
46. *Ibid.*
47. Felder, Rufus K., letter dated September 23, 1862, The Hood's Texas Brigade Letters Collection, Harold B. Simpson History Center, Hill College, Hillsboro, TX.
48. Daniell, pp. 341–42.
49. Geo. W. Kerby to Eliz. McRee, October 14, 1862, Archives of Chappell Hill Historical Society.
50. *Galveston Tri-Weekly News*, November 7, 1864, Archives of Chappell Hill Historical Society.
51. Felder, Rufus K., letter dated September 23, 1862, Hill College Research Center, Hillsboro, TX.
52. Felder, Rufus K., letter dated October 1, 1862, The Hood's Texas Brigade Letters Collection, Harold B. Simpson History Center, Hill College, Hillsboro, TX.
53. Simpson, *Touched With Valor* (Hillsboro, Tx: Hill Junior College Press, 1964), p. 12.
54. Priest, J. M., *Antietam, The Soldiers' Battle* (Shippensburg, PA: White Mane Publishing, 1989), pp. 60–70.
55. *Ibid.*, p. 308.
56. Sears, Stephen, *Landscape Turned Red: The Battle of Antietam* (New York: Ticknor & Fields, 1983), 197–199, p. 202.
57. Felder, Rufus K., letter dated October 1, 1862, The Hood's Texas Brigade Letters Collection, Harold B. Simpson History Center, Hill College, Hillsboro, TX.
58. *Ibid.*
59. *Ibid.*
60. Felder, Rufus K., letter dated January 30, 1863, The Hood's Texas Brigade Letters Collection, Harold B. Simpson History Center, Hill College, Hillsboro, TX.
61. *Ibid.*
62. *Ibid.*

5. Capture at Arkansas Post

1. Texas State Archives, Austin.
2. Zuber, William P., *My Eighty Years in Texas* (Austin: University of Texas Press, 1971), p. 133.
3. Personal communication with Rev. Bill Hedges, historian of the Methodist Church's Texas Conference.
4. Seat, William, "An Address Delivered at the Commencement of Soule University, June 30, 1858" (Texas Christian Advocate, 1858).
5. Personal communication with Rev. Bill Hedges, historian of the Methodist Church's Texas Conference.
6. "Soule University, Minutes of Board of Trustees 1856–1887," Archives of Chappell Hill Historical Society, Entry dated November 26, 1859, p. 54.
7. Wilkes, F. C., Archives of Chappell Hill Historical Society.
8. Zuber, p. 231.
9. Vernon, W. N., *The Methodist Excitement in Texas* (Dallas: Texas United Methodist Historical Society, 1984), p. 98.
10. Vernon, W. N., p. 98.
11. *Ibid.*
12. Burns, Laura, letter dated January 20, 1861, in possession of Fred and Mary Brandt, Chappell Hill, Texas.
13. Bailey, Anne J., *Between the Enemy and Texas: Parson's Texas Cavalry in the Civil War* (Fort Worth: Texas Christian University Press, 1989), p. 26.
14. Zuber, p. 141.
15. Elliott, Thomas A., letter to wife dated July 3, 1862, Archives of Chappell Hill Historical Society.
16. Zuber, p. 141.
17. *Official Records*, vol. XIII, serial 19, p. 770.
18. Martin, H. N., "Texas Redskins in Confederate Gray," *Southwestern Historical Quarterly* 70 (April 1967): 589.
19. *Ibid.*
20. McCaffrey, *This Band of Heroes* (Austin: Eakin Press, 1985), p. 40.
21. *Official Records of the Union and Confederate Armies* (Washington, D. C.: U.S. Government Printing Office), vol. 17, 783; hereinafter referred to as *Official Records*.
22. *Official Records*, vol. 17, 793.
23. Smith, C. S., "Battle Report of Arkansas Post," in *Galveston Tri-Weekly News* (March 24, 1863).
24. *Official Records*, vol. 17, pp. 784–85.
25. *Ibid.*
26. *Official Records*, vol. 17, p. 793.
27. McClernand to Grant, January 14, 1863, *Official Records*, series II, vol. 5, p. 176.
28. Hesseltine, W. B., *Civil War Prisons* (Columbus: Ohio State University Press, 1930, reprinted 1998), p. 89.
29. Curtis to Grant, January 23, 1863, *Official Records*, ser. II, vol. 5, p. 203.
30. McCaffrey, p. 54.
31. *Ibid.*, pp. 55–56.
32. *Ibid.*
33. Hesseltine, p. 178.
34. Levy, G., *To Die in Chicago: Confederate Prisoners at Camp Douglas 1862–1865* (Evanston, IL: Evanston Publishing, 1994), p. 102.
35. Levy, p. 101.
36. McCaffrey, p. 57.
37. "Patrick Henry Swearingen," National Archives, Record Group 109, Microfilm Series M323, Military Service Records for Confederate Volunteers, Roll 123.
38. *Ibid.*

6. Glory at Galveston

1. Pennington, M. A. W., *History of Brenham and Washington County* (Houston: Standard Printing, 1915), p. 37.
2. Wallis, Jonnie Lockhart, *Sixty Years on the Brazos: The Life and Letters of Dr. John Washington Lockhart* (New York: Argonaut Press, 1966, orig. 1930), p. 18.
3. Plummer, B., *Historic Homes of Washington County* (San Marcos: Rio Fresco Books, 1971), p. 100.

4. Del Perkins, military service record, National Archives, National Archives, Record Group 109, Microfilm Series M323, Military Service Records for Confederate Volunteers, Roll 406.
5. Ibid.
6. Johnson, F. W., *Texas and Texans*, vol. 4 (Chicago: American Historical Society, 1914), p. 1624.
7. Ibid.
8. Taylor, Lonn, "Furniture," *The Handbook of Texas Online*, http://www.tsha.utexas.edu/handbook/online/articles/view/FF/lpf1.html.
9. Chappell Hill Historical Society.
10. Wallis, p. 73.
11. Ibid.
12. Ibid.
13. Cotham, Ed, *Battle on the Bay: The Civil War Struggle for Galveston* (College Station: Texas A&M Press, 1998), p. 116.
14. Wallis, p. 74.
15. Ibid.
16. Ibid.
17. Cotham, p. 115.
18. Wallis, pp. 74–75.
19. Cotham, p. 116.
20. Ibid.
21. Wallis, p. 75.
22. Yeary, Mamie, *Reminiscences of the Boys in Gray, 1861–1865* (Dallas: Smith and Lamar, 1912), p. 419.
23. Spindler, "The History of Hempstead," *Southwestern Historical Quarterly* 63 (January 1960), p. 415.
24. Kliewer, T., "Confederate Prison Camp Long Forgotten" (*Houston Chronicle*, December 19, 1999).
25. Read, John, Testimony, "Treatment of Prisoners of War by the Rebel Authorities" *House Report No. 45, 40th Congress, 3rd Session, No. 1391* (National Archives), pp. 926–27.
26. Duganne, A. J. H., *Twenty Months in the Department of the Gulf* (New York: J. P. Robens, 1865), p. 243.
27. Speer, L. R., *Portals to Hell, Military Prisons in the Civil War* (Mechanicsburg, PA: Stackpole Books, 1997), p. 131.
28. Kliewer, T., "Confederate Prison Camp Long Forgotten" (*Houston Chronicle*, December 19, 1999).
29. Read, pp. 926–27.

7. Marauding Cavalry

1. Brooksher, W. R. and Snider, D. K., *Glory at a Gallop: Tales of the Confederate Cavalry* (Washington: Brassey's, 1993), p. 118.
2. "Clothing and Horses For the Rangers," *Houston Tri-Weekly Telegraph*, September 24, 1862.
3. Ibid.
4. "Glenblythe, near Brenham," *Houston Tri-Weekly Telegraph*, September 26, 1862.
5. Cutrer, T. W. "We are Stern and Resolved: The Civil War Letters of John Wesley Rabb, Terry's Texas Rangers," *Southwestern Historical Quarterly* 91 (July 87–April 88), pp. 206–7.
6. Brooksher, W. R. and Snider, D. K., p. 118.
7. Brooksher and Snider, p. 122.
8. Ibid.
9. Ibid., p. 123.
10. Browning, Daniel H., letter dated February 1863, Archives of the Chappell Hill Historical Society.
11. Harcourt, A. P., "Terry's Texas Rangers," *The Southern Bivouac* (November 1882).
12. Browning, Daniel H., letter dated February 1863, Archives of the Chappell Hill Historical Society.
13. Ibid.
14. "Letter from the Rangers," *Houston Tri-Weekly Telegraph*, June 15, 1863.
15. Bailey, Anne P., *Between the Enemy and Texas: Parson's Texas Cavalry in the Civil War* (Fort Worth: Texas Christian University Press, 1989), p. 32, referencing the *Bellville Countryman*, April 11, 1863.
16. Letter from Thomas Bates dated February 21, 1862, Archives of the Chappell Hill Historical Society.
17. Letter from George W. Kerby to Elizabeth Cocke dated September 12, 1854, The Archives of the Chappell Hill Historical Society.
18. Letter from Thomas Bates dated October 14, 1862, Archives of the Chappell Hill Historical Society.
19. Oates, S. B., *Confederate Cavalry West of the River* (Austin: University of Texas Press, 1961), pp. 124–25.
20. "Letter from Arkansas," *Houston Tri-Weekly Telegraph*, June 15, 1863.
21. Zuber, William P., *My Eighty Years in Texas* (Austin: University of Texas Press, 1971), pp. 186–87.
22. Ibid., p. 187.
23. Ibid., p. 188.
24. Walton, W. M., *An Epitome of My Life: Civil War Reminiscences by Buck Walton* (Austin: Waterloo Press, Austin, 1965), p. 41.
25. Ibid., p. 53.
26. Ibid., p. 54.
27. Smith, David Paul, "William Quantrill," *Handbook of Texas Online*, http://www.tsha.utexas.edu/handbook/online/articles/view/QQ/fqu3.html.
28. Archives of Chappell Hill Historical Society.
29. "Soule University, Minutes of Board of Trustees 1856–1887," Archives of Chappell Hill Historical Society, May 9, 1861, p. 67.
30. Ibid., May 29, 1858 and November 2, 1858.
31. Archives of Chappell Hill Historical Society.
32. "Andrew Keller," National Archives, Record Group 109, Microfilm Series M323, Military Service Records for Confederate Volunteers, Roll 37.
33. Brown, W. L., *A Life of Albert Pike* (Fayetteville: University of Arkansas Press, 1997).
34. Griscom, G. L., *Fighting with Ross' Texas Cavalry Brigade* (Hillsboro: Hill Junior College Press, 1976), pp. 22–23.
35. Britton, W., *The Union Indian Brigade* (Kansas City: Hudson Publishing, 1922), p. 34.
36. Griscom, p. 10.
37. Ibid.
38. "B. T. Kavanaugh," National Archives. Record Group 109, Military Service Records for Confederate Volunteers.
39. "The Knight Line" (Ruthven Commandery No. 2, Houston, vol. VII, no. 1, January 1979).
40. "The North-West ripe for Revolution," *Galveston Tri-Weekly News*, July 2, 1863.
41. Ibid.
42. Ibid.
43. Levy, p. 103.

44. "The North-West ripe for Revolution," *Galveston Tri-Weekly News*, July 2, 1863.
45. *Ibid.*
46. Levy, p. 105.
47. "The North-West ripe for Revolution," *Galveston Tri-Weekly News*, July 2, 1863.
48. *Ibid.*
49. *Ibid.*
50. *Ibid.*
51. *Ibid.*
52. *Ibid.*
53. *Ibid.*
54. *Ibid.*
55. *Ibid.*

8. Vicksburg and Gettysburg — The Turning Points

1. *Bellville Countryman*, June 13, 1863.
2. Felder, R. K., letter dated May 2, 1863, The Hood's Texas Brigade Letters Collection, Harold B. Simpson History Center, Hill College, Hillsboro, TX.
3. Johnson, Frank W., *A History of Texas and Texans* 4 (Chicago: American Historical Society, 1914), p. 1630.
4. Burns, Laura, letter dated January 20, 1861, in possession of Fred and Mary Brandt, Chappell Hill, Texas.
5. Archives of the Chappell Hill Historical Society.
6. "Henry C. Brandt," National Archives, Record Group 109, Microfilm Series M323, Military Service Records for Confederate Volunteers, Roll 426.
7. Affleck, T., *Houston Weekly Telegraph*, July 17, 1861, reprinted in: *Afternoons on New Year's Creek, Washington County, Texas: 1861, 1862, 1988* (Brenham: New Year's Creek Settler's Association, 1989), pp. 4–5.
8. Knolle, Herman, Diary in: Hasskarl, R. A. and Hasskarl, L. R., *Waul's Texas Legion 1862–1865* (Ada, OK: R. A. Hasskarl, 1985), p. 33.
9. *Ibid.*, p. 34.
10. *Ibid.*
11. *Ibid.*, p. 38.
12. Hesseltine, W. B., *Civil War Prisons* (Columbus: Ohio State University Press, 1930, reprinted 1998), p. 189.
13. Knolle, p. 40.
14. Felder, R. K., letter dated July 9, 1863, The Hood's Texas Brigade Letters Collection, Harold B. Simpon History Center, Hill College, Hillsboro, TX.
15. Floca, Samuel W. Jr., "Hood's Protest," *Confederate Veteran* 6 (1995), p. 27.
16. Barziza, Decimus, *The adventures of a prisoner of war, 1863–1864* (Austin: University of Texas Press, 1964).
17. West, J. C., *A Texan In Search of a Fight: being the diary and letters of a private soldier in Hood's Texas Brigade* (Texian Press, 1969, reprint of 1901 edition).
18. Felder, R. K., letter dated July 9, 1863, The Hood's Texas Brigade Letters Collection, Harold B. Simpson History Center, Hill College, Hillsboro, TX.
19. Scott, Dr. John O., "The Texans at Gettysburg," *Galveston Daily News*, July 1913.
20. *Ibid.*
21. Floca, Samuel W. Jr., "Hood's Protest," *Confederate Veteran* 6 (1995), p. 36.
22. Scott, Dr. John O., "The Texans at Gettysburg," *Galveston Daily News*, July 1913, from Rosenberg Library.
23. *Ibid.*

9. The Home Front 1863–1864

1. Johnson, J. P., "February 1864 Inspection Report of Trans-Mississippi Department," in: *Official Records*, ser. I, vol. 22, part 2, p. 1130.
2. Shalhope, R. E., *Sterling Price: Portrait of a Southerner* (Columbia: University of Missouri Press, 1971), p. 246.
3. *Ibid.*, p. 102.
4. Wooster, R., *Texas and Texans in the Civil War* (Austin: Eakin Press, 1995), p. 101.
5. Josephy, Alvin M., Jr., *The Civil War in the American West* (New York: Alfred Knopf, 1991), p. 377.
6. Shalhope, p. 248.
7. Steele, F., Dispatch to N. P. Banks, March 7, 1864, *Official Records*, ser. I, vol. 34, part 2, p. 5
8. "B. T. Kavanaugh," National Archives, National Archives. Record Group 109, Military Service Records for Confederate Volunteers.
9. George Washington Carter, Military Service Record, CSA, National Archives.
10. *Galveston Tri-Weekly News*, October 5, 1863, from microfilm in Houston Public Library.
11. Burkalter, L. W., *Gideon Lincecum: 1793–1874, A Biography* (Austin: University of Texas Press, 1965), p. 160.
12. *Ibid.*
13. *Ibid.*
14. "Death of Rev. George W. Carter," obituary in: *Texas Christian Advocate*, June 6, 1901.
15. *Ibid.*
16. *Ibid.*
17. *Galveston Tri-Weekly News*, October 5, 1863, from microfilm in Houston Public Library.
18. *Ibid.*
19. *Ibid.*
20. *Tri-Weekly News*, October 9, 1863.
21. Farber, James, *Texas, C. S. A.* (New York: The Jackson Company, 1947), pp. 176–177.
22. Wooster, Ralph, *Texas and Texans in the Civil War* (Austin: Eakin Press, 1996), p. 120.
23. Pilcher, Walter, "Francis Jarvis Cooke," Handbook of Texas Online, http://www.tsha.utexas.edu/handbook/online/articles/view/CC/fcoeg.html.
24. Archives of the Chappell Hill Historical Society.
25. Johnson, Frank W., *A History of Texas and Texans* (New York: American Historical Society, 1916), vol. IV, p. 1609.
26. Winfield, Nath and Judy, "Forgotten Towns Along the Brazos, Part Two," *The Chappell Hill Historical Society Review*, 1998, vol. IV, p. 14.
27. *Galveston Tri-Weekly News*, January 22, 1864, from the Archives of the Chappell Hill Historical Society.
28. Christian, Carole E., "Washington County," *The Handbook of Texas Online.* http://www.tsha.

utexas.edu/handbook/online/articles/view/WW/hcw4.html.
29. Christian, Carole E., "Chappell Hill," The Handbook of Texas Online, http://www.tsha.utexas.edu/handbook/online/articles/view/CC/hlc21.html.
30. *Galveston Daily News*, July 19, 1865.
31. *Soule University, Minutes of Board of Trustees 1856–1887*, Archives of Chappell Hill Historical Society, September 17, 1861, p. 77.
32. *Ibid.*, July 4, 1861, p. 77.
33. Freeman, James W. Papers, letter dated January 18, 1864, Center for American History, University of Texas at Austin.
34. Freeman, James W. Papers, letter dated January 27, 1864, Center for American History, University of Texas at Austin.
35. "Socks for Soldiers," *Houston Tri-Weekly Telegraph*, October 9, 1863.
36. *Ibid.*
37. Keller, Andrew M., letter to T. J. Jackson, dated October 25, 1863, Archives of the Chappell Hill Historical Society.
38. *Ibid.*
39. Miers M. Felder, Military Service Record, National Archives, Record Group 109, Microfilm Series M323, Military Service Records for Confederate Volunteers, Roll 298.
40. Archives of the Chappell Hill Historical Society.
41. *Galveston Tri-Weekly News*, January 22, 1864.
42. *Ibid.*
43. *Ibid.*
44. *Ibid.*
45. *Soule University, Minutes of Board of Trustees 1856–1887*, Archives of Chappell Hill Historical Society, April 16, 1859, p. 44.
46. *Soule University, Minutes of Board of Trustees 1856–1887*, Archives of Chappell Hill Historical Society, August 6, 1864, p. 84.
47. *Soule University, Minutes of Board of Trustees 1856–1887*, Archives of Chappell Hill Historical Society, October 5, 1864, p. 81.
48. "Death of Rev. George W. Carter," obituary in: *Texas Christian Advocate*, June 6, 1901.
49. Archives of Chappell Hill Historical Society.
50. Phelan, Macum, *A History of Early Methodism in Texas, 1817–1866* (Nashville: Cokesbury Press, 1924).
51. Yeary, Miss Mamie, *Reminiscences of the Boys in Gray 1861–1865* (Dayton, OH: Morningside, 1986), p. 441.
52. Yeary, p. 442.
53. Archives of the Chappell Hill Historical Society.
54. Cutrer, Thomas, "Williamson Simpson Oldham," *Handbook of Texas Online*, http://www.tsha.utexas.edu/handbook/online/articles/view/OO/fol2.html.
55. Archives of the Chappell Hill Historical Society.

10. Eastern Tennessee Campaign

1. Swearingen, Richard M., Swearingen, Richard M., "Four Year in the Confederate Army or My Part in the Great Rebellion," unpublished manuscript, p. 1, Call Number 2G450, Swearingen Narrative, Center for American History, University of Texas.
2. *Ibid.*
3. *Ibid.*, p. 9.
4. *Ibid.*, p. 11.
5. *Ibid.*, p. 13.
6. *Ibid.*
7. "Thomas Keesee" National Archives, Record Group 109, Microfilm series M323, Military Service Records for Confederate Volunteers, Roll 301.
8. Swearingen, p. 17.
9. *Ibid.*, pp. 17–21.
10. *Ibid.*, p. 25.
11. *Ibid.*
12. Brooksher and Snider, *Glory at a Gallop: Tales of Confederate Cavalry* (Washington, D.C.: Brassey's, 1993), p. 120.
13. Felder, Rufus K., letter dated May 2, 1863, The Hood's Texas Brigade Letters Collection, Harold B. Simpson History Center, Hill College, Hillsboro, TX.
14. Felder, Rufus K., letter dated October 12, 1863, The Hood's Texas Brigade Letters Collection, Harold B. Simpson History Center, Hill College, Hillsboro, TX.
15. Foster, Samuel, *One of Cleburne's Command: the Civil War reminiscences and diary of Capt. Samuel T. Foster, Granbury's Texas Brigade, CSA*, edited by Norman D. Brown. (Austin: University of Texas, 1980), p. 52.
16. McCaffery, James M., *This Band of Heroes: Granbury's Texas Brigade* (Austin: Eakin Press, 1985), p. 73.
17. *Official Records*, ser. I, volume 30, part II, pp. 194–95.
18. Foster, 54. McCaffrey, p. 76.
19. *Official Records*, p. 195.
20. Felder, Rufus K., letter dated October 12, 1863, The Hood's Texas Brigade Letters Collection, Harold B. Simpson History Center, Hill College, Hillsboro, TX.
21. Woodworth, p. 111.
22. McCaffrey, p. 79.
23. Felder, Rufus King, letter dated October 12, 1863, The Hood's Texas Brigade Letters Collection, Harold B. Simpson History Center, Hill College, Hillsboro, TX.
24. *Official Records*, vol. 31, p. 540.
25. *Official Records*, p. 541.
26. *Official Records*, pp. 541–42.
27. Archives of Chappell Hill Historical Society.
28. *Official Report*, p. 544.
29. *Galveston Tri-Weekly News*, December 28, 1863, from the Archives of the Chappell Hill Historical Society.
30. *Galveston Tri-Weekly News*, December 28, 1863, from the Archives of the Chappell Hill Historical Society.
31. Anonymous, "In Memory of My Brother," [Confederate Soldier's Death Poem], Box 2L 259, Center for American History, University of Texas.

11. The Defense of Atlanta

1. *Galveston Tri-Weekly*, March 2, 1864, from the Archives of the Chappell Hill Historical Society.

2. *Galveston Tri-Weekly*, March 9, 1864, from the Archives of the Chappell Hill Historical Society.
3. Garrett, Hosea, letter dated August 1, 1864, manuscript MS 119F, Hosea Garrett Manuscript Collection, Atlanta History Center, Atlanta, GA.
4. William. H. Harmon to Miss Mollie Jackson, June 14, 1864, Archives of the Chappell Hill Historical Society.
5. Felder, Rufus K., letter dated October 12, 1863, The Hood's Texas Brigade Letters Collection, Harold B. Simpson History Center, Hill College, Hillsboro, TX.
6. George W. Kerby to Mrs. Elizabeth McRee, dated July 20, 1864, The Archives of the Chappell Hill Historical Society.
7. Garrett, Hosea, letter dated August 1, 1864, manuscript MS 119F, Hosea Garrett Manuscript Collection, Atlanta History Center, Atlanta, GA. Remaining quotations from Garrett in this chapter are all drawn from this same letter.
8. Seaton, Benjamin, *The Bugle Blows Softly: The Confederate Diary of Benjamin M. Seaton*, ed. by Simpson, Col. Harold B. (Waco: Texian Press, 1965), p. 59.
9. Ibid.
10. "Hosea Garrett," National Archives, Record Group 109, Microfilm Series M323, Military Service Records for Confederate Volunteers, Roll 339. Also *Daily Intelligencer* (Macon, Georgia), September 17, 1864.
11. Ibid.
12. *Galveston Tri-Weekly News*, November 9, 1864, Archives of the Chappell Hill Historical Society.
13. Fischer, Noel C., *War at Every Door: Partisan Politics & Guerrilla Warfare in East Tennessee*, (Chapel Hill: University of North Carolina Press, 1997), p. 150.
14. Brown, Hohn Henry, *Indian Wars and Pioneers of Texas* (Austin: L. E. Daniell, 1890), p. 748.
15. Ibid., p. 177.
16. Ibid., p. 178.
17. Ibid., p. 192.
18. Wooster, R. A., *Texas and Texans in the Civil War* (Austin: Eakin Press, 1995), p. 168.

12. The Wilderness and Petersburg

1. *Official Records*, vol. 30, part 1, January, 24, 1864, p. 470.
2. Felder, Rufus K., letter dated July 14, 1864, The Hood's Texas Brigade Letters Collection, Harold B. Simpson History Center, Hill College, Hillsboro, TX.
3. "Lee to the Rear," *Texana*, 11(1973, no.2), pp. 115, 121.
4. Rhea, Gordon C., *The Battle of The Wilderness, May 5–6, 1864* (Baton Rouge: Louisiana State University Press, 1994), p. 303.
5. Ibid.
6. "James Edward Landes," Military Service Record, National Archives, Record Group 109, Microfilm Series M323, Military Service Records for Confederate Volunteers, Roll 301.
7. Felder, Rufus K., letter dated July 14, 1864, The Hood's Texas Brigade Letters Collection, Harold B. Simpson History Center, Hill College, Hillsboro, TX.
8. Kerby, George, letter dated July 20, 1864, George Kirby File, Archives of the Chappell Hill Historical Society.
9. Felder, Rufus K., letter dated August 13, 1864, The Hood's Texas Brigade Letters Collection, Harold B. Simpson History Center, Hill College, Hillsboro, TX.
10. Felder, Rufus K., letter dated August 13, 1864, The Hood's Texas Brigade Letters Collection, Harold B. Simpson History Center, Hill College, Hillsboro, TX.
11. Felder, Rufus K., letter dated September 18, 1864, The Hood's Texas Brigade Letters Collection, Harold B. Simpson History Center, Hill College, Hillsboro, TX.
12. Felder, Rufus K., letter dated September 18, 1864, The Hood's Texas Brigade Letters Collection, Harold B. Simpson History Center, Hill College, Hillsboro, TX.
13. Felder, Rufus K., letter dated September 18, 1864, The Hood's Texas Brigade Letters Collection, Harold B. Simpson History Center, Hill College, Hillsboro, TX.
14. Brinsfield, John, "The Battle of New Market Heights," www.army.mil/soldiers/feb 96/p50.html (accessed January 4, 2003).
15. Clay, T. T., *War Letters of Tacitus T. Clay, C. S. A.* (Winfield, Judy and Nath, 1968), pp. 14–15.
16. Toland, Gracey Booker, *Austin Knew His Athens* (San Antonio: Naylor Co., 1938), p. 16.
17. Felder, Rufus K., letter dated December 18, 1864, The Hood's Texas Brigade Letters Collection, Harold B. Simpson History Center, Hill College, Hillsboro, TX.

13. The End of the War

1. Felder, Rufus K., letter dated February 23, 1865, The Hood's Texas Brigade Letters Collection, Harold B. Simpson History Center, Hill College, Hillsboro College, TX.
2. "From the Texas Rangers—Casualties," undated piece of *Galveston Tri-Weekly Telegraph*, from the Archives of the Chappell Hill Historical Society.
3. *Official Records*, vol. 47, part II, p. 533.
4. Hampton, Wade, "The Battle of Bentonville" in *Battles and Leaders of the Civil War* 4 (New York: T. Yoseloff, 1956), p. 704.
5. *Official Records*, vol. 47, part I, p. 1057.
6. Johnson, Frank B., (ed. by Barker, E. C.), *A History of Texas and Texans* (Chicago and New York: The American Historical Society, 1916), p. 1738.
7. Jeffries, C. C., *Terry's Rangers* (New York: Vantage Press, 1961), pp. 125–26.
8. Simpson, H, "Hood's Texas Brigade at Appomattox" in *Lone Star Blue and Gray: Essays on Texas in the Civil War*, p. 339.
9. Simpson, H. B. (ed), *Touched with Valor: Civil War papers and casualty reports of Hood's Texas Brigade. Written and collected by Jerome B. Robertson* (Hillsboro, TX: Hill Junior College Press, 1964), pp. 102–4.

10. Trudeau, N. A., *Out of the Storm, The End of the Civil War April–June 1865* (Boston: Little, Brown and Company, 1994), p. 149.
11. Gordon, J. B., *Reminiscences of the Civil War* (New York: C. Scribner's Sons, 1904), pp. 443–48.
12. Chamberlain, J., *The Passing of the Armies* (New York: G. P. Putnam's Sons, 1915), pp. 258–65.
13. Simpson, p. 344.
14. *Ibid.*, p. 346.
15. *Ibid.*, p. 129.
16. *Ibid.*, pp. 134–35.
17. *Ibid.*, p. 129.
18. "Sketches of the Famous Eight Texas Cavalry," *Confederate Veteran* 5 (1897).

14. Texas at the Close of the War

1. "Franklin C. Wilkes," National Archives, Record Group 109, Microfilm Series M323, Military Service Records for Confederate Volunteers, Roll 123.
2. *Ibid.*
3. McCaffery, James M., *This Band of Heroes: Granbury's Texas Brigade, C.S.A.* (College Station: Texas A&M University Press, 1996), p. 65.
4. Foster, Samuel T., *One of Cleburne's Command: The Civil War reminiscences and diary of Capt. Samuel T. Foster, Granbury's Texas Brigade, CSA* / edited by Norman D. Brown (Austin: University of Texas Press, 1980), p. 93.
5. War Department letter dated February 20, 1932, "Franklin C. Wilkes," National Archives, Record Group 109, Microfilm Series M323, Military Service Records for Confederate Volunteers, Roll 37.
6. *Galveston Tri-Weekly News*, July 18, 1864.
7. Foster, 93.
8. "Franklin C. Wilkes," National Archives, Record Group 109, Microfilm Series M323, Military Service Records for Confederate Volunteers, Roll 123.
9. Speer, L. R., *Portals to Hell, Military Prisons of the Civil War* (Mechanicsburg, Pa: Stackpole Books, 1997), p. 196.
10. *Ibid.*
11. *Official Report*, series II, volume 8, pp. 215–16.
12. "Franklin C. Wilkes," National Archives, Record Group 109, Microfilm Series M323, Military Service Records for Confederate Volunteers, Roll 123.
13. Hesseltine, W. B., *Civil War Prisons* (Columbus: Ohio State University Press, 1930, reprinted 1998), p. 232.
14. Josephy, Alvin M., Jr., *The Civil War in the American West* (New York: Alfred Knopf, 1991), p. 384.
15. Edwards, *Shelby and His Men* (1867), p. 470.
16. *Ibid.*, p. 474.
17. *Ibid.*
18. Kavanaugh, B. T., Military service record, National Archives.
19. Kavanaugh, B. T., *Texas Masonic Mirror* (August 13, 1873, volume II, no. 32), p. 371.
20. Edwards, *Shelby and His Men* (Cincinnati: Miami Printing, 1867), 475 and Rea, R. R., *Sterling Price, the Lee of the West* (Little Rock: Pioneer Press, 1959), p. 157.
21. Josephy, p. 377.
22. Rea, p. 157.
23. *Galveston Daily News* (Houston) April 8, 1865.
24. Spurlin, C., *West of the Mississippi with Waller's 13th Texas Cavalry Battalion* (Hill Junior College Press, 1971), p. 11.
25. "Campaign from Hempstead to Red River," *Houston Tri-Weekly Telegraph*, May 24, 1865.
26. Perkins, R. P., *Heroes and Renegades: A History of the Arizona Brigade* (website of the Colonel Sherod Hunter Camp 1525, Sons of Confederate Veterans, Phoenix, Arizona).
27. "Campaign from Hempstead to Red River," *Houston Tri-Weekly Telegraph*, May 24, 1865.
28. *Ibid.*
29. *Ibid.*
30. *Houston Tri-Weekly Telegraph*, April 15, 1865.
31. *Ibid.*, April 24, 1865.
32. *Ibid.*
33. *Galveston Tri-Weekly News*, March 20, 1865, from Archives of Chappell Hill Historical Society.
34. *Houston Tri-Weekly Telegraph*, April 24, 1865.
35. *Ibid.*
36. *Ibid.*
37. *Ibid.*
38. *Ibid.*
39. *Ibid.*
40. *Houston Tri-Weekly Telegraph*, April 25, 1865.
41. *Ibid.*, May 11, 1865.
42. *Ibid.*, May 16, 1865.
43. Wilkes, F. C., letter dated April 27, 1865, Archives of Chappell Hill Historical Society.
44. *Houston Tri-Weekly Telegraph*, May 24, 1865.
45. *Ibid.*, May 12, 1865
46. *Ibid.*, May 24, 1865.
47. *Ibid.*
48. *Ibid.*
49. *Confederate Military History* (Atlanta, 1899, volume XI), pp. 138–39.
50. Blessington, J. P., *The Campaigns of Walker's Texas Division* (New York: Lange, Little, 1875), p. 307.
51. *Ibid.*
52. Young, K. R., *To the Tyrants Never Yield* (Plano: Wordware Publishing, 1992), p. 193.
53. Hunt, J. W., "Battle of Palmito Ranch," *The Handbook of Texas Online*.
54. Marten, J. A., "Rio Grande Campaign," *The Handbook of Texas Online*.

15. Texas Homecomings

1. Swearingen, R. M., "Diary of R. M. Swearingen in the Confederate Army," unpublished, Center for American History, University of Texas at Austin, p. 29.
2. *Ibid.*
3. Brown, John Henry, *Indian Wars and Pioneers of Texas* (Austin: L. E. Daniell, 1890), p. 748.
4. J. T. Swearingen, Military Service Record, National Archives.
5. Daniell, L. E., *Types of Successful Men* (Austin: E. Von Boeckmann, 1890), p. 149.
6. *Ibid.*, p. 150.
7. Knolle, p. 50.

8. Personal communication with Fred and Mary Brandt, Chappell Hill, Texas.
9. "Mrs. H. C. Brandt, Widow's Application for a Pension, No. 51722," Texas State Archives, Austin.
10. Brandt, Henry C., Diary of Trip Home, Chappell Hill Historical Society Archives.
11. Archives of the Chappell Hill Historical Society.
12. Letter of O. H. P. Garrett to Florence Garrett— "Character and Experiences of the Civil War," Special Collections, Atlanta History Center.
13. *Ibid.*
14. Johnson, Frank W., *A History of Texas and Texans* 4 (Chicago: The American Historical Society, 1916), 1829.
15. Johnson, 1830.
16. Johnson, 1830.
17. Johnson, 1830.
18. Coco, Gregory, *The Civil War Infantryman* (Gettysburg: Thomas Publications, 1996), p. 136.
19. Cutrer, Thomas W., "Martin McHenry Kenney," *The Handbook of Texas Online.*
20. Jeffries, C. C., *Terry's Rangers* (Vantage Press, 1961), p. 138.
21. *Galveston Daily News* (September 21, 1865).
22. Hargrove, J. A., "Memoirs" (1903), p. 13.
23. Crane, W. C., "Centennial Address Embracing the History of Washington County, Texas," delivered July 4, 1876, reprinted in Brenham *Banner*, 1939.
24. Oldham, William S. Jr., letter to A. B. Thompson dated November 18, 1865, J. W. Thompson papers, Archives of Chappell Hill Historical Society.
25. *Ibid.*
26. *Ibid.*
27. *Ibid.*
28. *Ibid.*
29. *Ibid.*
30. Letter from Andrew Frederick Buchanan to his daughter Eulalie Buchanan Granberry, dated January 18, 1935, provided to the author by Mr. and Mrs. Samuel Rice Buchanan.
31. *Ibid.*
32. *Ibid.*
33. Callaway, Nancy Ruth Buchanan, "The Journey of Mary Eugenia Felder Callaway," narrative written for the family in November 1999, provided to the author by Mr. and Mrs. Samuel Rice Buchanan.
34. Letter from Andrew Frederick Buchanan to his daughter Eulalie Buchanan Granberry, dated January 18, 1935, provided to the author by Mr. and Mrs. Samuel Rice Buchanan.
35. Letter from Andrew Frederick Buchanan to his daughter Eulalie Buchanan Granberry, dated January 18, 1935, provided to the author by Mr. and Mrs. Samuel Rice Buchanan.
36. Hill, L. F., "The Confederate Exodus to Latin America," *Southwestern Historical Quarterly* (April 1936, vol. 39, no. 4), pp. 315–22.
37. Hill, 323.
38. Nunn, W. C., *Escape from Reconstruction* (Fort Worth: Texas Christian University, 1956), p. 75.
39. Letter from Eugenia Felder Buchanan, dated April 30, 1869, provided to the author by Mr. and Mrs. Samuel Rice Buchanan.
40. *Ibid.*
41. *Ibid.*
42. Callaway, p. 4.
43. Patrons of Husbandry, certificate dated December 3, 1874, provided to the author by Mrs. Samuel Rice Buchanan.
44. Provided by Samuel Rice Buchanan and Amy Ruth Mayo Buchanan.

16. Occupation and Reconstruction

1. *Houston Daily Telegraph*, July 7, 1866.
2. Richter, W. L., *The Army in Texas During Reconstruction* (College Station: Texas A&M University Press, 1987), p. 14.
3. *Ibid.*, p. 16.
4. Archives of the Chappell Hill Historical Society.
5. *Ibid.*
6. Haskew, C. P., *Historical Records of Austin & Waller Counties* (Houston: Premier Printing, 1969), p. 117.
7. Richter, W. L., *The Army in Texas During Reconstruction* (College Station: Texas A&M University Press, 1987), p. 19.
8. Richter, W. L., "The Brenham Fire of 1866," in: *Louisiana Studies* (volume 14, Fall 1975), p. 294.
9. *Ibid.*, p. 294.
10. Richter, W. L., *The Army in Texas During Reconstruction*, p. 52.
11. Richter, W. L., *The Army in Texas During Reconstruction*, p. 13, from U.S. Grant papers in the Library of Congress.
12. Gillespie, C. C., "Doings in Congress," *Houston Daily Telegraph*, June 19, 1866.
13. Gillespie, C. C., "Doings in Congress," *Houston Daily Telegraph*, June 19, 1866.
14. Gillespie, C. C., "The Celebration of the Anniversary of Their Freedom," *Houston Daily Telegraph*, June 21, 1866.
15. Gillespie, C. C., "The Reconstruction Report," *Houston Daily Telegraph*, June 21, 1866.
16. *Ibid.*
17. Read, John, Testimony, "Treatment of Prisoners of War by the Rebel Authorities" *House Report No. 45, 40th Congress, 3rd Session, No. 1391* (National Archives), p. 927.
18. Gillespie, C. C., "The Fourth of July," *Houston Daily Telegraph*, July 4, 1866.
19. Chappell Hill Historical Society.
20. Chappell Hill Historical Society.
21. Crockett Family Records, Chappell Hill Historical Society Archives.
22. *Galveston Daily News*, June 10, 1866, 2 (in *The Chappell Hill Historical Society Review*, vol. 2, 1996, p. 15).
23. *The Chappell Hill Historical Society Review*, vol. 2, 1996, p. 18.
24. *Ibid.*, p. 19.
25. "Sketch of the Famous Eighth Texas Cavalry," *Confederate Veteran*, vol. 5, 1897.
26. Richter, W. L., *The Army in Texas During Reconstruction* (College Station: Texas A&M University Press, 1987), p. 51.
27. Moneyhon, Carl, "Black Codes," The Hand-

book of Texas Online, http://www.tsha.utexas.edu/handbook/online/.
28. Richter, W. L., "The Brenham Fire of 1866," in: *Louisiana Studies* (vol. 14, Fall 1975), p. 290.
29. Richter, W. L., *The Army in Texas During Reconstruction* (College Station: Texas A&M University Press, 1987), p. 29.
30. *Ibid.*, p. 28.
31. *Ibid.*, pp. 29–30.
32. *The Chappell Hill Caller*, Newsletter of the Chappell Hill Historical Society, April 2000.
33. Richter, W. L., "The Brenham Fire of 1866," p. 299.
34. Gillespie, C. C., "Texas Items," *Houston Daily Telegraph*, June 20, 1866.
35. *Ibid.*
36. Pennington, M. A. W., *History of Brenham and Washington County* (Houston: Standard Printing, 1915), p. 37.
37. Thompson, Jerry, "When General Albert Sidney Johnston Came Home," in: *Southwestern Historical Quarterly* 103 (April 2000), p. 473.
38. *Ibid.*, p. 475.
39. *Ibid.*, ref: Johnston, W. P., *Life of Albert Sidney Johnston* (Austin: State House Press, 1997), p. 712.
40. Young, K., *To The Tyrants Never Yield*, (Plano: Wordware, 1992), pp. 98–102.
41. *Houston Telegraph*, June 12, 1867.
42. *Ibid.*
43. *Ibid.*
44. Winfield, *All Our Yesteryears*, p. 37.
45. Vertical file, Brenham City Library.
46. Nieman, Donald G., "Black Political Power and Criminal Justice: Washington County, Texas, 1868–1884," *The Journal of Southern History* (August 1989), vol. LV, no. 3), p. 394.
47. Pitre, Merline, "Matthew Gaines," The Handbook of Texas Online, http://www.tsha.utexas.edu/handbook/online/.
48. Hatley, Allen, *Bringing the Law to Texas: Crime and Violence in Nineteenth Century Texas* (LaGrange, TX: Centex Press, 2002), p. 51.
49. Hatley, p. 86.
50. Hailey, James and Leffler, John, "Washington County," *The Handbook of Texas Online*. http://www.tsha.utexas.edu/handbook/online/articles/view/WW/hcw4.html.
51. Barr, Alwyn, *Black Texans: A History of African Americans in Texas* (Norman: University of Oklahoma Press, 1996), p. 48.
52. Hatley, p. 57.
53. Barr, p. 49.
54. Baum, Dale, "The Matthew Gaines Memorial," http://www.tamu.edu/gaines/feb ruary.html.
55. Kavanaugh, B. T., "Negro Masons," *Texas Masonic Mirror* (volume 1, no. 9, February 28, 1872).
56. Kavanaugh, B. T., "Western Tract Society," *Texas Masonic Mirror* (volume 1, no. 48, November 27, 1872).
57. Harper, Cecil Jr., "Freedmen's Bureau," Handbook of Texas Online, http://www.tsha.utexas.edu/handbook/online/articles/view/FF/ncf1.html.
58. Hailey, James and Leffler, John, "Washington County," *The Handbook of Texas Online*. http://www.tsha.utexas.edu/handbook/online/articles/view/WW/hcw4.html.
59. Richter, William, *Overreached on All Sides: The Freedmen's Bureau Administration in Texas 1865–8* (College Station: Texas A&M University Press, 1991), p. 20.
60. *Ibid.*
61. Winfield, Judy, "Providence Baptist Church," *The Chappell Hill Historical Society Review*, 1995, vol. 1, p. 7.
62. Chappell Hill Historical Society.
63. Chappell Hill Historical Society.
64. Nieman, p. 398.
65. Hardman, Peggy, "Exodus of 1879," *The Handbook of Texas Online*.
66. Nieman, p. 396.
67. Carter, G. W., letter dated September 4, 1865, Chappell Hill Historical Society Archives.
68. Pitre, Althea D., "Collapse of the Warmoth Regime," *Louisiana History* (Spring 1965, vol. VI, no. 2), p. 166.
69. Warmoth, H. C., *War, Politics and Reconstruction* (Macmillan Company, 1930), p. 109.
70. Harris, F. B., "Henry Clay Warmoth, Reconstruction Governor of Louisiana," in: *The Louisiana Historical Quarterly* (volume 30, no. 2, April 1947), p. 550.
71. Pitre, Althea D., "Collapse of the Warmoth Regime," in: *Louisiana History* (Spring 1965, vol. VI, no. 2), p. 166.
72. Harris, 622, from: *New Orleans Times*, August 13, 1871.
73. Harris, p. 610.
74. Wetta, Frank J., "Bulldozing the Scalawags: Some Examples of the Persecution of Southern White Republicans in Louisiana During Reconstruction," *Louisiana History* (Winter 1980, vol. XXI, no. 1).
75. Taylor, J. G., *Louisiana Reconstructed 1863–1877* (Baton Rouge: LSU Press, 1974), p. 213.
76. Wetta.
77. Taylor, p. 476.
78. Harris, p. 613.
79. Pitre, p. 348.
80. Harris, p. 621.
81. Wetta.
82. Pitre.
83. Pitre.
84. Wetta, p. 46.
85. Dufour, C. L., "The Age of Warmoth," *Louisiana History* 6 (Fall 1965, no. 4), p. 350.
86. *Ibid.*, p. 351.
87. Harris, p. 622, from: *New Orleans Times* (August 15, 1871).
88. Dawson, J. G., *Army Generals and Reconstruction: Louisiana, 1862–1877* (Baton Rouge: LSU Press, 1982), p. 118.
89. *Ibid.*, p. 123.
90. *Ibid.*, p. 124.
91. Dufour, p. 356.
92. *New Orleans Bee*, January 23, 1872, in: Dawson, p. 128.
93. Taylor, J. G., *Louisiana Reconstructed 1863–1877* (Baton Rouge: LSU Press, 1974), p. 227.
94. Letter from Thomas & Wells, representing Carter in Virginia, to James W. Thompson in Chappell Hill, TX, dated August 22, 1874, Archives of Chappell Hill Historical Society.

17. Yellow Fever

1. Walker, Dale, *The Boys of '98: Theodore Roosevelt and the Rough Riders* (New York: Forge, 1998), p. 253.
2. Baker, D. W. C., *A Texas Scrapbook: made up of the history, biography and miscellany of Texas and its people* (Texas State Historical Assoc., 1991, orig. publ. 1875), p. 487.
3. Kavanaugh, B. T., *Texas Masonic Mirror* (September 17, 1873, volume II, no. 37), p. 437.
4. Brown, J. H., *Indian Wars and Pioneers of Texas* (Easley, SC: Southern Historical Press, 1978), p. 749.
5. Winfield, Nath and Judy, "The Yellow Fever Epidemic in Chappell Hill, 1867" in: *The Chappell Hill Historical Society Review*, vol. 1, pp. 14–15.
6. Winfield, Nath and Judy, *All Our Yesteryears* (Waco: Texian Press, 1969), pp. 18–19.
7. Archives of Chappell Hill Historical Society.
8. Archives of Chappell Hill Historical Society.
9. *Texas and Texans* (volume 4), p. 1611.
10. Archives of Chappell Hill Historical Society.
11. Winfield, *All Our Yesteryears*, p. 19.
12. Winfield, "The Yellow Fever Epidemic in Chappell Hill, 1867," p. 16.
13. Archives of Chappell Hill Historical Society
14. Winfield, *Cemetery Records of Washington County 1826–1960* (Chappell Hill: Winfield, 1974).
15. Texas and Texans, vol. 4, p. 1624.
16. Winfield, Judy and Nath, *Cemetery records of Washington County, Texas*, p. 31.
17. Baker, p. 487.
18. Personal correspondence with Beverly Maurice, a descendant.
19. Carlisle, James, Military Service Record, National Archives.
20. Zuber, W. P., *My Eighty Years in Texas* (Austin: UT Press, 1971), p. 230.
21. Speer, L. R., *Portals to Hell, Military Prisons of the Civil War* (Mechanicsburg, Pa: Stackpole Books, 1997), p. 129.
22. Walker, D. A., "Texas State Penitentiary at Huntsville," *Handbook of Texas Online*.
23. Zuber, W. P., p. 231.
24. Thompson, Barney, *The Thompson Family* (Indianapolis: Barney Thompson, 1995), p. 104.
25. Hesler, "Taliaferro, Robert H.," *Handbook of Texas Online*.
26. Swearingen, R. M., "Diary of R. M. Swearingen in the Confederate Army," unpublished manuscript, Center for American History, University of Texas at Austin, p. 163.
27. Brown, p. 749.
28. Winfield, "The Yellow Fever Epidemic in Chappell Hill, 1867," p. 16.

18. National Reconciliation

1. Crane, Stephen, *Red Badge of Courage* (New York: Harcourt, Brace & World, 1960), p. 24.
2. Ashabranner, Brent, *A Grateful Nation: The Story of Arlington National Cemetery* (New York: Putnam, 1990), p. 109.
3. "Meeting of Hood's Brigade," *Houston Telegraph*, July 17, 1866.
4. "Hood's Texas Brigade," *The Handbook of Texas Online*.
5. Robertson, Jerome B., *Touched With Valor: Civil War Papers and Casualty Reports of Hood's Texas Brigade* (Hillsboro, TX: Hill Junior College Press, 1964), p. 19, written and collected by Jerome B. Robertson and edited and with a biography of General Robertson by Harold B. Simpson.
6. "Bryan, 1902," *Minutes of Hood's Texas Brigade Association Meetings, 1895–1905*, p. 154.
7. Ibid., p. 157.
8. Ibid., p. 154.
9. Simpson, Harold B., *Hood's Texas Brigade in Reunion and Memory* (Hillsboro, Tx: Hill Junior College Press, 1974), p. 331.
10. Groom, W, *Shrouds of Glory* (Atlantic Monthly Press, 1995), p. 290.
11. Barr, Alwyn, "Franklin Collett Wilkes," *The Handbook of Texas Online*.
12. Personal communication with Shirley Jacob, First United Methodist Church, Austin.
13. "Bayland Orphan Home," *Dallas Herald*, July 27, 1872.
14. Ibid.
15. *Dallas Herald*, July 20, 1872.
16. "F. C. Wilkes," obituary in *Texas Christian Advocate* (January 7, 1882).
17. "Bayland Orphan Home," *Dallas Herald*, July 27, 1872.
18. "F. C. Wilkes," obituary in *Texas Christian Advocate* (January 7, 1882).
19. Ibid.
20. Barr, Alwyn, "Franklin C. Wilkes."
21. "F. C. Wilkes," obituary in *Texas Christian Advocate* (January 7, 1882).
22. Cocke file, ancestry.com.
23. "Memorial Service, Col. P.H. Swearingen, March 16, 1880," Center for American History, University of Texas.
24. Ibid.
25. Winifred McCraw and Patrick Henry Swearingen Papers, University of Texas at San Antonio Archives.
26. "Galveston, 1874," *Minutes of Hood's Texas Brigade Association 1895–1905*, Harold B. Simpson History Center, Hill College, p. 9.
27. Ibid.
28. Ibid.
29. Christian, Carole, "D. C. Giddings," *The Handbook of Texas Online*.
30. Giddings, D. C., "Addresses at the Brenham Reunion in 1881," in file at Hill College: *1881 Brenham Reunion*.
31. Winfield, Judy and Nath, *Cemetery Records of Washington County, Texas* (1974), p. 31.
32. Boatner, Mark Mayo III, *The Civil War Dictionary* (New York: David McKay Company, 1959), pp. 563–564.
33. The Archives of the Chappell Hill Historical Society. Also, Brown, Lawrence, *The Episcopal Church in Texas, 1838–1874* (Austin: The Church Historical Society, 1963), p. 131.
34. Crute, *Units of the Confederate States Army* (Midlothian, VA: Derwent Books, 1987), p. 179.

35. Rable, G. C. "Fire in the Streets: The Assault on Fredericksburg," *North & South* (volume 3, no. 6), p. 77.
36. Sadler, Augustus David, *Memoirs written at Chappell Hill in 1901*, p. 36, provided by Eleanor Crockett Camp.
37. Rable, p. 82.
38. Crute, p. 33.
39. Haley Obituary, Archives of Chappell Hill Historical Society.
40. Crute, pp. 35–36.
41. Archives of Chappell Hill Historical Society.
42. "Huntsville, 1875," *Minutes of Hood's Texas Brigade Association 1895–1905*, Harold B. Simpson History Center, Hill College, Hillsboro, TX, p. 17.
43. *Ibid*.
44. "Bryan, 1876," *Minutes of Hood's Texas Brigade Association 1895–1905*, Harold B. Simpson History Center, Hill College, Hillsboro, TX, p. 27.
45. "Bryan, 1876," *Minutes of Hood's Texas Brigade Association 1895–1905*, Harold B. Simpson History Center, Hill College, Hillsboro, TX, p. 26.
46. "Waco, 1877," *Minutes of Hood's Texas Brigade Association 1895–1905*, Harold B. Simpson History Center, Hill College, Hillsboro, TX, p. 31.
47. *Ibid*.
48. Frazier, John, *Reunion of the Blue and Gray, 1118 and 1906* (Philadelphia: Ware Bros. Co., 1906), p. 70.
49. *Brenham Banner*, May 23, 1887, in Brenham City Library, Brenham, TX.
50. *Brenham Banner*, May 25, 1887, in Brenham City Library.
51. *Ibid*.
52. *Brenham Banner*, April 15, 1887, in Brenham City Library.
53. *Brenham Banner*, October 7, 1886, in Brenham City Library.
54. Benner, J. A., *Sul Ross, Soldier, Statesman, Educator* (College Station: Texas A&M Press, 1983), p. 185.
55. *Ibid*.
56. *Texas Methodist Newspaper Abstacts*.
57. Archives of Chappell Hill Historical Society
58. *The Philomathean* (Chappell Hill, September 1886), Center for American History Newspaper Collection, University of Texas, Austin.
59. *The Philomathean* (Chappell Hill, November 1886).
60. *Ibid*.
61. Archives of the Chappell Hill Historical Society.
62. Crute, Joseph H Jr., *Units of the Confederate States Army* (Midlothian, VA: Derwent, 1987), p. 40.
63. *Biographical Souvenir of the State of Texas* (Chicago: F. A. Battery & Co, 1889), Archives of Chappell Hill Historical Society.
64. *The Philomathean* (Chappell Hill, December 1866).
65. *Ibid*.
66. *Ibid*.
67. Tourgee, Albion W., "The South as a Field for Fiction," *Forum* 6 (1888–9), p. 405.
68. Jones, John William, *The Davis Memorial Volume* (Dallas: A. P. Foster, 1890), p. 649.
69. Jones, p. 649.
70. Brown, J. H., *Indian Wars and Pioneers of Texas* (Easley, SC: Southern Historical Press, 1978), p. 750.
71. *Ibid*.
72. *Brenham Daily Banner*, July 17, 1890.
73. Archives of the Texas State Library.
74. Blight, David W., "Race and Reunion: Soldiers and the Problem of the Civil War in American Memory," *North and South* (April 2003, volume 6, no. 3), p. 31.
75. Wyeth, John A., "Cold Cheer in Camp Morton," *Century Magazine* (March 1891, XLI, no. 5), p. 852.
76. Holloway, W. R., "Treatment of Prisoners at Camp Morton: A Reply to 'Cold Cheer at Camp Morton,'" *Century Magazine* (September 1891, XLII, no. 5), p. 757.
77. *Ibid*.
78. Wyeth, John A., "Rejoinder," *Century Magazine* (September 1891, XLII, no. 5), pp. 774–75.
79. *Ibid*.
80. Fouts, Frederick W., Military Service Record, National Archives, Washington, D.C.
81. Kelly, Patrick J., "The Election of 1896 and the Restructuring of Civil War Memory," *Civil War History* (September 2003, vol. 49, no. 3), p. 254.
82. "Hood's Brigade Reunion," *East Texas Pinery* (Livingston, July 2, 1891), Hill College Research Center.
83. Wallis, J. L., *Sixty Years on the Brazos: the life and letters of Dr. John Washington Lockhart* (1930), p. 133.
84. *Brenham Banner*, May 19, 1895, in Brenham City Library, Brenham, TX.
85. Hood's Texas Brigade Association papers, Harold B. Simpson History Center, Hill College, Hillsboro, Texas.
86. *Brenham Banner*, May 21, 1895, in Brenham City Library.
87. *Sponsor souvenir album: history & reunion, 1895* (Terry Engraving, 1895), p. 31.
88. Bailey, F. A., "Free Speech and the Lost Cause in Texas," *Southwestern Historical Quarterly* 97 (1994), p. 457.
89. *Ibid*., p. 462.
90. *Ibid*., p. 468.
91. Underwood, John Cox., *Report of proceedings incidental to the erection and dedication of the Confederate monument* (Chicago: W. Johnston Print Co, 1897), p. 25.
92. "Calvert, 1895," *Minutes of Hood's Texas Brigade Association Meetings, 1895–1905*, Harold B. Simpson History Center, Hill College, Hillsboro, TX, p. 83.
93. *Ibid*.
94. "Floresville, June 30, 1897," *Minutes of Hood's Texas Brigade Association Meetings, 1895–1905*, Harold B. Simpson History Center, Hill College, Hillsboro, TX, p. 110.
95. "Floresville, June 30, 1897," *Minutes of Hood's Texas Brigade Association Meetings, 1895–1905*, Harold B. Simpson History Center, Hill College, Hillsboro, TX, p. 106.
96. Swearingen, R. M., *Diary of R. M. Swearingen in the Confederate Army* (unpublished), Center for American History, University of Texas, Austin, p. 159.

Notes — Chapter 18

97. Kelly, Patrick J., "The Election of 1896 and the Restructuring of Civil War Memory," *Civil War History* (September 2003, vol. 49, no. 3), p. 255; citing *New York Times*, October 12, 1896.
98. United Confederate Veterans, *Reunion of United Confederate Veterans, June 4,5, 6 and 7, 1917* (Government Printing Office, Washington, D.C., 1918), p. 25.
99. Skinner, Maria W. (Mrs. T. J.) editor, Alabama, Division United Daughters of the Confederacy, The "Angel of Santiago" p. 8, from "The Wheelers: General Joe and Miss Annie" (Alabama Essay Contest, 1999).
100. "Dr. Irene Toland of St. Louis Gave Her Life To Save Suffering Santiago Soldiers," *St. Louis Post-Dispatch*, October 2, 1898.
101. Archives of Chappell Hill Historical Society.
102. "Haley, William," Archives of Chappell Hill Historical Society.
103. Thompson, C. W., letter dated July 3, 1895, in possession of Cornelia Hurley, Franklin, Texas.
104. *Brenham Daily Banner*, October 19, 1876.
105. Daniell, pp. 341–42.
106. "Austin, May 2, 1899," *Minutes of Hood's Texas Brigade Association Meetings, 1895–1905*, Hill College Research Center, p. 113.
107. *Ibid.*, p. 114.
108. Sears, Rev., "Sketch of Rev. Henry M. Haynie," *Rev. John Haynie: Ancestry, Life & Descendants*, Hill College Research Center, pp. 86–88.
109. *Ibid.*
110. *Ibid.*
111. Wallis, p. 29.
112. Archives of Chappell Hill Historical Society.
113. Tompkins, Shannon, "Storm ripped Brenham structures, trees," *Houston Chronicle*, September 9, 2000, p. 39A.
114. "Bryan, 1902," *Minutes of Hood's Texas Brigade Association Meetings, 1895–1905*, Harold B. Simpson History Center, Hill College, Hillsboro, TX, p. 142.
115. "Ennis, 1904," *Minutes of Hood's Texas Brigade Association Meetings, 1895–1905*, Harold B. Simpson History Center, Hill College, Hillsboro, TX, p. 172.
116. Simpson, p. 204.
117. "Ennis, 1904," *Minutes of Hood's Texas Brigade Association Meetings, 1895–1905*, Harold B. Simpson History Center, Hill College, Hillsboro, TX, p. 172.
118. Hill, James E., *Addresses of Hon. James E. Hill and Judge J. M. Crosson at the Confederate Monument unveiling, Livingston, Texas, October 10, 1901* (Livingston, TX: T. M. M'Clure, 1901), p. 4.
119. *Ibid.*
120. Hill, W. T., *Address of Captain W. T. Hill, President of Hood's Texas Brigade Association at Jacksonville, Texas, June 25, 1903*, Harold B. Simpson History Center, Hill College, Hillsboro, TX.
121. Sadler, p. 30.
122. *Proceedings of the 11th Annual Convention of the Texas Division of the United Daughters of the Confederacy, Bryan, Dec 4–7, 1906*, Hood's Texas Brigade Reunion Files, Harold B. Simpson History Center, Hill College, Hillsboro, TX.
123. *Proceedings of the Eleventh Annual Convention of the Texas Division of the United Daughters of the Confederacy* (1907), p. 46.
124. *Ibid.*, p. 137.
125. *Ibid.*, p. 37.
126. *Ibid.*, p. 38.
127. Tourgee, Albion W., "The South as a Field for Fiction," *Forum* 6 (1888–9), p. 413.
128. "Galveston, June 27, 1901," *Minutes of Hood's Texas Brigade Association Meetings, 1895–1905*, Harold B. Simpson History Center, Hill College, Hillsboro, TX, p. 129.
129. *Ibid.*, p. 131.
130. Stone, Cornelia Branch, *U.D.C. Catechism For Children* (Galveston: Veuve Jefferson Davis Chapter UDC, 1904), p. 11.
131. Bailey, F. A., "Free Speech and the Lost Cause in Texas," *Southwestern Historical Quarterly* 97 (1994), pp. 463–64.
132. "Noted Character Dead: Rev. Dr. George W. Carter," *New Orleans Times-Democrat*, May 12, 1901.
133. "Death of Rev. George W. Carter," obituary in *Texas Christian Advocate* (June 6, 1901).
134. Letter from Thomas Wells to James W. Thompson, dated August 1874, Archives of Chappell Hill Historical Society.
135. Bailey, Anne J., "George Washington Carter," *The Handbook of Texas Online*.
136. "Noted Character Dead: Rev. Dr. George W. Carter," *New Orleans Times Democrat*, May 12, 1901.
137. *Ibid.*
138. Carter, George Washington, "Application for Admission," The Maryland Line Confederate Soldiers' Home, Pikeville, Maryland Collection, 1883–1932, MS 256. H. Furlong Baldwin Library of the Maryland Historical Society.
139. *Ibid.*
140. Carter, George Washington, "Application for Membership," Society of the Army and the Navy of the Confederate States in the State of Maryland Collection, 1871–1926, MS 2825. H. Furlong Baldwin Library of the Maryland Historical Society.
141. Bailey, Anne J., "George Washington Carter," *The Handbook of Texas Online*.
142. Crute, pp. 253, 259.
143. "Dr. Hammond Bouldin," *Confederate Veteran* (June 1905, vol. XIII), 281.
144. Hargrove, J. A., "Memoir," unpublished manuscript, 1903, Archives of Chappell Hill Historical Society, p. 3.
145. Ashabranner, p. 40.
146. Kellbach, J., "Maj. Gen. Fitzhugh Lee," *Spanish American War Centennial Website*.
147. "Ennis, 1904," *Minutes of Hood's Texas Brigade Association Meetings, 1895–1905*, Harold B. Simpson History Center, Hill College, Hillsboro, TX, p. 172.
148. *Ibid.*, p. 165.
149. McKay, S. S., "Shepard, Seth," *The Handbook of Texas Online*.
150. *Bellville Times*, August 12, 1904, Bellville Library, Bellville, Texas.
151. *Ibid.*.
152. "The Lynchings in Georgia," *Bellville Times*, August 26, 1904, Bellville Library, Bellville, Texas.
153. *Bellville Times*, June 3, 1904, Bellville Library, Bellville, Texas.

154. Frazier, John, *Reunion of the Blue and Gray, 1887 and 1906* (Philadelphia: Ware Bros. Company, 1906), p. 21.
155. Simpson, *Hood's Texas Brigade in Reunion and Memory*.
156. Chilton, Frank, *Unveiling and Dedication of Monument to Hood's Texas Brigade ..."* (Houston: Frank Chilton, 1911), p. 21.
157. Cutrer, Thomas W., "William Hamby," *The Handbook of Texas Online*.
158. Chilton, p. 23.
159. *Fourteenth Annual Convention of the United Daughters of the Confederacy* (1910), p. 72.
160. Walstein Keesee, Military Service Record, National Archives.
161. Bentley, Edward, "Soule University from 1872 to 1887," *The Chappell Hill Historical Society Review*, 1997, vol. III, p. 5.
162. *Ibid.*, p. 16.
163. Archives of the Chappell Hill Historical Society.
164. Campbell, J. D., *Vale, Soule University*, undated newspaper clipping in the Archives of the Chappell Hill Historical Society.
165. Christian, Carole, "Chappell Hill Female College," Handbook of Texas Online, http://www.tsha.utexas.edu/handbook/online/articles/view/CC/kbc15.html.
166. *Brenham Banner*, June 26, 1913, Brenham City Library, Brenham, Texas.
167. *Bellville Times*, January 8, 1914, Bellville Library, Bellville, Texas.
168. "Mrs. Kate A. Landes, Widow's Application for A Pension, No. 41388," Texas State Archives, Austin.
169. Frizzel, I., *Bellville: The Founders And Their Legacy* (New Ulm, TX: New Ulm Enterprises, 1992), pp. 197–98.
170. Scott, Dr. John O., "The Texans at Gettysburg," *Galveston Daily News*, July 1913, from Rosenberg Library in Galveston.
171. *Brenham Banner*, June 23, 1913, in Brenham City Library, Brenham, Texas
172. "Gettysburg, Gettysburg," *Confederate Veteran* 21 (1913), p. 377.
173. *Bellville Times*, October 24, 1912.
174. "Gettysburg, Gettysburg," *Confederate Veteran* 21 (1913), p. 381.
175. *Bellville Times*, November 7, 1912.
176. "Gettysburg, Gettysburg," *Confederate Veteran* 21 (1913), p. 377.
177. "Gettysburg, Gettysburg," *Confederate Veteran* 21 (1913), p. 377.
178. United Confederate Veterans, *Reunion of United Confederate Veterans, June 4,5, 6 and 7, 1917* (Government Printing Office, Washington, D.C., 1918), p. 7.
179. *Ibid.*, p. 9.
180. Winfield, J. and N., *Cemetery Records of Washington County, Texas 1826–1960* (Winfield, 1974), p. 28.
181. Nicks, Mary, *Garrett-Buster-Estes Family History* (1956), p. 37.
182. Nicks, Mary, p. 76.
183. Ellis, Hugo, "Edward Benjamin Cushing," *The Handbook of Texas*.
184. Benner, J. A., *Sul Ross, Soldier, Statesman and Educator* (College Station: Texas A & M University Press, 1983), p. 233.
185. Chappell Hill Historical Society newsletter.
186. Reminiscences of Thelma Crockett of Chappell Hill.
187. *Brenham Banner*, January 9, 1929, from the Brenham City Library, Brenham, Texas.
188. *Brenham Banner*, January 10, 1929, from the Brenham City Library.
189. *Ibid.*
190. "Mrs. Lula N. Felder, Widow's Application for a Pension, No. 49577," Texas State Archives, Austin.
191. Simpson, Harold B., *Hood's Texas Brigade: Compendium* (Hillsboro, Tx: Hill Junior College Press, 1977), p. 562.
192. Hoar, J. S., *The South's Last Boys in Gray* (Bowling Green State University Popular Press, Ohio, 1986), p. 39.

Epilogue

1. Nath Winfield, Chappell Hill Historical Society, personal communication.
2. Wallis, J. L., *Sixty Years on the Brazos: the life and letters of Dr. John Washington Lockhart* (1930), pp. 247, 252.
3. Christian, Carole E., "Soule University," *The Handbook of Texas Online*, www.tsha.utexas.edu/handbook/online.
4. Personal communication with Fred and Mary Brandt, Chappell Hill, Texas.
5. Browning Plantation.
6. Matthews, Col. Harvie, "Record of Assignment," National Personnel Records Center, Army Reference Branch, St. Louis.
7. Wooster, Ralph, "Texans in World War II," *The Handbook of Texas Online*.
8. Nicks, Mary, *Garrett-Buster-Estes Family History* (Nicks, 1956), p. 44.
9. *Ibid.*, p. 69.
10. *Ibid.*, p. 49.
11. *Ibid.*, p. 80.
12. Newspaper clipping from Chappell Hill Historical Society. McElroy, H. B., "Joseph Eugene Routt," *The Handbook of Texas Online*.
13. *Houston Post* (April 21, 1949), from: Chappell Hill Historical Society.
14. *Houston Daily Telegraph* (July 4, 1866).

Bibliography

Primary Sources

The Archives of the Chappell Hill Historical Society was the most important historical collection providing primary source material for this book. Ladonna Vest, Director of the Museum and Archives, estimates that perhaps 85 percent of the artifacts and archival material derived from the personal collection of Judy and the late Nath Winfield, long-standing residents of Chappell Hill. The archives contain a great deal of biographical information on the people of Chappell Hill and include a large number of letters from the Civil War era. Extracts from approximately 25 letters were incorporated into this book. A number of the photographic images used in this book came from the historical society's archives. The Archives of the Chappell Hill Historical Society also was the source of "Soule University, Minutes of Board of Trustees 1856–1887," John Alexander Hargrove's "Memoirs" (1903), Augustus Sadler's "Memoirs written at Chappell Hill in 1901" and an old newspaper clipping of an article by J. D. Campbell, "Vale, Soule University," concerning the opening of the cornerstone of the main building at Soule University many years later.

Fred and Mary Brandt, residents of Chappell Hill and members of the Chappell Hill Historical Society, provided the diary that Henry C. Brandt kept on his long journey home after the war, as well as a vintage photographic portrait of Brandt and a letter from Brandt's wife, Laura, dated January 20, 1861.

Samuel Rice Buchanan and Amy Ruth Mayo Buchanan of Navasota provided a number of important letters from the 1930s, which included considerable information on the Buchanan and Felder families. Nancy Ruth Buchanan Callaway's "The Journey of Mary Eugenia Felder Buchanan" was a useful narrative for understanding those families. The Buchanans also provided two valuable photographic images of Confederate ancestor John Jackson of Terry's Texas Rangers.

Several other archival holdings provided primary source material that contributed significantly to this book. The Harold B. Simpson History Center at Hill College in Hillsboro, Texas (Peggy Fox, Director), maintains an important collection of material on Hood's Texas Brigade. The discovery of the Rufus King Felder letters in the Hood's Texas Brigade Letters Collection was an important find. This file consists of approximately 20 letters, dated from August 1861 to February 1865, written home to Chappell Hill by the young infantryman. The Rosenberg Library in Galveston, Texas, was the source for several letters written in early 1862 by Daniel Harvie Browning of Chappell Hill to his friend Dr. John Washington Lockhart, also of Chappell Hill. These letters augmented the numerous Browning letters in the Archives of the Chappell Hill Historical Society. The Special Collections Department of the Atlanta History Center provided an important letter written by Hosea Garrett during the Battle for Atlanta, as well as the letter of Oliver Hazard Perry Garrett to Florence Garrett, "Character and Experiences of the Civil War." The H. Furlong Baldwin Library of the Maryland Historical Society provided George Washington Carter's "Application for Membership" in the Society of the Army and the Navy of the Confederate States (MS2825) and his "Application for Admission" to The Maryland Line Confederate Soldiers' Home in Pikeville (MS256). The Texas State Archives was the source of the pension filings of the Confederate widows of Chappell Hill.

The unpublished manuscript of Dr. Richard M. Swearingen from the Center for American History at the University of Texas was an important primary source for this book. Swearingen's wonderful manuscript, catalogued as the "Swearingen Narrative," Call Number 2G450, is titled "Four Years in the Confederate Army or My Part in the Great Rebellion." The Center for American History was also the source for a number of other important items, including the James W. Freeman Papers (Chappell Hill, 1864), the Memorial Service for Colonel Patrick Henry Swearingen, March 16, 1880, the anonymous, "In Memory of My Brother," [Confederate Soldier's Death Poem], Box 2L 259 and *The Philomathean*, a literary publication published in Chappell Hill, from September, November and December 1886.

The Harold B. Simpson History Center at Hill College was the source of many important items in addition to the Felder papers, including the Hood's Texas Brigade Association papers. These were invaluable for information on the post-war reunions of Texas Confederates:

"Galveston, 1874," *Minutes of Hood's Texas Brigade Association 1895–1905*.
"Huntsville, 1875," *Minutes of Hood's Texas Brigade Association 1895–1905*.
"Bryan, 1876," *Minutes of Hood's Texas Brigade Association 1895–1905*.
"Bryan, 1876," *Minutes of Hood's Texas Brigade Association 1895–1905*.
"Waco, 1877," *Minutes of Hood's Texas Brigade Association 1895–1905*.
Giddings, D. C., "Addresses at the Brenham Reunion in 1881," *1881 Brenham Reunion*.
"Hood's Brigade Reunion," *East Texas Pinery* (Livingston, July 2, 1891).
"Calvert, 1895," *Minutes of Hood's Texas Brigade Association Meetings, 1895–1905*.
"Floresville, June 30, 1897," *Minutes of Hood's Texas Brigade Association Meetings, 1895–1905*.
"Austin, May 2, 1899," *Minutes of Hood's Texas Brigade Association Meetings, 1895–1905*.
"Galveston, June 27, 1901," *Minutes of Hood's Texas Brigade Association Meetings, 1895–1905*.

Hill, James E., *Addresses of Hon. James E. Hill and Judge J. M. Crosson at the Confederate Monument unveiling, Livingston, Texas, October 10, 1901* (Livingston, TX: T. M. M'Clure, 1901).
"Bryan, 1902," *Minutes of Hood's Texas Brigade Association Meetings, 1895–1905.*
Address of Captain W. T. Hill, President of Hood's Texas Brigade Association at Jacksonville, Texas, June 25, 1903.
"Ennis, 1904," *Minutes of Hood's Texas Brigade Association Meetings, 1895–1905.*
Proceedings of the 11th Annual Convention of the Texas Division of the United Daughters of the Confederacy, Bryan, Dec 4–7, 1906.
Proceedings of the Eleventh Annual Convention of the Texas Division of the United Daughters of the Confederacy (1907).
United Confederate Veterans, *Reunion of United Confederate Veterans, June 4,5, 6 and 7, 1917* (Government Printing Office, Washington, D.C., 1918), 7.
Sears, Rev., "Sketch of Rev. Henry M. Haynie," *Rev. John Haynie: Ancestry, Life & Descendants*

Secondary Sources

There were many secondary sources of importance to this book. Perhaps most important was Nath Winfield's *All Our Yesteryears: A Brief History of Chappell Hill*, published by Texian Press in Waco in 1969. The Winfields included in this thin volume a preliminary listing of the Confederate veterans of Chappell Hill. The listing from this book and the information from the white headstones in Chappell Hill's old Masonic Cemetery were the early basis for the book. Nath and Judy Winfield's *Cemetery Records of Washington County, 1826–1960* (published by the Winfields in 1974) was also important in the early period of researching this book. The Winfields also collected and published *War Letters of Tacitus T. Clay, C. S. A.* (Winfield, Judy and Nath, 1968) and a number of important articles in *The Chappell Hill Historical Society Review*. Among the important articles were "The Yellow Fever Epidemic in Chappell Hill, 1867" (vol. 1), "Providence Baptist Church" (vol. 1) and "Forgotten Towns Along the Brazos, Part Two" (vol. 4). Nath Winfield was co-author of *Sandbars and Sternwheelers: Steam Navigation on the Brazos* (College Station: Texas A&M University Press, 1976).

I would be remiss if I did not follow the Winfields' works with those of the late Colonel Harold B. Simpson, the long-recognized authority on Hood's Texas Brigade. The following were used in the course of this book and by no means represent the complete works of this legendary historian.

Robertson, Jerome B., *Touched With Valor: Civil War Papers and Casualty Reports of Hood's Texas Brigade* (Hillsboro, TX: Hill Junior College Press, 1964), p. 19, written and collected by Jerome B. Robertson, edited and with a biography of General Robertson by Harold B. Simpson.
Seaton, Benjamin, *The Bugle Blows Softly: The Confederate Diary of Benjamin M. Seaton*, ed. by Simpson, Harold B. (Waco: Texian Press, 1965).
Simpson, H. B., *Hood's Texas Brigade: Lee's Grenadier Guard* (Waco: Texian Press, 1970).
Simpson, Harold B., *Hood's Texas Brigade in Reunion and Memory* (Hillsboro, TX: Hill Junior College Press, 1974).
Simpson, H. B., *Hood's Texas Brigade: A Compendium* (Hillsboro, TX: Hill Junior College Press, 1977).

Simpson, H., "Hood's Texas Brigade at Appomattox" in: Wooster, Ralph, *Lone Star Blue and Gray: Essays on Texas in the Civil War* (Austin: Texas State Historical Association, 1995).

An important source for this book, as for any work on the Civil War, was:

U.S. War Department, *The War of the Rebellion: A Compilation of the Official Records of the Union and Confederate Armies* (Washington: U.S. Government Printing Office, 1881–1900). Also known as *Official Records of the Union and Confederate Armies* and commonly referred to as *Official Records*.

This massive compilation was invaluable for official dispatches and reports pertaining to actions involving the Confederates of Chappell Hill.

The following list of secondary sources includes volumes with information specific to Chappell Hill, Washington County, Confederates of Chappell Hill or Confederate units in which men from Chappell Hill served:

Baker, D. W. C., *A Texas Scrapbook: Made Up of the History, Biography and Miscellany of Texas and Its People* (Texas State Historical Assoc., 1991, orig. publ. 1875), 487.
Barziza, Decimus, *The Adventures of a Prisoner of War, 1863–1864* (Austin: University of Texas Press, 1964).
Battey, F. A. & Co., *Biographical Souvenir of the State of Texas, Containing Biographical Sketches of the Representative Public and Many Early Settled Families* (Chicago: F. A. Battery & Co, 1889). From the Archives of Chappell Hill Historical Society.
Blessington, J. P., *The Campaigns of Walker's Texas Division* (New York: Lange, Little, 1875).
Brown, John Henry, *Indian Wars and Pioneers of Texas* (Austin: L. E. Daniell, 1890).
Chilton, Frank, *Unveiling and Dedication of Monument to Hood's Texas Brigade ..."* (Houston: Frank Chilton, 1911), 21.
Crute, *Units of the Confederate States Army* (Midlothian, VA: Derwent Books, 1987).
Daniell, L. E., *Personnel of the Texas State Government, with Sketches of Distinguished Texans* (Austin, 1889).
Daniell, L. E., *Types of Successful Men* (Austin: E. Von Boeckmann, 1890).
Ford, John Salmon, and Oates, Stephen B., *Rip Ford's Texas* (Austin: University of Texas, 1987).
Foster, Samuel, *One of Cleburne's Command: the Civil War reminiscences and diary of Capt. Samuel T. Foster, Granbury's Texas Brigade, CSA* / edited by Norman D. Brown. (Austin: University of Texas, 1980).
Giles, Leonidas B., *Terry's Texas Rangers* (Austin: Pemberton Press, 1967, originally published 1911).
Houston, Sam, *The Writings of Sam Houston 1813–1863*, 8 (Austin: Pemberton Press, 1970).
Johnson, Frank W. (updated by Eugene C. Barker and E. W. Winkler), *A History of Texas and Texans* (Chicago: American Historical Society, 1916), 5 volumes.
Johnson, Frank W. (updated by Eugene C. Barker and E. W. Winkler), *A History of Texas and Texans* (Chicago: American Historical Society, 1914), 5 volumes.
Johnson, Barker, Winkler et al., *Texas and Texans* 4 (American Historical Society, 1914), 1617.
Knolle, Herman, Diary in: Hasskarl, R. A. and Hasskarl, L. R., *Waul's Texas Legion 1862–1865* (Ada, OK: R. A. Hasskarl, 1985).
McCaffrey, James M., *This Band of Heroes: Granbury's Texas Brigade, CSA* (Austin: Eakin Press, 1985).
New Year's Creek Settlers Association, *Afternoons on New Year's Creek, Washington County, Texas: 1861, 1862, 1988* (Brenham: New Year's Creek Settler's Association, 1989).
Pennington, M. A. W., *History of Brenham and Washington County* (Houston: Standard Printing, 1915).

Plummer, B., *Historic Homes of Washington County* (San Marcos: Rio Fresco Books, 1971).
Polley, J. B., *Hood's Texas Brigade* (New York: Neale Publishing, 1910), 124.
Polley, J. B., *A Soldier's Letters to Charming Nellie* (New York: Neale Publishing, 1908).
Read, John, Testimony, "Treatment of Prisoners of War by the Rebel Authorities," *House Report No. 45, 40th Congress, 3rd Session, No. 1391* (National Archives), 926–7.
Stone, Cornelia Branch, *U.D.C. Catechism For Children* (Galveston: Veuve Jefferson Davis Chapter UDC, 1904).
Toland, Gracey Booker, *Austin Knew His Athens* (San Antonio: Naylor Co., 1938).
Vernon, Walter N., *The Methodist Excitement in Texas* (Dallas: The Texas United Methodist Historical Society, 1984).
Wallis, Jonnie Lockhart, *Sixty Years on the Brazos: The Life and Letters of Dr. John Washington Lockhart* (New York: Argonaut Press, 1966, orig. 1930).
Walton, W. M., *An Epitome of My Life: Civil War Reminiscences by Buck Walton* (Austin: Waterloo Press, Austin, 1965).
West, J. C., *A Texan In Search of a Fight: Being the Diary and Letters of a Private Soldier in Hood's Texas Brigade* (Waco: Texian Press, 1969, reprint of 1901 edition).
Winkler, Earnest W., *Journal of the Secession Convention of Texas, 1861. Ed. from the Original in the Department of State* (Austin, 1912).
Wooster, R., *Texas and Texans in the Civil War* (Austin: Eakin Press, 1995).
Wooster, Ralph, *Texas and Texans in the Civil War* (Austin: Eakin Press, 1996), 120.
Yeary, Mamie, *Reminiscences of the Boys in Gray, 1861–1865* (Dallas: Smith and Lamar, 1912), 419.
Young, Kevin, *To the Tyrants Never Yield: A Texas Civil War Sampler* (Plano: Wordware Publishing, 1992).
Zuber, William P., *My Eighty Years in Texas* (Austin: University of Texas Press, 1971).

The following is a list of additional secondary sources used in this book:

Ashabranner, Brent, *A Grateful Nation: The Story of Arlington National Cemetery* (New York: Putnam, 1990).
Bailey, Anne J., *Between the Enemy and Texas: Parson's Texas Cavalry in the Civil War* (Fort Worth: Texas Christian University Press, 1989).
Barr, Alwyn, *Black Texans: A History of African Americans in Texas* (Norman: University of Oklahoma Press, 1996).
Benner, J. A., *Sul Ross, Soldier, Statesman, Educator* (College Station: Texas A&M Press, 1983).
Boatner, Mark Mayo III, *The Civil War Dictionary* (New York: David McKay Company, 1959).
Boritt, Gabor S. (ed.), *Jefferson Davis's Generals* (Oxford University Press, 1999).
Bouldin, J. W., *The Bouldin Family: A Genealogy* (Texas City, Texas: J. W. Bouldin, 1994).
Brooksher, W. R. and Snider, D. K., *Glory at a Gallop: Tales of the Confederate Cavalry* (Washington: Brassey's, 1993).
Britton, W., *The Union Indian Brigade* (Kansas City: Hudson Publishing, 1922).
Brown, Lawrence, *The Episcopal Church in Texas, 1838–1874* (Austin: The Church Historical Society, 1963).
Brown, W. L., *A Life of Albert Pike* (Fayetteville: University of Arkansas Press, 1997).
Burkalter, L. W., *Gideon Lincecum: 1793–1874, A Biography* (Austin: University of Texas Press, 1965).
Burns, E. B., *Patriarch and Folk: The Emergence of Nicaragua 1798–1858* (Cambridge: Harvard University Press, 1991).
Chamberlain, J., *The Passing of the Armies* (New York: G. P. Putnam's Sons, 1915).
Coco, Gregory, *The Civil War Infantryman* (Gettysburg: Thomas Publications, 1996).

Cotham, Ed, *Battle on the Bay: The Civil War Struggle for Galveston* (College Station: Texas A&M Press, 1998).
Crane, Stephen, *Red Badge of Courage* (New York: Harcourt, Brace & World, 1960).
Dawson, J. G., *Army Generals and Reconstruction: Louisiana, 1862–1877* (Baton Rouge: LSU Press, 1982), 118.
Doegey, L. M., "Sam Houston: Southern Spokesman for the Cause of the Union" (Southern Illinois University, Ph.D. dissertation, 1968).
Duganne, A. J. H., *Twenty Months in the Department of the Gulf* (New York: J. P. Robens, 1865).
Edwards, John N., *Shelby and His Men* (Cincinnati: Miami Printing & Publishing, 1867).
Evans, Clement, and Bridgers, Robert, *Confederate Military History: A Library of Confederate States History in seventeen volumes* (Wilmington: Broadfoot, 1987).
Farber, James, *Texas, C. S. A.* (New York: The Jackson Company, 1947).
Fischer, Noel C., *War at Every Door: Partisan Politics & Guerrilla Warfare in East Tennessee* (Chapel Hill: University of North Carolina Press, 1997).
Frazier, Donald S., *Blood & Treasure: Confederate Empire in the South* (College Station: Texas A&M University Press, 1995).
Frazier, John, *Reunion of the Blue and Gray, 1118 and 1906* (Philadelphia: Ware Bros. Co., 1906).
Frizzel, I., *Bellville: The Founders and Their Legacy* (New Ulm, TX: New Ulm Enterprises, 1992).
Gallagher, Gary W., *The Confederate War* (Cambridge: Harvard University Press, 1997).
Gordon, J. B., *Reminiscences of the Civil War* (New York: C. Scribner's Sons, 1904).
Griscom, G. L., *Fighting with Ross' Texas Cavalry Brigade* (Hillsboro: Hill Junior College Press, 1976).
Groom, W., *Shrouds of Glory* (Atlantic Monthly Press, 1995).
Haskew, C. P., *Historical Records of Austin & Waller Counties* (Houston: Premier Printing, 1969).
Hatley, Allen, *Bringing the Law to Texas: Crime and Violence in Nineteenth Century Texas* (LaGrange, TX: Centex Press, 2002).
Hennessey, J. J., *Return to Bull Run: The Campaign and Battle of Second Manassas* (Simon & Schuster, 1993).
Hesseltine, W. B., *Civil War Prisons* (Columbus: Ohio State University Press, 1930, reprinted 1998).
Hoar, J. S., *The South's Last Boys in Gray* (Bowling Green State University Popular Press, Ohio, 1986).
Jeffries, C. C., *Terry's Rangers* (New York: Vantage Press, 1961).
Johnson, Robert U., and Buel, Clarence C., *Battles and Leaders of the Civil War*, four volumes (New York: T. Yoseloff, 1956).
Johnston, W. P., *Life of Albert Sidney Johnston* (Austin: State House Press, 1997).
Jones, John William, *The Davis Memorial Volume* (Dallas: A. P. Foster, 1890).
Josephy, Alvin M., *The Civil War in the American West* (New York: Alfred Knopf, 1991).
Krick, Robert, "Robert E. Lee's First Victory at Gaines' Mill," talk presented to Houston Civil War Round Table, January 20, 2000.
Levy, G., *To Die in Chicago: Confederate Prisoners at Camp Douglas 1862–1865* (Evanston, IL: Evanston Publishing, 1994).
May, Robert E., *The Southern Dream of a Caribbean Empire, 1854–1861* (Baton Rouge: Louisiana State University, 1973).
McCutchan, Joseph D., *Mier Expedition Diary*, (Austin: University of Texas Press, 1978).
Nevin, D., *The Texans* (New York: Time-Life Books, Old West Series, 1975).
Nicks, Mary, *Garrett-Buster-Estes Family History* (unknown, U.S., 1956).
Norwood, Frederick A., *The Story of American Methodism* (Nashville: Abingdon Press, 1974).

Nunn, W. C., *Escape from Reconstruction* (Fort Worth: Texas Christian University, 1956).
Oates, S. B., *Confederate Cavalry West of the River* (Austin: University of Texas Press, 1961).
Phelan, Macum, *A History of Early Methodism in Texas, 1817–1866* (Nashville: Cokesbury Press, 1924).
Priest, J. M., *Antietam, The Soldiers' Battle* (Shippensburg, PA: White Mane Publishing, 1989).
Rea, R. R., *Sterling Price, the Lee of the West* (Little Rock: Pioneer Press, 1959).
Reynolds, Donald E., *Editors Make War: Southern Newspapers in the Secession Crisis* (Nashville: Vanderbilt University Press, 1970).
Rhea, Gordon C., *The Battle of The Wilderness, May 5–6, 1864* (Baton Rouge: Louisiana State University Press, 1994).
Richter, W. L., *The Army in Texas During Reconstruction* (College Station: Texas A&M University Press, 1987).
Richter, William, *Overreached on All Sides: The Freedmen's Bureau Administration in Texas 1865–8* (College Station: Texas A&M University Press, 1991).
Scott, O., *The Secret Six: John Brown and the Abolitionist Movement* (New York: Times Books, 1979).
Sears, Stephen, *Landscape Turned Red: The Battle of Antietam* (New York: Ticknor & Fields, 1983).
Sears, Stephen, *To the Gates of Richmond: The Peninsula Campaign* (New York: Ticknor & Fields, 1992).
Shalhope, R. E., *Sterling Price: Portrait of a Southerner* (Columbia: University of Missouri Press, 1971).
Skinner, Maria W. (Mrs. T. J.) editor, *Alabama Essay Contest*, "The Wheelers: General Joe and Miss Annie" (Alabama: United Daughters of the Confederacy, 1999).
Spaw, P. M. (ed.), *The Texas Senate* (College Station: Texas A&M University Press, volume 1, 1990).
Speer, L. R., *Portals to Hell, Military Prisons in the Civil War* (Mechanicsburg, PA: Stackpole Books, 1997).
Spurlin, Charles, *West of the Mississippi with Waller's 13th Texas Cavalry Battalion CSA* (Hillsboro, TX: Hill Junior College, 1971).
Taylor, J. G., *Louisiana Reconstructed 1863–1877* (Baton Rouge: LSU Press, 1974).
Thompson, Barney, *The Thompson Family* (Indianapolis: Barney Thompson, 1995).
Thompson, Jerry, *Westward the Texans* (El Paso: Texas Western Press, 1990).
Trudeau, N. A., *Out of the Storm, The End of the Civil War April–June 1865* (Boston: Little, Brown and Company, 1994).
Underwood, John Cox, *Report of Proceedings Incidental to the Erection and Dedication of the Confederate Monument* (Chicago: W. Johnston Print Co, 1897).
United Confederate Veterans, *Reunion of United Confederate Veterans, June 4,5, 6 and 7, 1917* (Government Printing Office, Washington, D.C., 1918).
Wakelyn, J. L., *Southern Pamphlets on Secession, November 1860–April 1861* (Chapel Hill: University of North Carolina Press, 1996).
Walker, D. L., *The Boys of '98*, (New York: Forge, 1998).
Warmoth, H. C., *War, Politics and Reconstruction* (Macmillan Company, 1930).
White, V. D., *Index to Mexican War Pension Files* (Waynesboro, TN: National Historical Publishing, 1989).
Williams, John Hoyt, *Sam Houston* (New York: Promontory Press, 1998).
Winders, Richard B., *Mr. Polk's Army: The American Military Experience in the Mexican War* (College Station: Texas A&M University Press, 1997).
Wood, W. J., *Civil War Generalship: The Art of Command* (Westport: Praeger, 1997).
Young, B. H., *Confederate Wizards of the Saddle* (Kennesaw, Ga: Continental Book Co., 1958).

Zemler, J. A., "The Texas Press and the Filibusters of the 1850's: Lopez, Carvajal and Walker" (North Texas State University, M. A. Thesis, 1983).

The Handbook of Texas Online, www.tsha.utexas.edu/handbook/online/, served the author well. The author extracted pieces of information from over 30 articles.

Southwestern Historical Quarterly, the publication of the Texas State Historical Association, is a valuable source of information for any work on Texas. The following articles were among the most important for the purpose of this book:

Bailey, F. A., "Free Speech and the Lost Cause in Texas," *SWHQ*, vol. 97 (1994).
Cox, C. C., "Reminiscences of C. C. Cox," *Texas Historical Association Quarterly* (initial title of *SWHQ*), vol. 6 (1902).
Cutrer, T. W. "We are Stern and Resolved: The Civil War Letters of John Wesley Rabb, Terry's Texas Rangers," *SWHQ*, vol. 91, no. 2 (October 1987).
Fornell, Earl W., "Texans and Filibusters in the 1850's," *SWHQ*, 59 (April 1956).
Hicks, Jimmie, "Some Letters Concerning the Knights of the Golden Circle in Texas, 1860–1861," *SWHQ*, vol. 65, no. 1 (July 1961).
Hill, L. F., "The Confederate Exodus to Latin America," *SWHQ*, vol. 39, no. 4 (April 1936).
Martin, H. N., "Texas Redskins in Confederate Gray," *SWHQ*, vol. 70, no. 4 (April 1967).
Oates, Stephen B., "Recruiting Confederate Cavalry in Texas," *SWHQ*.
Oldham, W. S., "Colonel John Marshall," *SWHQ*, vol. 20, no. 2 (October 1916).
Spindler, "The History of Hempstead," *SWHQ*, vol. 63, no. 3 (January 1960).
Thompson, Jerry, "When General Albert Sidney Johnston Came Home," *SWHQ*, vol. 103, no. 4 (April 2000).
White, William A., "The Texas Slave Insurrection of 1860," *SWHQ*, vol. 52, no. 3 (January 1949).

Confederate Veteran was a good source for material, including:

"Gettysburg, Gettysburg," *Confederate Veteran* 21 (1913).
Floca, Samuel W. Jr., "Hood's Protest," *Confederate Veteran* 6 (1995).
"Sketches of the Famous Eight Texas Cavalry," *Confederate Veteran* 5 (1897).
"Dr. Hammond Bouldin," *Confederate Veteran* 13 (June 1905).

Other articles used for this book include:

Bentley, Edward, "Soule University from 1872 to 1887," *The Chappell Hill Historical Society Review*, 1997, vol. III, p. 5.
Blight, David W., "Race and Reunion: Soldiers and the Problem of the Civil War in American Memory," *North and South* (April 2003, volume 6, no. 3), p. 31.
Dufour, C. L., "The Age of Warmoth," *Louisiana History* 6 (Fall 1965, no. 4), 350.
Fitzhugh, L. N., "Terry's Texas Rangers: An Address before the Houston Civil War Round Table" (Houston Civil War Round Table, 1958).
Harcourt, A. P., "Terry's Texas Rangers," *The Southern Bivouac* (November 1882).
Harris, F. B., "Henry Clay Warmoth, Reconstruction Governor of Louisiana," *The Louisiana Historical Quarterly* (volume 30, no. 2, April 1947), 550.
Holloway, W. R., "Treatment of Prisoners at Camp Morton: A Reply to 'Cold Cheers at Camp Morton'," *Century Magazine* (September 1891, XLII, no. 5), 757.
Kelly, Patrick J., "The Election of 1896 and the Restructuring of Civil War Memory," *Civil War History* (September 2003, vol. 49, no. 3), p. 254.

Nieman, Donald G., "Black Political Power and Criminal Justice: Washington County, Texas, 1868–1884," *The Journal of Southern History* (August 1989, vol. LV, no. 3), p. 394.

Pitre, Althea D., "Collapse of the Warmoth Regime," *Louisiana History* (Spring 1965, vol. VI, no. 2), 166.

Rable, G. C. "Fire in the Streets: The Assault on Fredericksburg," *North & South* (volume 3, no. 6), 77.

Reynolds, D. E., "Vigilante Law During the Texas Slave Panic of 1860," *Locus* (Denton: University of North Texas Press, Spring 1990).

Richter, W. L., "The Brenham Fire of 1866," *Louisiana Studies* (volume 14, Fall 1975), 290.

Tourgee, Albion W., "The South as a Field for Fiction," *Forum* 6 (1888–9), 413.

Wetta, Frank J., "Bulldozing the Scalawags: Some Examples of the Persecution of Southern White Republicans in Louisiana During Reconstruction," *Louisiana History* (Winter 1980, vol. XXI, no. 1).

Wyeth, John A., "Cold Cheer in Camp Morton," *Century Magazine* (March 1891, XLI, no. 5), 852.

Wyeth, John A., "Rejoinder," *Century Magazine* (September 1891, XLII, no. 5), 774–5.

Newspapers

Contemporary newspaper accounts were an important source of information for this book.

Houston Tri-Weekly Telegraph, which covered the period of the war, and the *Houston Daily Telegraph*, which was the name after the war when paper for print was available, were most helpful in providing insight into conditions in Confederate Texas, as well as reporting details of local units in the fight. The Houston Public Library has an extensive collection of microfilm for these papers. The Houston Public Library was also the source for the *Galveston Tri-Weekly News*, as well as the subsequent post-war *Galveston Daily News*. Certain important articles, such as Dr. John O. Scott's "The Texans at Gettysburg" in a 1913 edition of the *Galveston Daily News*, were sourced at Galveston's Rosenberg Library. The Archives of the Chappell Hill Historical Society has an impressive number of original copies of these newspapers, as well. The *Houston Daily Telegraph* also was important in terms of providing insight into Clayton Gillespie, who for a time was editor of that paper in the period immediately following the war, specifically including June and July 1866.

Newspapers from two towns near Chappell Hill were useful. The Bellville, Texas, Library provided microfilm copies of the *Bellville Times* from 1904 through 1914. The Brenham, Texas, Library was useful for microfilm copies of the *Brenham Banner* from 1876 through 1939. The Center for American History at the University of Texas provided several newspapers and magazines, including pre-war newspaper articles from the *Texas Ranger* (Brenham), December 17, 1860, and the *Brenham Enquirer* (April 18, 1861). The *Texas Masonic Mirror*, also accessed through the Center of American History at the University of Texas, provided the editorials of Confederate B. T. Kavanaugh after the war, specifically for the periods 1872 (volume I) – 1873 (volume II).

The *Dallas Herald* of July 27, 1872, reported on Franklin Wilkes's efforts on behalf of the Bayland Orphan Home. The *Texas Christian Advocate* of January 7, 1882, carried the obituary of Franklin C. Wilkes and the same paper of June 6, 1901, carried the obituary of George Washington Carter. The *Texas Christian Advocate* was obtained through the Texas Conference Archives of the United Methodist Church at Lon Morris College in Jacksonville, Texas. The Texas Conference Archives also provided copies of the minutes of the Tennessee Conference of the Methodist Episcopal Church, South, which included a considerably detailed obituary on Wilkes. Carter's obituary was also found in the May 12, 1901, issue of the *New Orleans Times Democrat*.

MILITARY SERVICE RECORDS

The National Archives is the main repository for all military records, Federal and Confederate, from the Civil War. National Archives Record Group 109 contains Records of Confederate Soldiers Who Served in the Civil War. The index for Texas volunteers is Microfilm Roll M227. The Compiled Military Service records for Confederates who served in organizations from the state of Texas are in Microfilm Series M323, which consists of 445 rolls. Of course, the service of selected individuals, such as Richard M. Swearingen, who served with the Tennessee cavalry, would not be in M323, but in the series for that state.

The Archives of the Chappell Hill Historical Society has copies of certain military records for some of the men of that town. The George Memorial Library in Richmond Texas (within the Fort Bend County Library System), has microfilm copies for all Texas units for the Civil War.

Index

Aedes aegypti mosquito 181, 185
Affleck, Thomas 75, 89
Agricultural and Mechanical College for Colored Youth 174
Agricultural and Mechanical College of Texas 174
Alabama 7
Alabama-Coushatta Nation 62
The Alamo 22–3
Albuquerque, NM 38, 40, 41
All the Year Round 42
Allen, Amos 42–43, 189
Allen, Harry 163
Alta Vista Plantation 9, 156, 174
Ammen, Jacob 85
Anderson, Bloody Bill 81, 146
Apache Nation 38, 41
Appomattox 11, 140–1, 148–9
Arizona Brigade (C.S.A.) 148–9
Arkansas Post, Battle of 11, 58–65, 84, 102, 110, 120, 144
Arlington National Cemetery 187
Askew, Charles 191, 208
Atlanta, GA 12, 101, 144
The Atlanta Campaign 118–126
Austin, TX 18, 20, 21, 97, 163, 167, 171, 173, 174, 188, 194

Baber, Tom 135, 206
Badger, A. G. 180
Baines, Al 20, 29, 76–77
Baker, Austin Clay 30, 31 (photo), 190
Baker, Milton 31, 69
Baker, Presley 30

Bankhead, John 215
Banks, Nathaniel 43, 103–104
Banks, Thomas 7, 98
Barrilon, Catherine 46
Bartlett, Jesse 6
Barton, Tom 120
Barton, William 120
Barton Springs 188
Barziza, Decimus 92
Bates, Thomas 46, 49, 79, 93
Battles and Leaders of the Civil War 196
Bayland Confederate Orphans Home 188–189
Beaumont, TX 47
Beauregard, P. G. T. 50
Bell, Milton 160
Bentonville, NC, Battle of 11, 137–139
Bickley, Charles 20
Bickley, George 19–20, 85
Billingsley, W. 32
Blewett, Lizzie 34
boll weevil 5
Bonne Carre, LA, action at 42–43
The Bonnie Blue Flag 30
Bouldin, Edmund 29
Bouldin, Florence 212
Bouldin, Green 29, 189, 222
Bouldin, Hammond 29, 30 (photo), 34, 208
Bowling Green, KY 32, 34, 35
Brandt, Emma 184, 196
Brandt, Fred 222
Brandt, Frederick Dennis 158
Brandt, Henry Christian: taken

prisoner at Vicksburg 88–91; photo 157; release from Camp Morton and return home 157–158; yellow fever 184; friendship with Fouts 197; reconstruction of Methodist Church 205; photo 212; at opening of cornerstone 213; death and memorial service 216–217; grandson 222
Brandt, Laura 158, 184; *see also* Burns, Laura Jane
Brashear City, LA 44
Brazos 6
Brazos River 5, 9, 14, 22, 66, 73, 99, 100, 181, 219
Brazos Santiago, TX 23, 154
Brenham: castle of Knights of the Golden Circle 20; Sam Houston speaking against Secession 23–24; company organized at 38; Chappell as deputy sheriff in 68; Affleck plantation between Chappell Hill and Brenham 75; Carter address at 97; Francis Jarvis Cooke ill at 99; railroad through Chappell Hill through Brenham 100; Littlepage visit to 105; county meeting at 148; beginning of Federal occupation 166; George Armstrong Custer 167; Camptown 170; clash with Federal garrison 170–171; county meeting 172; State Police office at 174;

Presler letter 182; Texas brigade reunion at 190; ball at Opera House 192; impact of 1900 storm 205; Toland death 209
The Brenham Banner 171 192, 193, 196, 198, 214, 216
The Brenham Enquirer 25
Brenham Union League 176
Brown, John 17
Browning, Daniel Harvie: enlisting 28; first letter home 31; Woodsonville 34–35; letters from Tennessee 77–78; photo of his sister 83; killed in action near Knoxville 114–116; father's loss 128; return of body and burial at home 161; grave in Atkinson Cemetery 222; descendant in U.S. Army 223
Browning, Elizabeth 29, 116
Browning, Fannie 34
Browning, Mattie 117, 161
Browning, Sarah Ann: photo 83
Browning, William Westcot: move from Mississippi 7; photo 14; family life 29; photo of daughter 83; Board member of Soule University, loss of son Daniel 116; purchase of Confederate war bonds 128; letter to 177; Atkinson cemetery on the plantation 222
Brownsville, TX 23, 98, 154
Bryan, TX 174, 192, 206
Buchanan, John Millican 163–165
Buchanan, Samuel Rice 165
Burleson, Ed 14
Burnet, David 198
Burnett, Judge David 17
Burns, Laura Jane 88, 184
Burnside, Ambrose, at Knoxville Siege 114–115
Burr's Ferry 160
Burton, TX 173
Buster, Claudius: arrival in Texas 14; Somervell and Mier expeditions 15, 37; participation in Battle of Galveston 66, 70; commanding prison camp garrison at Camp Groce 73; descendants in First World War 215; descendants in Second World War 224–225
Buster, John Vaughn 62, 120, 125, 215
Buster, William 224
Buttry, Joab 126–127

Calvert, TX 189
Camden, AK 104
Cameron Parish, LA, creation of 177
Campbell, George 38
Campbell, J. D. 213
Campbell, William 169
Cape Girardeau, MO 79

Carlisle, James 184
Carmer, Charles 103, 183, 222
Carpetbagger 177
Carr, Mortimer 178
Carter, George Washington: early preaching career, president of Soule University and advocate of secession 21; resignation to go to war 25; formation of Texas Lancers 58–61; participation in Marmaduke's Raid 78–81; return to Texas and fame 97–98; settlement with Soule University 103; post-war address in Houston and Carter for Governor movement 150; paroled 166; rise to power in Louisiana 177; speaker of the Louisiana House 178; involvement in Reconstruction struggle in New Orleans 179–180; later years and death 207–208
Carter, James 107
Carter, Solomon 190
Casey, James 179
Centenary College, LA 60, 178
Century Magazine 196
Chambers, Thomas Jefferson 96
Chappell, Mrs. Bettie 212
Chappell, George W. 20, 148
Chappell, Mary 29; *see also* Haller, Mary
Chappell, Robert Wooding 7, 38
Chappell, Robert Wooding, Jr. 88, 189
Chappell, Thomas 68, 69, 120, 182–183, 222
Chappell, William 37, 40, 41, 60, 69, 100
Chappell Hill Confederate Convalescent Hospital 100–101
Chappell Hill Female College 194, 203, 213
Chappell Hill Male and Female Institute 9, 38
Chappell Hill Masonic Cemetery 1, 7, 205, 222
Chappell Hill Masonic Lodge 82
Chappell Hill Methodist Church 205, 216, 217
Chattanooga, TN 75, 114–115
Chickamauga, Battle of 11, 111–113, 120–121
Chickamauga and Chattanooga National Park 198
Chimbrazo Hospital, Richmond, VA 50
Chustenahlah Creek, Indian Territory 83
Cincinnati, OH 19
circuit riders (Methodist) 18
Clark, J. L. 120
Clay, Bettie 134
Clay, Tacitus 46, 68, 93, 134–135
Clay Castle 46, 135
Cleburne, Patrick 128, 200

Cocke, J. Norfolk 78–79, 189, 222
Cocke, James H. 6, 78
Cocke, Mattie McDade 189
Code of honor, Southern 9
Coffield, Theodore 30
Coke, Richard 176
Coke-Davis Controversy 176
Colbert, William 9
Collins, Nannie 214
Comanche Nation 170
Condren, Riley N. 30, 190
Confederate Brigades and Divisions: Arizona Brigade 148–149; Barksdale's Mississippi Brigade 181; Carter's Cavalry Brigade 222; Churchill's Infantry Division 104; Cleburne's Division 110, 113, 116, 125–127; Deshler's Brigade 61, 110–112; Granbury's Brigade 127–128; Green's Brigade 192, 222; Hood's/Gregg's Texas Brigade 47–51, 55, 57, 92–94, 110–111, 121, 129–134, 139–141, 148; Humphrey's Mississippi Brigade 130; Longstreet's Corps 130; McIntosh's Brigade 83; Parson's Brigade 183; Ross' Cavalry Brigade 101, 119, 128, 152; Tarrant's Battery 194; Van Dorn's Cavalry Division 84; Walker's Texas Division 42–44, 103–105, 152–153, 206, 222; Wheeler's Cavalry Corps 143
Confederate currency valuation 97–98
Confederate Regiments, Battalions and Legions by state: *Alabama*: Seventeenth Alabama Infantry 196; Eighteenth Alabama Infantry 191; Fifty-Seventh Alabama Infantry 191; Eufala Light Artillery 191; *Arkansas*: Third Arkansas Infantry 57; *Georgia*: Eighteenth Georgia Infantry 47, 57; *Mississippi*: Twenty-First Mississippi Infantry 191; *North Carolina*: Forty-Second North Carolina Infantry 184; *South Carolina*: Fourteenth South Carolina Cavalry Battalion 208; *Tennessee*: Brazelton's Third Tennessee Cavalry Battalion 106–109; First Tennessee Cavalry 109–110, 114, 119, 126; *Texas*: First Texas Infantry 45–47; First Texas Lancers 58, 59; Second Texas Infantry 190; Fourth Texas Infantry 26, 45–47, 92–93, 211; Fourth Texas Mounted Volunteers 38–41; Fifth Texas Infantry 45–47, 50–54, 56, 92–93, 107, 113, 130–131, 141, 198, 202, 216, 217; Fifth Texas Mounted Vol-

unteers 37–41, 209; Sixth Texas Cavalry 82–84, 101; Eighth Texas Cavalry (Terry's Texas Rangers) 28–36, 75–78, 101–102, 115, 119–120, 136–139, 141, 143, 162, 165, 170, 183, 190, 198, 203, 210–211; Tenth Texas Infantry 116, 119–120, 122–127, 189, 215, 216; Fifteenth Texas Infantry 176; Sixteenth Texas Infantry 61, 184; Seventeenth Texas Infantry 103, 183–184; Twentieth Texas Infantry 66–74, 162, 170, 183, 184, 215, 222, 225; Twenty-First Texas Cavalry 60, 78–81, 161, 184, 190, 207; Twenty-Fourth Texas Cavalry 60–63, 65, 111–113, 116, 119, 127, 144–145, 156, 165, 173, 183, 212, 222; Twenty-Fifth Texas Cavalry 60–63, 65, 127, 168; Brown's Cavalry Battalion 148–149; Giddings' Cavalry Battalion 154; Dave Terry's Cavalry Regiment 102; Val Verde Battery 41–43, 161–162; Waller's Cavalry Battalion 41–44; Waller's Thirteenth Cavalry Battalion 42–44, 148–149, 203; Waul's Texas Legion 88–91, 182, 183, 184
Confederate Veteran magazine 208, 214
Confederate war bonds 100, 128
Cook, Gustave 136, 139
Cook, Joseph 71
Cooke, Francis Jarvis 7, 99 (photo)
cotton 5, 6, 99
Cox, C. C. 43
Craig, William 43
Crane, Stephen 187
Crawford, Jennie 182
Creek Nation 82–83
Crockett, Eva Sadler (Mrs. W. D.) 191, 212
Crockett, J. R. 69
Crockett, John E. 69, 183
Crockett, John Jesse 183
Crockett, Sallie 69, 183
Crockett, William Davie 183, 191, 212–213
Crockett, W. R. D. 169, 183
Crump, George and J. W. 69
Cuba 16, 201–202
Cumberland gap, TN 106–110
Cupples, Dr. George 20
Curtis, Samuel 63
Cushing, E. H. 167, 215
Cushing, Edward Benjamin 215
Custer, Elizabeth 167, 192
Custer, George Armstrong 167, 192

Dallas, TX 17, 25, 193
Dallas Herald 188
Dalton, GA 120
Danville, VA 146
Darbytown, VA 206
Davidson, Thomas 88, 183, 189
Davis, Edmund J. 173, 174, 176
Davis, Jefferson: petitioned for formation of Terry's Texas Rangers 28; petitioned for formation of Texas brigade, perceived lack of support by in Trans-Mississippi 96; defense of Atlanta 121; replaced Johnston with Hood 122; allowed Johnston to return to command in North Carolina 137; imprisoned by Federal government 169; fierce post-war dialogue with Sherman 193; death and funeral in New Orleans 195; birthday a Texas holiday 209; quote on Texas brigade monument 211
Davis, Winnie 198
Deggs, James 46
DeKalb 90
Diana 43–44
Dickens, Charles 42
Dover, TN 77
Drane, Robert 158–159
Dresler, James 62
Duganne, A.J., 169
Duggan, Edmund 25, 45
Dumfries, VA 47
Dunn, Oscar 179
Durham, NC 141
Dwyer, E.C. 197–198

Edwards, the Rev. Jonathan 21
Eldridge, Bolling 198, 217
Eldridge, Frank 135
Elgin, Gansello 183
Elgin, Mary Stanchfield 183
Elgin, Robert: enlistment in Terry's Texas Rangers 30; participant in post-war jousting tournament at Chappell Hill 170; death by yellow fever 183; buried in Chappell Hill's Masonic Cemetery 222
Elliott, George 133
Elliott, Emma Felder: letter from husband Thomas 61; letter from brother Rufus King 110; mentioned in letter by Rufus king Felder 113; grieving loss of her husband 133; daughter Emma married 165
Elliott, Thomas A.: enlistment in Twenty-Fourth Texas Cavalry 60; letter home to wife Emma 61; freedom by prisoner exchange mentioned in letter of Rufus King Felder 110; father 111; killed in action at Chickamagua (photo of cenotaph) 113
Elmore, Henry 66
El Paso, TX 38
Eltham's Landing, Battle of 50
Emancipation Proclamation 98
Enfield rifles 47
Ennis, TX 209
Estes, Clifford 224
Estes, Clifton 215
Estes, Greer 224–225
Estes, John Thomas 225
Evans, Green 173
Ezra Church, Battle of 123

Fairfield, TX 161–162, 169
Farmer, D.C. 171
Felder, Catherine 101; see also Barrilon, Catherine
Felder, Gabriel 9, 46, 60, 73
Felder, Frank, J. 46
Felder, Hans 46
Felder, Jesse 46
Felder, Lula (Mrs. Rufuf King) 196, 212, 213, 217
Felder, Margaret Matthews 142 (photo)
Felder, Miers: arrival in Chappell Hill 46; photo with cousin Rufus King 48; mention of photo in letter home 49; participation in victory at Gaines' Mill 51; wounded at Second Manassas 53–54; photo with wife and son 53; discharged from service 101; photo 202; post-war career and death 203–205
Felder, Rufie 213
Felder, Rufus King: arrival in Chappell Hill, youth and student at Soule University 46; letter home from Richmond 47; photo with cousin Miers 48; letter home regarding photo 49; letter home regarding Captain John D. Rogers 50; ill at Chimborazo Hospital 50; letter home regarding forced marching with Stonewall Jackson 51; letter home regarding Second Manassas 52–53; letter home regarding Sharpsburg/ Antietam 56; letter home regarding winter camp and The Great Snowball Fight 56–57; letter home on eve of Spring 1863 fighting 88; letter home regarding march into Pennsylvania 92; letter home regarding Battle of Gettysburg 93; letter home regarding missing Battle of the Wilderness 130; letter home regarding entrenchments at Petersburg 132; letter home regarding horrors of war 133; letter home regarding Battle of New Market Heights and Union African American soldiers 133–134; letter home regarding desire to be transferred to defend Texas

135; letter home regarding Sherman's ravaging the Carolinas 136; surrender at Appomattox and long walk home 141; photo of Rufus and wife with tarpon 142; attendance at Texas Brigade Association Reunion in 1874 189; delegate to 1895 United Confederate Veterans gathering 198; photo with fish 199; attendance at 1910 dedication of Texas brigade monument in Austin 211; photo with Landes and Brandt at opening of Soule University cornerstone 212; death of son Rufie 213; death in 1922 216; burial in Atkinson Cemetery 222
Field, Scott 200
Fifteenth Amendment 173, 175
Five Forks, VA, Battle of 139
Flournoy, George 20, 61
Floyd House and Ocmulgee Hospital, GA 126
Ford, Ermine 34
Ford, Rip 13, 23, 41, 153–154
Forrest, Nathan Bedford 36, 75, 77–78, 124
Fourteenth Amendment 172, 173, 175, 196
Fouts, Frederick 197
Franklin, TN, Battle of 127–128, 191
Fredericksburg, Battle of 191
Freedmen's Bureau 175

Gaines, Matthew 173–175
Gaines' Mill, Battle of 51–52, 188
Galveston 6, 15, 20, 25, 60, 86, 88, 97, 105, 164, 166, 170, 171, 177, 182, 184, 188, 189, 198, 207, 219
Galveston, Battle of 66–74, 76
Galveston, Storm of 1900 205, 217
Galveston Daily News 16, 93, 100, 148, 162, 205, 214
Galveston Tri-Weekly News 55, 85, 97–98, 101, 116, 118, 119, 126, 136, 140, 145, 150, 153
Garland, Robert R. 63, 144
Garrett, Hosea: at Arkansas Post 62; move to Chappell Hill from South Carolina 119; letter home covering the defense of Atlanta 120–125; wounded at Jonesboro 126; homecoming at end of war 160; death 189
Garrett, the Rev. Hosea 104, 119, 123
Garrett, Isaac 124
Garrett, John 124
Garrett, Oliver Hazard Perry 104, 123, 169
Gary, John 120
Gatewood, John 163–164
Gay, Hill, TX 88

Gee, A. D. 170
Gee, Leonard Groce 131
George, Major 141
Georgetown, TX 221
Gettysburg, Battle of 92–95, 110, 129
Gettysburg post-war reunions 192, 211, 214
Giddings, D. C. 190, 192–193
Giddings, George 154
Gillespie, Clayton Crawford: Methodist minister turned Confederate cavalry officer 58; recruitment of Texas Lancers 59; pre-war career as prison superintendent and newspaper editor 60; given command of Twenty-Fifth Texas Cavalry (dismounted) 61; Rogers as staff courier 103; militant post-war address in Houston 150; editorial statement regarding Texas 166; new role as anti-Republican editor with *Houston Telegraph* in 1865 167; photo 168; investigated for war crimes as superintendent of prisoner-of-war camp 169; facing Reconstruction 172; death to yellow fever while prison superintendent at Huntsville 184; editorial support for formation of Hood's Texas Brigade Association 187
Glass, Mary 182
Glenblythe (plantation) 89
Glorieta Pass, Battle of 40
Goforth, Alex 107, 109
Goliad, TX 19, 182
Goliad Messenger 18
Gordon, John 140, 198
Granbury, Hiram 191
Granbury, TX 128
Grand Army of the Republic 193
Granger, Gordon 166
Grant, Ulysses S.: capture of Forts Henry and Donelson 35; Vicksburg campaign 63, 87; promoted to general-in-chief of Union Armies 129; Petersburg campaign 134, 136, 137; regarding *Brenham Banner* 171; U.S. president 173; Reconstruction 175, 176, 177, 179, 180; funeral 192; use in textbook 207
Green, Tom 37, 39, 44, 72, 104
Gregg, John 134
Griffin, Charles 171, 185
Griscom, George 83
Grissett, John 29, 203
Groce, Camp 61, 72, 152, 166, 169
Groce, Leonard 35
Guyton, A. W. 69

Hackworth, Stephen 176
Haley, William 191, 202

Haller, Jacob 7, 221
Haller, Mary 7, 29
Hamby, William 211
Hamilton, Andrew Jackson 166
Hammond, Alex 170, 222
Hampton, Wade 137, 198
Hardee, William 137–139, 143
Hardeman, William 163–164
Hargrove, Charlotte 221
Hargrove, John A. 15, 148, 162, 209
Hargrove, Robert 46, 51, 148, 209
Hargrove, William 6, 7
Hargrove House Hotel 7
Harme, F. C. 189–190
Harmon, William H. 120–121
Harriet Lane 72
Harrison, Thomas 35, 76–77
Haynes, Harry 192
Haynie, Henry M. 205
Haynie-Gunn House 221 (photo)
Heard, William Jones 7, 10 (photo of grave marker)
Helena, AK 95
Hempstead, TX: Wharton youth spent in 35; Lancers companies raised near 38; Camp Waller near 42; Camp Groce POW camp near 72; Texas troops from Louisiana near at end of war 152; Federal occupation forces 166, 167; investigation of war crimes at Camp Groce near 169; passing through of remains of A. S. Johnston 171; Alta Vista Plantation and College for Colored Youth 174; yellow fever at 182
Hero Tales from American History 200
Hill, G. G. 207
Hill, George 120
Hill, James E. 206
Hill, T. W. 206
Hindman, Thomas 33, 41, 152, 163
Holland, Emma 170
Holly Springs, MS 84, 185
Holmes, Theophilus 95–96
Hood, John Bell: lieut. colonel in Fourth Texas Infantry 45; promoted by Lee to brigadier general to command Texas brigade 50; led division at Antietam 55; wounded at Gettysburg 92; presented with artificial leg 121; replaced Johnston in defense of Atlanta 122; taking offense to defend Atlanta 123, 125, 126, 127, 128; appearance at HTB reunion and death by yellow fever in New Orleans 188, 192, 195
Hood's Texas Brigade 11, 26, 45–57
Hood's Texas Brigade Association: formation 187–188; early

Index

reunions 191, 192; first attempt at reconciliation 193; raising money for TX Confederate Veterans' Home 194; Federal veteran speaking at 1891 reunion 197–198; urging for unity 200; reunion photo 204; Rufus King Felder at reunion honoring deceased Miers Felder 205; African American veteran introduced at 1902 reunion 206; woman from UCV named as honorary member 207; 1904 reunion 209; dedication of monument on state capitol grounds in Austin 211
Houston 17, 18, 20, 23, 30, 46, 53, 73, 78, 86, 97, 100, 105, 141, 151, 153, 163, 166, 171, 188, 198, 219
Houston Telegraph 16, 17, 19, 40, 41, 43, 44, 53, 75, 80, 100, 149, 150, 152, 167, 168, 169, 171, 172, 187, 226
Howth, William Edward 7, 8 (photo of grave marker)
Huisache tree 7
Huntsville, TX 191
Huntsville (TX) State Penitentiary 60, 73, 184
Hutchinson, Burrel B. 20, 22
Hutchinson, Jim and Julian 56

Iankes, Albert 29, 170
Iankes, Charles 29, 183
Iankes, Mary 183
Independence, TX 17, 26, 46, 68, 92, 119, 131, 134, 170, 188
Indianola, TX 181
Iuka, Battle of 84

Jackson, Clairborne 96
Jackson, John A.: photos 32, 33; wounded at Woodsonville 34; returning to Terry's Texas Rangers 101; in Joe Wheeler's command in Tennessee 114; return home at war's end 161; marriage of daughter 165; participation in jousting tournament 170; photo of reunion gathering 210; mention in photo caption 211; move and death 216
Jackson, Mrs. John A. 206
Jackson, John Day 194
Jackson, Laura 165
Jackson, Mollie 120–1
Jackson, Terrell A. 15, 33, 154
Jackson, Terrell J. 7, 9, 33–34, 101, 161, 183, 190
Jacksonville, TX 104
January, James 43
Jenkins, Micah 129
Jenkins Ferry, Battle of 104
Jesse, Lea 107

Jessie, Jennie 107, 126
Jessie, Sallie 126
Johnston, Albert Sidney 32, 35, 171, 207
Johnston, Joseph E. 199–122, 137, 206
Jones, Hess 79
Jonesboro, Battle of 125–126
jousting tournament 11, 170
Juarez, Benito 164
Justice, Emma Toland 190
Justice, John C. 7, 30, 31 (photo), 190
Justice, Mary Jackson 190
Justice, T. H. 7

Kavanaugh, Benjamin, T.: assistant surgeon and chaplain to Sterling Price 84; return to Chappell Hill, resignation from service and return to Soule University faculty 96; death in battle of man who boarded with him 120; letter in defense of Sterling Price 147; editor of *Texas Masonic Mirror* 175; editorial opinion on yellow fever 182; loss of a son and a daughter to yellow fever 183; move to Kentucky and death 193
Kavanaugh, Charles T. 88
Kavanaugh, Margaret 193
Keesee, Gideon 38, 39, 209, 222
Keesee, Mrs. Gideon 196
Keesee, Thomas Milton 107–108, 114, 189
Keesee, W. G. 154
Keesee, Walter 170
Keesee, William 6, 38
Keesee, William, Jr. 60
Keller, Andrew: stonemason on Soule University building 81; accepted to Chappell Hill's Masonic Lodge and enlisted in Sixth Texas Cavalry 82; wounded at Chustenahlah Creek 83; taken prisoner near Lagrange, TN 84; escape from Camp Douglas and exploits in Illinois 85; article published regarding support in southern Illinois 85–86, 96; traveling with John Jackson back to the front 101; role in defense of Atlanta 119; covering the retreat from Nashville 128; brigade commander as governor of Texas 193
Kellogg, William 180
Kenedy, Mifflin 99
Kennesaw Mountain, Battle of 121
Kenney, Martin 161
Kerby, George 54, 79, 122, 132, 148
Kilgore, C. B. 197
King, Richard 99

Kinney, Henry 16
Kirby, Helen Marr Swearingen 156, 174
Kirby, Jared 9, 174
Kirby Smith, Edmund 81, 96, 104, 109, 147, 150–153
Kirkpatrick, Judson 137
Knights of the Golden Circle 19, 22, 38, 85, 202
Knights of the White Camellia 179
Knolle, Henry 91
Knolle, Herman 89, 90, 91, 157–158
Knox, Robert Wallis 215, 225
Knoxville Siege 113–116, 129
Kolb's Farm (GA), Battle of 121
Ku Klux Klan 174

LaGrange, TX 20, 75, 104, 175
Lamar, Mirabeau 17
Lampasas, TX 189
Landes, Colonel 67
Landes, Elmina Lockhart 184
Landes, Henry: enlistment in Elmore's Regiment 67; recalling Battle of Galveston 72; loss of wife to yellow fever and move to Galveston, where he became mayor 184; photo and commercial success 185; death 216
Landes, James E.: to Virginia with Texas brigade 67; Battle of Gettysburg 92–94; Siege of Knoxville 115, 129; wounded in Battle of the Wilderness 131; at Appomattox 141; commanding officer 171; attendance at 1870's Texas brigade reunions 189, 192; at dedication of monument on state capitol grounds 211; photo of opening of Soule University cornerstone 212; death 213; Methodist memorial service at Camp Ground 214
Landes, Mrs. James 196, 212, 213
Landes, John Lockhart 184
Landes, Kate 67
Lang, Willis 39
LaVergne, TN 76, 110
Lea, Albert and Pryor 19
Lee, Abraham 46, 54–55
Lee, Robert E. 19, 45, 50, 52, 55, 56, 91, 110, 129, 130–131, 132, 162, 209, 212
Lee, Stephen 198, 200
Lincoln, Abraham 11, 20, 24, 25, 126, 129
Linecum, Gordon 97, 165
Little River Ford (TN) 114
Littlepage, Samuel C. 104
Livingston, TX 197, 206
Lockhart, John Washington: planter and slaveowner 9; friend of Sam Houston 24; letters from Daniel Harvie

Index

Browning 34, 35; lieutenant in infantry 66; medical practice and plantation (photo of manor) 67; letter on the eve of combat 70; letter regarding Battle of Galveston 71–72; letter from Browning 77; recruiting for the Confederacy 81; photo 82; mentioned in postwar letter 177; address at dedication of statue in Galveston 198; Galveston Storm of 1900 and death 205; reflection on liberation of the slaves 219–220; burial in Atkinson Cemetery 222
Lockhart, Mary Eliza 184
Lockhart, Sarah Ann Elizabeth Browning 83
Lockridge, Samuel 38–39
Lockridge, Widow 120
Lodge, Henry Cabot 200
Long Point, TX 97
Longley, Bill 173–174
Longstreet, James: Battle of Gettysburg 92; Knoxville Siege 114–115; court-martial charges against Robertson 129; Battle of the Wilderness 131; Appomattox 140; Reconstruction 172, 179; New Orleans 195; Houston UCV gathering 198; in Chicago 200
Lookout Mountain (TN) 76, 110
Lost Cause 196, 200, 206, 209, 211
Lubbock, Frank 96
Lubbock, Thomas 15, 28, 35
lynchings 209, 214

Magruder, John: Battle of Galveston 70–72; Wilkes to report to 145; signed Brandt discharge 160; self-imposed exile in Mexico 163
Maine, battleship 201
Maine, planter from 9
Malone, H. D. 120
Manning, T. D. 185
Marmaduke, John 78–79, 81
Marshall, John 45, 50, 52
martial music 127–128
Martin, John 70
Maryland Confederate Soldiers' Home 208
Maryville, TN 114
Matamoras, Mexico 98
Matthews, Arnie 161
Matthews, Harvie 223–224
Matthews, Jacob 29
Matthews, James Fiske "Doc": move to Texas from Mississippi 29; taken prisoner at Murfreesboro 77; in Wheeler's cavalry command 114; burying Daniel Harvie Matthews after action at Stock Creek near Knoxville 115; photo with brother Joseph 138; leads last great cavalry charge of war at Bentonville 139; address to Terry's Texas Rangers at end of war 143; return for body of Browning and its burial in Chappell Hill 161; buried in Atkinson Cemetery 222; photo of grave marker 223
Matthews, Mrs. James Fiske 206
Matthews, John F. 60
Matthews, Joseph Wier 138 (photo)
Maximilian 164
McClernand, John 63
McCown, Jerome 38
McCulloch, Benjamin 14, 22, 83
McCulloch, Henry 81
McDade, Jacob 42, 43
McDade, James 42, 43
McDade, John R. 41
McDade, Mrs. John 196
McDade, Thomas 42, 43
McDade, William 42, 43, 148
McDonald, John 169
McGary, Dan 171
McInnis, Malcom 225
McIntyre, Hugh 24, 99, 173
McNeely, J. W. 194
McNeil, John 79
McPhail, Hugh 38
McPherson, James 122–123
McRee, Elizabeth Cocke 49, 54, 79, 132
McRee, Robert 46, 49
Methodism in Texas 18, 58–60, 104, 179, 220
Mexia, TX 162
Mexico 13–15, 19–20, 98, 103, 163
Meyer, Henry 208
Mier Expedition 66
migration to Kansas 176
Mill Creek Bridge, action at 137–139
Millican, TX 166
Mills, Roger 120
Milton, Phil 32
Missionary Ridge 114–116, 119, 120
Monuments to Hood's Texas Brigade and Terry's Texas Rangers on grounds of Texas state capitol 211
Moore, John 158
Moore, John Creed 190
Morgan, George 107
Morse, Bill 32
Morton, Oliver 196
Murfreesboro, TN 11, 76–77, 109
Murrah, Pendleton 96, 163
Muse, Tom 47

Nashville, Battle of 128, 191, 194
Nashville, TN 32, 35, 76, 127–128
National Board of Health 185
Navasota, TX 20, 75, 182
Nelville, G. L. 75
New Hope Church, Battle of 120
New Market Heights, Battle of 133–134
New Orleans, LA 16, 42, 68, 95, 151, 177–179, 182, 188, 195
New Orleans Advocate 60
New Orleans Picayune 180
New Salem, TX 104
New Years' Creek 88, 181
Nicaragua 16–17, 38
Nicholson, James 15
Nolensville, TN 110

Oakwoods Cemetery, Chicago 200
Oldham, Williamson Simpson 105, 162
Oldham, Williamson Simpson, Jr. 162–163
Onins, L. M. 194
Opothyleyahola 82–83
Orangeburg, SC 111, 163
Owens, Joe 124

Packard, Stephen 179
Palmito Ranch, Battle of 154
Palmyra, TN 77
Pea Ridge, Battle of 83–84
Peachtree Creek, Battle of 122, 191
Perkins, Del 46, 49, 68, 170, 222
Perkins, John 183
Perkins, Nannie 165
Petersburg Siege 130–135, 136, 139
Phalen, H. J. 69
The Philomathean (of Chappell Hill) 194
Pickensville, AL 101
Pickett's Mill, Battle of 120
Pike, Albert 82
planters 5, 7, 9, 11, 20, 54, 60, 61, 66, 73, 88, 116
Pleasant Hill, Battle of 104
Pope, John 52
Port Isabel, TX 153
Powell, Robert 93–94
Presler, James 60, 182, 183
Presler, Mary 182, 183
Preston, C. C. 188
Price, Sterling: driven from Missouri 82; former Missouri governor defeated at Pea Ridge 83; commissioned major general, CSA, move into Tennessee 84; conflict with Holmes 95; extended furlough 96; public dispute with Governor Reynolds 146–147; looking back at Missouri raids 149; self-imposed exile in Mexico 163–164
Prohibition (of alcohol) 192
Providence Baptist Church 176

Index

Quantrill, William 81

Raleigh, NC 141
Rancho Las Rinas, Battle of 154
Raysor, Peter 194, 208
Read, John 169
Reagan, John 18
Reconciliation movement 196
Reconciliation, racial (abandonment of) 197, 214
Reconstruction 166–180
Reconstruction Act of 1867 177
Red Badge of Courage 187
Republican Party 11, 20
Reynolds, Thomas G. 96, 146–147, 163
Rice, Hiram 30
Rice, William Marsh 99
Richmond (KY), Battle of 109
Richmond, VA: +++Terry to Richmond for permission to form Terry's Texas Rangers 28; Felder letter from camp outside 47; Battle of Gaines' Mill saved 52; letter from George Kerby in 54; threat to 110; Atlanta second only to 119; Overland Campaign focused on 130; George Kerby letter from 132; Darbytown as last resort to save 134; Felder letter from position outside 136; Wilkes court-martial in 144; Brandt release from prison during siege of 157–158
Rio Grande River 13, 39, 99, 154
Robertson, Jerome B.: formed Company I of Fifth Texas Infantry 45; promoted to command of Fifth Texas Infantry 50; collapsed on march to Antietam due to wounds 55; Tom Bates enlistment in Robertson's company 79; Battle of Gettysburg 92; wounded at Gettysburg 93; court-martial and dismissal from service after Knoxville 129; key role in formation of Hood's Texas Brigade Association 188; proposal to reconcile through joint Blue-Gray reunion 192
Robinson, A.J.: enlistment in Fifth Texas Mounted Volunteers 37; participation in Sibley's Brigade to west 38; transferred to Val Verde Battery 41; fighting in Louisiana in 1863 43; burial of artillery pieces after the war 161–162
Rogers, Edward W. 102, 183
Rogers, John D.: to California for Gold Rush 15; formed Company E of Fifth Texas Infantry 46; Felder letter regarding departure of Rogers 50; photo and brief biography 51; family history 102; attendance at 1870's reunions of Texas Brigade 189, 192; officer who replaced Rogers to lead Company E 206; offered Cornelia Branch Stone as honorary member of HTBA 207; death in 1908 208
Rogers, Joseph D. 102, 103 (photo)
Rogers, Patrick 102
Rogers, William S. 102 (photo), 182
Ross, Lawrence Sullivan "Sul" 84, 101, 193, 216
Rough Riders 201
Routt, Joe Eugene 226
Routt, John 32
Routt, Joseph 60, 99
Routt, Lafayette 113, 222
Routt, Spelman 32, 189, 222

Sadler, Augustus David 191, 206, 216
St. Charles Hospital, Richmond 108
St. Francis River 79–80
St. Louis, MO 63, 84, 85, 90, 202
Sallis, David 69
San Antonio 7 22, 37, 38, 40, 41, 152, 161, 173
San Jacinto, Battle of 7, 23, 37, 58, 60, 99
Sayers, Joseph 41
Sayles, John 172
scalawag 178
Schofield, John 127–128
Scott, Sir Walter 9, 11
Scurry, Thomas, Jr. 176, 189
Scurry, William Read 38, 40, 176
Seat, Benton 38–39
Seaton, Ben 125
Second Manassas, Battle of 11, 52–55, 101
Seven Pines, Battle of 50
Sharpsburg, Battle of 55
Shattuck, Horace 203
Shelby, Jo 163–164
Shelby, John S. 79
Shelton, W. E. 197
Shepard, Seth 209
Shepard, Thomas T. 148, 216
Sherman, Sidney 17, 198
Shiloh (TN), Battle of 35, 89
Shreveport, LA 61, 101, 103, 116, 151
Shreveport News 147
Sibley, Henry Hopkins 11, 37–38
Slaughter, James E. 153
slaves and slavery 5, 7, 9, 11, 13, 18, 47, 60, 89, 140, 145, 167, 170, 172
Sledge, William 222
smallpox 85, 103
Smith, C. H. 62
Smith, E. M. 69
Smith, G. W. 171
Smith, James 116
Smith, John Sterling 99, 220 (photo of house)
Smith, P. A. 183
Sneedville, TN 107, 126
Somervell Expedition 15, 37, 45
Soule University 9, 21, 25–26, 46, 58, 60, 78, 81, 96, 100, 102, 103, 147, 162, 177, 178, 190, 194, 212, 213, 221
Southern ethos 9
Spring Hill (TN), Battle of 127
Stagecoach Inn 5 (photo), 7
Stamps, John 172
Stanchfield, Bartley 9
Stanchfield, Mrs. 183
Stanton, Edwin 141, 173
Stark, Thomas, Jr. 225
Starring, F. A. 151
Steele, Frederick 96, 104
Stewart, Alexander 198
Stock Creek (TN) 114–115
Stockton, Emily 99
Stone, Cornelius Branch 207
Stone, Warren 82, 84
Strong, William E. 175
Sumter, Fort 24–25
Swearingen, Helen Jesse 182
Swearingen, John Thomas 106, 156
Swearingen, Patrick Henry: attorney before enlistment 60; lieutenant colonel 61; Battle of Arkansas Post 62–63; cited in Deshler's report for gallantry 63; received parole 166; sister Helen 174; honored by District Court of Washington County upon his death 189
Swearingen, Richard J. 6, 9, 16, 60, 102, 174
Swearingen, Richard M.: law student at outbreak of war 22; enlistment to serve under Rip Ford and in action at Brazos Santiago and Brownsville 23; to eastern Tennessee to substitute for brother 106; ill and under care of Lea family in Sneedville and falling in love 107; photo 108; recon in force 108–109; defending Cumberland Gap in First TN cavalry 110; in Wheeler's cavalry command 114; in defense of Atlanta 119; marriage of 126; captured but released 127; feelings for the flag at war's end 155; danger and escape from Tennessee 156; medical school after war 157; orator at jousting tournament 170; sister Helen 174; loss of daughter to yellow fever 182; medical authority on yellow fever 185; memorial address in honor of Jefferson Davis 195; address to graduation class at

Soule University and death soon thereafter 201
Swearingen, Mrs. Richard M. 206

Taliaferro, Robert 184–185
Tapscott, R. C. 69
Tapscott, Mrs. R. C. 196
tariffs 11
Tarrant, Edward W. 194
Taylor, Richard 103, 104, 154
Taylor's Creek, Battle of 80
Terry, Clinton 35
Terry, Frank 15, 28, 31, 33
Terry's Texas Rangers Association 170, 210 (reunion photo), 211
Texas A&M Corps of Cadets 198
Texas Baptist Herald 184
Texas Christian Advocate 25, 60
Texas Confederate Veterans' Home 194–195
Texas Legislature: Eleventh 170–171; Twelfth 174–175
Texas Masonic Mirror 175, 182
The Texas Ranger 20
Texas Republican 146–147
Texas State Gazette 16, 18, 45
Texas State Militia 129
Texas State Police 174
Texas Troubles 18–19
Thaxton, A. M. 32
Thirteenth Amendment 167, 172, 175
Thompson, Alexander (A. B.) 162–163, 182–183
Thompson, Charles W. 162, 203
Thompson, J. W. (Bill Dick) 68, 182, 216, 222, 225
Thompson, James P. 191
Thompson, Lulu 194
Throckmorton, James 170–172
Toland, Carrie 209
Toland, Emily 66
Toland, Irene 194, 202
Toland, Joe 215
Toland, John Francis Williamson 46, 54, 208–209
Toland, Joseph 7, 66
Toland, M. E. 61
Toland, Rebecca 202
Traveling Masonic Lodge of Eighth Texas Cavalry 190
Travis, Susan 29
Traynham, J. H. 69
Tuxpan, Mexico 164–165

UDC Catechism 207
Umland, Jacob 69, 222
Umland, Johann 69
Union Army, Brigades and higher: Kilpatrick's Cavalry Division 137; Mower's Division 137, 139
Union Army Federal units: Seventeenth U. S. Infantry 170–171; Duncan's Brigade

United States Colored Troops 133–134
Union Army Regiments by state: *Illinois*: Ninety-Ninth Illinois Infantry 166; *Indiana*: Seventh Indiana Cavalry 167; Fifteenth Indiana Artillery 197; Twenty-Fifth Indiana Infantry 84; Thirty-Second Indiana Infantry 33–34; *Kentucky*: Eleventh Kentucky Infantry 114; *Massachusetts*: Forty-Second Massachusetts Infantry 70, 72; *New York*: Fifth New York Zouaves 52–53, 201; *Ohio*: Seventy-Seventh Ohio Infantry 36
United Confederate Veterans 192, 193, 195, 198, 200, 205, 207, 215
United Daughters of the Confederacy 206, 207, 212

Val Verde, Battle of 39
Val Verde Battery 41, 43, 161–162
Val Verde Ford 39
Vanderbilt, Cornelius 16
Velasco (TX Revolution), Battle of 7, 203
Vicksburg Siege 11; Marmaduke Raid as diversion for 78; Holly Springs Raid 84; Grant's victory at 86; Brandt at Vicksburg 87–91, 157
Victoria, TX 43, 182

Walker, James and John 69
Walker, John 120, 153
Walker, William 16–17, 38
Walker, William H. T. 123
Waller, Edwin 41, 42
Wallis, Elmina 66
Wallis, James E. 87
Wallis, John C. 60, 66, 68–70, 71
Wallis, John Edmund 208, 215
Wallis, Joseph 66, 67, 72
Walton, Buck 80
Warmoth, Henry Clay 177–180
Warren Town 6, 15
Washington 6
Washington County Railroad 33, 222
Washington on the Brazos 45, 170, 221
Waul, Thomas 88, 190
Wave 154
Waverly Plantation Manor House 222
Wear, Madison 42
West, John C. 93
Westfield 72
Wharton, John 28, 35, 77–78, 100
Wheeler, Annie 198, 201–202
Wheeler, J. B. 26
Wheeler, Joe: given cavalry command by Braxton Bragg, Battle of Murfreesboro 76;

failed assault on Dover 77; denounced by Forrest 78; Knoxville campaign 114–115; defending North Carolina 137; farewell address 143; Houston UCV gathering 198, 200; command of cavalry in Spanish American War 201; burial in Arlington 209
Whitten, Noah 196
Wigfall, Lewis 47, 49
Wilburn, James 29
The Wilderness, Battle of 11 129–132
Wilkes, Franklin C.: recruiting for Texas Lancers 58, 59; command of Twenty-Fifth Texas Cavalry (dismounted) 60; assigned to Deshler's Brigade 61; ordered to Arkansas Post 62; surrender flags among Wilkes' regiment 63; taken prisoner and taken to Camp Chase in Ohio 64; released and given command of brigade 65; Battle of Chickamauga 111–112; relieved of command after wounded 112; son killed near Atlanta 120; facing court-martial charges 144; taken prisoner in Louisiana 145; photo 145; letter to Washington prison authorities 146; attempt to negotiate Texas surrender 151–152; mayor of Chappell Hill 169; removed from office by Federal authorities 173; loss of daughter to yellow fever 183; general agent for Bayland Home 188; death 189
Wilkes, Josie 183
Williams, Walter Washington 217
Williamson, F. M.: enlistment in Fifth Texas Infantry 46; under command of John Rogers 51; wounded at Second Manassas 54; transfer to First Tennessee Cavalry 113–114; death by yellow fever 182–183
Willich, August von 33
Wilson, President Woodrow 214–215
Winston, Dan 206
Wirz, Henry 169
Woodsonville (KY), action at 33, 35, 101
Wyeth, John 196–197

Yazoo City, MS 89–90
yellow fever 73, 181–186, 188, 220
"The Yellow Rose of Texas" 46
Young, Maude 188
Young, S. O. 213

Zuber, William 58 61, 62, 80

www.ingramcontent.com/pod-product-compliance
Ingram Content Group UK Ltd.
Pitfield, Milton Keynes, MK11 3LW, UK
UKHW050537150426
5217IPUK00026B/1975